LUTON TOWN: BACK WHERE WE BELONG.
A SEASON OF DREAM, OR A LESSON IN REALITY?

BY CHRIS LUKE

FOREWORD BY MIKE THOMAS.

Text Copyright © 2015 Chris Luke
All Rights Reserved

Other Titles by Chris. Luke

MEMORIES FROM THE GREEN CARPET.
(Sports, Horse Racing)
By Christopher Luke

**Dedicated to the memory of good friend and fellow Hatter
David Stanyon.
January 14th 1960 to November 13th 2010**

**A loyal Hatter, who loved his football but worshipped Luton Town along with twin brother
Paul.**

NEVER FORGOTTEN MY DEAR FRIEND.

**Thank you to my family for putting up with my constant ravings regarding Luton Town over
the past months, including the locking of myself away to the confines of one's desk.
Mike Thomas, who endured hours of passing back and forth comments, chapters via email
and texting.
Without Paul Wright, it would not have, at times been possible to have included the game
reports in such detail. His perseverance was at times wondrous, to keep his travels moving
throughout the season. Thank you, Paul.
Finally, Jimmy Duggan, for giving one the confidence required of oneself. Together also with
our mutual friend Alan Hudson who inspired to realise that through adversity one can
triumph.**

Table of Contents.

Foreword 5

Introduction. 6

August 14

September 39

October...63

November..81

December 99

January 112

February 134

March 161

April 195

May 230

1959 and All the Razzmatazz. 234

The Final Chapter..239

Supporters Games of the Season. 242

Acknowledgements: 243

The final word goes to the surviving twin brother Paul, of whom this book was dedicated at the very beginning. I will say it again, a miserable old so and so, but he is my mate, and that counts more to me than anything and he deserves the last say as he missed not one game this season home or away. 244

JE SUIS CHARLIE. 245

Foreword

What an honour and pleasure it is to be able to write a foreword to this book that started life as a bit of wacky idea and has evolved into a diary of an extraordinary and unique football club as it starts its life back where it belongs in the Football League after 5 years in exile.

In my forty odd years as a supporter, there has barely been a season that has passed where there hasn't been tears of joy as we have seen the team triumph at Wembley and glorious seasons of promotion. To the tears of despair of being ejected from the football league and watching in ignominy as "worst result ever followed worst result ever in non-league." What has stayed constant is the incredible and unwavering support of the fans, who travel the country in numbers which quite frankly are astonishing. This season is a reward to those hardy souls who have travelled from Barrow to Braintree and all points in between during the years in search of finally righting a wrong. Finally realising promotion back into the Football League. Maybe in years to come we will all look back and think it was a 5 years which made the club stronger for it in the long term even if at the time it didn't feel that way.

One of these hardy stalwarts Paul Wright has very kindly been the poor sod that has been entrusted to write the bulk of the match reports, we've rewarded him with £1.50 expenses per game enabling him to warm up at half time with a cup of tea for his trouble and we are eternally grateful for his contribution and incredible dedication in the face of adversity during trips to Newport and Bury on cold Tuesday evenings!

The writing of this piece comes as a great relief to me, a few may know of me, I am sure. I have upset a few people in the past , in fact I know I have, on social media with a few well intended casts of the rod, to the point where I have been banished from many a supporters group. With that I am now in hiding within the deep wilds of the Peruvian woodland with just a laptop, an old transistor to keep me company along with my league ladders and a signed Kevin Blackwell book of tactics.

No longer, though, will I have to spend half my nights reading the mysterious emails to proof read from Chris which have been sent in true John Gurney style in the early hours and bounce ideas back and forth to each other during the days over the last 9 months.

There are other books available from good book shops, and some rubbish shops too, about Luton Town and all are very valid and commendable. However, I do not think one has ever been written which covers the ups and downs of a season in such detail but also tackles issues which have arisen in the wide world of football at all levels and as such it has been an absolute honour to have played a very small part in this.

I am immensely proud of that, but mainly of Chris for his work, bravery and honesty in putting all this together.

Luton fans can be a diverse bunch, lots of moaning after a bad result, lots of disagreed views bought out by the wonders of Facebook, Twitter and the internet, but surely that's the beauty of the game isn't it? You may not agree but it all adds to the fun for me, football should be talked about and discussed for enjoyment.

As one wise wily old fox once said "the stronger the team, the stronger the team" Whatever happened to him?

I hope you enjoy this book and COYH!!!
Mike Thomas.

Introduction.

Here we are at last, the season we have all been waiting for has finally arrived, following five seasons in the basement of professional football, the Conference Premier, we are back in the Football League, it all starts here.

I speak plainly, I will upset many along the way and I have been in the past called a happy clapper, if only those that make such claims really knew.

I have for the sake of peace and goodwill to all men, in the past kept many of my thoughts to myself regarding certain things to do with the second sporting love of my life. Luton Town FC, my first being National Hunt racing, but that deserves my number one spot for one reason and one reason only, jump racing was my life it gave me so many emotional roller coaster rides, similar in fact to the rides that the "Hatters" have given us all over the years in many ways. As like our beloved club, I bounced back on numerous occasions, I was nowhere near successful, however I had the time of my life, and now I have found another love apart from NH racing and LTFC and that is simply to write about both. I am also not one of those that lives and breathes Luton Town. May I point out at this point that I am not criticising in any way those that are. I would just like it known that I am extremely passionate about many things in life and I will not be just aiming this book down one path. It shall meander, digress and go off the pathway now and again, of which I will not apologise for because when all said and done this is a journal of my thoughts, not just Luton Town but other interests in my life also.

I am not writing and publishing this book in the hope of selling a certain number of copies. To a degree, I doubt if I will even keep count, I am writing for my own enjoyment if I sell two copies I will be as pleased as if I sell two hundred thousand copies, which is not going to happen anyway. The fact is I am under no illusions that I can keep you interested throughout, but if I am able, well I will be a happy individual and I thank you for taking your valuable time to read and even more thanks for spending your hard earned pounds to purchase, I am eternally grateful to you.

One of my main regrets will be the lack of photographs available within this publication due to copyright restrictions, that as I write, I am doing my utmost to take care of, however in case of failure on this point I apologise in advance.

SO HERE WE GO!

Speaking for myself, it has not all been doom and gloom. Despite, what we could only define as a dubious choice of managers following the departure of Mick Harford, at least with Mick we knew he had the club at heart, the proof of the proverbial pudding being when he more or less admitted he just could not take the club any further than he had and resigned gracefully. To be honest the remainder up until the arrival of our saviour, John Still to take the reins three quarters through the 2012-2013 season, were farcical to a degree. Although, Gary Brabin did have the club at heart. Brabin's problem in fairness was he was not up to the job, but at least tried. For myself I enjoyed visiting and playing the non-league sides, met some great characters along the way, that is what football is about, as much as the winning, watching your team play, it's about the journey and the people we meet during that adventure.

Something else that caught my eye also, the players of these clubs at the lower end of the scale. It was a joy to see the likes of Edgar Davids when player-manager at Barnet, some of his touches were superb, although his temperament did let him down at times, for a player such as he is, at that level it was obviously difficult. However, players in the Conference and lower have much to teach those who earn millions at the higher levels, because we saw passion, commitment and determination, that at times would put many, if not most of our so-called stars to shame with their will to play and perform to the extremes of their ability. Maybe not so pretty to watch at times, not the same finesse, but hey what passion.

Each and every one of those managers that we gave the reins to, apart from Mick Harford and John Still, made the promise that they will get us back into the Football League at the first season of trying, and each failed, I will not say necessarily miserably, but they never the less failed. Mick, I recall said that it would not be an easy task, whilst on his arrival John Still told us in no uncertain terms that being realistic it will not be for a couple of seasons. However, I somehow felt at the time that he was as always being astute in winning the fans over from the start, no big announcement that we will do this and do that, just a calm and sensible approach to what was going to be a difficult job ahead. It was already obvious to the fans, that some players that he had inherited did not really have Luton Town at heart. He made it quite plain, if you do not want to "really" play for Luton Town, or himself, then they should leave there and then, and within weeks many of those that we already had doubts about were gone, either given free transfers or sold on.

The 2013-14 season was, in all a testament to the shrewdness of John Still and his assistant Terry Harris. They bought in players from the lower leagues and made them into good players. Not great players, but good, one player in particular benefitted from Stills' coaching and man management and that was Andre Gray, originally plucked from Conference North's Hinckley United by previous manager Paul Buckle, I said I was not going to mention the likes of, however this is the exception to the rule simply for signing Gray. For me at least Gray developed by a further 30% with the JLS input, he scored the same number of goals as his increased percentage, coincidence I have to admit, in his 45 appearances throughout the season. Gray was scouted through the latter parts. It was inevitable that he would leave the "Hatters" before this season got under way. In the end for a reported half a million pounds fee to Championship side Brentford, already in pre-season looking quite impressive for them. I for one will watch him with much interest this coming season and sincerely wish him well in his new venture.

One other player that has left the club in the close season is last season's skipper Ronnie Henry. The two parties were not able to agree terms beneficial to him and re-joined his former club Stevenage Town. I am sad to say, some were glad to see him go. Those same people may come to rue that later in the season. For myself a very influential captain last season and will be dearly missed.

Luton made a number of new signings during the summer, notably the return of Andy Drury who Luton sold to Ipswich Town in 2011, after playing 23 games and scoring 6 goals for the Hatters in a short spell during the 2010-2011 for £150,000. After a surge of bids to his current club at the time Crawley Town, the "Hatters" finally secured his services after paying out £100,000 on the 30th June 2014. It will be most interesting to see how he fares this time around. To be perfectly honest I am not a great fan of players returning to the club following a long spell away, unless still in their mid-twenties they are invariably lacking the pace they possessed during their past tenure. We have experienced the likes before, with much better players than Drury.

Paul Benson who had played a good part of last season for the "Hatters" on loan from Swindon Town also put pen to paper on a two-year contract.

So following what seems at least to have been a good solid start with the pre-season friendlies the time is nearly upon us as I write this, three days from the kick off. Luton's return to the Football League begins in earnest on Saturday August 9th 2014, at Carlisle United's Brunton Park. An interesting affair with both clubs playing their first games in League Two for a while, following Carlisle's relegation from League One at the end of last season.

Players.
Let us take a fleeting look at the players with whom Luton Town commence the new campaign.

He may, to some when first seeing him between the posts get the impression Mark Tyler is not that imposing a figure, but as the saying goes, looks can be deceiving, he was by a long way the best goalkeeper playing in the Conference throughout our time there. He is agile, quick to come off his line, and commands his area with authority, defenders and attackers alike are aware of his presence at all times. I have no concerns regarding "Tyles" this season at all.

Fraser Franks acquired from Welling United during last season, for me was always dependable. Strong in tackles, happy to go forward with the ball, he made several appearances for England C until recently, now because of Luton's league status he is no longer eligible, I am in the belief that Fraser will be quite an asset this coming season, however I am aware some do not agree with my thoughts.

Danny Fitzsimmons, one of those players that the manager recruited from a lower league club, Histon. There is little one can say in regards to Danny, Therefore he is one of many that I shall be following with interest and by the end of the season and of this book will have good things to add. Time will tell.

I believe given a full season and his leg withstands, Jonathan Smith will do reasonably well this season, he broke his leg at Barnet last season and this time round will seriously want to impose himself in the side.

Now the man who is the epitome of players, one who gives his utmost. He may not be the most talented or prettiest of players to watch. Nonetheless, would make my side week in week out purely on his commitment and obvious love for this club. I will admit that when Steve McNulty signed from Fleetwood Town I groaned, but the man grew on me as time went on. He looks overweight and clumsy, but either is not true, he has so much influence at the back for me, takes no prisoners, but not a hacker, just a hard tackling defender who does his job perfectly, most of the time. For me, despite being a defender scored the goal of the season, in 2013-2014 in the home game against Southport. Many, I have heard and read are waiting for him and hoping it seems to fail, I believe they will be waiting a while yet. Known too many these days as "Sumo" for his rather deceiving build, looks like an unfit Sumo wrestler hence the name, but kid you not, as I just said looks can be so deceiving. We shall have fun watching his showboating antics that is for sure.

Now to one of those I have earmarked as a potential star for the future. Twenty-one year old Alex Lacey, a defender by trade. Alex has much scope for improvement. I personally would be happy as punch if he pulls it off this season.

One of the senior players in the squad is Alex Lawless, our dependable Welsh wizard, a defensive midfielder who loves to come forward, scored what turned out to be the Town's winning goal against Wolverhampton Wanderers two seasons ago during our famous cup run. Always looks comfortable on the ball and an accurate passer in addition. For myself one of the best players on the park. Barring injuries and the like, I would expect Alex to be forever present.

There is much expected from Andy Drury as mentioned in my introduction, many expect him to fail as they do McNulty, but I dearly hope that they are proven to be totally wrong with their assumptions. Very effective player on the wing and in midfield, his pinpoint crosses may be a serious factor to Luton's success this season.

Stalwart Paul Benson signed a new two-year contract before the season commenced to the delight of most fans. The 6ft 2in striker will be in the goals again this season I am sure, having netted 17 in 36 appearances last season.

This next player exasperates me. He is capable of so much and I hope this season he will settle himself down and steady his nerve in front of goal. He does have a tendency to rush his shots and they go wide, out of bounds or upwards towards the space station, but on those occasions that he does connect, not many goalkeepers get a chance when on target. Living not far from Dartford, I decided to go watch him on a couple of occasions last season whilst he was on loan there. He netted some amazing goals, but missed even more through reckless shooting, he really does just need to calm himself take his time and with that he could be a force to contend with in League Two this season. His temperament does at times tend to take over which could also prove problematic though, Alex Wall just needs the JLS Midas touch to turn him into the player he has the potential to be, if nurtured correctly.

For the length of time Jake Howells has been playing as a regular first team player for Luton Town, one could not help but think that he must be turning 30 years of age, when in fact the lad is still only 23 years young and yet since making his debut on the final day of the season in 2007-08. He has gone on to make 276 appearances scoring 26 goals for the club. He can play most positions from defence to midfield on the left hand side and has plenty of pace and accuracy when running forward in a wingers role, something I enjoy immensely watching, there is for me not enough wing based play in English football at the moment. I am looking forward to much of the same this coming season. A very exciting player when he goes forward.

Scott Griffiths, I believe his appearances record for last season speaks for volumes, dependable and hardworking, resulted in him being forever present in both league and cup and has nothing to prove for me this season. An effective left sided defender. More of the same please Mr. Griffiths.

For Mark Cullen, this must be the season of make or break for him, hopefully his coming of age. He has the potential to be part of the main strike force. I have a good hunch for this young man, I am going to stick my nose out and say he could be one of the top marks-men in League Two.

A sensible player, who likes to play the wings, is how I see Andy Parry, signed last season from Southport at the same time as Shaun Whalley, is becoming quite a favourite with the Town fans and I would like to see him flourish this season and hold his own in the Football League. "Rooneeee", something we never expected to be singing from the terraces at Kenilworth Road. However, here we are doing exactly that, Luke Rooney, for me could, if he gets it right be a phenomenal player for the "Hatters" this season, signed from Maidstone United at the back end of last season on a short-term contract, which has been extended to a one-year contract. When at Swindon Town alongside Paul Benson they linked well, it would be something if the pair could do likewise this season for Luton.

Elliot Justham, a player for the future without a doubt, being understudy to first choice 'keeper Mark Tyler, obviously his opportunities of first team appearances will be limited, but he is a formidable replacement for Tyles if things go wrong through injury etc. When his time does arrive he has the talent and the confidence to do a sterling job.

Next, a player who could be one of a few that has the credentials to be awe inspiring, something special. Pelly Ruddock Mpanzu signed from West Ham during the summer following a successful loan period at Kenilworth Road. Pelly scored an absolute scorcher to bring the Town level at Dartford when the "Hatters" were looking as if they could suffer a shock defeat, the goal made a massive difference to the game that the Town eventually won two goals to one. He is capable of some amazing through balls. If anything his downfall may be from what I have interpreted, his desire to be successful and please everyone, maybe at times he tries too hard. With the help of the coaching staff to curb that enthusiasm just a tad he could be a real force in the Luton attacking midfield. A very strong looking player, with great potential and further scope to improve further.

Another close season signing that I was able to watch a few times last season as I only live two miles from the ground is Ross Lafayette, signed from Welling United and joining up with his former team mate Fraser Franks again. With Welling, he made it count in front of goal scoring 16 goals in 41 appearances that included three as a substitute. Formerly with Wealdstone, I will be watching with interest in the hope he will be able to cut it in League Football.

An unknown quantity for now is Ricky Miller, another summer signing from the non-league community, Boston United. An Ambitious Miller is quoted "I am not here to make up the numbers," One to watch with interest.

Shaun Whalley, signed together with Andy Parry from Southport United. Initially he is seen as a wing playing midfielder who likes to run forward with the ball, but can just as easily slot into a centre forward position, something that may well confuse some defences in the coming season hopefully. Definitely looking forward to his contribution.

What can I say about Luke Guttridge? The players Player of the Year, that says it all really. The much-travelled midfielder has remarkable experience at this level, and Guttridge will be an important asset to the squad this season.

Young Matthew Robinson, Made 39 appearances including substitutions last season for the "Hatters" bagging three goals in the process. Will be an important contributor in midfield I hope this season.

Yet another summer signing, this time from Lowestoft Town, is defender Curtley Williams. Apparently he enjoys going forward, so the Luton trend having defenders of that ilk continues from the days of Tim Breacker, Mitchell Thomas and the likes. Looking forward to seeing what this young man has to offer.

Youngsters are very much to the fore at Luton Town this season which has been one of Luton's policies for many years now, another rising up through the ranks is midfielder Jim Stevenson who had a welcomed loan spell at Dartford last season, he will be hoping to add to that experience as the season progresses without a doubt.

An experienced right back is Paul Connolly, who has played at League level with Millwall, Derby County, Plymouth Argyle, Leeds United and more. Therefore, the hope is he will have much to offer the squad in general.

Luke Wilkinson joined the "Hatters" in the summer from Borehamwood. John Still will know full well what Luke is capable of having been with him at Dagenham and Redbridge.

Brett Longden another youth protégé, a defender who will be hoping to get some regular first team experience through the season. One for the coming years' maybe?

Mark Onyemah signed from Thurrock in pre-season, he has represented England at school-boy level, I wonder if this is one of JSLs very shrewd moves, there is another young lad I will mention after going through the squad of whom I believe the boss has made a very clever move with.

Youth team striker Zane Banton signed professional forms in the summer and it is a fitting testament that he is included in the first team squad.

Charlie Walker comes to Luton from Ryman League South champions Peacehaven, following a 43-goal season, for the team that also went on to win the Sussex Senior Cup. I am impressed with Still's knack in finding players of this calibre from the lower leagues, bringing them into the club and coaching them on to be competent League players, he did similar at both Barnet and Dagenham and Redbridge.

We have another proper Charlie, in the guise of Charlie Smith, last year's youth team captain signed his professional forms in the summer, a very influential midfielder who can the pass the ball with impeccable skill, with the credentials he has already surmounted we can expect much from this talented young man in the future, hopefully with Luton Town.

Eighteen-year-old Ian Rees concludes the members of the squad that start the season for Luton Town, Rees a midfielder well thought of by Mr. Still and recently rewarded with his professional forms.

As I mentioned earlier there is one more summer signing that I would like to make a comment on, regarding that of young Lee Angol who upon signing, has been sent on loan for the season to Borehamwood. On his arrival he was put straight into the side to play Arsenal XI and watched by Arsene Wenger, at times Lee ripped his way through the Arsenal midfield and impressed Wenger a great deal. A season out on loan at Borehamwood can only be a plus for a young man who has so much talent to prove to us in the future, I for one will be watching his progress this season quite avidly.

The Squad numbers:

1. Mark Tyler.
2. Fraser Franks.
3. Danny Fitzsimons.
4. Jonathan Smith.
5. Stephen McNulty.
6. Alex Lacey.
7. Alex Lawless.
8. Andy Drury.
9. Paul Benson.
10. Alex Wall.
11. Jake Howells.
12. Scott Griffiths.
13. Mark Cullen.
14. Andy Parry.
15. Luke Rooney.
16. Elliot Justham.
17. Pelly Ruddock Mpanzu.
18. Ross Lafayette.
19. Ricky Miller.
20. Shaun Whalley.
21. Luke Guttridge.
23. Matthew Robinson.
24. Curtley Williams.
28. Jim Stevenson.
29. Paul Connolly.
30. Luke Wilkinson.
32. Brett Longden.
33. Mark Onyemah.
34. Zane Banton.
35. Charlie Walker.
36. Charlie Smith.
39. Ian Rees.

August

Run up to the opener.
As the opening game gets closer, the calming effect of manager John Still will be paramount, not only for the players but the fans also. The euphoria that has been building since that day when Luton Town were officially crowned Champions of The Skrill Conference Premier has been growing daily. Feet have to make contact with the floor again. There is much to do this coming season if many supporter's dreams of back-to-back promotions are to prove to be not just dreams but fact. Reality has to kick in from this point for many, which this is not going to be a walk in the park. As I write this the "Hatters" are 15/2 joint favourites with one of our old sparring partners Portsmouth, it could be a royal battle indeed, but there are twenty two other clubs to do battle with out there and each one starts the season with the same expectations as we have. There are some formidable opponents just waiting to take all six available points from us this season.
Technically, this season also realises Luton Town defending their Johnson's Paint Trophy crown. Still unbeaten in the competition since Sunday 5th April, 2009, when the virtually relegated "Hatters" took a horde of 40,000 supporters down the M1 to Wembley stadium with the task of facing League One outfit Scunthorpe United, winning 3-2, after an early battering, with a superb finish from Frenchman Claude Gnapka. Not only winning the trophy, but also putting two fingers firmly up the nose of Football League chairperson Lord Mawhinney. Mawhinney was instrumental in orchestrating Luton's demise from the Football League that same season by deducting thirty points from the outset. Effectively sending the Town into the abyss, the Blue Square Premier, virtually before a ball had even been kicked, in to what even to this day some look upon as not only a personal vendetta against the club but also an illegal act. Since that time, many bigger clubs have made much larger dishonest dealings than Luton but have walked away with hardly a blemish to their records. However, that is now in the past and as saying we always used to use in horse racing after a knock was as I say now, we get up, dust ourselves off, get back in the saddle, onwards and upwards, it's the only way we know.
As we await the start of the season Luton have a bye into the second round of the "Paint Pot" competition.
The first big news for the coming season, following the signings of the new members of the squad is that Steve McNulty is named as captain, which I am sure has gone down well with many of the supporters and more importantly the players. Yorkie Bar as I have called him since first watching him play for the "Hatters", something in large to do with his chunky appearance, is for me the perfect choice, he commands the defence vociferously and with his attitude towards the game. He was quoted as saying, "That if it wasn't for coming to Luton I would maybe even have made the decision to quit football, joining Luton is the best thing I have done in my footballing career." His love of the club is obvious every time he walk out onto the park. He will in time be one of the cult figures of LTFC, joining the ranks of our past cult type figures that included Wayne Turner and marvellous Marvin Johnson, to name but a couple.

Friday August 8th 2015
It is one day from kick off. The squad that will travel to Carlisle United later is named and good to learn that Luke Guttridge will travel as a member of the squad, he had been out since 1st March,

when injured against Alfreton Town, so it is great to see him return ready for the fray at Brunton Park.
Not so lucky are Alex Lawless nursing a slight hamstring problem, Jonathan Smith and Shaun Whalley, both missed a couple of days training and therefore will not be risked for the long trip northwards. The fourth absentee being Andy Parry, who took a knock against Biggleswade Town in a pre-season game. Otherwise, the Town have a fully fit side ready and eager to hit the trail.
The team leave on a 550 mile round trip, in the newly acquired King's Ferry coach. Starting with a training session at Preston North End's training ground later in the afternoon.

Saturday August 9th 2014

The day all "Hatters" supporters have been waiting five very long years for, following a period that felt like purgatory. The day has arrived. It should be said, with relief, yes, we are back.
It is a four and a half hour journey, up the M1 and M6 to Carlisle, 275 miles of orange and white flags, banners and the like, more like a convoy travelling in military precision. People waving and shouting to each other with so much expectation in their hearts. To be honest, win draw or lose it is going to be a fantastic atmosphere this afternoon at Brunton Park. The Football League really will realise today that Luton Town are back where they belong. Of course we want to win or at least bring an away point home with us tonight, but let's face it today is just as much about showing those that tried so hard to kill the spirit of our great club they could never do that, we are bigger and better than they will ever be. "WE ARE BACK TO ROCK THE WORLD", just one of many quotes heard this week.
What I will add, is that during this week many "Hatters" fans have received "tweets" and other social media messages from football fans from nearly all of the other 72 football league clubs sending the club best wishes, many saying we should never have been in such a dilemma at all considering the circumstances that sent us down. It shows the support we have witnessed throughout our plight, and the only losers' long term are those that did their utmost to bring our club down to its knees. Thank you to every one of those who sent their best wishes.
The sun is shining down on Carlisle, and the city is in for a treat, as the sea of orange floats its way forward. Over 1,200 travelling supporters are converging on what was a Roman settlement in the past, so it is well used to being invaded, if there are any naughty shenanigans this afternoon from any Town fans and they get locked up for a while, they will be in good company because Mary Queen of Scots was a prisoner in Carlisle.

The pubs are packed to the rafters with Luton fans taking over the town, all in good spirit. As 2.15 approaches the bars begin to empty out as the band of orange raiders slowly descend upon the area of Brunton Park reserved for away supporters. The banter between both sets of supporters is of a friendly nature. Expectations are high for both sides on this first day of the season. It is a good turnout from both clubs. The rattle of the turnstiles hidden by the growing crescendo of both sets of fans chants and songs.

The team sheet arrives, not many surprises for Luton Town, two debutants in centre-half Luke Wilkinson, playing alongside the newly appointed skipper, Steve McYorkie (McNulty), who it has to be said is looking fitter and leaner than he ever seemed to be last season and newly signed right back Paul Connolly.

One landmark for the "Hatters" is the fact that it is goalkeeper Mark Tyler's 200th League appearance between the sticks. That being 199 appearances in the Conference Premier and his first in League Two. Quite apt when one thinks about it, congratulations Tyles

The team line up reads:

Mark Tyler, Paul Connolly, Scott Griffiths, Luke Wilkinson, Steve McNulty, Alex Lacey, Matty Robinson, Andy Drury, Jake Howells, Mark Cullen and Paul Benson.

Substitutes; Elliot Justham, Fraser Franks, Alex Wall, Pelly Ruddock Mpanzu, Luke Guttridge and Jim Stevenson

Carlisle United 0 Luton Town 1

Following the customary huddle by the Town player's it is down to the real business. Their first touch of a ball in league football for five years, the fans are having celebrations at the away end, Luton win a corner in the very first minute but comes to nothing. The game is slow to take off and there are not many chances to shout about, but that does not quieten the delighted Luton fans. With thirty minutes on the clock, Paul Benson picks up the ball just inside the Carlisle half. He runs with it a few yards before finding Jake Howells running down the right touchline. Howells' dances past a defender sliding in on him and pulls the ball inside. Getting close to the bye line crosses the ball across the home goalmouth beating two defenders. With the goalkeeper stuck to his line striker Mark Cullen slips in behind two other Carlisle defending players to the far post and easily slides the ball across the line. GOAL! Luton have a deserved 1-0 lead on the balance of the play. I earlier predicted this could be young Cullen's season, a good start, and the perfect confidence booster for him

At the other end of the stadium, the crowd erupts with sheer delight… "LUTON ARE BACK, LUTON ARE BACK…" the fans are calling out. Around the rest of the ground there are obvious signs of unrest, with many of the home support, after relegation the previous season it is too much of the same for many of them. The remainder of the first half is on the whole as it was before, a quiet affair. At the interval whistle, the unrest of the home supporters is obvious, their team booed off the pitch. How often have we heard that in the past five years from "Hatters" fans? Therefore, it is quite refreshing in some ways for the boot to be on the other foot, despite the fact I am not a fan of booing your own side whatever the situation, let me be clear on my thoughts regarding such, not the best morale booster on the planet that is for certain.

One thing about half time intervals that make me laugh there are these days almighty queues for the toilet. Not many though there for natural relief. The smell of cigarette smoke is chokingly obvious. Despite the signs plastered all over the place advising that the stadium is a no-smoking zone, as for me all I ever want to do is relieve my aching bladder of the excess beer that has been building up throughout the lunch time drinking period, normally downing as many as possible in a limited period of time.

That reminds me of some years ago when travelling to St. James Park, Newcastle for an evening game against The Magpies, I was travelling for one of the only times I ever did so in all these years of supporting the "Hatters" with the "Bobbers" club on their official coach. Stopping just outside Newcastle at a small town called Washington, we clambered into the only pub near to the coach park we were situated. The driver, or whoever was in charge of the coach at the time, maybe even Mr Luton himself, John Pyper (that's another story for another time), declared that we had a thirty minute break before making the rest of the journey. Well, as I mentioned quite a few of us clambered into the pub, mainly for a visit to the toilet. However, I bee-lined to the bar and ordered a pint, believe me it never touched the sides. A second quickly ordered. That one also dispatched with ease. As I was ordering my third pint, another guy from the group kept looking over. For some reason I got the impression he wanted to say something. However, hesitating to do so, after ordering the third pint in the first ten or so minutes, yes travelling in a coach can be a thirsty job. I looked down the bar again with the corner of my eye and started to realise that this fella with long straggly hair and glasses was actually trying, and succeeding it must be said to keep up with me. I started to grin and could not resist asking if this was so. Upon which he said quite matter of fact anything that I drink he can equal, so that started it, we must have downed about seven pints of bitter in that thirty minute stop, I must admit though I remember feeling quite unsteady on the plates of meat afterwards. Well, this guy and I got talking and I learnt his name was Dave. He usually travelled to games with his twin brother Paul, who unfortunately could not get time off work for this particular match. We stood together throughout the goalless draw that evening and became good mates along with him and his brother. For many years now whenever able to make a game, because I was in horse racing at the time and getting away to games was not easy, we would meet up. They have always been thought to many as an odd pair, some I recall called them the bookend twins, which to me seemed a little cruel, but I suppose that's how life is at times, bloody cruel. Dave passed away four years ago now, from a rare form of throat cancer, to me he is sorely missed, but I do still frequent games with his brother when able, where conversation always and I mean always returns to memories of Dave.

Well I certainly digressed there a little, it takes up the time waiting for the sides to come out again though I suppose.

Carlisle come out a lot more lively in the second half and if not for some good 'keeping from Mark Tyler, Billy Paynter could have scored once if not twice. They bought the game to Luton and there was some staunch defending for our boys to deal with. Andy Drury for the "Hatters" had a good long distance effort beat the Carlisle keeper, but go just wide of the post, before being substituted for Jim Stevenson after 69 minutes, with Jake Howells being replaced by Luke Rooney after 83 minutes.

There were a couple of good chances late into the game for both sides, but Luton managed to hold on and record a win on their return to the Football League, securing all three points with a clean sheet as well. Therefore, that long journey home was thankfully not going to be one of misery.

After the game John Still said that Luton still need to get better, and that it is now important to carry the momentum on, he also praised young debutante Luke Wilkinson, who impressed with his defending, he played extremely well for a young lad.

The only card of the game, a yellow, went to Luton's Paul Connolly.

The games attendance was 6,760, which included 1,088 orange shirted Luton fans. Not a bad turn out, considering the distance.

The biggest win of the day in League Two was Morecambe's 3-0 thrashing at Dagenham and Redbridge, therefore finding themselves top of the tree after one game.

It is good to see that the "Hatters" supporters have received recognition already this season having been awarded the FL72 supporters of the weekend award, in recognition of over 1,000 travelling fans making such a long round trip from Luton to Carlisle

Tuesday 12th August 2014

On what is a sad day we learn of the passing of one of my most favourite comedy actors Robin Williams, apparently from his own hand? Depression is such a frightening illness that can creep up on any one of us without any warning whatsoever, even to the best of us. Just for the record, my all-time favourite film of Mr Williams was not one of his more well-known productions but a very beautifully made and touching film named "What Dreams May Come", with Annabella Sciorra and Cuba Gooding Jnr. About a man, portrayed by Williams, who was killed in an accident but his spirit and soul will not accept the fact that he is dead. One great actor who will be dearly missed for a good time to come.

Back to business, Town are preparing for their first home game of the season.

The first game at Kenilworth Road in competition mode and the visitors are Swindon Town in the first round of The Capital One Cup, our first venture in the competition for five years, a competition we won in 1988, when known as the Littlewoods Cup, when beating Arsenal at Wembley.

The atmosphere a little muted, as it always was in the past when it came to the early round of this competition, I see nothing has changed there then.

Swindon are located in League One and having a good start themselves beating Scunthorpe United 3-1 in their opening fixture of the season.

The line-up has changed from Saturdays' game at Carlisle with Luke Rooney, Fraser Franks and Jimmy Stevenson all getting starts.

Mark Tyler, Paul Connolly, Scott Griffiths, Fraser Franks, Steve McNulty, Luke Wilkinson, Luke Rooney, Matt Robinson, Paul Benson, Mark Cullen and Andy Drury.

Substitutes; Alex Lacey, Alex Wall, Jake Howells, Elliot Justham, Pelly Ruddock Mpanzu, Ross Lafayette and Luke Guttridge.

Luton Town 1 Swindon Town 2

John Still experimented with three centre backs, some will say not the way to go, but this was a game where it would be worth the try at least.

Swindon had much the better of the possession from the off, but Luton defended admirably, not giving Swindon time on the ball. Their best efforts described as hopeful pot shots. They played a patient passing game that seemed to frustrate Luton at times with a number of silly fouls being committed. Swindon bossed the midfield, maybe Luton giving them too much respect and standing off too much. It's ironic that one of the many loanee's Paul Buckle introduced into the club during his short tenure of the team, was the player holding the game up for them, Yaser Kasim whom we had loaned from Brighton at the time, I always thought would have been a decent signing to make, throughout the game

It was hard work for the Luton midfield but as half time loomed ever closer they were at least starting to get into the game more.

The second half saw the "Hatters" tempo rise a gear.

Mark Tyler looking for route one, kicking the ball upfield found Paul Connolly who rose majestically and his powerful header went goal-wards only to be handled by Nathan Thompson in the area, the linesman did not hesitate in putting up his flag, penalty to Luton, against the run of play in all fairness. Despite a mass of Swindon players surrounding the guilty linesman, but neither he nor the referee, Paul Tierney, were going to be swayed. Luke Rooney keeping his calm stepped up to take the kick and cleanly stroked the ball low to keeper Mark Fotheringhams' right, 1-0 to Luton, their first real effort on target for the night so far.

Luke Rooney was in fact having his best performance for the Town since his dazzling display at Dartford on April 1st last season, when most instrumental in the teams turn around which looked like it was going the home sides' way until he and Pelly Ruddock Mpanzu entered the battle.

Soon after the penalty, Paul Connolly had a great chance when he powered in a shot on target with Fotheringham forced into what was a rare save on the night.

With Mark Cullen receiving hardly any service from the midfield all evening, John Still decided to change the formation and bring Luke Guttridge for the somewhat redundant Cullen, who unlike Saturday at Carlisle never got into the game.

Despite being a goal behind Swindon were looking on the ascendancy and it was not long before their hard work paid off. Luton's defence were defending with tenacious intent, it seems that JSL experimentation was working with good effect, the problems came in midfield once the ball cleared, as they were unable to hold the ball up. Most of Swindon's efforts were continually of the long-range kind.

Luton made their second change of the night, Paul Benson replaced by Russ Lafayette for his first senior appearance in a Luton town shirt. The Swindon support gave Benson rousing applause as he left the field of play, always being a respected player for them in the past.

As time drew on Swindon's constant pressure was starting to take its toll, and finally its mark made. A superb turn and cross-field pass by Michael Smith found Nathan Byrne and a clumsy attempt at winning the ball. Paul Tierney did not hesitate in pointing to the spot. Smith struck the ball low and hard into the right side of Tyler's net, he guessed right as to where the ball would be sent, but the pace and the power of the shot was always going to be quite impossible to get even a touch to, 1-1.

Pelly Ruddock Mpanzu was Luton's final change in the 77th minute, replacing Matty Robinson. It was Pelly unfortunately, who played a hand in what was to be the winning goal of the game. Slow to sense the danger of Massimo Luongo, Steve McNulty did his best to rectify the situation and it left him out of position to allow Luongo to play a pass into the path of Michael Smith who for the second time finished quite clinically giving Tyler no chance whatsoever.

On the night as he has been during every minute of his service for Luton Town, Mark Tyler was superb between the sticks, making yet again some superb saves, to keep the Town at least in contention in a as much as it was only a single goal deficit.

Six minutes added time following a nasty clash of heads earlier in the game between Swindon's Jordan Turnbull and the "Hatters" Paul Benson.

Late into injury time, Luke Guttridge found the other Luke, Rooney, on the edge of the box. Rooney did one of his infamous step-overs before going down in the box, it was quite upsetting to see the Swindon players making a most concerted effort to have Rooney sent off, quite ironic really when all evening they had been going down much too easily when tackled. Typical Paul Cooper tactics I have noticed down the seasons, to think he was at one time favourite to take the Luton hot seat, would not have been many Luton supporters' favourite managers that is for sure.

To be fair to referee Tierney he was at least consistent, something else that has been sorely lacking from the game at all levels for way too long, consistency between referees', as Rooney had already been booked earlier in the game he had no choice but to show him a red card.

Well, at least we have averted the ghastly horror of being involved in the tedious Europa League next season. We won the League Cup when it meant something rather than the afterthought it is these days, so it would be greedy to win it again.

A defeat, but one in which the players showed fight and determination, however in truth not enough quality against an excellent Swindon side, whose ability to go to ground when someone breathed on them was quite awe inspiring. Credit where it's due, Swindon passed and moved the ball extremely well. After watching Conferences lesser players over the past five years, it was novel to see someone pass the football rather than taking three hundred and seventy four touches to miscontrol the ball. Nonetheless, we made a very good side work hard to beat us.

Wednesday 13th August 2014

It's the morning after the night before, the Rooney affair still sticking in the throat of John Still it seems, especially as now comes to light the same Swindon players that were demonstrating and insisting Rooney be sent off were later saying the player was clipped and it should have been a penalty. The manager makes a good point when asking the question "Why would the lad need to dive when he has a clear run at goal and a scoring opportunity?"

However, what is done, is done the game over and it is time to begin concentrating on the forthcoming home game against another club whose supporters have suffered over recent years. AFC Wimbledon who rebuilt themselves from the ashes of a club that turned tail and ran to Milton Keynes, leaving many without a club, but whose tenacity built a club worthy of league status again, much respect to them. Usually we would wish such a club well, but not this week, we are on their case, determined to take all three points to give us a one hundred per cent start to the season in League Two.

John Still decides it a good idea to keep yours truly on his toes this evening, no sooner am I about to throw the towel in for the day, the alarm bells sound, Luton Town have an announcement to make, please don't tell me Wayne Turner is coming out of retirement, that I could not handle today believe me. But no something much more mundane and less exciting, the signing that we had been anticipating, despite not knowing who it would be until now, he had hinted before the Swindon game that there was another imminent signing of a young player. So at ten minutes to eight this evening the announcement is made that he has signed a player who had featured in a couple of pre-season friendlies, former Reading under 18, Oxford City and of late Banbury United winger, 20 year old Kynan Isaac.

Quite a controversial figure it seems though, in January 2014 having been given a seven game ban following alleged racist comments to an assistant referee during a Banbury United v Bedford Town match in 2013. Isaac recommended to Luton by Banbury boss Edwin Stein who was quoted as saying that Isaac was capable of playing at a much higher level than he was at Spencer Stadium. This I suspect will be the "Hatters" final signing for quite a while and it will be interesting to see how quickly Isaac's will be slotted into the side, or is he yet another young player designed for Luton's long term future, whichever it may be welcome to Kenilworth Road young man.

Thursday 14th August 2014

Well, it's not exactly Luton Town, but what a shocker, probably the best manager/coach Crystal Palace have had in many years, just resigned. Tony Pulis, saved them from what looked like certain relegation last season in the Premiership, and voted Premier League manager of the year, something drastic must have gone on there, I would hazard a guess and say that he could not get on with Chairman Steve Parish, and the club statement on their website was most informative and really showed their appreciation to the man that most probably made them millions last season ….

This is the Club statement.
Crystal Palace Football Club can confirm that Tony Pulis has left the club by mutual consent with immediate effect.
Keith Millen will be in temporary charge of the team for our opening Barclays Premier League game against Arsenal this Saturday.
The club would like to thank Tony for his efforts with the club during last season and wish him all the best for the future.

Simple as that nothing more. What an insult.

Friday 15th August 2014

One day to go before the first League home game for over 5 years. How fitting that our opponents are AFC Wimbledon, themselves having a raw deal in the past. I usually watch their results with interest as I am known to throw back a few beers with a group of the original Dons' fans and now staunch AFC supporters which is great, in Weatherspoon's at Thornton Heath, a good bunch of lads it has to be said.

Neal Ardley, the Dons manager actually believes they now have at their disposal the best squad they have had since the club was re-formed and for many tomorrow's game will be an interesting contest without a doubt. They have a player in Adebayo Akinfenwa who could outweigh any other player in the football league I would imagine, weighing in at a staggering 16 stone and yet the media constantly take the piss out of our own Yorkie bar mountain Steve McNulty, who is a mere boy in comparison to Bayo. A great contest will be had if centre back McNulty and striker Bayo Akinfenwa come to together, it could be something to measure on the Richter scale. Earthquake warnings will be sounding off around Kenilworth Road tomorrow, which is by all accounts a sell-out game.

AFC's opening game of the season was at home to Shrewsbury Town and resulted in a hard fought 2-2 draw with their goals coming from two debutants Sean Rigg and a player of whom the "Hatters" were chasing a couple of seasons ago Matt Tubbs.

Thomas Palmgren, awaiting his flight to Luton.

Luton will be welcoming a fan from Lidköping in Norway, Thomas Palmgren, who comes over to watch the Town as often as possible, an ardent Luton Town supporter from afar, it will be good to see you at the Kenny Thomas enjoy the game.

Saturday 16th August 2014
Luton's manager John Still has called for the players to take care not to become entangled within the atmosphere at Kenilworth Road that has the makings of being a magnificent afternoon for our first home match back in League Two. Last season, when the Skrill Premiership was all but ours to take, we played Braintree in what was a carnival atmosphere. If the game won we would have been Champions that day, but we were all stunned when Braintree took a 3-0 lead, the "Hatters" did pull it back to 3-2 but all too late, the players it seems got caught up in the celebrations and took their eye off the ball. I was talking to someone regarding this and he tried to tell me that it was most unprofessional of the players to allow that the happen! I cannot agree with that statement, players are human just as much as the fans, and when surrounded by such an atmosphere, of course it is easy to become embroiled in the euphoria of the moment. However today is a little different, we are not on the verge of a Championship trophy, we are gearing up for a fight to the end, and I feel that the players will be fully charged for this afternoons contest. I am hoping for a great atmosphere and one hell of a game.

Luton is filling up with both "Hatters" and "Wombles" alike, the White House pub is close to overfill with both Luton and Wimbledon supporters and the visitors are reported to be bringing over 800 fans up from their South London home. Nice to have a few pints before the game. The only downside being the numerous journeys we often have to make to relieve one's self during the match itself that maybe doesn't go down too well with your neighbours in the seats, it was perfect one season when I managed to get a seat at the end of the row, makes life much easier that's for sure.

I often wonder why they called down the side of the where the Billy Butlin chalets are now situated, did his son play for the "Hatters", Barry Butlin?, the "Bobbers", could it be the fact that when the seats were introduced it was a matter of bobbing up and down for those requiring the room of thrones? That is a thought! I know the Stanyon twins used to get well pissed off with me for my ups, downs and on my way. However, by the second half there were times that they had consumed so much one of them at least would have a crafty kip whilst the game was in play, most probably dreaming of faraway places, such as the Premier League. Miss you Dave mate!

Just a little thought before the game as another one in Manchester finishes. I wonder what my mate Alan Hudson will make of this, Manchester United 1 Swansea 2, he predicted earlier this week it will not all be roses for United, like myself that pre-season drubbing of Liverpool in America meant nothing in reality, despite the United band wagon fans thinking this season is going to be a walk in the park, Well they have had their thirty seconds of fame in this book, now back to real football.

Well the game is nearly upon us, make way for the toilet trolls…

The Luton Town line up is as follows:

Mark Tyler, Fraser Franks, Scott Griffiths, Steve McNulty, Luke Wilkinson, Matt Robinson, Andy Drury, Luke Guttridge, Jake Howells, Mark Cullen and Paul Benson.

Subs: Alex Lacey, Alex Wall, Pelly Ruddock Mpanzu, Ross Lafayette, Curtley Williams, Luke Stevenson, Elliot Justham

So Two changes from the starting line up at Carlisle last Saturday, Fraser Franks replaces Paul Connolly and Luke Guttridge comes in for Alex Lacey.

Luton Town 0   AFC Wimbledon 1

Following the celebrations of last Saturday at Carlisle, the parachutes were out as the Town came back down to earth with a slight crunch, not a big one mind you. Carlisle gave us the space allowing us to play football, from Wimbledon it was the complete opposite, never allowing us time on the ball. Despite a good ratio in regards to possession.

In a game which lacked quality, apart from Tubbs' finish.

We started well enough, reasonable tempo, although even from the early stages, it looked like it would be difficult to break Wimbledon down or get behind them.

They were more streetwise than many of our rising stars, who for a good few are still learning the ropes of how demanding and ruthless League football can be. Wimbledon more often than not quicker to the ball with their midfield winning more second balls. With a weak referee, they had the awareness to make use of that fact, using every situation when put their way to time waste to the letter. Time wasting is not something I condone from any team to be honest, however you cannot blame the opposition players, of course they are going to take advantage of every opportunity the blame is solely at the feet of the referee who did not stamp on it when he could and should have done. Maybe a couple of the Wimbledon players could sign up to be starring on WWE rather than playing league football. Luton had three very reasonable penalty appeals waved away. Scott Griffiths was the first to go in the book, for what yes was admittedly those officiating the game the fact only minutes before a foul on Mark Cullen by Fuller totally missed, or even ignore a late tackle on Francomb, what really did rile the Luton support and the players.

The winning goal and the only one of the game to be fair a well taken one. Bayo Akinfenwa flicked a long ball on to Matt Tubbs, after beating McNulty for speed hitting a powerful strike past Mark Tyler, who in total fairness had no possible chance of getting to it leave alone stopping it, so that was it 0-1 to Wimbledon.

The Hatters had a number of good chances but it was not to be their day, in fact, in the final quarter of the game, the "Hatters" were peppering the Wimbledon goal from all angles, sadly, though with nothing of power and purpose, also they seemed to lack any imagination when going forward.

However, despite the loss, fans are still surrounding the area of the tunnel and singing their hearts out in support to the team, it was a hard fought game. How pleasing for once to see the team applauded in such a way following defeat, how different is that from this time last season, when starting to get on players backs already. The truth is this league is going to be difficult. So I hope this trend continues in an upward spiral from the supporters, because my thoughts are and always have been, get behind the players not on their backs. A happy club brings success, which has been one of the problems in the past, the fans discord rubbing off on the players and sapping their confidence. Continue knock a player he will start to think he is as bad as some may be saying, that results in heads dropping, give a player confidence with solid remarks, his chest expands his heart quickens and he gets in there and has a go. That is my philosophy any way and always worked for me when I was coaching, it does not matter who the players are professional or community team kid's, positivity works.

In addition, yes, as always with some Luton Town fans, if you can truly call them that at time, the moaners and groaners are out. Homing in on the games with our return to the football league and they appear from nowhere, it's the same ones every season, it's funny though, at the end of last season they were there with everyone else shouting the praises from above, how times change, but then do they change really? Nope not really, they are just as weak and fickle as ever.

Sunday 17th August 2014

The dust has settled somewhat and now the analysis begins, Facebook is being peppered with all the armchair managers and coaches having their two penny worth, to be honest on the whole mostly on a positive note with some very good points. I did love the banter regarding the battle of the giants, our skipper Steve McNulty and Wimbledon's Adebayo Akinfenwa, how they kind of squared up to each other, to be fair the media hyped this meeting of two over-sized professional footballers and were looking for it to happen, and to their joy yes the boys duly obliged.

I wonder if in reality there were not looking for an opportunity to please the expectant fans and media. Surely not.

I have just read an article on the London 24 website. Low and behold, there is the Wimbledon manager claiming that they could have won by three or four goals easily. Mr Ardley I suggest you watch again, the Town could just as easily been awarded three separate penalties we had more clear cut chances to score than your side and yes you did admittedly hold your own in the midfield area, but win by three or four goals? No sir, come back down to reality, you won a game where a draw would have been a fair reflection. You got the run of the green today and a referee who was not able to stamp his authority on the game, I am not bitter that we lost, far from it, but I do live in the world of realism, his verdict on the game much different and much more realistic in comparison.

John Still was adamant the team played okay. There was a problem in the final third with the lack of passes and finishing, but limiting the opponents to only a few real chances. Yes agreed we needed more force in front of goal, no real power. However, we started much the same last season also but when the players found their feet it all came together nicely. These things take time. He was always in the mind-set that we would eventually equalise, but it did not happen this time round and that is football.

Therefore, Neal Ardley I suggest you go away and watch the game as a neutral not a manager in rose tinted glasses that you could not have bought from Specsavers. Vision Express maybe?

Monday 18th August 2014

Time to move on. It is the turn of Bury on Tuesday evening, again at the Kenny. They are hoping to sign striker Danny Rose from Barnsley later today or tomorrow I hear.

Manager John Still quoted as saying that he is in the belief that Bury will be one of the clubs vying for promotion at the end of the season, but did question their signing of older experience players to get them in to such a position. The problem he quite rightly assesses is that come next season if they were to win promotion where would they really be. That comes back to the philosophy behind the way he is preparing Luton, for the future rather than the present. He says, "I just believe if you can start a process of those young, hungry, ambitious players and gradually keep adding to it and adding to it, then in three or four years, you've got a reasonable young, experienced, energetic, athletic, ambitious team and that's how I believe the right way to do it is. You need your experience, you do, but gradually your experience becomes your 24-year-olds." Those who may be braying for blood at the end of the season if we do not win promotion or finish closer to the bottom rather than the top will stop think and reflect.

On a previous page I mentioned a name most familiar to many Luton supporter and somewhat ridiculed by many, yes I think in fairness most of us know him just as "Pyper", but John Pyper, bless his little coat tails must be the "living legend", when it comes to Luton Town supporters. He does get some stick the poor old sod. Well this is Teflon country mate so hold on to all those Luton hats you've got mate because here we go again, but don't worry it's all in good faith, actually maybe not, with a sinister little grin on my face as keyboard clicks over and over.

It was a summer's afternoon and we were playing a pre-season in the evening at Brisbane Road against The Orient as Leyton Orient were known for a while at least. Having arranged to meet Paul and Dave Stanyon later I had arrived early as I took the advantage of a little visit elsewhere beforehand, of that I will not go into for now, number one she was a Spurs supporter so that is something to keep quiet about. Anyway following my spot of afternoon delight, thank you kindly to the Starland Vocal Band for that little ditty, I took my way over to Leyton. Upon where I went into one of the local hostelries, as you do, there at the bar was one of Luton Town's welsh wizards. We had a trio if I remember correctly at the time. John Hartson, Mark Pembridge and the fellow at the bar Ceri Hughes. Because glass at his side, it is obvious he was not playing on this particular evening. I asked him what he was drinking, why not the bar was relatively empty anyway. I had already ordered whatever my drink of the moment was, no not a soft one, I was on leave from racing or something more sinister like I had took a sickie when not really sick or injured, anyway to my amusement Hughsie replied "I'll have a treble vodka and slim tonic if that okay", sure I said, why not? At that, the ole lad called to the barman on second thoughts hold the fucking tonic. Following a good chat, no there is nothing more to tell though, apart that he was out of his face and I would just add that as a little salad filling. I had to make my way back to Leyton tube station to meet Paul and Dave Stanyon as we had arranged, When they eventually turned up, who was tagging along? None other than that most amiable of fellows John Pyper. It was still early so there was time to take in a couple of pubs at least, as you do.

As it happened, I knew some good people not far from the station who had a pub. I suggested we go there. We will at least get a decent pint. Therefore, off we trudged, it was not far so did not take very long at all. On the arrival at our destination, I walked in first and greeted with great gusto by a few of the regulars and my good friend Sonny, who owned the place, closely followed by Dave and Paul, Pyper no sign of him. I step outside and there he was standing there with a look of horrified concern on his face. "But, Chris it's a black mans' pub we can't go in there, they don't like us going into their bars." It took a while but I was able to convince the poor soul it was fine. That I know them. We were there for about half an hour. I have never seen anybody looking terrified as John did that evening. I was pissing myself with laughter and doing my best not to let it show. What was funniest that he had a collection of bags with him, I don't think he ever let go of those bags the whole time we were in that pub. As the time passed, I realised the nervousness was not dissipating from the poor guy, he was totally bricking it. Obviously too many stories heard, all unfounded I can assure you, the regulars in the bar even tried to make him feel welcome but to no avail. Eventually for the sake of reasoning, we decided to go elsewhere, sad really, because in reality one could feel more at ease there than most of the other bars around. Without doubt, the friendliest bar in the area when there was a game at Brisbane Road. After that evening, I cannot recall him ever tagging along with the brothers when I was with them again. He most probably thinks I am too dangerous to know. Whenever I saw him after that he would acknowledge but never really speak. Except one time at Wembley when we played Nottingham Forest in the Littlewoods Final of 1989. John was sitting in the row in front and a couple of my mates from my home town of Kempston, one happened to be a Forest supporter who I had bought a ticket for. Halfway through the second half, it must have been, I got into a friendly but loud argument with Tony. Pyper turns round and says "You should not be in these seats, Chris do you want me to get a steward or copper to get him moved, my friend Richie looked at him and laughed, that was another time I saw Pyper looking a little on the concerned side. It took my other mate Mick who was incidentally a Spurs supporter to calm him down and explain the situation, so after that, to add to the Leyton thing deemed even more of a liability I think. What really made me think about him is the fact, a few nights ago I was watching something on the History Channel, or similar, there was Maggie Thatcher telling us to "just be thankful for that." In her speech outside number 10 after the Argies' had surrendered in the Falkland Islands, the camera pans round to a group of cheering supporters of hers or whatever and blow my socks into space who was standing there with his infamous grin? None other than John bloody Pyper, a younger version obviously, but yep there he was!

Even now he comes back to taunt me. I love ya really John mate.

Enough, back to the game in hand John Still this afternoon pledged his faith in Andy Drury, who is not playing in the position familiar for him during his last stint at Kenilworth Road and certainly not playing to his full potential as of yet, but maybe hopefully as JSL states he is still finding his feet. I hope so.

In comparison to Saturday, let's be fair it is a midweek game, the town centre is relatively quiet, midweek matches can be a little more subdued fan wise than the weekend games, but those who are making their way to the match are in good spirit, things haven't gone totally to plan, but when do they in football anyway? I do predict a tough game tonight and in Hatters Talk, a forum type page on Facebook, I have in the prediction League plumped for a 1-1 draw, Bury are going to be a force this season I feel, a great youth set up these days and have made some decent signings. Soon enough we shall see for ourselves.

The "Hatters" starting line-up is as follows:

Mark Tyler, Luke Wilkinson, Fraser Franks, Scott Griffiths, Steve McNulty, Luke Rooney, Andy Drury, Luke Guttridge, Matt Robinson, Mark Cullen and Paul Benson.
Substitutes; Alex Lacey, Alex Wall, Jake Howells, Elliot Justham, Pelly Ruddock Mpanzu, Ross Lafayette, Jim Stevenson.

Luton Town 1 Bury 1
Luton did well to snatch a point from a side whose passing and movement was excellent, but thankfully their attack contained all the bite of a pacifist wearing dentures, and making the game more open for the fact they did not park a giant black pudding in front of their goal.

John Still also proved why he is different to those gone before him. He read the game and made changes to shore up the midfield putting more life into the attack. Effectively matching the formation Bury had been using all evening, we started to push them back and had the game lasted a further ten minutes, the signs were that we could have even stolen the victory, in a game where Bury were the better side for the best part of the game.

Four points from the opening three games, is a reasonable return considering our injury and fitness concerns now and not replacing Gray, we have at this time little width, outnumbered in midfield, in games when the opposition have strikers with movement. John Still is an outstanding manager and there are no doubts whatsoever in my mind that he will rectify the mistakes and improve the team. The late goal and thereafter a surge in performance, will give us some momentum to take to Accrington with us.

On return from his one game suspension Rooney was the only attacking player who looked to run at a composed Bury defence. For all his endeavour and effort, not to mention going to ground easily, something I personally would be very happy to see eradicated from the game weighing in at 13 stones than that happening. Both sides as guilty as the other.

Just the one change from Saturday. Jake Howells unlucky to be replaced by Rooney. Sadly no balance to the team. However, I recall the same said this time last season as JSL was looking for his best line-up.

Bury have done well to recover from being Blackwelled so recently, the man should have a health warning attached to his C.V., he is a total menace to any club he gets his claws into. They look a good side, should be in the shake up for automatic promotion. Their defence looks solid and strong with Mills and Cameron looking like bouncers at the door of my local nightclub,

playing wingbacks Bury always looked to have options on the ball. Their passing and movement was excellent for a side at this level. Etutu marshalled Guttridge effectively, Guttridge is building up his game time and the quicker he hits form again the better. Adams and Tuttle broke from midfield and managed to expose plenty of space between defence and midfield although Adams blotted his copybook, by producing a pitiful and embarrassing dive with Wilkinson near him. Not even booked either! Typical of the English game, which is in such a wretched state, the only thing we pick up from football abroad is diving and now the latest fad it seems, taking an age to walk from the field of play after being replaced.

Even from the word go, we lacked any tempo or cohesion to our play, although Rooney made a bright impact, a fierce cross from the left aimed for Benson was cut out by Mills, it dropped to Griffiths who put his headed effort over the bar. Rooney cleverly defeated Soares. However, the final pass hit with too much venom for Benson to control.

Bury soon dominated the midfield. Having an extra man in that area might have helped. We sat back and both midfielders far too deep, allowing the likes of Rose, Tuttle and Adams to sweep the ball around and play some eye catching football.

We seemed to be giving them too much respect. If you stand off any team they will look good in possession, allowed to gain control of the match too easily, so we limped to half time, just as well Bury did not have a cutting edge to their neat approach play.

We started the second half with more of an edge, sharper and with a bit more tempo.

Pelly Ruddock Mpanzu replaced Guttridge, who is still not 100% match fit following a long injury lay off, allowing the formation to change. Franks going back into centre back. Pelly and Griffiths wing backs, Rooney playing more central, with Cullen closer to Benson. It was the right change, although before it had time to take shape, Bury scored with a very soft goal, McNulty tried to run the ball out, but Tuttle capitalised , Tyler appeared to be barged by Lowe, leaving Rose a gift of an open goal to put the Lancastrians ahead. McNulty is a very good defender when the play is in front of him, but the last couple of games, the movement by Tubbs on Saturday, followed tonight with another basic error, you can see why Fleetwood binned him in this league, maybe a nano-second or three too slow in turning.

Mark Tyler being clearly frustrated by basic errors in front of him, was further exasperated as Rose refused to retreat the ten yards for a free kick, Tyler pushed Rose over and after an unseemly passage of play, both players were booked.

Pelly's introduction was starting to take effect giving us the pace, energy and strength we had lacked beforehand.

Luton made a double change, Howells for Griffiths and Lafayette for Benson. Lafayette gave us more mobility and Howells is a more effective attacker from left wing back, as Bury begin to time waste and sit on their lead. Why teams do this, I will never understand. A man with two broken legs could have walked off quicker than Mayor did. You could have walked from Luton to Bury quicker than his departure off the field, clapping the sizeable following from Bury on a work night. It is another thing that needs to be eradicated from the game, the slow walk off after being replaced. We have done it and it is equally poor. Managing the game is just another word for cheating the game.

At least the referee awarded six minutes additional time, so their efforts to slow the game down had not fulfilled its desire, a case of chronic backfiring, like farting in your own face

Wilkinson headed wide from Rooney's free kick, then just as the fourth official signalled six minutes, the Town equalised, a long ball played forward nudged on by Cullen, Pelly took it in his stride, keeping the ball away from Mills and smashing into the top far corner, with their keeper Lainton helpless.

Then came the grand stand finish, far more tempo and pace, going at Bury, they looked far removed from the side who had played unruffled football for the majority of the match. They looked very nervy. An excellent Drury run beating both Lowe and Sedgwick, Lafayette's shot was powerful but well held by Lainton. Andy Drury's pass found Rooney who jinxed past two Bury defenders, but after getting time and space disappointingly ran into a cluster of white shirts at the near post.

Luton piled it on after the goal but Bury held on for the 1-1 draw, which in the end was a fair result for both sides.

Griffiths had another good game, probably been our most consistent player in the first few matches.

Elsewhere in League two both Morecambe and Burton Albion are the only sides left with a 100% record, both gaining 1-0 home wins against Oxford United and Exeter City respectively. Whilst at the bottom end of the table four sides still waiting for their first points of the campaign Oxford United, Newport County, Hartlepool United and the "Hatters" next opponents Accrington.

Wednesday 20th August 2014
In the aftermath of the first four games in both League Two and Capital One Cup competitions, with only three goals to Luton's name it seems that John Still and Terry Harris are thinking of one more signing before deadline day on 1st September. However, they are insistent that it will not be a panic buy, although if the right player does not become available they will leave well alone, not having to sign someone just for the sake of signing. I have to agree though that a more experienced front player is required, no disrespect to the guys just bought in but we need that experience, and it will surely in the long term view more beneficial to those young players already bought in for the future of the club.

I have heard Mick Harford is available. Oh for another Mickey to arrive on the scene. I was talking earlier this morning actually, to a young man who would have fitted so well into our side right now if just a couple of years younger. He had the reputation of being one of the fittest player in English football. George Best called him the greatest player he ever played against. He had an edge about him. Something we need right now. A young Alan Hudson would be the perfect candidate.

It really is quite incredible, I have just been reading some comments on a "Hatters" Facebook page and I cannot believe the mentality of some of the supporters of Luton on there and believe me they do class themselves as supporters.

One, well I will let you the reader use your own imagination as to what I have called him as I am doing my utmost to use diplomacy throughout this book, made the comment and I quote: "Why is John Still intent on not playing Andre Gray this season? It's time the board realised his failings and kick him out", I do not think I need to say much more than that really. By the way, for the record the culprit was being serious, I thought it was a wind up when I first read, but no, they were serious.

Then there are also those that are just moaning because the team have only won one game in three. Well that is also a little ludicrous in my eyes. There are complaints about the players in general and the team's inadequacies. For me personally, even if things do not go to plan this season we the supporters should not lose heart. This has been a long time coming, now we are here let the man get on with his job. If one listens carefully to what he said, we are still on a learning curve. We are building for the future, not right now, it makes me boil with frustration when people are already bemoaning the team, it is on the whole a very young and inexperienced squad league wise, confidence comes from having positive backing, these youngsters need nurturing, It's a totally different game from what they are used to. Surely, these people should have learnt something from the past five years. We have in JLS the most intelligent manager / coach we have had for many a year, don't let the few drive him away, he has done a fabulous job since coming here and long may he be with us. I dread, by the end of this book, which will conclude with the last ball kicked in anger by a Luton Town player, for this season that I am not writing about yet another manager at the helm. This club is desperately crying out for continuity, in the management team and the playing squad, as we had in the Pleat era. I always tell such people that keep moaning about this and that within the club, be careful what you wish for, you may get it!

Thursday 21st August 2014

Some will say what has this to do with Luton Town, well if its football and good for football it is worth a mention.

News has just come in that on September 16th Coventry City FC will again grace the turf of The Ricoh Arena, following nearly a year at Northampton Town's Sixfields Stadium, following a rent row with the Arena's owners that nearly put the club out of existence a year ago. Congratulations to them.

Danny Fitzsimons went out on loan today to Conference South side Bishops Stortford, JSL is hoping it will assist in bringing the defender back to match fitness following a knee injury that has plagued him since last season. He will be out on-loan for an initial three months.

It's strange you know, to think that four months ago I was telling myself that this writing game was not for me, when an old friend from my days in horse racing called me up after seeing my blogs on trainers and jockeys of the past asked if I would be interested in writing his official biography. Jimmy Duggan the former National Hunt jockey of the 80s and 90s wanted little old me to write for him, I was dumbstruck to be honest. After some serious deliberation, all of thirty seconds, I agreed to at least have a try, since then I have not looked back. Suddenly everything has dropped into the place, apart from Jim's biography there is this book, inspired by former England player Alan Hudson I decided to attempt to write this book on the "Hatters" and well so far so good at least, we shall plod on regardless of whatever and see what happens. So yes guys you are totally stuck with me until the end of Luton's 2014-15 League campaign that's for sure.

On an unhappy note, the word is that former England star Paul Gascoigne is back in hospital and on the verge of being homeless following another drinking binge. Troubled with alcoholism for quite a few years now, according to some his health is again deteriorating and close friends are most concerned of his well, we should well, he gave us all so much pleasure watching his footballing genius during the 1990s.

As I am writing this segment, it is announced that the voice of football results on the BBC, James Alexander Gordon has passed away. We had been graced with his so familiar voice for many years, this is my opportunity to give my thanks for the pleasure he gave to us all whilst giving us the results we either waited for or dreaded, your distinctive sound will never be equalled and forever missed. On behalf of all football supporters thank you and condolences to his family.

Well, back to Luton town and tomorrow the lads travel north to Accrington, Lancashire for our second away game of the campaign to bottom of the table Accrington Stanley. Their season has yet to take hold having lost all three of their opening games. They have a minus goal difference of six going into the game with Luton Town. JSL will be trying to ensure the boys do not get complacent I am sure, to come back with a win tomorrow evening, giving them a 100% away record so far would most definitely be a massive boost to their confidence.

One piece of interesting news coming out of the Stanley camp this week so far is the theft from the stadium of some of the players' boots, following a break in. with Sky Bet popping up and purchasing for those that had lost their boots a new pair in time for Saturdays' game.

Saturday 23rd August 2014

So Accrington here we come, second league away game of the season and a difficult one at that. The best part of a 400 mile round trip for both players and fans, to the North of England. For both parties let's hope we can return to winning ways, the last time Luton played at Accrington was an evening match on 24th February 2008 when the game finished in a goalless draw.

Accrington's manager James Beattie will be looking for a change of fortune against the "Hatters." Luton will have to be at their best this afternoon. Maybe though it may be a welcomed respite for the Luton players away from the cauldron of pressure that is Kenilworth Road, we are a most critical band of supporters. Therefore, the pressure is off a little on their travels maybe allowing them to play a more flowing game, who knows!

The Hatters tem news is not as good as we could hope, with Alex Lawless still not fully fit, together with Shaun Whalley and defender Curtley Williams, also missing are Andy Parry, Jonathan Smith and Ricky Miller through injury, so John Smith may be pushed to find some right side players in the starting line-up.

Accrington are without their regular 'keeper Luke Simpson who will be serving suspension following his sending off on Tuesday night against Shrewsbury Town in their 0-4 defeat.

Team sheets out, Luton Town line up as follows: Mark Tyler, Steve McNulty, Alex Lacey, Andy Drury, Paul Benson, Jake Howells, Mark Cullen, Luke Rooney, Matt Robinson, Paul Connolly and Luke Wilkinson. With subs: Fraser Franks, Alex Wall, Elliot Justham, Pelly Ruddock Mpanzu, Ross Lafayette, Luke Stevenson and Luke Guttridge.

I personally would have liked to see Pelly Ruddock Mpanzu in the starting line-up, but I am sure John Still has his reasons and maybe it is tactical also.

After a rocky first half an hour, with the "Hatters" going two goals down, the comeback was on with two goals before the break from Luke Rooney and Jake Howells to make it 2-2 at the break. One thing I have learnt since John Still arrived at Kenilworth Road, never write the Hatters off until the final whistle, I am not saying we will make a famous comeback this afternoon, but JSL sides do not throw in the we need to shore up that defence.

The attendance today is 1,562 and 586 of those are Luton Town fans. Yet again a following to be proud of away from home.

Accrington Stanley 2 Luton Town 2

Despite the sunny afternoon in Lancashire, it was in reality not such a sunny time for Luton Town, to be brutally honest they were poor. I believe they turned up embedded in their thoughts that the game was just a formality and the result would go their way with ease, wrong!

For the first twenty or so minutes, they were not even at the event, more likely at home on their sofas, because yes that is how abysmal they honestly were. Two goals down in just 16 minutes and deservedly so, It was not until Luke Rooney pulled it back to 2-1 that Accrington really began to wobble, and then just before half time Jake Howells made it 2-2 with a left footed free kick to the centre of the goal.

The second half began to show glimpses of what they are capable of but in all honesty very poor, there were chances to snatch the game but the firepower just was not that convincing.

There were some positive points, especially Luke Guttridge who came on for Alex Lacey early in the game, which most certainly did seem to make an impact on the game for Luton. Jake Howells having a formidable game in comparison to most of the team, Paul Benson was more involved than usual than he has been so far this season, also Drury showed snatches of what he is capable of. Wilkinson had an absolute nightmare, most of the time defending too deep, not so bad in aerial situations, but most of the time looked like an accident waiting to happen.

John Still selected the same formation that won our away previous game at Carlisle. Can see the thinking, but unhappy to see Pelly remain on the bench, he gives some something different, energy, pace, strength and makes things happen. Our football so far has been bland this season. Ignoring the obvious lack of pace, there has been a lack of tempo in our play. Lawless and Smith, in the travelling party, along with Williams, Miller and Walker, will return. It will be good to witness their return.

With Griffiths out, Howells replaced him at left back. Connolly replacing Franks at full back. Lacey in for Guttridge, who played the holding role behind Drury and Robinson, with Rooney and Cullen either side of Benson.

Thankfully we have a manager who will not tolerant that rancid opening. It has been a very puzzling start to the season, not a bad points return, but we have not gelled or got to grips with the higher standard of the opponents yet. Much to ponder for the manager and staff ,with a very hard looking game next Saturday at Shrewsbury and their handily located new ground. No parking in or around the ground. Well, that is bloody marvellous planning. Not!

Following the game manager JSL was not in the best of moods that is for sure, he made it quite clear that the rubbish displayed at Accrington was intolerable to say the very least. After giving them what must have been a right royal roasting at full time he made a short interval where he commented on the game to BBC Three Counties Radio, "I felt that our general play in the second half meant we deserved to win the game, but I think we were quite rightly behind.

"We battled back well, but it's not good enough. I think the players are aware it was not good enough. Our approach to the game not as disciplined or professional as we usually are and I'll have to look into that.

"Luke Rooney can come up with the unpredictable sometimes and I like that in a player, particularly attacking players, but his all-round game wasn't that consistent "We want to win. But we won't win by giving goals away, and we're not a team that gives goals away."

A long journey back to Luton for all after that display.

Elsewhere in League Two, Morecombe are the only remaining side with a 100% percent record. Two points clear at the top of what has to be said a rejuvenated Portsmouth side, following all their misfortunes in recent years. It is good to see them on the road to recovery, not unlike ourselves, the Pompey fans have had one hell of a roller coaster ride, at times they were not sure if they would even have a team to play some weeks. Good luck to them with all sincerity. It has been a hard year so far losing a club like Hereford United from the Conference and Salisbury United also because of financial matters. Something that gets me quite angry when the bigger clubs play with money like its sand on Southend beach. At the other end of the table Hartlepool picked up their first points of the season with a shock win away at AFC Wimbledon, coming away 2-1 victors. Oxford United now up the whole of the Football League still without a point after four games.

Monday 25th August 2014

Well, Liverpool rid themselves of one troublesome "super star" and then go right out and sign another today when paying AC Milan £16m for Mario Balotelli. Yet another interesting season in store for the Anfield club I should think, then straight after they go to Manchester City and get slammed 3-1, I wonder what was going through Mario's mind whilst sitting in that so familiar setting, it sure is going to be a most interesting season I feel.

Anyone for a third round FA Cup drawing together, Luton Town v Liverpool? It does happen you know!

Yet another day of sad news as it is announced that veteran British movie actor Richard Attenborough has passed away at the age of 90, I absolutely loved him in one of his earliest Films "Brighton Rock" as the young gangster "Pinkie". When the film was released in the States they renamed it "Young Scarface" eat your heart out Mr. Pacino, we had the first Scarface.

Tuesday 26th August 2014

To be honest, I really thought this week was going to be reasonably quiet considering the "Hatters" have no mid-week game for us to contend with. However, even this evening the keyboard is crunching with the news that the club one cannot give a true name to, the Milton Keynes Franchise, took on the "mighty" Manchester United in the second round of the Capital One Cup better known to us as The League Cup. Although the red devils did not take along a full quota of their Premiership squad they were still it has be said graced with the likes of de Gea, Januzaj, Hernandez, Vermijl and the England World Cup failure Danny Welbeck in their side. What must have been going through head Coach Louis Van Gaal and assistant Ryan Giggs minds after this game is anyone's guess. I would dearly have loved to be a fly on the wall in their dressing room after the game. Because their devilish tails were left cold to freezing after the "Franchise" from League One gave them a true lesson in football. Not just beating them but humiliating them 4-0, what will have made it the more sweeter for Arsenal manager Arsene Wenger is the fact that two of the four goals came from the "Gunners" loaned out player Benik Afobe and the other two coming from Will Grigg. I would not usually have bothered to tell you the truth, but with all the hype being thrown in our faces by the media and the plastic fans that strut the country in their red shirts, when they would be better off helping their local sides out with a pound or two. Instead of giving support to a local club. Many of them I can boast to that I have been to their so-called "Stadium of Dreams" more times than they ever go. However, believe me not to see those in red that is a fact. Giving it large about how good this team will be this season, it was too much to handle, I sat in the arm chair thinking shall I shan't I, well in the end these weary old legs lifted me up and here I am at desk crunching the keyboard for all its worth.

How I see it right at this moment, we have all of those "Hatters" having their moan and groan because our team of new boys to the Football League are still trying to find their feet. Yet here is the great and mighty Manchester United having not what I would call a blip, I would call it more of falling into a fucking great abyss and do I feel even a little bit of sympathy for them? No! I can put it as simply as that No!

One last sentence came to mind, "Where the fuck is David Moyes when you need him? However, let us wait for the media hype tomorrow. It will be Manchester United this and Manchester United that. Not many words will portray the feat of the Franchise players, which will be a travesty, because loath the club as we may do because of the way it was formed, it is not those who play for the clubs fault, at the end of it all they have to earn their bread and butter somewhere. So well done to those guys tonight. Now I think I can again lift these weary old pins to this time carry me off to my bed where a pillow is so loudly calling my name.

Thursday 28th August 2014

Some good news coming from both the development team and the Youth team this week, firstly the Development team that will be playing in a brand new league consisting mainly of Southern based sides, Luton Town being by the Football League along with AFC Bournemouth as founder members. They are joined by, AFC Wimbledon, Cambridge United, Gillingham, Leyton Orient, Peterborough United and Portsmouth in the inaugural Final Third Development League Southern Division.

The side played their final pre-season friendly this week against a strong Wycombe Wanderers side and coming out 6-1 winners with a superb hat trick from Alex Wall, the other goals coming from Curtley Williams, Ricky Miller and Charlie Walker the line-up was as follows:

Elliot Justham, Curtley Williams, Fraser Franks, Alex Lacey, Mark Onyemah (Luke Trotman), Trialist (Solomon Taiwo 72), Pelly Ruddock Mpanzu, Jim Stevenson, Alex Wall, Ricky Miller, Charlie Walker.

The first game contested in the newly formed league for the "Hatters" is on September 9th against AFC Bournemouth, at Kenilworth Road. This will be where to see John Stills young players in action, the future of Luton Town.

Just to add to the good news in regards to our future, the under 18s side who are competing in the Football League Youth Alliance South East division have made a superb start to their season. Winning their opening game against MK Dons 3-1, followed by a very pleasing 2-1 victory away to AFC Bournemouth in the cup competition. Returning to the league campaign, they drew 1-1 at Stevenage Town. This followed by another two wins at Cambridge United 2-1 and most recently smashing a 5-0 victory at Dagenham and Redbridge, leaving the boys in second place in the table behind Peterborough on the goals scored basis as both teams are on 10 points and the same goal difference of plus nine. Well done to those boys and let us hope they can keep the momentum running. Great things happening at the club right now. Despite the first team experiencing a slow start.

The countdown has begun for Saturday's League Two game away at Shrewsbury Town and it does look like as if we will have another 600 plus following travelling up there. To be honest, I have a feeling this could be one of our most difficult tests so far along with Bury. It will be interesting to see how the lads fare, that is for sure and Shrewsbury will more than likely be showing off their latest signing Anthony Griffith following his released from Port Vale earlier this week after making 45 appearances for the last season.

I see that Neil Warnock is to replace Tony Pulis at Crystal Palace, as much as I do rate Warnock as a coach. I wonder how long his second stint at Palace will last, previously being there from 2007-10. Last time round the then chairman Simon Jordan was a good mate of his, not so sure how he will get on with Steve Parish and Stephen Browitt, let's face they didn't give Pulis much support despite his miracle act at the end of the last season, this will be a most interesting partnership I am sure.

Friday 29th August 2014

One day away from another away day for the "Hatters" of this world, unless of course you really are on those Hatters that live not too many miles away from Manchester, thieving sods nicked our name.

The 12th man for Luton town is growing with momentum as I speak, metaphorically speaking, hmm okay, the total of tickets for Luton fans travelling to Shrewsbury is just over 1,000, some call it the New Meadow others the Greenhous Meadow, some will say more politically correct than the previous ground, Gay Meadow. But then the politically correct regime are load of politically correct people I suppose, best I stay politically correct don't you think?

Luton will be going into the game with a weeks' "rest" under their belt, however knowing Mr Still, they would not have been experiencing much rest, as there has been much work to do following the last couple of outings. I think though, that I may be repeating myself a little here. That can often happen following a few glasses of the claret stuff, as is the case this evening. As many who have joined me in the revelries at both football and racing and let's face it anywhere else I end up for that matter, so sometimes you will just have to put up with me on the odd occasion, like now.

As I was saying, to be fair we have been missing our better right sided players for the beginning of the season, therefore I reserve judgement for the time being at least.

Just this morning, JSL admitted to the media that strong words followed after the game at Accrington. One has to applaud him the way he did it though, there was no individual blame, it is a team out there, and they should all have to share the bad with the good. I firmly believe that when a player is picked out of the pack by the management team as not pulling their weight or things are not going as well as hoped it causes animosity throughout the squad, its more diplomatic to keep it inside the changing room or the training ground for me. What was equally pleasing to read was the fact that after the game he did not need to ask, the players told him what was wrong out there. For me that is the sign of a very good and a united squad, what a difference from 18 months ago. As Bob Dylan sang "The Time they are a changing…"

For Shrewsbury Town, they come into the game with a great deal of confidence after the midweek Capital One Cup second round win against Premier League side Leicester City away at The King Power Stadium. Beating a very strong but at times disjointed Leicester side 0-1 with a goal from former Forest Green striker Andy Mangan, another player not unlike AFC Wimbledon's Matt Tubbs who gave the defence a hard time a couple of weeks ago.

Saturday 30th August 2014
Well, as I am not at the game I cannot tell you what the weather was like or the atmosphere, so I will most probably just end up rambling on about this and that no doubt.

The line-up reads as follows: Mark Tyler, Luke Wilkinson, Jake Howells, Paul Connolly, Steve McNulty, Luke Guttridge, Matt Robinson, Jim Stevenson, Paul Benson, Luke Rooney and Mark Cullen. The subs: Alex Lacey, Alex Wall, Elliott Justham, Pell Ruddock Mpanzu, Ross Lafayette, Ricky Miller and Curtley Williams.

Shrewsbury Town 2 Luton Town 0
With Alex Lawless, Jonathan Smith and Scott Griffiths out injured the Town were yet again nowhere near full strength and against a side as strong as Shrewsbury are, that was always going to make today an uphill struggle. There was little chance of the taming of the Shrews this afternoon. Ever the misty-eyed optimist, I was expecting a defeat today against a strong side, who will sure to be up there in the mix for the automatic promotion, with the team we had available. However, made the more galling, last week's abject, pitiful start at Accrington in a very winnable game. Had we won that game, a defeat today to a vastly superior side, who are going to be challenging for promotion would not have been a big problem. My pessimism reflected in the "Hatters Talk" Facebook pages prediction league where I actually for once predicted that the "Hatters" would lose this game 2-0.

Rooney's antics when being subbed as early as the thirteenth minute were not the most professional it has to be said, as John Still tried in vain to stop Shrewsbury's tight vice like grip on the match. Sure, no player likes being withdrawn so early in the game. Nevertheless, I do not recall Alex Lacey walking down the tunnel in similar circumstances last week. It looks poor and a lack of respect towards your teammates. What is that saying about "The stronger the team, the stronger the team"? Looks wonderful when a player wanders off back to the dressing room. Actually, in some respects it might have saved a lot of time, if the whole team had followed Rooney's suit.

In a very one-sided match, Shrewsbury were stronger and showed more class throughout. From working harder, passing the ball quicker on the floor and more accuracy, they dominated proceedings from the first to the last whistle. Considering Shrewsbury having signed approximately two billion players in the window, they have gelled remarkably quickly and entitled to have a strong season.

In all fairness, playing the likes of Bury and Shrewsbury it was a hard start to life at the higher level. It is asking a hell of a lot for Robinson and Stevenson to excel against superior players. With Griffiths still out, Drury injured and Franks not in the eighteen, we are starting to run out of players only three weeks into the season.

In what was by all accounts a rather chastening half, which the plus points were being only 1-0 down from a Jordan Clark goal as early as the third minute when the midfielder slotted home from a Connor Goldson through ball.

The second half was no different from the first in as much as Shrewsbury dominated every inch of the pitch. The second Shrewsbury goal came about following a clumsy challenge on Jordan Clark by Skipper Steve McNulty on the right flank. Clark took the ensuing free kick, floated the ball across the goal mouth, Tyler reaching the ball with bare finger tips, minimal contact from Collins, which on another day may well have been classed as an infringement, such is the inconsistency with refereeing throughout the world, the ball got away from him and was over the line, 2-0. To be fair, without Tyler's tenacity between the sticks it could have been a much wider margin of victory. However as is very often the case he was in superb form. It totally amazes me how I can read that he was to blame for the second goal. Berating him for the fact, even the best make mistakes and with the amount of work he was asked to do I find it rather uncalled for, but then that's football, especially when it comes to Luton Town, one cannot please all, all of the time. Things deteriorated when the "Hatters" were down to ten men following a red card handed to Matty Robinson for a rather cynical foul by all accounts on Cameron Gayle. So that was that, despite a magnificent following of 1,003 travelling fans to make up the twelfth man Luton were played off the park by a more superior side. One plus, I got maximum points for the correct score in the prediction league, sigh, there are times I truly hate it when I am right.

It had to come, the last side in the Football League with a 100% record, Morecambe, went down 2-1 at Prenton Park. Despite going in front with an early goal against Tranmere Rovers. That means there are no sides with a Norwegian style nil points, with Accrington Stanley holding up the table with one solitary point. Yes correct, taken from our very own Luton Town. One other side also languish down there on one point, our old adversaries Oxford United. The Town themselves sitting only five places above the dreaded relegation zone, in eighteenth place, with five points from five games. However, hey its early days, isn't it?

Now the fun begins in earnest, as I am not at the game I am in the position to see the comments and remarks posted on our dear old friend Facebook. Which in recent years has allowed as the luxury of pub style banter from the confines of our sitting rooms, bedrooms and some of us even retreating to the little throne room for some well-deserved peace from marauding kids and for some nagging wives, sorry ladies but for some, not all my I add, it has to be said.

Back to the joy that is Facebook. Some of the lunacy coming across makes you shiver with fear, but for the grace of crack cocaine, marijuana, some people would maybe be in seats of power, oh sorry they are already there, well in Canada at least that is true. The ludicrous remarks, posts and comments that are appearing this evening does not surprise me one bit, however, after five games for a side that has just come back into the Football League, which we have to take into account is in better shape football wise this season than ever before, in my opinion. I blame it on the foreign influx of players to the upper echelons of our national game, because those English players who have not lost all faith in the game and are still willing to earn a living in the lower divisions are making for a stronger based league throughout in my humble and misguided opinion anyway.

I have said throughout my previous blogs and articles relating to Luton Town Football Club and their most fanatical supporters. I will never mince my words despite knowing I will upset many, because some have the opinion that they are right and nobody else has the right or the intelligence to go against their thoughts and opinions. However, guys, dream on because I and many like me do have other opinions, and I do not give a stuff whom I upset on my journey, because lets be fair we all have our opinions, and all should be valued and accepted as such. With that said hey-ho let's go.

The only post I placed after this game is this and I quote.

"Anyone who thought that it was going to easy this season for Luton Town, their first season back in the Football League for five years truly do need a reality check, the class of football is a great deal different to the Conference, this season for me was never going to be easy. Patience required, I have said it on many occasions already in this first month that it is going to take a while for these players to acclimatise. We have three of our best players injured. Benson is not fully fit. I am not going to get into any arguments because that is my opinion and I will stick by it, I am not a happy clapper, far from it, but I am a realist"

The reason I wrote that was that since we won promotion back to the Football League, I have read and heard much talk that we will win back-to-back promotions. In previous season's we have witnessed the likes of Crawley Town and Fleetwood Town do exactly that. However, let us be very honest the standard of League Two football over the past couple of years has raised somewhat. Promoted from what in all honesty, for me any ways, an inferior Conference Premier in relation to seasons before, York City had one of the best squads seen in the non-league competition when they beat us at Wembley, but look how they struggled on their return to the Football League. Some will argue my point there and I challenge those to the fact that yes, we had some very good players, but we also had a handful of players who were at Luton Town for the good of their own being rather than for the good of the club. I am not going to name any names, I am not into that, but we as a collective know whom they were and we salute them not. We did have two players who have since proved their worth and one has gone on to greater things in the Championship and quite rightly, so, he will improve even more as the season goes on I truly believe. Our veteran youngster, because that is what he is in reality, a veteran of the club but still a youngster, Jake Howells is finding it harder this season than ever before. That though is not because he has lost what he has, its simply because we are now competing in a much higher standard of football, a different kind of football, no longer is it, as for a long time, the kicking, bundling off the ball style of game, the bar his risen to a new level, good football. Time to adjust is taking longer than expected, but with the skills and coaching of Mr Still, I will say it again, the best we have had in a long time, we will improve as the season progresses. However, let us also be realistic, we will not be fighting for promotion of that I am seventy percent certain. We simply are not good enough. Even more realistic, is the fact that if we did manage to gain promotion at the end of this season would we be ready for such a journey next season? For me no, therefore I believe a nice steady middle of the table campaign would be much more beneficial to the club and the squad, enabling them to gel for a real push next season, as Del Boy would say with the same enthusiasm, "You know it makes sense Rodney, Good boy".

I have even noticed this morning, yes it's now Sunday 31st August 2014, one ludicrous idiot saying it's time for Still to think about stepping down and letting someone who knows what they are doing take over. That takes me back to those who must be doing crack cocaine and marijuana, that

or he is an in-patient at the infamous Maudsley hospital at Denmark Hill in Camberwell, South East London, closer to Millwall's New Den than Kenilworth Road. Yes, I know I said I would not remark about others opinions, or close to that anyway, but come on what lunacy is that.
Time for church, well a certain public house in Barnehurst anyway. I shall return though, this book has a long way to go.
The lure of real ale and the sensational aroma it brings, caused a momentary lapse in concentration, because from out of the depths of Hatteresque despair a light of hope rises from within the gloom.

It is mid-evening, a glass of wine and some soothing music. Just the ticket for a journey back in time. Apart from this book I am also in the throes of writing the official biography of former National Hunt jockey from the 1980s and 90s, Jimmy Duggan. Let me just point out to you, this lad had it all in his grasp, but like another certain lad from the other side of the Irish border, he had his demons too. George Best was for me the greatest player ever to grace the football fields of England. Jimmy Duggan had the world at his feet in a similar vein. He had the raw talent to be one of the best we had seen in National Hunt racing at the time, what has this to do with Luton Town you may ask, well apart from the fact that Jimmy was in those days a "Hatter" himself in some ways. A good friend of Stevie Foster, Ashley Grimes and others of that great 1980s side we were fortunate to have witnessed at Kenilworth Road.
My mind goes back to a story told by a mutual friend of the affable Mr. Duggan and myself. It was a typical day at Chepstow in the middle of winter, bitingly cold. He was riding a very nervous young novice hurdler, Amari King, for that wonderful trainer of the old school variety, the kind of whom are greatly missed these days, Captain Tim Forster. One of the best trainers of his time. Amari King finished a reasonable sixth or seventh beaten about twenty or so lengths. After he had dismounted, gave his account of how the race had gone the Captain turned to the lad that took care of the horse and Pete Feltham the travelling head lad, saying, "If I could tell a jockey how I want my babies educated in their first runs that would be exactly how they would be instructed. That was just incredible." Jimmy had something special that not many other jockeys bore, the ability to put a horse to sleep during a race, totally turn it off. Not in the way of cheating or anything of that sort, he nursed many a nervous or difficult horses throughout a race. This in effect, gave the horse more confidence in itself and therefore a better prospect in later races. There is nothing wrong in giving a horse an easy first few outings, it educates them for the task ahead as they develop and go forward in their racing careers. That particular race helped in the quest in transforming the horse Amari King from a very nervous novice to a confident young racehorse, Jimmy gave him a good experience, the first race can either make a horse or break them and Jim had the knack of making these horses. The proof in the pudding, Amari King went on to be a profoundly successful jumper. The point I am getting at is this. John Still in my eyes does similar to the young inexperienced players he has bought into Kenilworth Road. He nurses them in slowly, giving them the confidence to perform and succeed, maybe not immediately but in good time, that for me is one reason JLS has so much success with the young players he plucks from the lower leagues, patience and understanding. To lose this man from Luton Town at this stage of our resurgence would be a complete travesty, I believe we can trust this man implicitly, he has the clubs future at heart, how many of his predecessors can we say that about in recent years, I can tell you with ease, none.

September

Monday 1st September 2014

Its deadline day today for the transfer window. I am reading on that infamous social media page, which no doubt is going to prove quite a regular player in this book, people discussing who JLS will sign and who he won't sign before 11pm tonight. To be honest I am not convinced that he will, I would be more prone to the thinking that if the injuries persist and some take too long in their recovery he will rather look at maybe a couple of loans later in the month. Some of the remarks, comments whatever you would wish to call them are quite ludicrous to be honest, I have to admit yes the team is unbalanced at present but what else can be expected when we have most of our more experienced right sided players out with injury.

I say this every season it seems when, let's face it the same individuals year in year out, people start complaining at the weaknesses of the team, the season is not a 100 metre dash, it is more akin to the London Marathon, so please a little patience if you care.

One place though where the patience has run a little too thin is at Carlisle United, the first managerial victim of the season has been sprung, after just five games they have sent Graham Kavanagh to the car park with file box in hand and asked to leave the premises. Damn it is a tough place this football world, however for Luton Town at least, hopefully onwards and upwards.

On a sad note, I did not know if I should actually include this story of my own recent experience, but yes, I think I shall. Earlier, last week I was reading my friend Alan Hudson's, the former Chelsea, Stoke and Arsenal legend and yes he is just that. George Best quoted that he was the best player he ever played against, that is some testimony, book "From the Playing Fields to the Killing Fields." I arrived at page 127, a point at which he was reminiscing about the time he sat at the bed of his former manager at Stoke City, Tony Waddington, as he passed away from cancer. Alan was asking himself how he would deal with if told he had cancer and the aftermath of that news. Ironically, the following morning I receive an email from Alan, nothing new there. Until I read the contents, he was diagnosed with prostate cancer. After all he had endured over the past 18 or so years I find it so damned unfair following his fight from the brink of death that he now be hit with this new test of his character. Now my friend has a new battle to deal with. However, I know he will get through this, because the man is a fighter of the highest level, I know he detests sympathetic attention. Therefore, all I can really say keep fighting Al. They have tried once and failed, so they throw this at you. Show them you have the strength and will to win this fight also, in my thoughts matey.

Back to the transfer deadline and we have sent two players on loan to Dover I see, Ricky Miller and Solomon Taiwo, hopefully they will get some first team football in at the Conference Premier side.

Now, with the deadline done and dusted, it transpires that I was correct in my assumption. There were no signings from JLS and guess what, with that news the pessimists are out in their droves on Facebook. Admittedly, each person is entitled to an opinion so I will not say much apart from, if there is no one available who fits what we may possibly need it is stupid to sign someone just for the sake of panic, which I do not understand why at this stage we should be panicking. We have been down that road before in the not too distant past and more often than not it has ended up disastrously. As we all used to say when those thirty points were illegally in my humble opinion stolen from us and my dear friend Kenny Cook quoted to me recently, "KEEP THE FAITH".

Friday 5th September 2014

Well due to circumstances beyond my control, I went down with a bug, only a near overdose of Beecham's Night Nurse, sexy little green bottle, seems to have done the trick and a lot more workable today thankfully. Together also with some thieving bastard who has disappeared with my earnings, an agency has done a runner after I did some work for them, apart from that everything is rosy.

I missed the England v Norway game, not because I would rather watch that Bake off programme that got more viewers, but it's not just the football that's putting people off is it, the incessant drivel that Andy Townsend spouts out does not make the viewing that inviting either.

From what I have been reading thought we were worse than awful. I have my own reasons for why our national side is on the decline.

Let us face it, we have been hearing over the past few weeks now since England's early departure from the 2014 World Cup finals in Brazil how the side was well below our expectations, and how the players were lacking motivation. To a certain degree yes that can be argued so, however, let us be honest with ourselves it's not something that has happened overnight. It has been coming for a good while now. Well I have definitely been waiting, with much unease I have to say, for the situation we find the national side to arrive for a while, therefore not at all surprised where we find ourselves at this time.

Those in charge have been burying their heads in the sand for way too long now, that stance should change to holding their heads in shame. They for too long have been sitting comfortably in their gilded cages expecting it all to change automatically.

Yes, we do and rightly so have to put apportion of the blame on the players shoulders, but I argue not all.

Being a twenty two year old footballer in the Premier League means that one is, if sensible, covered financially for life. Therefore, the incentive has already dropped a couple of quavers that is in fairness a human trait.

There was a time when to play for England was an absolute privilege to be savoured every step of the way. Unfortunately, I personally do not see that passion any longer, many, myself included see players using the opportunity to perform on the international scene as purely a shop window exercise these days.

There is also the argument that the influx of foreign stock is one of the over-riding factors.

To a point yes.

However, the England problem goes much deeper than this foreign influx of players. My honest belief is that it actually rests heavily on the shoulders of the F.A. they are too arrogant, self-centred and stubborn to admit that they have to change our set up drastically before we slip into an abyss that we will never recover from in the foreseeable future. The England side at present are moderate at the very best and sliding further away from those countries at the top of the ladder.

More investment is desperately required, not just at top level, but throughout the whole footballing pyramid including the grassroots. I myself was involved for quite a few years at the grassroots level and believe it; the struggle to find adequate funding and sponsorship was enormous. That for sure is very much still a massive and continually worrying problem. It is therefore no surprise that there will be a great deal of incredible talent slipping through the net simply because of this reason. For me St. Georges was a token gesture to keep certain factions happy, it is nowhere near enough that is for sure. We need to work as a nation when it comes to football not a group of organisations who answer to the FA and are scared to cross them.

The FA, Football League, Football Conference and others below need to band together and build a Football Federation and work together with each other not against one another, which seems to be a problem at this time. We clearly need something more concrete.

We boast apparently the best and most exciting football competition in the world, so why can we not equal that with one of the most impressive national sides in the world.

Time is running out for England as we sit here now. It really is time to act.

Matty Robinson receives a three-match ban despite the Town appealing, to be honest I didn't think it was a red card offence seeing it on video replay, however it's done and dusted now, maybe Pelly Ruddock Mpanzu will get his chance to shine. Many people think that he is not in favour with JSL I tend to believe otherwise. I believe the wily old fox is up to his tricks, making sure that there is going to be cover in that position and role before giving the young man a permanent place. Also, I do not care how good he is or the potential he possesses, put a player like that into the game too early may just burn him out in the latter stages of the season. Again, as I mentioned in the introduction stages of this book and when I was giving my personal assessment of the players, I believe there are times he tries too hard to please and can be a little erratic.

Another player who it seems is at the other end of the scale to some, Luke Rooney; I hear it said he is not good enough. I tend to disagree with that. If, later in the season I happen to be proved otherwise I will hold up my hands, I actually honestly in my heart of hearts sternly believe that he has much to offer. As with many players it is a matter of acclimatising, as I will keep on reiterating until proved otherwise, we cannot jump from non-league to Football League and become an overnight success. Unfortunately, there are a good few that think because we are Luton Town FC we are going to turn every other side with ease. I am sorry but that is not going to happen, we need a season to learn this league and as I have mentioned, it is the best standard I have seen from this level in many years. Patience from many quarters of the Kenilworth faithful is required I think.

Early kick off tomorrow with the visit of Plymouth Argyle to the Kenny, also for the first time since 2009 we shall be welcoming Sky Sports TV back.

Saturday 6ᵗʰ September 2014

Match day arrives, an early 12.15 kick off today thanks to SKY SPORTS.

Myself, I am in truth not a great admirer of early kick offs, I am of the belief that players are tuned to either a 3.00 or 7.45 kick-off, anything else is not acceptable in my mind. The likes of SKY SPORTS and now BT have really turned our game upside down for me and not for the better that is for sure. The TV culture in my humble opinion has ruined our game, okay more money has been invested into it that is true, however much of that money has been utilised in much the wrong way, it is a factor in the decline of our national side, as I wrote earlier in yesterday's segment.

Although I have to look back to something Alan Hudson said. Not only in his books, "The working man's ballet" and "From the playing fields to the killing fields", but also in conversation. The start of the decline began way back in the 60s with Sir Alf Ramsey, playing without wingers and trying to make football too technical, people trying to be clever instead of players being given the freedom to play to their skills and strengths. I would willingly go back to those days of seeing George Best being able to have a free role running at defences. With his imp like build, dancing away from tackles as if they were not really there, or, that canny little Scotsman Georgie Armstrong flying down Arsenal flanks, I always used to call him "The flying Scotsman", how I dream of such days, but alas that will never again be. The likes of such players gone forever, although in honesty that young Argentinian guy, what's his name? Ah yes Messi, he at least brings back some of that enjoyment. Also too many foreign owners, managers/coaches and players who do not appreciate our traditional competitions. The Money side is, in my opinion immoral, I am not saying all players, that would be most unjust of me, but let's face it, let's be honest as we contemplate it, do not have football at heart do they, all they are interested in is their next big pay day when transferred. My heart is broken when I watch England these days, there is no true passion and no commitment for their country, these players it comes across to me is as if they are simply going through the motions. The pride in some totally non-existent. The proof for me is the attendance last week at Wembley against Norway, because of not feeling too well I did not see, be thankful for that some will say and the performance itself during that game said it all. Luton Town a side facing relegation out of the football league took as many fans of our own to support our club against Scunthorpe United in what is known as a tin, paint pot trophy. So no, I am not a fan of Saturday lunchtime or any lunchtime football just so that it can be shown on TV. Another factor as to why I do not enjoy watching Luton playing league games on TV, is that it seems each time we are on TV, unless playing a side like Liverpool, we tend to freeze. Maybe the pressure gets too much, who knows, all I seem to recall is the fact that we never fare too well in front of live cameras'.

Therefore, to the game, not much time for a drink it seems, although many would have enjoyed a hearty full English and washed down with a few beers before marching off to Bury Park and the shrine that is Kenilworth Road.

The "Hatters" starting line-up is named; Mark Tyler, Paul Connolly, Steve McNulty, Alex Lacey, Scott Griffiths, Wayne Rooney, Pelly Ruddock-Mpanzu, Andy Drury, Jake Howells, Luke Guttridge and Mark Cullen. With Subs: Jonathan Smith, Alex Lawless, Alex Wall, Elliott Justham, Ross Lafayette, Luke Wilkinson and Jim Stevenson.

Luton 0 Plymouth Argyle 1

Despite Argyle wearing yellow, their fans taking up a good section of the Oak Road. Which we have to applaud really taking in the kick off time, the distance and the fact it was being shown live on SKY, were quite bizarrely shouting "Come on you greens", maybe they were still half asleep and thinking they were at the previous game and seeing green.

In contrast to recent games, we played some great football. The passing at times a joy to watch. Reminiscent of last season, and other years gone by when we had some true passing masters in our midst. Unfortunately, our best two opportunities fell to Jake Howells. Let's not be too harsh on him though, a true striker he definitely isn't. He did well in getting into a scoring position on the two occasions, was really in all honesty the wrong man in the right place, and good keeping from the Argyle goalie Luke McCormick also a contribution to our not going in at half time with what would have been a deserved two goal cushion.

On the whole we played some good football in the first half, Pelly Ruddock Mpanzu making his first full league start of the season, not before time, as some were declaring, gave us some much needed power and strength in the midfield battle, also getting back when required to assist the defence. The way we were playing in the first half, it was imperative that we got our nose in front, but we were not utilising our chances, so half time came and it was still stalemate.

Plymouth came out for the second half, maybe it was closer to the traditional three o'clock kick off now, because they seemed to find the spring in their foot that was so badly missing in the first forty-five minutes. Ruben Reid turned the tables on his own, he was running past our defenders with ease, his pace had picked up drastically that's for sure, every time the ball fell to his feet I would feel that something is going to happen, our defence had to work much harder in the second half that's for certain. When Bray, the Argyle substitute, who had earlier been booked after his second touch, when dangerously catching Alex Lacey, with what for me was a cynical act of going in late. Only minutes later himself going down with what looked like a muscle pull, play carried on and the Luton defence seemed to lose concentration with Bray down on the floor in obvious pain. Dominic Blizzard blitzed his way through as Ruddock Mpanzu, Lacey and Griffiths looked more like that row of statues that line the centre of Whitehall in London, he placed a low threaded shot past a hapless Tyler into the net, 0-1. Tyler was quite rightly absolutely ranting at his defence, there were a couple of half-hearted attempts by sticking out feet, but there again catch him and the chances were he would have gone down for a penalty anyway, but yes, it was a well taken goal, together with "Hatters" glorious incompetent defending to assist.

Luton did make a few chances late on but in all honesty we never really looked like scoring in the second half, apart from a back header by one if their defenders following Tyler's clearance that McCormick gratefully caught under the crossbar, it would have been a bizarre but much welcomed equaliser though.

On a more happy note, it was pleasing to see Alex Lawless back following his hamstring problem, when bought on as substitute he made some good passes, however, he is clearly not back to his best yet and we look forward to him being a first team regular again as soon as possible.

So another defeat, and as the fixture list continues not to do us any favours, high flying Cheltenham at home, followed by a trip to unbeaten York and then Cambridge who have started the season pretty well. We are looking an inexperienced side lacking leadership on the field and without the ability of being able to earn points when not playing all that well. Whilst he has made some mistakes, have no doubts John Still will be able to turn around this recent slump.

I am now waiting for the infamous Facebook bells to start sounding, all the moaners groaners and armchair managers will be out in their droves tomorrow and I cannot wait. So that will be my Sunday well and truly tied up, trying to find someone with positivity in his or her souls, oh Christopher please, dream on my dear.

Meanwhile, in the league we drop one place to nineteenth. Now that the day has finished, it is quite difficult to take that the team that hammered us quite unmercifully last week, Shrewsbury Town, lost to the same score at Jeff Stelling's beloved Victoria Park. More delight for the quirky Mr. Stelling, his team are above the "Hatters" in the League two table, yes folks, can it get any worse than that?

Our next opponents Cheltenham Town now top the table, so next Saturday really is something to savour, unless you support the "Hatters" that is. Then the next week we have York City away, and do I have a lovely little ditty for you guys on that day of sweet reminisce, winking saucily, read on folks read on.

I am off for a sandwich and a pint with the joy of Facebook awaiting me tomorrow.

Sunday 7th September 2014

Firstly, the news is that defender Fraser Franks will be out for a while, as he requires a hernia operation.

Looking at the players out on loan, Ricky Miller and Lee Angol both scored for their respective sides. Miller scoring in his debut for Dover, when bought on as Substitute and scoring in their 4-1 away victory at AFC Telford. Young Lee Angol, a player I rate very highly scored his fifth of the season with the only goal of the game in Borehamwood's win at Gosport in the Conference South. As expected, the moaners and groaners are out in force, some people really make me want to scream from the rafters, but then I think I suppose every club has similar, some more than other though and I honestly believe we are one of the latter. I have just read that our captain had a right go at one of our supporters during the game yesterday, when the guy, yes some of us do know he was or is, a prolific moaner it has to be said. I think if he had been at the game when Joe Payne put ten past Bristol Rovers in 1936 he would still have found fault, McNulty though left the man red faced after the short altercation. Just thinking actually we could do with dear old Joe now to slot a few home. There are even a couple of dead beats shouting for John Stills head again, yes I will upset some of you, in fact actually you are the first I would love to buy this book and read. Luton Town need people like these just as much as football needs Sep Blatter. Some will argue that they pay their money so therefore they are entitled to their opinion, in reply to that, Luton Town would rather you didn't bother most probably. All of this negativity gets to the players, it is not assisting the cause at all. It was proved two seasons ago, and then last season, following Ronnie Henry's similar altercation, maybe it was the same guy, but I do not think so. I will not call them a fan or supporter, just guy, the mood actually changed and Luton's game also changed, positivity set in around the ground and the rest as they say in that famous cliché, is history.

Monday 8th September 2014
Now unrelated to football, and of course our happy "Hatters", I am having a lovely cup of tea earlier and watching the BBC news channel and the news is breaking that there is to be a second baby for the Royal couple. Now, I am a staunch supporter of the Royal family, have no doubts about that.

No, this is not me. All my pictures were destroyed some months ago. However, this is a Royal Postilion in action

In my younger day's I took a year's break from horse racing, following a serious leg break. An old friend from my short, but superb army days in The Kings Troop Royal Horse Artillery asked me, if I would like a temporary job at the Royal Mews. It was 1977, the year of the Queens' Silver Jubilee, as a state coachman and postilion; I jumped at the opportunity, not only a prestige appointment but also a rent-free flat in the grounds of the palace and more importantly to me in central London, all amenities free and £125 after taxation spending money per week, the perfect job. However, I dread the newspapers, the news channels and all those daytime magazine programmes for the next nine months. I say nine because yes she is already two months gone, the two months following the birth are going to be just as painful. Already the big news of the day is the fact that Her Highness is being treated to the delights those better known for their lowness are also made to suffer at such times, morning sickness, is that really news with all that is going down in the world today? I have not heard much reported lately for those poor Nigerian girls still being held hostage by those rebels, has such a travesty really been forgotten, I hope not. So on that note let me congratulate the Royal couple, yes, that's great news for them, however, can we please be spared all the women journalists and presenters and some of the guys as well, the cooing and pathetic chat about what the poor woman is going through, it's called having a baby dears, not a terminal illness.

I mentioned Sep Blatter yesterday and now hearing he does not intend to hand over the reins at FIFA, when will people like him get the message? He is one of the many scourges within our beloved game. It is time to go Mr. Blatter. PLEASE!

On that note, back to the real job, is that my phone ringing…?

Tuesday 9th September 2014

I do not just want this book to bounce around the Luton roads all the while, otherwise tedium sets in, for me anyway and then maybe with a little luck it will when finally get it way out onto the road itself go a little further afield escaping the confines of Bedfordshire and her rolling fields of mustard yellow.

Yet again Alan Hudson has rattled my cage. He can be quite thought provoking at times with his well-tuned articles. This morning he was pointing his finger firstly in the direction of the "Racing Post" sports newspaper that has, without doubt made quite a dip in his estimations and my own. Once upon a time, we could respect the papers views and take note of their predictions and tips, but for me that ended a good while ago. Alan was complaining about the feature yesterday regarding the game later in the evening, England's 2016 European Championship qualifying game in Basle against Switzerland. The back page emblazoned with the headline, "Roy's Boys in for More Misery" something to mislead the punters in both Alan's and my opinion, which is the way the "Racing Post" plays these days.

I have realised that since Jim McGrath, the former Channel 4 racing presenter, got involved with the "Racing Post" that the paper has gone downhill with the speed of an Olympic bobsled team hurtling down the luge. It is also most apparent that the "Post" is working for or at least with the major bookmakers to mislead the everyday punter into a sense of false security with some quite ludicrous statements, such as the one mentioned regarding the England game of last evening. There is worse than there is good about the "Post" these days that is for sure. I remember, when it first came onto the shelves. Bright and most refreshing, giving the "Sporting Life" a good run for its money. More compact than the regular broadsheet, was one of the many formats that made it more appealing to some. It was definitely easier to read when travelling for hours to every corner of the country. From Newton Abbot, Haydock Park, Carlisle and Ayr to Perth in a cramped horsebox not having to fight with the pages of the much more "Times" like "Life". Yes, in 1986 it was generally accepted with open arms. Especially within the racing industry. It was made for the owner, the trainer, the jockey and the lads. Plus of course the trusting punter. Then in those days a pure racing fanatic, not a bookmaker's friend, conceived it. That is the difference in now to then, Sheikh Mohammed Bin Rashid Al Maktoum certainly did not have the "bookies" running the wings for him, or should I say he and the newspaper were not running the wings for the "bookies", as it certainly is these days from all accounts.

Back to the "Hatters".

It is was good to see Jonathan Smith get a full 90 minutes in for the first time since Boxing Day. Nearly eight months ago, following the leg break, he had a solid game in the Development teams Final Third Development League Southern Division game earlier today where the "Hatters" side easily overhauled Bournemouth with a most convincing 5-0 win, which included a Jim Stevenson hat-trick, and other goals coming from Russ Lafayette and youth team centre half Frankie Musonda. The only blemish of the game came when Alex Wall received a red card in injury time for dissent. Smith later confirmed that he came through the game without any problems from his leg and insists that is all behind him now and just requires to get back to match fitness and fight for a return to first team football. It will be good to see him back in the throng of it all that is for sure, maybe with Lawless back to full fitness very soon and the return of Smith we may begin to witness a much stronger midfield. The "Hatters also had three trialists in the line-up and will be interesting to see if JSL will sign at least one of them, former Dagenham & Redbridge midfielder Matt Saunders, Ex Norwich City defender Ewan McNeill and full back Jordan Brown who was on West Hams' books in the past.

Bloody hell, I'm sorry guys but damn all I seem to hear is why did John Still, just in case you are lost, he is the Luton Town manager, not sign someone before the transfer window closed? That easy, there was no one available, or, maybe he isn't one of those idiots we have had in the past who bought or signed players just for the sake of it. Now it's thought that will he sign someone on loan. Okay, yes we are going through a bad time, but let's look at it from sensible point of view, we have arrived back in the football league. We are therefore in a period of transition, the quality of football having risen considerably in the past couple of seasons. It's going to take our new side time to acclimatise to it, yes a good number of our players have played in the football league before, but those players are now older and a little slower, the younger ones are less experienced, they will come good but it is not going to happen overnight. Now, I hear another cry and this one really makes me laugh in pain at the ridiculousness of the quotes. People asking the question, why are our players on loan scoring freely whilst our first team are not? The simple answer is they are as John Still has quite rightly mentioned young players with great potential to shine, but nowhere near ready to compete at football league level. They need real time football, hence sending them out on loan; the potential that JSL has recognised is shining through, therefore in my humble opinion a bloody good move. I do hope that answers many questions. Can we now please take the needle off the record and hear something new. Thank you kindly, it is getting a little tedious reading or hearing the same old crap every day.

Thursday September 11th 2014

News is coming in that we have signed a midfielder, Nathan Doyle, on a one-year contract. Doyle has extensive Championship and League One experience with Bradford City.

John Still says of the player "Nathan is a top quality player and I think we're very fortunate to be able to bring him to Kenilworth Road. "He is only 27 but has played over 250 games – most of them in the Championship, which underlines his ability."

"He barely missed a game for Bradford last season and was a driving force behind their success the season before last. He has masses of big-game experience and knows what it takes to get out of League two."

"He is a very good player, capable of playing in a number of positions and he is a central midfielder who can pass, create and break-up play. We are confident he has the potential to be a great success with us."

Mr Still is certainly showing his hand in public for the first time, that I can recall, when dealing with a player who is apparently not pulling his weight in training. Also being quite immature not only in training but also on the pitch following his red card in the development game against Bournemouth earlier this week for dissent. The consensus being that he called the referee something along the lines of vaginal content. For JSL to come out and publicly complain about a player's attitude, one can only imagine that things must have truly come to a head because I can never recall him doing this in the past. I have an inkling that he has had enough of the all the criticism from the Luton supporters as to why such and such are not starting games. Some are saying this is the end for Alex Wall as a Luton Town player; I myself reserve judgement on such thoughts for now, as this may be a wake-up call for him, if not yes he will be walking away from Kenilworth Road. For me this is Wall's opportunity to either make or break his Luton Town career. Back to the manager, I have a feeling he has not experienced such vociferous supporters in the past. We are a breed like no other that is for sure when becoming a "Hatter".

Friday September 12th 2014

Despite the signing of Nathan Doyle, it transpires that he is not anywhere near to match fitness and in the same vein Alex Lawless has received a knock back in his return to fitness from his hamstring problem along with Shaun Whalley and the suspended Matty Robinson are all definitely missing from tomorrow's squad against table topping Cheltenham Town.

Saturday September 13th 2014

Admittedly, I am not very optimistic about this afternoon. In the hope of being proved totally wrong I have gone onto the prediction league in the "Hatters Talk" forum on Facebook and predicted Luton Town 0 Cheltenham Town 3, it is a ploy I have found sometimes works, maybe the score will now be reversed and we will win 3-0. Well one can wish.

It is a pleasant morning at least, that is something I suppose. The condemned man ate a hearty meal and all that…

This if for me, where the season needs to change. I am not saying we are in a crisis but we just need to start collecting a few points, the only real worry we could get used to losing and then the rot sets in and that is a rut that as time passes it gets more difficult. The other worry, after today's game we travel to York City for Tuesday evening and that is going to be no easy game either, as I write this they are on a twenty three game unbeaten run in the league, reminiscent of our fabulous run last season in the Conference Premier. And as we well know when a side are on a run as York are now everything seems to go the way of that side, so a win today would make all the difference to the attitude we go into Tuesdays game.

Usually for me, the name Cheltenham brings back such superb memories from my days in racing, having many runners there over the years, some of my greatest times had there. The 1986 Champion Hurdle, my brave little fellow Aonoch, who the pundits fancied to take See You Then's crown. However, right from the starters' flag he was always struggling. He suffered from corns. Horses suffer from that same ailment as we humans do, but the pain so much more severe for them. What a day to for the annoying varmints to decide it would be fun to flare up. To make it worse five hurdles from home Corporal Clinger fell in front of him, a flaying hoof catching Aonoch plumb centre of his face, as the faller somersaulted. He ran on gamely but with that and his corn-ridden feet. He was always going backwards in comparison to the rest of the field. Following the race, he suffered the worst nosebleed I have ever experienced seeing from a horse, terrible. The next year he started joint favourite with Irish challenger Galmoy in the Waterford Stayers Hurdle, also at the festival meeting, losing at least six lengths coming into the home straight looking for the best ground, subsequently beaten three lengths by the Irish contender and Tommy Carmody. Despite the defeats, such superb memories stick in the mind forever, Cheltenham then, usually a name synonymous with fun and great sporting moments, however today that is all out the back door, for the next few hours its Cheltenham, the enemy within. So let us make it down the road to the "Kenny".

The "Hatters" line up as follow Mark Tyler, Alex Lacey, Steve McNulty, Pelly Ruddock Mpanzu, Scott Griffiths, Luke Guttridge, Jonathan Smith, Curtley Williams, Mark Cullen and Ross Lafayette. Substitutes being: Andy Drury, Alex Wall, Jake Howells, Luke Rooney, Elliott Justham, Jim Stevenson and Charlie Walker.

How good to see young Jonathan Smith back in the line-up, following his Boxing Day break at Barnet last season, to be honest I am surprised to see Alex Wall on the bench following John Still remarks in mid-week. Nevertheless, it warms me to know that unlike some JLS will give him an opportunity at some time to redeem himself.

Luton Town 1 Cheltenham Town 0

A hard fought win full of graft, grit and desire against a hitherto unbeaten team. Leaving off from last week, we played some very good fast flowing, high tempo stuff against Cheltenham, who really did not come to the races today.

Leading though a deft header by Cullen, getting his head to a cross from Scotty Griffiths at the centre of the box and heading it down wide of the keeper, we made them look an average side. Smith was fantastic, considering his nine months out; he played with more energy than a Duracell bunny on Speed. He protected the back three superbly and set up numerous attacks for us. That type of performance typifies him. Sensing danger and blocking it before it happened.

Second half, Cheltenham could have galloped away with the game, and put us under some intense pressure, we struggled to hold the ball up, pressure kept building. McNulty was excellent, but against sides that look to bang the ball forward quickly, he excels in, the teams who show that extra movement and a bit of pace, where he looks most exposed, metaphorically not literally, thankfully. Wilkinson came on and was reliable. Pelly was all over the place, disgracefully targeted by Cheltenham, who tried to kick him out of the game. Personally, I would expect better behaviour from residents of a Spa town of such note.

A couple of superb blocks by Tyler kept our noses ahead, as the finishing line approached. That and some greedy novice finishing by Kobi Arthur, who finished more like Steptoe's cart horse than Dawn Run. Those bloody pink booties he wore probably did not help his cause. Yes folks the keeper wore pink boots, reminds me of someone else I know, but you will have to read my other book to get that one.

But for a very strange and late decision by the assistant referee to chalk off Jim Stevenson's goal from close range, seconds after he replaced Lacey, would have meant a more comfortable win. No one seems to know exactly why disallowed. It could not have been offside, as there was a defender on the line. The linesman's flag went up very late, strange one that really, not even the spooks at GCHQ could positively work out that little conundrum.

Whatever the limitations of the team, you cannot say they did not give their all for the cause. It is something to build on ahead of the two difficult away games this week.

If anyone says they guessed the correct starting line-up today, they either have the powers of Mystic Meg or are a bit of a Jackanory writer. Tyler in goal, three centre halves in Wilkinson, McNulty and Lacey. Williams, the Lowestoft Cafu, and Griffiths as wingback. Smith and Pelly the midfielders, with Guttridge playing behind the attacking two-some of Cullen and Lafayette.

Both debutants, well it was Lafayette's full debut, did pretty well, until stamina and rather like our old friend Oscar Pistorius they ran out of legs, milady. Lafayette benefited from having a forward front-runner aside him, as did Cullen. He struggled to hold the ball up in the second half, when Cullen moved to the right. Although in his defence, Lafayette is not suited to playing as the only man up front.

Williams, it's safe to say, is far better going forward, he could be an asset with his attacking play, but defensively his positional sense is lacking somewhat. Appreciate he is inexperienced and it is a big jump up from playing for Lowestoft, but positional sense is like common sense, you either have it or you don't.

Cheltenham, a big strong powerful unit. On the evidence of today, it is hard to see them push for automatic promotion. We have come up against far better teams already this season. They will be a hard team to oppose in mid-Winter, when Football becomes a haphazard, joyless lottery on pitches with only the barest hint of grass cover. They are a typical modern lower division side. You can decide if that is a compliment or insult, they lined up with three centre halves, all the size of a beast you would find in a sanctuary for Shire horses with footballing skills to match.

So there we have it, the "Hatters" first home win of the season. As mentioned our next opponents, York City, go and suffer their first defeat in twenty-four games away to Burton Albion by two goals to nil. We can only hope they are on a downward spiral right now.

The Town's Youth Alliance fixture at Peterborough on Saturday morning was abandoned after 40 minutes when " Hatters" defender Luke Trotman suffered a serious injury.

The second year scholar broke his leg in a 40th-minute incident with the Hatters 2-1 up against Posh. Trotman taken to Peterborough Hospital with his mum by his side.

Our thoughts are with Luke at this difficult time and wish him a speedy recovery.

Tuesday September 16th 2014

York City, are they on the slide or was Saturday at Burton Albion just a one off? Well this evening we shall see for ourselves. Their twenty-three game unbeaten run came to an abrupt end at Burton. Last season we suffered a mini blip after suffering the same fate, it stops that momentum and so shall we see likewise from the Minsters? We could be in for a drubbing also, the backlash may be one we live to regret, it all depends on their character and attitude as to how they respond.

I love visiting York. My historical and archaeological head takes over whenever I go there. However, it also holds other memories of visits to watch Luton Town F.C. Well most times I get there. There was though one particular occasion I was somewhat misguided in my attempts to get the ground. For example, I cannot remember exactly, over the years my mind has grown a little fuzzy, to be expected I suppose. Anyway, I will not name a certain person as that will not be fair and if I do, she may just jump out of the shadows one evening and crunch no more me. She is renowned for over-react sometimes, laughing quite profusely as I type that. Let us just say in her youth she was in the wrong company and found herself working for her Majesty's own pleasure. At the time in question, she was residing in one of those open type hostels and allowed out for a few hours on occasion. We were able to wrangle it so that one of those weekends was coincidentally one that the "Hatters" were playing at Bootham Crescent, therefore I travelled up on the Friday afternoon and arranged to meet a fellow "Hatter" Chris up there for a drink on the Friday evening, yes it has to be said we had a few bevvies. Usually I stayed at The Moat House Hotel when there, on the riverside and friendly staff. I had some rather happy evenings in the bar at times it has to be said. But this particular weekend I found a lovely hotel just opposite the turn into Bootham Crescent, The Bedford Hotel, family run and very nice people with a bar that stayed open until the last man dropped, I actually stayed there again a few times after. Anyway, I got tickets for myself and, let us for safety reasons call her Naomi, always had a thing for a certain Ms Campbell. I got tickets for both of us to go the game, usually I would have been out with the boys having a few jam jars before kick-off, but because Naomi had a day pass, so we decided to go back to the hotel to enjoy our little time we had together. Bianca is Jamaican by birth and most attractive, twenty years my junior and great fun to be with in every sense of the term. Time passed and was quite comfortable in the surroundings and the company, suddenly I hear a familiar voice, from outside on the street, our room was on the second level and looked right down onto the main road. All I heard was Danny Clubb's dulcet tones "Lukey, what you up to the game is due to start in a while. I slide myself to the window, the bed being right at the side. There down below us were Chris from the night previous. Who actually came back to hotel bar for a few after the pubs kicked us out. Richard White, Terry Alder, the Stanyon twins Paul and David. Also a couple more guys and Danny's lovely wife Elsie all gaping up to get a glimpse of my bare torso as I responded, "sorry guys I am having a meal right now, in fact the only one actually eating was Naomi as I was shouting down, if you get my drift. At the same time being ordered to get back and stop bringing attention to the room, she was not shy but at the same time, well you know a little private also. It does not need to be said really, we did not make the game, but I was made aware of the score as they passed by again, I did not miss much a boring 0-0 if my memory serves me correctly. Nevertheless, a most enjoyable weekend was had. Oh sweet memories of days now passed. Tonight's game has drawn about 150 "Hatters" fans up north, such a long journey on a week night is not the most easy of places to get to, so it cannot go without noting a thank you to all that travelled.

York are under the capable and watchful eye of Frank Worthington who it has to be said turned the club around somewhat since his arrival.

So the team lines up as follows, there is no skipper Steve McNulty who has been given special leave to be with his partner who has gone into labour, the very best wishes to all three.

Mark Tyler, Curtley Williams, Alex Lacey, Scott Griffiths, Luke Wilkinson, Andy Drury, Jake Howells, Pelly Ruddock Mpanzu, Jonathan Smith, Luke Guttridge and Mark Cullen. With subs: Alex Wall, Luke Rooney, Elliott Justham, Ross Lafayette, Shaun Whalley, Luke Stevenson and Paul Connolly.

York City 0 Luton Town 0

A decent point, which should have been more, against apparently our old foe according to the York based media. Some of their supporters seem to have more chips on their shoulders than even McCain's can produce, it's nice to see some people are mature enough to put the past behind them and move on.

Two changes from the Cheltenham win, Drury and Howells replacing McNulty who as mentioned earlier has been given leave to be with his Partner who is in labour, I am not too sure if I can condone this sex before marriage situation though and Russ Lafayette (who isn't pregnant, as far as I know) respectively. Back to a 4-4-1-1 formation. Tyler in goal. Back four of Williams, Wilkinson, Lacey and Griffiths. The midfield of Drury, Smith, PRM and Howells with Guttridge playing behind Cullen the lone central striker.

The main disappointment from the evening was that we were unable to turn our supremacy over an average side for long periods into goals. On the bright side, it continues our rather splendid and perfectly formed goal less run at Bootham Crescent to six visits.

The fact that the hosts' goalkeeper Ingram was the stand out player of the evening does tell a tale. In particular a reaction save from Rooney's snap shot was quite brilliant.

For many it was the best all round performance of the season, some of our play on the break was excellent, fast flowing football. Guttridge, orchestrating move after move. With Ruddock Mpanzu available to charge though and cause problems for York's rather flat-footed defence.

On the balance of the play, it was two points dropped rather than one gained. Now with Smith back, Ruddock Mpanzu coming into form and Guttridge close to full fitness again, the team has improved significantly, not surprisingly. If by any small chance we can maintain the type of performance of last night and the first halves of the last couple of home matches, we will before too long be climbing up the table. Goals do continue be somewhat elusive but we have cut out individual errors at the back which were giving the opposition some soft goals.

York did create a few chances, but let themselves down through a lack of creativity, Tyler was forced into a few saves, but all were relatively comfortable, whilst both our centre halves played well, but neither had to do anything remarkable to put paid to any of York's rather lacklustre efforts.

York will need a miracle to replicate last season's play-off place. Goalkeeper apart they need to improve all areas of the team. Ponderous defence, both fullbacks better going forward than back. Apart from Penn, they lack of talent in midfield, so the forwards starved of service.

After the game JLS had this to say "It was a first-class performance, without a doubt. Everyone is doing their jobs now. We are in our groove.

"I thought people should have taken their chances. They did not, we have played terrific, but we do have to take our chances, there is no doubt about that.

"These young ones that we have brought in will gradually become the future of this football club. It's really, really pleasing."

Another away game this weekend. This time to those, we love to hate, Cambridge United. With it comes another encounter with our former manager Richard Money who seems to be in the habit of attempting to wind us up with many ridiculous remarks, the only way to put him to bed in reality is the lads talking with their feet and knocking the mouthy old sod for six or seven would be a perfect lesson. Realistically I do see us coming out with something from the game, which will be good enough. Today a game to relish for many reasons though, last season they looked as though they were in an unassailable position. However, they never reckoned on JLS and the boys, could it be a case of onwards and upwards again this season for the "Hatters". Time will tell.

Wednesday September 17th 2014
Well done and congratulations to Sumo, our captain Steve McNulty, along with of course his girlfriend who now have a new daughter Lillia. Good fortune to the new family Skip.
Following their dour performance last night, York City manager Nigel Worthington really stuck into them publicly calling them "Diabolical at times". So all you moaners out there take note we are not that bad, York have now failed to score in four of their last five games.

All the news this week is focused quite rightly so on the Scottish referendum, however I am going to stay well away from politics to the best of my ability in this book, this is about sports and a little extra curriculum of sorts, not politics. So good luck Scotland in whatever you decide.

Saturday September 20th 2014
Following the York game, I have to admit to placing my priorities elsewhere in preparing a database for my new project, The National Sixties, a look at the first decade of televised coverage of our national institution that is The Aintree Grand National from 1960 to 1969. I hope in time you will look out for it, just a subtle hint from yours truly.

Today for many of us today is a "must" win day and not just for the reason of points. We have to rub salt into the festering wound that we made for our former illustrious leader Richard Money. When at the club berated the fans quite publicly in the local media, following a defeat by Kidderminster Harriers. If I remember correctly, although I may be well off track. "It does not matter what players Luton possess, who the manager is or how much money they may have in the bank, Luton Town will never run away with the Conference Premier." Three seasons later, a season in which for the early part it looked like his side Cambridge United were going to run away with it themselves. Not only did we turn around what at one time was a fourteen point lead, but totally overturned to win the league by a massive nineteen points and seeing them finish of course a very distant second. Egg in the face? More like a tray full.

To be honest today got off to the worst of starts for myself at least, from the moment of waking to see a certain newspaper trying to besmirch the sport that has given myself the life I have and many people so much pleasure also. This morning the front page of the Daily Mirror had the front-page picture story of a vet holding a gun the forehead of a poor unfortunate racehorse, which had broken its leg so badly that there was no other way than to euthanise. Such actions are never an easy decision for anyone to make. However, this scurrilous newspaper decided how wonderful a headline it would make on a peaceful Saturday morning where there is no other scandal to be had regarding some over indulging non-talented so called celebrity. Their actions so irresponsible, not only for what it was but also for the fact on the front page where vulnerable children visiting a newsagents able to see this awful image. I an addition to the picture shown they were trying to say that the only reason the horse put to sleep was that it was worth in value £1.3million pounds and so accusing the connections of doing it purely for insurance, in order to recompense their monetary loss. This is not at all how it works. An independent veterinarian professional always makes the decision, especially on this occasion at a racecourse. The leg in question was obviously so badly damaged that it would for a horse be virtually irreparable and the horse was already in a great deal of pain and discomfort, sometimes therefore such a disturbing and upsetting decision has to be made. From experience I can assure anyone that this is one of the most harrowing, stressful and heart-breaking moments I have ever had to endure in my lifetime and on a number of occasions. It is something one never forgets.

I was though also angry at the racecourse officials who failed to put up the usually mandatory sightscreens that in all fairness would have eradicated this picture from being able to have been taken and subsequently published.

These are the words of my friend, racing journalist Andrew Pelis.

"I want to applaud the British Horseracing Authority statement made by Robin Mounsey, which addresses that awful article and is quoted on the Racing Post website at present.

"We are appalled by the Daily Mirror's decision to publish these photos, and also to contextualise the images in the manner that they have.

"All that the images show is a veterinary surgeon doing his job and carrying out an act of humanity to prevent an animal from suffering. They show the same actions as would be taken by a vet whether the incident was occurring on a racecourse or at home in a field and we do not understand where the public interest lays in publishing these images or why they should be used to open a debate about horseracing.

"We will be seeking a meeting with the editor of the Daily Mirror in regards to this issue and the use of these photos in such a manner."

Thank you Andrew could not have put it better.

So with daily rant over, it is that time.

With well over 2,000 "Hatters" fans making their way to Abbey Stadium this afternoon there is sure to be a superb atmosphere.

The "Hatters" will line up this afternoon as this: Mark Tyler, Curtley Williams, Scott Griffiths, Steve McNulty, Alex Lacey, Luke Wilkinson, Pelly Ruddock Mpanzu, Luke Guttridge, Jim Stevenson, Mark Cullen and Alex Wall. Subs: Andy Drury, Shaun Whalley, Ross Lafayette, Matt Robinson, Nathan Doyle, Charlie Walker and Elliott Justham.

I am thrilled to see such a positive starting line-up. With Cullen and Alex Wall up front. What is also pleasing, despite many trying to say Wall was definitely on his way out after the public blasting from JLS, which I now realise what I wrote previously regarding the situation to be correct. Not to embarrass the young man but to give him a hefty shove and to get himself back on track, here is given the opportunity to shine. Let battle commence I say.

Cambridge United 0 Luton Town 1

The performance was inferior to that of the York game, the first half as bad as any we have played apart maybe from the first half at Accrington, yet we won today. As expected a feisty game, in truth the quality of the games-manship was more apparent than the quality of football. We have played Cambridge, unlike Richard Money, I am not small minded or petty enough not to name the opposition, a lot over the last few years, games are generally tight, well-contested affairs against our apparent rivals. The only reason one can truly call Cambridge United our rivals for me is the connection with Mr Money and yes, I suppose the manner in which we not only caught them last season but also ran away from them points wise, no running away though in any other context that is for sure.

For the first half we seemed to have stayed back at the Kenny. Apart maybe from Luke Wilkinson who was exceptional, sweeping up danger and hardly gave the much-lauded Appiah a chance, he looks to becoming a handy player to have, he has limitations but does what he is there to do and one cannot really ask for more than that.

Cambridge looked the brighter of two poor sides in the first half, but failed to take their chances, it was lucky that most of them fell to Elliott who not only has the height of a Giraffe but the footballing talent of one as well. Their final ball was not good, with Donaldson and Dunk two of their more creative players having pretty subdued matches.

The second half brought more intensity to our performance, to be honest it would have been a somewhat difficult to get more lacklustre, which was the case even before Naylor, on loan to Cambridge from Derby County, on his debut was sent off for a rash tackle on Stevenson. Naturally the dynamics of the game changed, the Cambridge set up looked more central therefore some use of the width was required from the "Hatters", which Drury did, showing some of his class at last the, with some quality play on the right, after giving a passable impression of the Invisible Man in the week. Lafayette, who replaced the booked Wall, supported Cullen well and the pairing gave Nelson and Coulson a hard time, in the first half both centre halves would have been excused for falling asleep through boredom. Pelly Ruddock Mpanzu started to swagger his way through the opposition, his shot hit with the power of a sledgehammer. I dare say the goal post is still shaking now. He also won the penalty, inviting a defiant Tait to put in an unnecessary challenge close to the by-line. Cullen stepped up and played a cheeky one two with disillusions of grandeur come to mind when quoted as saying the keeper from the spot to put the Town in front. Six minutes of injury time signalled by the fourth official. I believe they must think of a number and double it just for a laugh. We saw out the game comfortably enough, keeping the ball well and not giving the ten men a sniff of the possession or a sight of Tyler.

It does amuse me somewhat as to how Richard Money has that unique knack of being able to wind up the Luton following from the first moment he opens his mouth. First, we hear his ridiculous comment, "And I'm also proud that I played some part in turning them from a club that got relegated three divisions in four years to a club that was ready to move forward."

The only thing both himself and his good mate Gary Brabin done for us was made us into a side of second bests, as also their successor a certain American schoolgirl's football coach these day did for us.

Thank God most graciously for John Leonard Still, forever to be called a Luton legend alongside the likes of Harry Haslam, Alec Stock, David Pleat, John Moore and Ray Harford.

As always, I would like to thank Paul Wright for his superb depiction of the game.

Elsewhere in League Two, there was a nine goal thriller at Sixfields where Accrington Stanley overcame the Cobblers to win 5-4, last Tuesdays opponent York finally scored two goals in a game for Nigel Worthington, however Southend scored one more to win 3-2, so following twenty three games unbeaten they are sliding disastrously to oblivion, or at least close to. As predicted by many, Bury tonight top the table after knocking Burton Albion off their perch with a most resounding 3-1 victory. Next Saturdays' opponents, Oxford United, could only muster a goalless draw against another side we are looking forward to meeting in a couple of weeks with relish, Stevenage Town. So the league table is beginning to take a more realistic shape. Now nine games into the season some will say I am being a little premature but it does look as I envisage the league to finish. The "Hatters" now in thirteenth place and yes, we are above you Dicky Dosh, which makes it even sweeter, another forty points and we will be relatively safe from relegation. Just a thought after all the moaning we have witnessed over the opening weeks of the season. The strangest thing is yes we won but not our greatest performance by a very long way so far this season, but certain moaners have not been heard at all, not even saying well at least we won, in fact not a whimper, how satisfying is that?

Another little dig at a handful who were a couple of weeks ago calling for the sacking of John Still I have one message, get a life and wake up you demented bunch of…, well that will suffice for now.

Very satisfying is my reply.

I am not for one minute gloating at those particular fans though, because we still have a great deal of work to do, but the confidence in the changing room and on the training ground must be flowing with more fluidity this coming week.

Let us remember for a moment or three, one of the greatest footballing managers who brightened up our lives with his antics during his managerial career. The loveable Brian Clough, how different

English football could have been if he had been as the people always wanted as England boss, but the blazer boys of what was in those days Lancaster Gate were too damned scared of him. Brian passed away ten years ago this weekend, sorely missed by football itself and the fans alike.

Sunday September 21st 2014

The morning after the day before and I have just been listening to BBC Radio Cambridgeshire's post match podcast last night. What a load of balderdash I have just had assault my shell likes. Firstly a few demented fans saying we only had one shot on goal and that was the penalty, is that why you still this morning have a distinct ringing in your own ears from the rattling of Pelly Ruddock Mpanzu rasping drive from outside the box. Then the inevitable I suppose, Dicky "Luton Town" Dosh. I call him that just to remind him of our name because it seems he has lost the ability to say the name for quite a while now, maybe it hurts him to mention the name of the club where he was a total failure after all his promises. It really must stick firmly in his throat. I quote, "We were the better side by far eleven versus eleven and I thought we could still hold our own with a ten men" well to be fair the way we had played in the first half that was a valid point I suppose, but the second half was a different game altogether. However, to say they were the better side throughout the game was another quote dug out of his pre match dreams. Cannot wait for the next instalment at Kenilworth Road.

I cannot help but smile recalling the pre-season noises coming from all of those Anfield supporters. How great they were going to be despite the loss of the two-legged man-eater. Even with the arrival of their so-called Messiah Mario Balotelli, why they signed him I am still trying to fathom out. I am sorry but after Aston Villa last week and West Ham this week they looked quite ordinary for me and the distinct dislike for claret and blue must be quite prominent today. I have to admit I do love it when the scouse supporters cringe into the shadows, I believe it could be a long season for them.

When one listens to John Still being interviewed post match, you have to sometimes stop for a while and take stock of the situation. Think hard and then go outside into the garden and shout at the top of your voice "Hallelujah", because let's face it when have we as "Hatters" in recent years been able to agree in harmony, apart from a few misguided imps of course, that this really genuinely is a Luton Town manager speaking. The man actually tells it how it is, the mannerisms and facial expression accentuate the fact that everything is tormenting him as much as it is us as fans. I sincerely believe the man has grown to love the club and not see it as just a job of work, the pain is there to see, maybe I am wrong, but if so I am seeing different to everybody else that is for sure. With the man in front of the camera, or just in a general press conference, he is no different. He always comes across as telling it how it is. No insipid nonsensical or lame excuses just the plain and simple matter of fact truth. I have like a manager who does not hide his emotions. Even Kevin Keegan used to do it for me in that sense, honest to goodness feeling from the heart, not just play acting in front of the cameras, a true passion. There are many managers out there up and down the country, in and out of the higher leagues that could, no not could, should watch and listen to this man, they would learn so much about themselves and the correct way to act. To me it is noticeable more now than ever before why this man we are most fortunate to have in our midst has never been out of work as a manager. As far as I can remember back he has always been the man sought not the man chasing, his dignity and attitude is the best in my book, it is easy to say that with him as Luton manager, but it has taken that for us to see the man in the real daylight, for many including myself an enigma.

Back to his interviews though, we do not hear the ball or the run of the green is not doing it for us now. We do not hear anything from him, like the match officials were abysmal, more often than not that is exactly the case, they have mostly been pretty awful at the level Luton have been at in recent years. What we do hear, his admission that the team he has been putting out most of this season so far has been unbalanced. That he is struggling to find a right sided player fit enough to play whole ninety-minutes. In fact, not just a right sided player, he would rather acknowledge but a whole team in general, who can play in their rightful positions. He does not mention a player is not pulling their weight, apart from once which to be honest was to gee the player on more than actually reprimand him in public. As I see it, he would rather come out and acknowledge the fact that the squad as a whole have worked their socks off in the hope of getting a result despite the problems. John explained to the media following the Cambridge game at the Abbey Stadium the reasons for not delving into the fiasco of bringing players in on loan. In his experience, it gives those youngsters that he has bought into the club an opportunity to not only get a feel for first team football, but also get them much valued experience in the football league where they can find out first-hand how tough it really can be out there. Valuable experience indeed for the future, because these young players are not in to fill gaps, they are as the manager himself states the future of Luton Town Football Club. It is largely thanks to John Still I personally believe we do have a reasonably bright future, when in recent years have we truly been able to say that with an ounce of confidence whereas now we can have sacksful of confidence.

Lately, I have read and heard supporters questioning young defender Curtley Williams. Some asking how good he really is, he has looked slow and not really up to the task, again following the Cambridge game Still tells us why he made the decision to substitute him so early in the game. From the terraces, it was so easy to think the manager had realised his mistake. The player was not good enough, this simply was not the case the young lad had been asked the day before the game whilst on the treatment table whether he thought his fitness would be up to playing the next day, Williams obviously agreed, such is the Towns injury problem and also William's obvious commitment to the club. Saturday subsequently placed in the side, but after a while, it was obvious he was struggling. We the fans were just not aware it was the effects of an injury, not because he is not up to the job. Despite having an injury he has gone out there and tried to get through the game unfortunately it was not be. Sometimes risks have to be taken. Not always the correct decision maybe, but all the same taken.

Some will argue not the best scenario to have, however what can one do with the injury situation as it is, that is why we should bring in players on loan many will say, I have thought that now and again if I am honest. I believe that JLS is trying not to be lured into loaning anybody. Maybe, he cannot see the point of bringing a player in for a month. By the time the player has learnt to gel into the side it's time to return to his parent club, defeating the object somewhat some will say, who knows we may still be in the same situation once the player has gone, short term loans are really not beneficial, but that's only my thoughts on the subject obviously. Therefore, I am thinking patience and understanding from everybody is the best answer for now.

Wednesday September 24th 2014
Yesterday the Development side faced a strong Portsmouth side, holding them to a more than creditable 2-2 draw. New signing from Bradford, Nathan Doyle being put through his paces for the first 71 minutes before being substituted. The "Hatters" side had to come from behind twice with goals from Charlie Walker and a Shaun Whalley penalty after he himself upended inside the box.

Thursday September 25th 2014

It was thirty years ago today that Luton participated in what was an amazing display of attacking football from both sides at Stoke City's Victoria Ground, Luton fielded what was just about the strongest side we had available.

The line-up being; Alan Judge, Kirk "Basher" Stephens, Richard "straight jacket" Money, Nobby Horton, Clive Goodyear, Mal "Mr Dependable" Donaghy, Ricky "When he gets the ball he beats them all" Hill, Brian "Bruno" Stein, Paul "Walshy" Walsh, Wayne "The legend himself" Turner and David "Mossy" Moss with Raddy Antic (future Real Madrid, Barcelona and Atletico Madrid, the only man ever to manage all three and Maine Road hero.

George Berry opened the scoring for Stoke from a corner after Mark Chamberlains initial header came off the bar onto the head of Berry who had the simple task of putting the ball over the line, 1-0 to Stoke.

Then came the equaliser, what a goal to make it 1-1 also, Paul Walsh struck the ball so beautifully from a good 30 yards out giving the Stoke keeper Peter Fox absolutely no chance of reaching. The combination of Chamberlain and Berry then struck yet again in the 22nd minute when Chamberlain ran the ball to the by-line leaving "Basher" stranded and crossed the ball for Berry to rise unopposed and head home to make it 2-1 to the home side.

Then a most bizarre moment, even in the annals of Luton's history. Hill chipped a ball over the Stoke defensive line that had pushed well up towards the half way line. Peter Fox ran out of his area to either head the ball away from the oncoming Walsh but totally made a hash of it, handling it maybe, the ball dropped to Walsh who calmly ran the ball into the goal to make it 2-2, but then with much dismay to Luton players and fans alike the referee called play back and gave a free kick to Luton and sent Peter Fox off, why not give the goal? David Moss took the ensuing free kick but straight into the safe arms of the replacement keeper, in those day's players seemed to wear their shorts so tight and high it was on the cusp of being in the realms of the obscene.

Mossy then makes one of his famous runs down the right flank and places a precision cross to the oncoming Brian Stein who heads home quite sublimely to at last make it 2-2 and no intervention this time from the referee.

Half time then and it's a crazy 2-2. The second half gets under way and well five minutes in and a cross from the right puts the Luton defence in sixes and sevens a right defensive mess up, yes guys even in those heady days we made defensive mistakes by the dozen at times,

Paul Bracewell pounced onto the ball and poked it past a sprawling Mal Donaghy and a stretching "Basher" to make it 3-2. But hey remember this is Luton Town in those days we always had a never say die attitude, we battled and foraged, the equaliser came when Ricky Hill slotted the ball between two Stoke defenders for Brian Stein to dance through the defence to put the ball beyond the keeper to equalise yet again, 3-3. Then a collector's item Nobby Horton chips over the Stoke defence for Mal Donaghy to place a looping header over the Stoke keeper to put the Hatters in front for the first time in the game. 3-4. But with five minutes or so of the game remaining up pops Brendan O'Callaghan to equalise with a shot through the defence from about twenty yards out, Judge having no chance of getting to.

4-4. However that was not the end of it. Luton had the chance to steal the game in the dying moments. Bruno Stein ran into the box with speed and blatantly bought down. Definite penalty. Dave Moss runs up to the ball on the spot could this be 4-5 and a famous victory for the "Hatters" Mossy rarely missed from the spot, puts it well clear of the keeper, but no to the delight of the Stoke supports the ball slams against the left hand post, so the game ends up an amazing 4-4 draw. Some superb finishing from Luton and some dismal defending also, but that what it is at Luton

Town FC, we will never be allowed to just relax and enjoy a game, there for us and off the pitch is and never will be as Rod Stewart's album suggests a dull moment.

Finally for today…
I was so saddened indeed to learn that another of the old school trainers of my era in horse racing has passed away, it is often easily said "One of the nicest guys' in racing", but on this occasion it is said with such feeling, a warm genuine man with always a smile. Gave us all some great memories. The irony of it, last night I was writing much about his first of two National winners Highland Wedding in 1969. The world and the family of racing is a much emptier place this morning. Blessings to his family on this very sad day. RIP dear man. Toby Balding, one of my favourite trainers of all time.

Racehorse trainer Toby Balding who sadly passed away yesterday.

Saturday September 27th 2014

It is that time again, the "Hatters" are at home and for once, I hope not a bad omen, I am for some reason super confident that we will collect three points today from one off the bottom, at the moment of course, Oxford United. However, despite my feeling of confidence this is not going to be no easy affair that is for sure. We are still struggling with a list of injuries that most probably causes JLS more nightmares and restless nights than calm peaceful sleep-time.

A good atmosphere today. I feel for what, although not a derby match of sorts, there are certainly two going on today, to whet the appetite of those partial to a touch of derby excitement. With the Merseyside derby and the North London one also, I have been to a number of the latter in my time and one sticks out quite prominently at Highbury many years ago. I travelled down to London from Kempston with my two very good mates, again brothers, Mick and Kenny Cook. Ken a staunch Arsenal supporter and you have guessed it Mick Spurs through and through, it was definitely a day to remember, however I will return to that day later in the book, this today is all about Luton Town versus Oxford United.

Oxford as I mentioned sit two places from bottom of League two at the beginning of the game today with seven points from nine games, with Hartlepool and Carlisle below them. Their previous game was a 0-0 draw at home against Stevenage Town, I am sure Michael Appleton their manager would be happy with a similar result today somehow, we certainly will not be. Our starting line-up will be interesting to say the least. There will be checks on players before the game including Paul

Benson, Luke Rooney, Jake Howells and Curtley Williams. Alex Lawless, Fraser Franks and Paul Connolly are definitely side-lined still though.

The team lists are out and well as I said an interesting line up, new boy Nathan Doyle is making his debut along with Sean Whalley starting for the first time this season.

So it is as follows; Mark Tyler, Scott Griffiths, Alex Lacey, Steve McNulty, Luke Wilkinson, Pelly Ruddock Mpanzu, Shaun Whalley, Nathan Doyle, Jake Howells, Jonathan Smith and Mark Cullen. With the subs: Andy Drury, Elliott Justham, Ross Lafayette, Luke Guttridge, Matt Robinson, Jim Stevenson and Charlie Walker.

Luton Town 2 Oxford United 0

It's good to see that Luton are taking advantage of the easier fixture list recently and moving to a decent position, without playing as well as we can whilst missing key players.

Even parading world-class superstar Tyrone Barnett, who perhaps needed to remove both of Nathan Doyle's ankles to be shown a red card. It was a terrible tackle on Doyle over the top. The standard of tackling this season has been woeful and pitiful.   It appear the only coaching that goes on these days is how to manage the game and not the game's basics. But given the dreadful state English Football is in, that should surprise nobody. I will say more about coaching in a while because I have to agree with my friend Alan Hudson on that count, but we shall come back to that. Oxford's football was neat, but their passing was fairly ponderous and predictable at times. Only O'Dowda on the left, who gave Lacey problems, was the likely source of a goal.

After only two minutes, the "Hatters" through Wilkinson's bullet of a header from Howells' in-swinging free kick played into an ideal position in the area. The most impressive part of our play was how we did not let Oxford settle in the opening twenty-five minutes. Naturally, we could not keep up that tempo or the energy levels for a whole game, Oxford came into the game, but lacked pace in their play to get behind us very often.

As was the case at Cambridge, Luke Wilkinson was faultless at the back. He does have an uncanny knack of being it the right place at the right time in our box. The problems with our performance were down the right side, right back has been a problem this season with injuries, Lacey struggled against a good player in O'Dowda, but by the sound of things, Williams and Connolly maybe back next week. It was a big opportunity for Whalley to make a mark, he looked like the Whalley of last season, rather than the Whalley who used to terrorise us at Southport. He had a bit of a nightmare, poor final ball and easily nudged off the ball at times.

Nathan Doyle had a steady enough debut, already proven at this level with Bradford, and should improve with a number of games. Sitting in front of the back four, he read the game well he has good positional sense, allowing the likes of Smith and Pelly license to roam.

Oxford have struggled so far this season and to be honest it is difficult to see them improving unless they bring in a player with a cutting edge. They were though better than we were at ball retention and they did have their moments. Howard is a clever player, getting into space and Mullins is good at bringing the ball well forward from centre half.

Luton looked to get the ball forward quickly, often Tyler would attempt to get the ball up to Cullen on the right and take advantage of their smallest defender Newby on that flank. It almost worked soon after Wilkinson's goal, a long kick by Tyler. Cullen nodded down to Whalley, a pass into Pelly who charged forward past Newby. To be fair it was not Ruddock Mpanzu's finest match, but he was effective tracking back.

We seemed happy enough to keep our shape and defend a deep line. Oxford during the early exchanges often caught in possession, they were telegraphing their passes, they were slow to release the pass and slow in thought. With Barnett and Hylton well-marked, their only outlet was the trickery of O'Dowda. He received the ball from Howard, took on Lacey but Lacey managed to turn it behind. A pass by Howard found O'Dowda getting into a central position, managed to get a shot in, but it was comfortable for Tyler to hold diving low to this right. Mullins allowed to jog through but Wilkinson came around and won the ball. One incident summed up the difference between the two sides, Griffiths moving forward, took a poor touch, Ruffels was favourite to get the ball, but Griffiths won the battle with a firm sliding tackle. Really, we wanted it more. Griffiths certainly ruffled Ruffels.

Tyrone Barnett as mentioned earlier should have received a straight red following his lunging tackle on Nathan Doyle, however the referee decided a yellow was the better option, at about the same time a certain Wayne Rooney did similar and justifiably received a red, inconsistencies throughout the game do not change that's for sure. From Lacey's floating free kick Russ Lafayette, who had earlier replaced the lacklustre Whalley, made a leap and headed the ball down hitting the hand of Mullins. Quite a good save considering he was not the keeper, surely a nomination for a red card again, but the penalty given so we could not complain really I suppose considering the severity of Barnett's foul not getting the red card treatment.

Jake Howells stepped up to take the spot kick, keeper Long, quite un-sportingly mouthing off at Jake before the kick was taken, guessed correctly diving to his right and pushing the ball away, but not unlike Cullen's penalty kick at Cambridge last week, Howells was quick to latch on to the rebound and slotted the ball home, 2-0. I wonder if the "Hatters" have been practicing such scenarios of late.

Andy Drury come on to replace Doyle, even before the awful tackle by Barnett he looked to have run his race. Whilst not fit, Doyle did well enough on his debut and should prove to be a decent acquisition for us.

Drury again played well coming off the bench. I know the people who count see him in central midfield, but since he has returned all his better games have been whilst playing on the right flank. He put in a good shift, helping Lacey.

Jim Stevenson replaced a tired looking Jonathon Smith late on.

So another win and just as pleasingly four games have now passed without conceding, so at least at last the defence seems to have worked it out. Overall, it has been decent start at the higher level. Only really at Shrewsbury have we looked outclassed. We are beginning to look much more organised overall, but still perhaps lacking enough quality to score goals, but September has proven to be a good month.

The "Hatters" man of the match again being Scott Griffiths, who as is always the case had a solid game at the back.

All of this tactical stuff is getting too complicated for many of the lower league players. Coaches trying to be too clever, how I miss those days when we would see Ray Whitaker, Graeme French, without his shotgun of course, Brian Stein and Ricky Hill when they it seems were allowed to get out there and express themselves, making the game a whole lot more entertaining. I am not though painting John Still and Terry Harris with that particular colour of paint. I am just using the example of players of Luton Town's past. I suppose I should have maybe mentioned George Best, Georgie Armstrong, my favourite player of his era and the pocket rocket that was the late but great Alan Ball. The likes of such players were allowed to go out and play with a freedom, to do what they did best with their talents. Along with my friend Alan Hudson, also who was phenomenal in his time at Stoke City under Tony Waddington, simply because allowed to go out there and do what he did best, running the opposition ragged. This for me is what is wrong with English football now, not even the over influx of foreign players but the denial of what talent we do have being able to get out there and do their own thing. Too much emphasis put on tactical movement these days. The Premiership has its exciting moments and is a spectacle like no other when the game is played properly, however we go to watch two sides play football not two coaches orchestrating a chess game.

I have just watched the incident in the Manchester United v West Ham game today, where Wayne Rooney dismissed for a most cynical lash out at his opponent. If Rooney had caught him properly, I think Downing would have been searching the pitch for his testicles for weeks to come and then we witness the mentality of United's followers by applauding the so-called tackle, more like an attempt at grievous bodily harm for me, caught his leg but could easily have been the manhood assault.

So it seems that we are witnessing a return of the Witch-Finder General, we could have Vincent Price re-immortalised as the infamous persecutor of innocent victims wrongly accused of ungainly deeds. Now that they have attempted to ruin the lives of celebrities for monetary gain, strange since the series of Michael Jackson cases it all suddenly appears on our shores, bringing up so-called allegations years after the fact. I am not saying such things did not take place but why wait this long to bring to the notice of the authorities, the evidence is long gone and that is the main problem in such matters. Some yes, did happen, maybe most, but I get the feeling others are of people trying to make a quick buck or three. However, when they do not get that private pay off that they hoped for they have to carry it on through to the end to save face and not look to be trying to pull a fast one. I do sympathise greatly for those victims of genuine cases but it is the other minority of cheats trying to besmirch and wrongly accuse that make it so much harder for the real cases to be believed.

Recently it has come to light in the media that former Stoke City goalkeeper Peter Fox, later to become the goalkeeping coach has been accused of assault in the way of initiation rituals held behind locked doors to young players within the clubs academy. Along with former England defender and captain Mick Mills, at the time of the alleged assaults, the club manager turning a blind eye.

Rituals are something that has become a tradition throughout many establishments all over the world, it is not something limited to football clubs. For hundreds of years it has been a much-documented tradition at the highest level of institutions including those so-called elite colleges of Eton and Harrow. So if the likes of Stoke City are investigated and Peter Fox's name dragged through the mud for all to see. Why not then those upper crusted bullies that we hear so much about? Are the likes of David Cameron and Boris Johnson going to be questioned and harassed to learn if they were ever involved in such? No, of course not, that is obviously forbidden territory, they are upper class so it is different, they are allowed what others are not, always has been always will be. To me this smells of persecution of the lower classes, but then that has been run of the mill these past six years or so anyway, so what is new.

Where will all this end? I ask myself, because first it is all these long time passed sexual assaults and now it's come down to initiation rituals, yes some are worse than others, some are over the top sometimes, however my real grouch is simple, why leave it until now if it happened in the 1980s? The saying, "after the horse has bolted", yet again comes to mind.

As I just said, if this is to be investigated surely every other establishment should be investigated also and believe me that will become a major embarrassment for many high profiled individuals as well as the organisations they now may represent, because we cannot persecute one without the other.

I myself was the victim in my youth of two such rituals they were not what I would call comfortable by a long shot, but I do not think either warrant complaint, let alone accuse, sue and look for conviction.

Even David Beckham, I read somewhere when joining Manchester United had to go through the indignation of being forced to masturbate whilst looking at a Clayton Blackmore calendar, maybe then there are limits after all, who would want to see him doing what he is already renowned for being.

The first being at the age of fifteen straight after leaving school I left home to do my jockeys apprenticeship for top trainer of the time Sir Jack Jarvis. On only my second day following last lot, the cleaning of the yard and tack, the feeding of the horses. I was grabbed and had water thrown over me, stuffed into a large hay net along with some hay and then hung in the stable box of what was one of the most notorious three year old colts at the time. If I remember correctly a chestnut by the name of Caballero, I was left there for quite a while, but being such a long time ago I cannot remember the length of time obviously, I was eventually let down and from the net by a well-known but no longer with us jockey. It was a little harrowing at the time yes of course, but we get over such things, it is what happens and we accept it as such, I now look back and laugh at the episode, harmless fun at the most.

My second such initiation again involved hay. It was with horses again so I suppose only to be expected. This time I was eighteen years of age and it was second week in as a gunner in The Kings Troop Royal Horse Artillery. Following evening stables, whilst at our temporary barracks in Windsor. Again, grabbed, this time stripped from the waist down, covered me in molasses, and rolled through the hay, seeds and all. Then left me there taking my trousers with them leaving me with only my boots, therefore having to make my way from the stable lines to the living quarters, which was quite a way. The only discomfort though was my nether regions itched for days after, but again why complain its part of tradition, no harm done, and it proves ones hardiness and trust, one who complains it shows not to be a member of the team and will never really fit in. Neither cases did any harm whatsoever.

If one complains of such so many years later, there has to be some other underlying reason, I will not be as bold as to accuse the accuser of Peter Fox though, that would be wrong and insensitive of me, but I will ask the question again why after all this time?

Initiations are a test of your character and resolve, we can learn much about a man from such, for me anyway, but then I am old school, we held tradition in high esteem, unlike these days of multi culture, tradition is no longer adhered to much the pity. Too much emphasis on politically correct and health and safety, which are fine in the right context, but please let's not go overboard as we seem to be doing right now on too many fronts.

October

Wednesday October 1st 2014

So October is upon us already, this year has nearly gone and left us, not too long ago, or so it feels anyway, I was complaining to myself that 2013 went way too quickly, this year even more so. Yesterday the Development side turned out at the "Kenny" against a Gillingham side that fielded several of its League One players, that made no difference to our boys coming out worthy winners' five goals to three and good to see Alex Lawless back in the throng of play along with Paul Benson also, following their recent injury problems. Some thought our defending was a little diabolical earlier in the season, well Gillingham certainly have problems if this game was anything to go by as it was way too easy for the "Hatters" at times.

Well, with what I have been reading today we as football fans are really getting shafted to the hilt, as many of us have always thought anyway. Virgin media have definitely come up with some interesting facts. Premier League clubs, for quite a while have been charging ridiculous prices for games in recent years, making it difficult for the normal man in the street to afford to go and watch their favourite side week in week out, which as a child of the 60s I was always able to do quite easily. Now, Virgin have compared the UK TV charges for the top flight football in our country and the other top four European countries and the results are staggering to say the least, in fact to me it is downright criminal. Between the F.A., who are responsible for the Premier League, Sky and BT the deals have hit such gigantic proportion that the average monthly charge to watch Premier League football from our homes is £51 per month, now that covers approximately 41% of the total Premier League games played over a season that are actually broadcast live. Now compare that with the other top four countries in Europe.

Germany's monthly cost for viewers to watch the Bundesliga is £21 per month and every game is broadcast live, not a percentage of the games but every one, so the fans get to choose what game they wish to watch from home.

Italy charge £25 per month, again all games broadcast live. France is only £10 per month and yes, you have guessed correctly I imagine, all games played are broadcast live.

To watch either Real Madrid, Barcelona or any other Spanish league game live whatever match you may choose, in Spain the monthly viewing fee is £18.

So why is it that despite not every game being shown live each week we here in the UK have to pay more than double at the very least than any other European country?

It is nothing more than sheer greed on the part of The F.A. and the bigger clubs of the Premier League.

But when a smaller club is going out of business where is the assistance from either the F.A., the football league or the bigger clubs maybe forfeiting a small of their annual percentage to help alleviate the certain demise of such clubs? Simple answer to that is, nowhere to be seen and yet those same bigger clubs get away with blue murder when it comes to financial irregularities. However, clubs in the lower leagues and beyond get docked points for being in financial difficulties whereupon in most cases they are at the end of that season relegated, which in effect long term wise places them into even more financial difficulty it is a vicious never ending circle from that moment on.

Yet again, it is simply a case of rip-off Britain, the problem is nobody seems to want to take a stance against these greed-ridden organisations.

In 1992 the big four or five clubs and the Football Association knew exactly what they were doing. The plan to form a break away league that would be for the elite clubs only and those able to afford to compete year in year out, they allowed promotion and relegation, yes of course, but knowing full well only the strongest would survive year in year out. The clubs over the years have slowly but surely hiked up the prices to ridiculous heights that the normal working man on the street just cannot afford to pay out every week as I mentioned earlier.

To be honest some of the drivel being played in the Premier League I would not pay £5 a month for, leave alone £51.

There is no consideration for the real football fans any longer at the top flight, the prices will forever rise that is a fact, soon the majority of tickets will be even more corporate based or for the higher paid working classes of our country.

Football as I knew it as a young lad in the 60s and 70s has gone forever.

Friday October 3rd 2014

One of the "Hatters" biggest games of the season with regard to grudge matches and a local derby to boot looms upon us all, it's Stevenage Town versus Luton Town two days from now and the proverbial knives are out. Stevenage sent a ticket allowance of only 2,000 which Luton sold out within hours of going public. It was a real scramble for the golden tickets, a game every one wants to be present at. There are a few variables to look at, Ronnie Henry, last season's Luton Town captain left the "Hatters" just before the commencement of this new season. Some argued not a great loss. There has been a mixed bag of emotions on that count, some sorry to see him go, whatever the case he was instrumental in no small way to assisting our promotion back to the Football League therefore he does deserve some respect, despite the fact he will be facing us on Saturday, I for one hope he gets such. Another factor of course is the disrespect certain Stevenage players showed to Luton when we met on the two occasions during the season they won promotion themselves, something I am not going to get entangled in this time around. Then there is the geographical factor not many miles between the two Towns in distance but many miles apart when it comes to fan rapport from each section. But the biggest factor for a great deal is Stevenage's manager at this time, Graham Westley. Not the most popular of characters within the Kenilworth Road factions that is for sure. A manager not renowned for his finesse in terms of footballing tactics. He was on two different occasions in line, or so some sections of the media reported anyway, to become manager of Luton Town. Well for this supporter at least that would have resulted in a plane crash waiting to happen, we would have struggled even more so losing a great many fans in the process, that I am also quite positive about. We thrive on entertaining football at Kenilworth Road, we always have done, with Westley that would have not been seen. This week he has rocked the proverbial apple cart again with some quite ludicrous and what's more to the point unnecessary comments regarding the two clubs, trying to stir it up no doubt, but in the process made a laughing stock of himself amongst the "Hatters" community. He claims that Stevenage are as big a club as Luton Town, well if he looks at it in the context that they have been in the football league this time around for us then okay leave him to his moment of glorified bullshit. But, let's look at the facts here, a few any way, I do not really want to give the man too much publicity in my book, so in counter attack mode Mr Westley I ask you this, how many International caps in total have Stevenage players won whilst on the books of your club? Next, how many major trophies have you won, agreed we have in effect only won the one ourselves, however how many divisional championships have you won? How many years has your club spent in total within the realms of the Football League? Now Mr Westley compare your totals to those of Luton Town and carrying on just a little further let's take a look at the fan base of each club, enough said, without my having to quote a single figure, dream on sir, dream on.

It's strange how certain managers react when they are about to or have just been the opponents of Luton Town. Even in recent weeks, it is also very clear of their intentions, to try and ruffle the feathers of the players the fans and our manager. Both occasions this season, the desperation of each opposing manager for me has been quite apparent to see, they have no ammunition on the playing field so they try their damnedest to rile us in other ways. It's so warming to me that our own manager John Still is a man of dignity and takes not one moment of his time to even listen to the nonsense that comes from these wannabee managers. Richard Money so clearly wants to be in John Stills shoes, but he messed up his time good and proper, Graham Westley obviously still a bitter individual because on two occasions of trying failed miserably to even get his foot in the door.

Following the win at Cambridge Richard Money's frustration and pain obviously got the better of the man. Launching a verbal attack on John Still, no dignity whatsoever, Mr Still calmly avoided confrontation, this week again he has totally ignored Westley's ridiculous claims and carried on with getting the squad in the correct frame of mind to do the talking on the pitch instead of in the gutter. Even if we lose the game we win the battle of two managers, because only one is worthy to be called manager of Luton Town F.C. and it's neither, Richard Money or Graham Westley.

Saturday October 4th 2014

Stevenage is about to be invaded by the Orange army and no the Netherlands are not coming to town, a side even more mightier, Luton Town "Hatters" are on the march.

It's a relatively warm Saturday and our fans are out in force, even paying to stand in the Stevenage Town supporters' enclosure, because of the number of Luton fans they have allowed for, trying to say that they are bigger than us has backfired, the stadium is more orange flavoured this afternoon that's for sure.

The Town starting line-up is as follows: Mark Tyler, Alex Lacey, Steve McNulty, Luke Wilkinson, Scott Griffiths, Andy Drury, Jonathan Smith, Nathan Doyle, Pelly Ruddock Mpanzu, Paul Benson and Mark Cullen, with subs; Alex Wall, Jake Howells, Elliot Justham, Luke Guttridge, Matt Robinson, Luke Stevenson and Charlie Walker.

A strong looking side despite the fact Alex Lawless, Paul Connolly and Fraser Franks are missing through injury.

Stevenage 1 Luton Town 2

It was a game that seemed to change with frequency. For the first twenty minutes Luton were completely dominant and the game could and maybe should have been sealed tightly up in that opening period.

Stevenage are always going to be difficult opposition. Their style of play, combative and extremely physical. They did apply some spells of pressure.

For The "Hatters" both centre halves were excellent, as was Doyle sitting in front of them. It was that type of game, all were required to show their physical strength and they did so with honours, Pelly Ruddock Mpanzu gave us the thrust going forward, he let himself down maybe though with his poor finishing on the day, which if had been more effective on the day his input would have been phenomenal.

Luton started very quickly, considering Stevenage had five in midfield against the Towns' four, we found plenty of space. Pelly ran rings around Charles, the makeshift left back. We almost scored from the first attack. Charles penalised for a hand ball straight from Doyle's kick off.

With Nathan Doyle controlling the midfield, he wins the ball and has an excellent passing range and possesses a touch of class that we have been missing until now, his experience and know how is going to prove invaluable as the season progresses, when he becomes fully fit he will be a superb force to have in our armour.

Bond was booked for a trip on Pelly. Wilkinson got enough of a touch from Drury's free kick to divert it past Day for a well-deserved lead. Day had to make a decent save again from Wilkinson from a Drury assist soon after.

Stevenage equalised with their first attempt on goal, excellent diagonal ball by Lee finding Whelpdale his volleyed centre, tucked in neatly at the far post by Pett, Tyler helpless to prevent the goal.

Stevenage invigorated by their goal, looked the stronger side as half time beckoned, excellent pass by Beardsley found Lee, Wilkinson covered the danger, from the corner it was rather fortunate for the "Hatters" that the referee missed a shove on Ashton who headed over.

The game became feisty as Smith and Benson were booked for fouls on Pett, Benson's tackle looked like he had gone in from behind. With another referee, he could have been sent off. Both players gave of their best, but looked tired and were shortly withdrawn. Stevenson gave us a more calmed approach and Walker gave us some much needed pace up front. Stevenage brought on a couple of subs, themselves and in particular Deacon looked a handful down the left, but his inability to pick out a colleague was something they would pay for. Walker's movement gave us some threat on the break and with both Ashton and Wells lacking pace they defended deep as the game become stretched.

With eight minutes to go, it looked like a well fought draw was on the cards, until the manager brought on Wall for Cullen. Within moments, Wall had won the game with a clinical finish. Stevenage lost possession from their own throw in, a superb pass from Pelly finding Wall, his first touch was to take the ball inside and second was to lift in over Day and into the unguarded net. Wall was subsequently booked for over celebrating a rather pointless rule, but it's there so that is that, over exuberance of youth is not in my book a punishable offence, but the Sep. Blatter's of this world obviously disagree with me on that count. There were five minutes of overtime but that did not assist Stevenage, in fact it could have put the game even more beyond reach, Luton for once were not asked to hold on to their lead and the final whistle sounded with a second away victory on the bounce. Happy days!

To be fair to Graham Westley post match he was gracious in defeat, unlike the man from Cambridge and I have to give him credit for that at least.

John Still was as always in his matter of fact mode, as I like to call it. Laughing off the fact that people had called the bringing on of Alex Wall for Mark Cullen an inspired substitution and sensibly replying that it was a substitution nothing more than that and the fact that Alex scored with the first or technically his second touch of the ball was nothing more than a chance dropping his way. As always he thanked and acknowledged the whole team's efforts, battling hard and supporting each other throughout the game.

The evening before league leaders Burton Albion had lost at home to Cambridge United, Richard Money must have been unbearable following that result and Exeter City won against John Stills former club before joining Luton, Dagenham and Redbridge, 2-1.

This afternoon Bury beat Tranmere 2-0 at home to return to the top of the table and with this win for the "Hatters" we moved into the play-off places to seventh, just five points off the leading side's total of 23. What a difference from three weeks ago sitting in the lowly spot of eighteenth place.

Tuesday will see the visit of Crawley Town in Johnson's Paint Trophy and Mr Still has made it clear that there will be changes in place to rest players before next Saturday home league game against 4th placed Southend United, a difficult game awaits the Town it has to be said.

Monday October 6th 2014

Five league games unbeaten is certainly a difference to the clubs situation three weeks ago and suddenly the moaners have dissipated, however do they come back with complimentary remarks? No, of course not, I ask myself in truth why these people attempt even, to call themselves true supporters of Luton Town or are they from one of the other clubs within our vicinity trying to cause disruption? Actually I believe they are Luton supporters, but the only happiness they have in life is to complain.

Tomorrow we are at home in the paint pot trophy. Some are claiming we are in effect still holders of this most coveted of competitions, there is a chance I am in requirement of a lobotomy for that, but no I will leave it in, such is the euphoria amongst some of our more salubrious supporters, again have I got that correct? Anyway the fact is maybe we haven't been beaten in the competition since beating Scunthorpe at Wembley, but come on guys it's been and gone, please get over it. Unfortunately I was drawn into that thought for a while, but I may have been in a state of manic depression at the time, so I will write it off as just that.

It will be good to see the legend that is "Keano", Keith Keane, if he is picked to play for Crawley tomorrow night in the JPT tie. He is at the moment on loan with them from his parent club Preston North End and I am sure he will be given a rousing welcome from those that venture out to the game and deservedly so.

Tuesday October 7th 2014

I mentioned one Keane yesterday whilst scribing and today I will mention the other lesser Keane, this time Roy, the former Manchester United player, good he was but man did he know how to kick a man as well as a ball! His new book was released this morning and he has even bought Luton into the limelight again. All be it from August 2007 when we annihilated the side he was managing at the time Premier Club Sunderland in the League Cup. Saying he was so relieved that one of his defenders Clive Clarke, who was at the time on loan to Leicester City, suffered a heart attack in the changing room at half time in a match at Nottingham Forest's City ground, because it deflected the news away from how diabolically bad his side were at Kenilworth Road that evening. That to me is one of the lowest sides of football I have ever encountered, sheer evil and makes me sick to the core, totally uncalled for

Then there was another book which I dearly cannot wait to read, one of my cricketing greats Kevin Pietersen, a player who could lighten up any cricket ground and yet treated like crap by the England set-up.

But I will maybe get back to those publications when I have read them in full. Maybe?

The line-up for this evening is: Elliot Justham, Alex Lacey, Luke Wilkinson, Steve McNulty, Scott Griffiths, Nathan Doyle, Jonathan Smith, Jake Howells, Alex Wall, Luke Guttridge and Paul Benson. Subs: Mark Tyler, Jim Stevenson, Matt Robinson, Alex Lawless and Charlie Walker.

Luton Town 0 Crawley Town 1

Out of the paint pot in the same space of time that it takes Watford to get through about a half dozen managers.

A few changes from Saturday. Justham in goal. An unchanged back four, Doyle and Smith sitting in front of them, Wall and Howells playing in advanced roles on the wings, with Guttridge behind Benson.

A strike by Edwards, the outstanding player on view, flew into the top corner to decide the airport derby and stop people banging on about defending our trophy. It's the Associate Members Cup, not the Champions League, which of course we will defend successfully in due course.

A good open game, which the "Hatters" were unlucky to lose, particularly after the turn around with the introduction of Lawless and Walker. It was good to see Keano back at the Kenny who in fairness was excellent for the visitors and got a good ovation at the end and quite rightly so.

The bigger picture tonight is that we have performed with credit against good opposition, some of Crawley's patient football, with turn of speed on the break was very impressive. It gave John Still, although it was Harris and Hayrettin who were in the dugout for this particular game. A chance to try a different formations and give players who have not been in the first team lately a run out to boost their match sharpness. Even in defeat it was a very worthwhile exercise.

It's pleasing that we competed against a higher grade opposition and created some chances than we have for a long while. Admittedly, the game was far more open than a normal league match.

Thursday October 9th 2014

With the injuries to Paul Connolly and Curtley Williams, John Still has been forced to make an emergency loan agreement with Queens Park Rangers to bring Michael Harriman for a period of twenty eight days. A sensible loan signing as far as I am concerned as we are desperately short of right sided defenders. However, still I hear some, all I can describe as demented idiots, say that they would rather see a striker bought in. Myself I give up with this fixation that we need more strikers, that to me is a load of rubbish, we have an adequate number of strikers within our squad already, it is only a matter of time before it all come right, just a matter of confidence.

Michael Harriman is an experienced defender, he has limited Premier League experience with Rangers, but has plenty of League one games under his belt whilst on loan with Gillingham last season and hopefully he will be a temporary asset to the club.

He will be available for the Southend United home game this coming Saturday.

Friday October 10th 2014

Luke Wilkinson has been named Sky Bet Player of the month for September, a superb accomplishment for both the player and the club to be so recognised. Wilkinson has scored in his last two games, it would be great if he could make it three in three tomorrow that's for sure against The "Shrimpers".

I have predicted that this game will end in a 1-1 draw, which considering the two sides positions in the league and the upsurge in the "Hatters" recent form, unbeaten in their last five league matches it to be a reasonable assumption and Southend are definitely no slouches that is quite obvious.

The team sheets are out and it's an interesting Luton line-up, quite pleasing to the eye, well mine at least: Mark Tyler, Michael Harriman, Luke Wilkinson, Steve McNulty, Scott Griffiths, Pelly Ruddock Mpanzu, Nathan Doyle, Andy Drury, Jonathan Smith, Alex Lawless and Mark Cullen.

With subs: Alex Lacey, Paul Benson, Alex Wall, Elliot Justham, Luke Guttridge, Jim Stevenson and Charlie Walker.

Luton Town 2 Southend United 0

In front of our biggest crowd of the season thus far a cracking 9,238 the "Hatters" certainly exceeded most expectations in what for many was our best performance of the season.

An excellent all around solid team effort grinding out another League win.

During the entirety of the first half we had two shots and both ended up in Bentley's net. The first a sublime curling effort by Lawless, the second couldn't have been more of a gift from Bolger, if it had been wrapped up with pretty little bows and a card. Bolger wearing a head band after a cut to his head, under no pressure, could have kicked the ball anywhere. However, he elected to pass the ball straight to Drury, very sociable of him, Drury almost slipped but kept his composure to feed Cullen, his shot too powerful for the advancing Bentley to prevent from hitting the back of the net. Loan signing Michael Harriman on paper looked a good signing having played for the Republic of Ireland at most age levels and a good amount of League experience. But loan players can be hit and miss. But he was very good indeed and he looked to fit in straight away. He's a mobile, athletic type, reads the game well and got tight but not too tight when marking and his all round game was impressive. He didn't get forward much, but had no requirement to as Drury revelled in the space allowed him and was at the heart of most of our better play. Smith, Cullen, Doyle and Wilkinson were also excellent.

The game was volatile at times, caused mainly by Southend's frustration. There was a moment of madness involving Ruddock Mpanzu and Dave Penney their assistant manager. As the ball went out for a throw close to the Southend bench Penney held onto the ball, before launching it at Pelly, who rather foolishly it has to be said decided to retaliate. A rather childish scuffle ensued which resulted in Mpanzu Ruddock and Andy Drury receiving yellow cards and Dave Penney sent to the stands, who was given a standing ovation by the Southend following in the Oak Road stand, that just about sums their teams display if that was all they could muster to applaud all afternoon.

Following this superb victory Luton Town now find themselves in fourth place in the league table, quite a difference from only three weeks ago and six games now unbeaten.

Where are those doubters and moaners now? I am not trying to sound like the happy clapper, as I have so easily been accused in the past, but in the same vein it is refreshing to realise my patience has been rewarded, I have never doubted John Stills ability at this level, as I have written throughout this book, we always needed time, as also predicted and suggested Andy Drury required time to adjust and now he is beginning to show the player he really can be, maybe not so pacey as before but his touches are still top notch. Alex Lawless in his first full game of the season also showed why he will yet again be a major force as the season goes on if he is able to steer clear of injury recurrences and Mark Cullen starting to prove his worth also. Pleasing times again in the pipeline.

Elsewhere in League One today, Cambridge United beat Oxford United in the University Cities clash five goals to one. A smug Richard Money being interviewed after the game was glowing, however Oxford are not going to break any records themselves this season, not positive ones at any rate unless they have a complete transformation over the coming months, in fact they are my early choice as relegation favourites.

Wycombe Wanderers climbed to the number one spot after beating Morecambe at Moss Road, at the other end Tranmere Rovers sit at the bottom of the Football League after a 0-1 home defeat to Plymouth Argyle.

Our next opponents Hartlepool United beat a struggling Exeter City side at St James Park 2-1 and the delight on Jeff Stelling's face must have been a sight to relish on Gillette Soccer Saturday this afternoon.

The most upsetting news of the day without a doubt is hearing that a cretin of the worst kind has attempted to steal the Eric Morecambe statue which is located on the sea front of the northern town where he grew up as a lad. Eric is without doubt the most famous and well-loved supporter of our beloved club, vice president for many years and during his heyday as one of the funniest men on British TV never missed a chance to publicise the "Hatters" on his TV show alongside his best friend and comedy partner Ernie Wise. If Morecambe do not want the statue, Luton Town, I am sure would dearly love it outside our stadium. When we do finally have a new stadium I have always insisted and will always do so that it be named after the funny guy, The Eric Morecambe Stadium, it has such a lovely ring to it do you not think!

For some time now, even before my earlier mention in this book about the Tony Pulis saga at Crystal Palace, I have had my concerns in regards to the way clubs seem to treat their managers these past few years, the term loyalty seems to be a one sided affair in football.

When we look back in history most clubs used to keep their managers for years rather than months. The clubs used to show a sense of loyalty.

It pains me greatly that when a manager does so well in a season. Sometimes pulling off a minor miracle, such as how Tony Pulis did at Crystal Palace last season, when he arrived there they looked like odds on favourites to go back down to the Championship, but they somehow avoided the job with his guidance, however before the season even got under way he left, the reasons why one can only assume. He earned the club millions just by keeping them in the Premiership, but when it came to the crunch the Palace board, well some of them anyway were only too happy to let him go.

We see managers winning clubs promotion from a shoe string and with total surprise. Nevertheless, the next season when they are finding it difficult to cope with the higher level of football that same manager is given his marching orders. Despite getting them there in the first place against all odds. I call that insanity, the man works miracles and yet he is fired for not being able to get results in a league they really are not prepared properly to be in anyway, the loyalty is none existent, however in the same breathe the same directors ask for the managers they have hired to give them total loyalty, a little hypocritical in my book.

The football authorities need to protect managers more, I have no solution or thoughts on how they can achieve this, but surely something should be done.

I will think hard about this over the coming months and get back to the issue when have done so. Staying with management, the situation at Watford football Club, yes I know this is a book about the "Hatters" first and foremost, but for me football is football whoever the club. Some of the narrow mindedness I see as a "Hatter" when it comes to the club from down the road is a little childish at times. I told you I would upset a few people, is a little strange to say the least, but to go through four managers in a few weeks must be quite frustrating for all involved in the club, from the board all the way down to the fans. However, despite all that turmoil within they somehow seem to manage a decent string of results that have them challenging for a top spot within the Championship.

It has been a relatively quiet time since the win over Southend. Apart from maybe some "Hatters" fans squabbling over such mundane things as hanging a couple of flags at a home game. I could think about more interesting topics to discuss myself, but hey some people have to complain about something or somebody and show their authority and get their way before the pram rocks too heavily and its more than flags that fall out of the proverbial vessel.

England, again made very hard work at prising open an Estonian defence. Similar to a few days before, against San Marino. Yet, some whoop whooping over the fact they are top of their group table in the 2016 European Championships qualifiers without dropping a point or conceding a goal. Well I would hope not since they have been playing the equivalent of Dulwich Hamlet, Kempston Rovers and at best Wycombe Wanderers, wake up guys, although I love my country and will support them through thick and thin we are not what one would proudly call world beaters are we now.

Then there is the slating that Roy Hodgson is getting for telling the world's public that Raheem Sterling asked not to play because he was tired, well what would one rather, that Roy tell lies or kept quiet altogether? At least he told it how it was when questioned and for me at least the lad, who let's face it is only nineteen years of age. Maybe it's as much mentally tired as physically, he has taken a great deal of stick since the World Cup finals in Brazil, he doesn't look the strongest of guys and at least he was brave enough in these days of the big I am to admit his tiredness. What would some rather he do, go out there in a game and have a mare and may even be instrumental in an embarrassing defeat, or admit his tiredness and allow a stronger and mentally fitter player to be out there? Some people are never satisfied that's for sure. The media in this country seem to look for anything to slate the England manager about and the players equally, instead of getting behind the team. A worthless bunch some of them, who really at times need to look in their mirrors before condemning others. Maybe the F.A. should really get a Mike Bassett to take charge. By the way, I notice they are making a sequel and apparently if one pays £5,000 pounds in to the kitty to make the film you could get a speaking cameo part alongside Ricky Tomlinson and others, as farcical as the character in itself, but a good idea also. Maybe we could petition for him to take over the country from our inglorious leader David Cameron also, let's face it there would not be much difference.

This Ebola outbreak that is rocking the west-side of the African continent is quite worrying. So how long will it be before Sep and his cronies at F.I.F.A. headquarters in Zurich decide that it would be in the best interest of mankind at this moment to suspend all International football in the affected countries to assist in keeping the dreaded virus at bay? Just a thought. Whenever there is an outbreak of foot and mouth disease in the United Kingdom they suspend horse racing and the transporting of livestock, so why not the equivalent in football now? Every little bit helps, surely.

Friday 17th October 2014
Happy Birthday bro, yes it's my brother Tim's birthday today, hope he gets his quota of Famous Grouse and John Smith's bitter.
Also it's the 78th anniversary of a great day in the town's footballing history, as on this day in 1936 Watford F.C. visited Kenilworth Road in a Division Three South league match. Yes you youngsters in those magical years before the second world war, the league was not a matter of Divisions 1, 2, 3 and 4, oh dear me no, it was Divisions 1, 2, and 3 North and 3 South.
A crowd of 20,956 packed into Kenilworth Road to witness a Luton Town line up of: Bill Dolman, Tom Mackay, Tom Smith, John Finlayson, Jack Nelson, Bill Fellowes, Jack Hodge, Joe Payne, Jack ball, Fred Roberts and George Stephenson, no not the one who invented the rocket, although by all accounts he was a bit of a rocket himself on the wing.
With thanks to Andrew Kingston we are able to see how a game of such standing was reported in those day, and the wording is a lot more colourful than anything you will read these days.
Watford's tactics have not changed much over the years though when one reads such sentences as "Luton's efforts were marred considerably by the methods of one or two of the visiting side, who showed ill-feeling towards Payne because of his liveliness in front of goal." How eloquently put, can you imagine reading such in this day and age?
Luton won the game 4-1 with yet another hat-trick from the lively Payne in front of goal, his third hat trick in a season's total of five three goal hauls and also two four goal matches throughout the season. Payne scored a total of fifty five goals in the season that saw the "Hatters" finish the season as division champions. The other goal of the game coming from Jack Ball. Incidentally the Town also won the Vicarage Road meeting by three goals to nil. A pleasing season on the whole would you not think.

One courageous little lady, Ellisha Hockham.

I think it only right and proper that I mention a very courageous young "Hatter", nine year old Ellisha Hockham whose family reside in Ipswich but are Luton Town supporters as is Ellisha herself, seen I photographs sporting a "Hatters" shirt. Ellisha has already had several major operations for a spinal curve. One of her ambitions is to give John Still a massive hug for getting the Town back where we belong, in the Football League, there will be a few who would want to likewise I am sure Ellisha, I hope you get your opportunity one day and knowing John Still he will most probably make sure you do.

When we hear of any child going through such rigours at such an early life it puts all the quibbling we do into perspective. A very brave young lady indeed, Ellisha Hockham.

Saturday October 18th 2014

With 500 plus supporters making the long trek up to the North-East of the country another great away support considering the distance.

Quite a pleasant day indeed, for that of mid-October.

Hartlepool United 1 Luton Town 2

One change from the Southend win. Miller in for Lawless, was he rested, not wanting to overdo after the injury problems he has experienced so far this season with John Still bringing him again slowly and carefully, otherwise it would seem strange Lawless not in the eighteen if he was available for selection. For me, most probably saving him for Tuesday evening's game against the managers other love, Dagenham and Redbridge.

On a bobbly pitch with the usual gale from the nearby North Sea meant that it wasn't much of a game, in fact tedium was the real winner, with few chances for either side. Cullen's goal was an instinctive finish, Ruddock Mpanzu's through pass from Harriman's throw, the highlight of what in truth was very tepid fare.

Second half, we improved markedly, Hartlepool didn't cause us that many problems, we broke away very well and always looked the more likely to score, Smith playing in his more advanced role did well to break the play and go forward. His welcome reappearance and the signing of Doyle have kick started the season.

Ricky Miller had a very promising debut, he is quick and direct, once he gets into possession he looks to attack his full back and get into the box. Good awareness, by no means the finished article, but like Walker, plenty of promise there. On the back of a good loan spell at Dover, he came into the game full of confidence.

It's quite amazing that every player who comes into the team as Michael Harriman did last week, knows his role in the side, what he is required to do, which is a tribute to the managers, coaching staff and the players themselves. Considering the amount of changes we have forced to make through unavailability and also players they have been forced to use already this season. Miller slotted in the same position on the wide left as Lawless performed last week. The formation was unchanged.

Hartlepool are in truth are a fairly modest team. Apart from Flinders, Bates and Miller, they are very young outfit. Like the majority of sides in the lower reaches of this league, they try to pass the ball, before hoofing the ball aimlessly. They did have a couple of comedy characters. Flinders for an experienced goalkeeper, had a real nightmare, his kicking was consistent, finding touch on most occasions.

The first half was a fairly quiet affair, few chances and even fewer glimpses of quality. The ball spent most of the in the sky. Luton as usual played no risk football, clearing our lines, but little service of quality to the likes of Cullen, Miller, Drury and Ruddock Mpanzu.

We had not been overly threatening, so it came as a surprise when from Harriman's throw Ruddock Mpanzu made a low pass to Mark Cullen who put himself between Jones and Bates to slot the ball past Flinders, 1-0 Luton.

Luton picked their game up in the second half, looking a great deal sharper than the first 45 minutes. Hartlepool needed, being a goal down, to take a gamble which allowed the Town to thrive on the space given them.

With Pelly Ruddock Mpanzu beginning to tire JLS made a change replacing him with Jim Stevenson which gave Luton a more solid look in midfield. It was not long at all, his second touch in fact that Stevenson made his mark on the game. Austin was penalised for wrestling Paul Benson, who had earlier replaced Mark Cullen, to the ground. What looked like an ideal situation for Andy Drury was actually handed to debutant Ricky Miller who elected to fire in a low fierce left footed shot. Flinders got down to the ball well enough but was only able to parry the ball straight into the path of Stevenson who was there to poke the ball over the line and make it 2-0 to the Town.

It certainly looked like game over, but instead of sitting back and soaking Hartlepool up the "Hatters" went on the hunt to add to their goal tally. Time ticked down and Luke Guttridge replaced Ricky Miller who received a much deserved ovation from the Luton faithful, a good solid debut.

Just as it looked as though the "Hatters" were going to cruise to a 2-0 victory, which would have pleased yours truly greatly, having earlier had a tenner on them to win at by that score, Hartlepool were rewarded with a penalty after Scott Griffiths went to ground diving in on Walker. Not the most sensible of challenges it has to be said. Austin gave Mark Tyler no chance at all, thumping the ball effectively into the top right hand corner of the goal, 2-1.

There was a heart in the mouth moment with only seconds rather than minutes remaining, when Tyler spilled the ball, but fortunately Nathan Doyle got to the ball first to and thumped the ball away from danger.

Luton held on to claim their fifth consecutive league win and also taking the unbeaten league run to seven games.

How many more books will Sir Alex Ferguson send out in order to make it known how good he was as a manager and how everyone else who had the balls to oppose him are valueless, clueless or just plain useless?

In the past he claimed that David Moyes got the Manchester United managerial post following his recommendations that Moyes was the perfect man for the job. Now I read he is contradicting himself to a degree by writing that the decision was not taken solely upon his say so, well to be fair nobody with an ounce of common sense would think that it was down to Fergie alone, the United board are not going to ever just take it on his say so. But, what a great get out for him. The time was coming when he retired for the United squad, despite winning the Premiership, to be replaced, he knew it many others knew it also, but rather than put his reputation on the line if he got it wrong he found a "patsy" to take the fall if and when it all went pear shaped, as it did. For myself, the man knew exactly what he was doing. It was always going to be a difficult time for United, it was going to take a good season or even two at that to get the squad up to scratch again, bringing new players in and getting them to gel effectively.

No, the results were not good under Moyes. But surely, patience should have been the key, Fergie claims in his latest publication that Moyes did not realise how big Manchester United is, what a load of tosh, even the most naïve of people are fully aware of the stature, of his attempt to belittle others, he has done it before and no doubt he will do it again.

Surely he should look back and remember the predicament he was in himself during his early years at United, maybe to the point of being 90 minutes from being fired. I think it quite inappropriate to lay all the blame on Moyes when it was obvious that Fergie himself has to take some of it after leaving Moyes with a squad of in the terms of footballers, pensioners on the verge of retiring. As always Fergie has made a concerted effort to take the pressure off himself. Clever yes, cowardice to a degree? Maybe. Now he is praising Louis Van Gaal, who is yes a very good manager / coach, but he isn't what one would call setting the Premiership on fire, but I get the impression Fergie is not so brave to question the Dutchman's qualities, the sure sign of a bully, pick on the weaker but make friends with the stronger.

Tuesday October 21st 2014

I can imagine this evening's game is going to be quite a difficult one and emotional one also for John Still, he has quite an affinity with our opponents Dagenham and Redbridge, whom he took into the football League from the Conference also and actually left to become the boss at Luton Town, following his second tenure with them.

That is the evening survives the lashing that the UK is being forecast to be on the receiving end of, from the remnants of a dying Hurricane Gonzalo, strong gale force winds and squalls of rain are being predicted for the afternoon and early evening. The weather has abated and so the game will go ahead with no real threats it turned out in the end.

The team line up is as follows: Mark Tyler, Michael Harriman, Steve McNulty, Luke Wilkinson, Scott Griffiths, Pelly Ruddock Mpanzu, Jonathan Smith, Nathan Doyle, Ricky Miller, Mark Cullen and Andy Drury with subs: Alex Lacey, Paul Benson, Alex Wall, Elliot Justham, Luke Guttridge, Jim Stevenson and Charlie Walker.

Luton Town 3 Dagenham & Redbridge 1

We have now managed six wins on the bounce and eight games unbeaten in the league, I will not say I told you so, but yes I honestly was never in any doubt it would come good, although I never for one moment envisaged such a fantastic run, I have to admit.

A perfect hat trick by Mark Cullen, a header, right foot, left foot in that order, to put a dagger through the Daggers hearts to win the Vauxhall – Ford derby and put us in the automatic promotion places.

Cullen's goals were of high quality. Pleased for him because he received a certain amount of criticism during the earlier part of the season despite always giving his all week in week out. His movement off the ball is excellent and that allows the likes of Pelly and Drury space to create or go on runs.

Dagenham should have been ahead at the break after playing by far the better football on display, you would have put the mortgage on a striker of the experience and quality of Jamie Cureton scoring one of several chances they created. However, they wasted their chances, a dangerous thing to do against this current Luton side, who are always likely to take their opportunities.

So it proved, Cullen started and ended the move which lead to our opening goal, a flick on to Drury on the right, he patiently worked the angle and hung a cross up to the far post which Cullen leapt like a salmon on its way to the breeding ponds to convert with a header. The second shortly after was courtesy of some kamikaze goalkeeping by Cousins after Smith won the ball, sending a delightful through pass down the right, Cousins decided to rush into no man's land, Cullen beat him and from not the easiest angle, deftly finished into the open goal, 2-0.

Luton had the worst of the conditions, defending into a strong, gusty wind and squally showers. With the pitch watered prior before kick-off, players struggled to keep their footing. We were quite careless in possession, and struggled at times to confirm our higher league standing over a decent little passing side, who looked lively on the break.

Cullen's hat trick came from one of Ruddock Mpanzu's famed runs and a low ball and slammed into the corner from Cullen left foot. Outstanding goal, 3-0.

Cullen was withdrawn for the usual standing ovation arranged by John Still which allowed Charlie Walker to make his home League debut.

The final goal on the evening was scored by the visitors, who deserved a goal for their efforts, particularly in the first half, Luton seemed to switch off in the latter stages. A well worked goal, McNulty had to come across to help out Harriman, who didn't have one of his better games, Doidge headed unmarked in the near post, the space which McNulty vacated to help his full back, fine timing header.

Now we have Saturday to look forward and another home game, this time Northampton Town will be the visitors, it will again be a most interesting game, a semi local derby to savour.

What the heck is going on at Liverpool? Not that I care too much in all honesty.

Firstly I am still not sure why they bought Balotelli in to replace Louis "the teeth" Suarez in the first place, from one bag of trouble to another just as volatile player, the one thing I will say about Suarez, at least he was worth the risk initially. Balotelli? No! Not a team player, never has been for me, all about the wonderful Mario. As a good friend of mine, Paul McCormack, mentioned in discussion and agree with him fully, they should have bought in one of their young protégé and groomed him to take over that shirt, much more sensible move in my opinion. It is too easy though, for a club of Liverpool's stature to just go out and buy any one they fancy, not think about the long term plan as much as the now time. Unlike Luton Town, who are more frugal of late. But that is how it seems to be done at the top flight, they have the resources to say think about the future later lets work for today. Well one day that will not be the case, all the walls eventually come crumbling down around them.

But really what was that all about with the half-time swapping of shirts? Yes I agree not the best of gestures, but wait a moment, as my friend Paul so rightly put it again, what if it had been either Jamie Carragher or Steven Gerrard, would the outcry had been so demonstrative? Again I doubt it very much. Did Real Madrid make the same fuss and reprimand Pepe, who after all was according to most the instigator? No they did not, if they did they kept it in house, a touch of class maybe, something not many of our own "big" clubs seem to possess, not just now but throughout recent years. We do seem to make a mountain out of a worm's droppings. Dear old Arsene Wenger, bless him. Must on the whole be a most relieved man that Balotelli though decided on signing for Liverpool instead, because let's face it as I have always thought, he just is not all that anyway, but then maybe Balotelli knew he could more easily take the piss out of Brendan Rodgers, as Suarez did, than the wily old Frenchman.

Tickets for the Northampton game are being gobbled up. Which is all good news for the club. The problem is if it can be done for one game why not all. No I do not make many games at the moment, but that is really not because I do not want to, it's more to do with commitments that at are more important. My children for one, I mention this solely because of comments recently, not made towards myself in general but all those that say they are "Hatters" but don't go to games. So for all of those that criticise those of us that just have more important priorities, like work and our children, get a life please.

Northampton Town are not having the best of seasons it has to be said, I honestly thought they would be quite a force to be reckoned with, however the defeat Tuesday evening gone to Oxford United, speaks volumes for me, no disrespect intended Oxford. I predict a 3-0 win for the "Hatters" but it will not be an easy contest as they are a strong physical side.

Saturday October 25th 2014

Match day, with the "Hatters" superb winning run of six wins on the bounce now putting us top of the recent form table for League Two it is a game that is obviously anticipated to be a cracker, hence the sell out that it has now been announced by the club, one word fantastic.

The "Hatters" lined up follows: Mark Tyler, Michael Harriman, Steve McNulty, Luke Wilkinson, Scott Griffiths, Pelly Ruddock Mpanzu, Jonathan Smith, Andy Drury, Nathan Doyle, Alex Lawless and Mark Cullen. With subs: Alex Lacey, Paul Benson, Alex Wall, Elliot Justham, Luke Guttridge, Jim Stevenson and Charlie Walker.

Luton Town 1 Northampton 0

Well first and foremost, another inspiring win for the Town. The winning streak is sustained to seven and that is amazing, not only that, but top of the table this evening. The perfect scenario. Following his last two performances I was a little surprised, if I am totally honest, to see that Ricky Miller was not included in the eighteen man squad. However, JLS knows what he is doing and maybe he is bringing this young man on slowly as he does with many of the younger players and fair play to him for that. So the only change from the superb win against Dagenham is that of Alex Lawless for Ricky Miller.

Not it has to be said the most entertaining of matches from either teams point of view, but a match to win none the less.

Northampton did not give Luton the opportunity to play the flowing football we have been accustomed to witnessing in recent games. They were well organised and did not give us any room for the freedom to create. On the balance of play in all fairness they were worth the point it looked as if they were going to be rewarded with until the dying embers of the game.

Since the installation of our Messiah of sorts, John Still, the Town have not shown much respect to the final whistle, being able to win very tight games in the last minutes of a match. The application, the never say die attitude that this squad most certainly have and the desire to win is complimentary of the highest being. At the beginning they were struggling to get to grips with the game in hand at the time, but with perseverance of the management and coaching teams all has been rewarded, I hate to say I told you so, but yes, I told you so. Patience does work eventually, especially when the manager despite the early criticism thrown his way at the beginning of the season was ignored, stuck to his laurels, as I said, the man knows what he is doing allow him to get on with it.

As I mentioned earlier, Northampton are a very strong and physical side and it was proving to be the case, unfortunately for the "Hatters". Nathan Doyle having taken a knock, was replaced at half time by Jim Stevenson. Then within seconds of the game resuming Pelly Ruddock Mpanzu was replaced by Paul Benson, not having the best of games, maybe a result of him being continuously kicked about by the opposition in far too many of our games recently. It is time the referees took note of this and not so much protected him but at least take action, but they seem to cast a blind eye far too often. Then to top it all Alex Lawless also limped out of the game to be replaced by Luke Guttridge, too many injuries piling up again, but we have a large squad so we should be able to cope as long as none are long term affairs.

It was getting, as is often the case late into the game and Luton did not look like scoring, but in truth neither did Northampton.

Andy Drury was having a good game forever teasing the Northampton defence. Time was ticking away the ninety minutes up with the fourth official holding up his board, four added minutes, but no sooner had he put it down and a good ball in from the right found Guttridge who managed to get in front of the defender and with a clinical finish put the ball past the "Cobblers" keeper. The Kenny erupted, the perfect time to score what must be the winning goal and the noise must have been heard as far away as Middlesbrough where the team in yellow were being held to a 1-1 draw in the Championship top of the table clash.

Hold on for the three minutes and it was going to be even noisier, seven wins on the bounce, nine matches unbeaten and only four goals concede in the last ten games, something to shout about? Yes.

The final whistle blown, other results were filtering through, Wycombe had been held at home by Dagenham and Redbridge, Bury held at Southend and Burton beaten at Broadhall.
The ground again erupted, "Top of the Football league we go" the "Hatters" from 18th place only seven games previous were now sitting on top of the perch. An amazing transformation.
Who would possibly dare complain about anything now?

Sunday October 26th 2014
Oh boy what were my final words typed last night?
Is it not amazing? But then again I have to remember this is not a normal set of fans, these are Luton Town Football Clubs' supporters.

Clowns in our Midst.

Where does one begin?
There are some great people on the "Hatters Talk" forum page of Facebook, but Oh my goodness, there are some complete tossers also. For example, following yesterdays' hard fought win against the Cobblers of Northampton Town I really am reading a load of old cobblers for real. The first post is this, "What did people think of Pelly Ruddock Mpanzu contribution in yesterday's match?" How can one question any of these players' commitment and contribution this season? Least of all Pelly. He has been kicked in the air by the opposition week in week out and yet, picked himself up and fought for the cause, yesterday he obviously got a knock early into the game and was never after that really able to play to the best of his ability. Then there are others that were alleging that John Still took him off like he did just after the start of the second half to make a statement. What a load of tripe these people love to serve up, it's quite obvious to me that Pelly wanted to see if it had eased when he got back out there, but it was not to be. I love these characters, only if it's because they are giving me so many page fillers for the book.
Then there is the classic that seems to rear its little spotty head every Sunday morning following the Football League programme on BBC late Saturday evening and also on Sunday mornings. They complain that Luton only get about a minute long review each week. For the sake of my sanity please get a faffing life guys, last season we were in the Conference, we never even got a mention, now you want to be treated as if we are Liverpool or Chelski. Please, why can you not be content with the fact that we are last back in the Football League and get a mention at all. Please as I have said GET A LIFE GUYS!!!!
To finish off for the day as I have other pressing appointments (smile), why do people keep making the point that the Football League and The FA need to sit up and take note? At the end of the day (Oh boy I do love that cliché… NOT!) Those that made all those decisions against us have all but a couple wandered into the obscurity of the human jungle, let it rest please, concentrate on the present and the future, not dwell on what was a spurious time at best.

One more thing, regarding Hatters Talk forum. It really peeves me that some people get quite overheated and abusive when they do not agree with someone else's opinions and nothing is done about it and that is to me offensive to a degree as some people on the said forum really believe that no other opinions are allowed to be aired. Too much of that is rife on the forum.

I am also just as annoyed when racist remarks such as pikey, etc. are displayed and nothing is said, it is offensive to some as I am offended greatly by any form of racism, nothing again is done about it. Get a grip of our forum Mr. Administrator, please.

Well I am certain I have made a few enemies in the Luton Town fan base camp by now and the "Fatwah" amount is growing on an hourly basis. However, I do need to point out, despite my ranting, such people as Stuart Hoare and Dave Bourne do a most amazing job, which I will not deny. They have the club at heart and are most generous in their charitable work, so please understand my raving lunatic views are not in any way shape or form aimed at them, apart from criticising the racism comment, as I saw it.

So onwards and upwards.

This weeks' entry is going to be somewhat bare due to my having a busy schedule. However I am looking forward to the Exeter game especially on Saturday as it is my father's place of birth and I still have much family around the Exeter, Exwick and Plymouth area.

My Grandfather Frederick Luke was the station manager at St Davids Railway Station throughout the 1950s. He used to tell me of how Circus Elephants would travel from the circus ground to board special box carriages to ferry to the next venue. An amazing sight as they walked down the streets of the city in a singular file, trunk to tail.

Let's hope though that on Saturday the only parade in town will be post-match as Luton parade around the pitch with three points firmly in the bag. However, this is not as some believe going to be a walk in the park for the "Hatters", the Grecians, a name that has a number of ideas how they came about to be called that. My father told me the story of how it derived from a bunch of orphans from St Sidwells, from where the football club originated were known as the greasy uns'. Although I really doubt that is so as I have gotten older over the years. They are a much organised side at the moment and defend well.

November

Saturday November 1st 2014

Who would have thought it was the first day of November or as some now call it Movember, when the guys grow a moustache for raising charity throughout the month. Will I be doing it? No, I detest having hair above my mouth and below my nose at the best of times, although I have to admit that should be even more reason to do it, to suffer like others truly suffer without complaint, not for a month but a lifetime, so hey if anyone wants to sponsor me I will maybe change my mind. Staying with the first of November, what beautiful weather we are experiencing, today the sun is shining on us again, may be a little chilly breeze in the air at times, but hey still sensational weather for this time of the year.

The Hatters line up is: Mark Tyler, Michael Harriman, Steve McNulty, Luke Wilkinson, Scott Griffiths, Mark Cullen, Nathan Doyle, Jonathan Smith, Jake Howells, Andy Drury and Paul Benson. With subs: Luke Rooney, Alex Lacey, Elliot Justham, Shaun Whalley, Ricky Miller, Luke Guttridge and Jim Stevenson.

Exeter City 1 Luton Town 1

Two changes from the home game against Northampton, Alex Lawless and Pelly Ruddock Mpanzu were replaced by Jake Howells and Paul Benson, not having played much first team of late they were both going to be a little ring-rusty.

It was the usual formation except that Benson played up front as the lone striker.

If anything, this was a game in which Luton gained a point rather lost two. Exeter proved that they are no push over this season, giving the "Hatters" a good game of football, they used the width of the pitch well and played with two upfront, if they stay clear of serious long term injuries they may well be a force at the top come the end of the season, particularly for a play-off place.

Steve McNulty and Luke Wilkinson were outstanding, however if there was a criticism concerning Luton's defence it was the amount of crosses allowed to get into the box.

Luton attacked the first half kicking up the famous St James Park slope, towards the end that "Hatters" fans were situated, it was a fantastic start, Andy Drury floated the corner into the box, Scott Griffiths getting above two defenders with inches to spare and heading the ball past the "Grecians" keeper to give the Town a third minute lead.

Following the goal, the "Hatters" settled into their usual pattern of play, without the strength and pace of Ruddock Mpanzu pushing forward it was proving not as successful as usual. Exeter had a good share of the possession, but mainly keep ball by the back four, they used Ashley Grimes, now there is a name to reminisce on, was by far the best passer of a ball that Luton have come up against all season so far, but all the play was in front of the Luton defence with not much getting past them.

Half time came and the sides went in with Luton holding on to that slender 1-0 lead.

The "Hatters" began the second period in a positive vein. Cullen had a fine shot from Jake Howells pass, towards the top corner of the Exeter goal and missed by just inches. Another chance dropped to Cullen when Jonathan Smith's through ball allowed the striker a decent effort but the Exeter keeper Pym was equal to it and parried when diving to his right.

The home side made two changes, Grimes began to play wider than he already had, these changes made the "Hatters" uncomfortable and Exeter started to move the ball wide enabling them to stretch the game.

The Hosts began to press for an equaliser and was not long in coming all be it from the penalty spot, Scott Griffiths turned villain from hero when he bought down Ribeno inside the box, no argument, a penalty all day long. Nichols dispatched the spot kick home with apparent ease, 1-1, a well-earned equaliser if totally honest.

Both teams had chances, but neither really testing the keepers following the penalty so the game ended with an away point for the "Hatters". On reflection a fair result. The winning run at an end but the unbeaten run moving on to ten league games.

Following the game John Still revealed that before the game began he would easily settle to come away with a point against such a good side as Exeter.

This could, if he is not asked to remain on loan, be Michael Harriman's final game for Luton Town. Personally I hope he is allowed to remain for a further period, as he has bought some experience and solidity to the defence since his arrival on a four week loan deal from struggling Premier League club Queens Park Rangers. If it is to be then thank you kindly for your contribution young man, much valued and appreciated by many if not all Luton Town supporters. Now, because I had to force myself to have some time off from writing, not just this book, but my others as well, I missed the fact that we have drawn Newport County in the first round proper of this seasons F.A. Cup competition at home, the game takes place on November 8th. Interesting game in store, Aaron O'Connor and Robbie Wilmott two former Hatters are regular first team players for County, although I am just learning that Wilmott may be absent with a long term foot injury.

Wednesday November 5th 2014
Remember, remember the fifth of November, a rather long standing saying that maybe I will live to regret within this book in the days ahead following publication.

Because I am about to be letting off a few fireworks here now. I do love a good firework display it has to be said.

I was a few days ago with my dear old fellow "Hatter" Paul Stanyon discussing the outcome of the hearing against Luton Town in 2008 when we were, I will admit as far as I am concerned anyway, illegally deducted those horrendous thirty points by the football League. Which virtually condemned us with relegation from the Football League into the non-league world of the Conference Premier. What I was saying then, was that not only did I feel it was illegal in as much as every club at the beginning of any football season in any competition should be allowed to start the competition on an equal footing with every other competing side. That season we were not alone, Rotherham and Bournemouth were deducted seventeen points each. All teams were informed that they were not allowed to appeal theses severe penalties and if they attempted and did not accept their punishments they would not be allowed to participate in the Football league that season and would therefore be expelled from the Football League altogether. This was where my argument of the legality of the ruling came in as surely as a point of law any punishment is worthy of one appeal at least. Even if they could have appealed I get the feeling that it would have fruitless against the might of the Football League lawyers. Also, costing a fortune in legal costs anyway, which unless one of the top clubs in the country these clubs could not realistically afford, the Football League knowing this, in my opinion, knew they could get away with these such ludicrous punishments. However, over the years we as fans have had our say, despite not being heard.

A good mate of mine, Mike Thomas, a fellow "Hatter" who is often accused himself of not being a true supporter because of his views, which are quite similar to my own in many cases bought up a good point to me yesterday. As already mentioned along with ourselves were deducted points at the beginning of the 2008-2009 season, granted their deductions were not as severe as our own, however following a short period of complaints and airing their views, they got on with life. We, as "Hatters" felt most hard done by because of the more severe points deductions, quite rightly so we were at odds with the authorities concerned, but at the end of it all we were guilty of what the football league decided were irregular acts. To be brutally honest with you all at the time I believed Luton Town were very fortunate not to be expelled from the League there and then, so to be a given a chance to at least fight for our league survival was something, in reality we should have been thankful for that. Although the points deductions to me were and are illegal, surely the directors of such clubs and other perpetrators such in Luton's case should be charged and banned from football other than the players and the supporters being punished as much as the clubs. Let's face it the team management and players are put under the biggest pressure to get results in such scenarios, whilst the guilty parties have more often moved on from the club and sitting cosily in other positions. But the decision was made so we had to get on with it. Yes all well and good we have our demonstrations. But for me still hearing the same old noises, "Fuck the FA and the Football League, really are getting quite tedious. We have to move on, let's face it those that dished out the punishments are no longer in those chairs of power, so it for me is a futile ranting, five years later? Getting back to what Mike was pointing out to me, Bournemouth got on with the job in hand, their energy used more in effect to getting out of the mire, they are now sitting on top of The Championship table, closing in on the riches of the Premier League. Good luck to them I say with sincerity. We are now back where we belong, let's use our energies to make such a climb through the leagues possible for Luton Town also, at last we have boardroom members capable of doing it and a management and coaching set up capable of getting us there also. We as supporters need to get behind them all totally, not start griping at every little blip, I honestly cannot think of another set of supporters who expect so much from a club that is picking itself from the verge of non-existence.

As Luton Town supporters we have been spoiled to degree. Yes I am serious, I look back to the beginning of the season, another club Hereford United virtually went into non-existence, but the supporters have got behind what remains of the club, they are not complaining they are working to keep the club going, they may still at this moment as I write this be taking their final breathes. Despite everything we are still here, I think we have to be most thankful for that and move on.

Something else in the same vein is when we were going through the transformation of the new squad players and all earlier this season and the side was finding it difficult to score I heard and read comments blaming Gary Sweet for not getting out his cheque book and forking out money for a seasoned striker. I was, to be quite truthful astonished at these comments, for a number of reasons. Have we not been down that path before? We buy a striker who has a good record, he comes to Luton and produces nothing of his past exploits, wasted money. Have we not in the past in the same vein blamed managers and directors alike for wasting good money? Look where it got us in the past, nowhere, we then suffered financial problems. In Gary Sweet and Nick Owen, we have two great guys who want to build this club back to where we belong, we are partially there, we have money in the bank, we have no real financial worries, they are being quite sensible in their approach to a new stadium, that we all are aware we do need to move on, but they are not shouting out how they will do this and do that, they are just as the Still regime also, doing it quietly and for me effectively. It has been a long time coming, let us rejoice at that, yes John Pyper will love that I am using the Maggie phrase.

Just as a passing shot, I always, as written earlier in this book had and still have full faith in all the players that JLS has bought into Luton Town. Not only last season but this season also, not many in English football can boast such a good eye for a footballer as the man at the helm at Luton Town, footballs answer to Sir Henry Cecil, a man who had the perfect eye for a horse. We are blessed believe me.

Thursday November 6th 2014
Another week begins and Luton have been graced with two awards from The Sky Bet Monthly awards for October, John Still for manager of the month and Mark Cullen for October's player of month for League Two, fully deserved by both.

Luke Trotman.

Also, congratulations to youth player, 17-year-old Luke Trotman, pictured above. Luke is offered his first professional contract by John Still, at the time recovering from a double leg break back in August, to date Luke has made one senior appearance in last season's FA Trophy tie against Cambridge United, another of our up and coming academy students to watch out for in the future. Good luck in your career young man.

Apart from that another quiet week, other than the fantastic news that Michael Harriman, on loan from Queens Park Rangers, has had his loan agreement extended by a further month, which is superb news, being a fantastic asset over the past month.

The FA Cup first round proper is finally here, a home tie against Newport County and hopefully a chance at least of going into the bag on Monday evening for the second round draw. However, not unlike Exeter City, who incidentally as I write this are on the verge of going out to Warrington FC of The Evo-Stick Northern Premier League, it is going to be a tough test for the Town. Newport County sitting six places below the "Hatters" in League Two with seven points dividing the two sides.

Saturday November 8th 2014

The Luton line up being: Mark Tyler, Michael Harriman, Luke Wilkinson, Steve McNulty, Alex Lacey, Jake Howells, Nathan Doyle, Jonathan Smith, Luke Guttridge, Mark Cullen and Paul Benson. With subs: Fraser Franks, Luke Rooney, Elliot Justham, Shaun Whalley, Charlie Walker and Ricky Miller.

Good to see Fraser Franks and Luke Rooney back amongst those in the dug-out following injuries. Let battle then, commence…

Luton Town 4 Newport County 2 (FA Cup 1st Round)
Into the second round bag of balls we go. A game that took some time to get going, but the second half definitely making up for the relatively dull proceedings of the first apart from one electric moment when Luke Guttridge blasted home from well outside the Newport box to put the "Hatters" into a 1-0 lead going into the break.

The stands not really overflowing, only three thousand plus braved the wet and quite unpleasant conditions, I remember the days when an FA Cup game whoever the opposition was would mean a packed house. Where has the tradition disappeared to, I ask myself, how extremely sad.

Early on our passing was laboured and predictable making life somewhat easy for Newport to sweep up the loose balls.

Against the run of play it has to be said the "Hatters" took the lead with a wonder goal from Luke Guttridge. Michael Harriman prodded the ball through to Guttridge who unchallenged struck the ball so neatly it just flew off his foot with what seemed an effortless strike, the ball found the top corner with precision, 1-0 Luton Town.

Newport started the second half looking much sharper, more tempo, proving to be better than Luton on the ball.

The equaliser came from some sloppy marking, a fine pass from Flynn finding the unmarked Klukowski whose neat control and firm finish flashed the ball past Tyler to his left.

Luton reacted positively following the equalising goal. Howells pressing forward, playing the ball to Nathan Doyle, who had the vision to spot Michael Harriman running into an empty space, he had plenty of time to set himself up for a shot on goal, but the resulting effort was a poor one and although looking to have taken a deflection off a Newport defender a throw to the visitors was given.

Jake Howells set up Mark Cullen who had a rasping shot, which Newport's keeper managed to push into the air, Paul Benson, climbing above the Newport defender Hughes nodded the ball over the line from close range to hand the lead back to the "Hatters" 2-1.

Despite the lead Luton looked quite vulnerable at the back, particularly on the flanks, Obeng skipped past the stretching Harriman, who attempted to push the attacking player off the ball, the referee waved the game on and a slick cross to the oncoming Aaron O'Connor showing good striking instinct to head the ball past Tyler, 2-2. O'Connor, who had taken a fair amount stick throughout the afternoon from a certain section of the Luton faithful rushed over towards that part of the ground to celebrate his equaliser, not the most intelligent moves maybe, but relief taking over from common sense prevailed somewhat, one cannot really blame him for that. If one wants to give a player some stick all well and good as long as you can take the backlash of that stick also.

Again, despite Newport's equaliser the "Hatters" started to use the ball more effectively, taking advantage of the gaps being left in the middle of the park. The game was becoming much more open. Ricky Miller replaced Mark Cullen up front who had as always had a good game. It was not long before the sub Miller made his own mark on the game and his first competitive goal for Luton, from Howells corner kick to the near post Miller capitalised from some poor Newport marking and steered the ball into the net, 3-2 to the "Hatters".

Brown missed an opportunity to put the visitor's level for a third time missing by a hairs breadth and then Loveridge sending a dipping shot just over. The game was far from over. Aaron O'Connor had a fantastic header saved just as brilliantly by Tyler.

Jake Howells picked up the ball just inside the Newport half and decided he would go on a solo run, reminisces of Scotty Oakes come to mind as he charged forward head down, danced past a defender and slammed the ball home for Luton's fourth.

Four minutes later the referee blew his whistle for time, a reasonably entertaining second half came to an end and the "Hatters" were in the bag for the draw on Monday evening.

Elsewhere in the round there were a couple of upsets with non-league Worcester City seeing off Coventry City at the Ricoh Stadium, Coventry and also newly formed from the ashes Chester FC winning at Roots Hall, the home of Southend United.

November 9th 2014

This morning the reading has been enlightening to say the least. Despite how I seem to be having constant digs at fellow Luton supporters I do not really enjoy or relish, however a handful of them are their own worst enemies it has to be said, some just seem to revel in the opportunity to give the likes of myself more fodder to feed on.

I mean come on guys, yes by all means let us see the question "Who would you like to be drawn against in the next round?" But the same question asked on the same forum at least ten times within five hours, a little excessive do you not think? Why not all reply to the original post, because let's face it opinions will not differ on one post to another, or will they? Some people it seems do not know who the faff they want. For myself, I did not comment on any of them by the way, I do not care who we are drawn against, it is enough for me to be in the draw. Don't misunderstand me though, for some there is the opportunity of visiting a new ground on their list of grounds to have in their time as a "Hatter." Also, there are those that would love to be playing a club close to where relatives or good friends are located. Alternatively, even play for that is the beauty of this competition, our unique FA Cup.

Then the one that really got my billy up, "If we draw MK Dons away would you go?"

Okay to be fair the MK Dons are not and will not be for many years to come be one of the most popular sides in English football after hi-jacking Wimbledon FC and moving the club lock, stock and barrel to Milton Keynes some good 50 miles northward from their original home. But, to say if Luton were drawn to play at Milton Keynes why would not one want to go and support their own side? Because I can tell you if those that had their chance, as they did a couple of seasons ago, who had their club taken from beneath their feet can do so with pride we can also. The question should not even be raised, wherever Luton go a supporter should follow, it's about Luton Town not Milton Keynes Dons. I sometimes wonder…

Another post that has niggled me more than any of the others is one that could have dangerous consequence for one or not two Luton supporters.

If it was done in jest initially or just a case of mistaken identity, or even a true fact I do not know, that is not for the likes of myself to decide.

One member accused another member of shouting racist abuse at the game yesterday, even producing a photograph of the alleged perpetrator. To be fair the accused stood up to be counted and categorically denied anything he had been accused of, with the accuser not saying another word or post, whichever way one would like to see it as.

Yes, I will have my say on this as racism of any form to me is abhorrent, what is even worse is when someone is wrongly accused, I have been on that side of the fence believe me and it is not a pleasant experience, the ripple effects are enormous if not nipped in the bud effectively early on. The majority were in total support of the accused, as I have to say I was also, his passionate pleas were to me most convincing, being prepared to face his accuser face on, the accuser I have to add did not respond therefore I can only therefore go one way on this. Stuart Hoare and Dale Williams, in afterthought dealt with it quite admirably I have to admit, Stuart finally having to call a halt to the comments for the good of the forum, at the time I will admit was a little upset at that move, however on reflection the best move possible. What did get me extremely worked up was the individuals, telling the accused he should just move on and forget it. Very easy to say when sitting wherever comfortably reading the comments. That is the problem these days, it is so easy to say "forget it and move on" when one is not the victim in the firing line.

As I wrote on the opening page, no holds barred, I am not doing this to be added in the popularity stakes that is for certain.

Monday November 10th 2014
John Still has apparently offered a contract to former Sunderland youth team captain, twenty year old Lewis Gibbons, who until recently was on a two year ban from the sport after being found to have both Cannabis and Cocaine in his system following what was a routine drug test at the time. John Still despite the players conviction has graciously given the guy a chance, it must be obvious that Gibbons has turned a corner otherwise he would not have even entertained the idea surely.

In life we all make mistakes especially at such a young age, temptation and experimentation are easily followed if in the company of one's peers. I for one wish the lad luck, he is obviously quite a talented player, so hopefully another future asset to the club. It is a certainty there will be some who will make much of his past, but let's at least give the young man a chance. Formalities at this time still though, to be completed.

It's 7.00pm, and so to BBC Two for the FA Cup draw. Wow, the first six numbers out of the hat are all crowded around Luton's number 25, low and behold, we too are pulled out of the goldfish bowl early. An away tie, a trip to Bury. For me a good draw, we have played them already and so are aware of their strengths and weaknesses and having drawn with them at home early on in the season when we were still getting to grips with the new look side we definitely held our own with one of the better sides in our division. An interesting tie in my opinion. Although I see the moaners and groaners are out in force and its only 7.10pm. But we all have our own opinions and some disappointed not to be going elsewhere, that's fine, at least those who were threatening will not now have to boycott the MK Stadium, how fortunate for them. As I said before I am not bothered who we have drawn, if we are good enough on the day we shall beat them, if not, well so be it.

Thursday November 13th 2014

Today is a very sad for some of us, four years ago today a very good friend of my own, of whom I mentioned earlier on, David Stanyon, lost his fight against a rare form of throat cancer at Luton and Dunstable Hospital. On that day his twin Paul was in Manchester for the Altrincham v Luton Town game. He received a call from his family telling of his brothers passing, upon which he called to give me the tragic news we had all been waiting for but dreading, I tried in vain to get the game dedicated to David, but to be fair it was a little late in the day. David and Paul I had known and attended games with for many years. When I was in the racing game, I would meet up with them home or away whenever circumstances allowed we had some great sessions together. There are many Town supporters who knew the guys but never really knew them and I know some saw them as odd, they were not odd, they were just more comfortable for the most with each other's company, nothing wrong with that at all. I think myself most fortunate to have been able to climb over the barrier as it were and enter their world. I hear and read these days of how many games so and so has been to over the years. Let me tell you here and now, not many can brag a better record than either of these brothers. I know of only a handful of games they have ever missed, until Dave was taken ill I could recall only about three or four games he alone had missed in about 30 years of following the Town and since then Paul has carried on that tradition these days mainly alone. Dave could reel off information as if he was a walking Encyclopaedia, I will not say Wikipedia because believe me not everything is correct in that little mine of information, from personal experience. That day in bitterly cold Altrincham Luton came away 1-0 victors with a goal from Alex Lawless if I remember correctly, at least in my heart I dedicated that win to Dave, which is why the result sticks in my memory so easily. It will be a difficult day for the Stanyon family and my heart goes out to the twins other brothers and sisters. In my memory you will never be forgotten, you bravely fought a terrible and painful disease my friend and in all honesty the relief for all was when you finally fell asleep and would suffer no more. I miss you mate, no more beer races, no more slinging insults at each other, no more hour long phone calls talking of one thing only Luton Town. Rest easy my dear friend, rest easy.

Saturday November 15th 2014

Our upcoming opponents' Tranmere Rovers are not having the greatest of times at the moment sitting second from the bottom of League Two, managed by Micky Adams following Rob Edwards sacking on October 14th. However since Adams took over they have started to pick up their performances so I doubt if it will be as easy a game as many expect it to be.

The last time Luton met with Tranmere was on December 22nd 2007, at Kenilworth Road, when Luton won 1-0 in League One, the only goal coming from Dave Edwards, now playing his football for Wolverhampton Wanderers

Today there were small scuffles of sorts between rival supporters. Not wanting to sound anti-scouse but it has taken a Merseyside based club to bring flares and firecrackers into the area of the Kenilworth Road stadium, sadly.

Another good turnout for a Luton home match. Tremendous support, let's hope that if as the season goes on and we have a dip in form the attendances do not drop. Also, that would be quite upsetting after all the good work thus far in winning over those that were complaining earlier as the season got under way, it really is quite encouraging to see and hear positive talk coming from the majority of Luton supporters.

Whilst watching some Bundesliga football a few days ago, it came to my attention how passionate and behind their team, the fans of Borussia Dortmund are. Despite the bad start they have made to the season, if only we could match that week in week out, which would make such a difference when the Town are having a lean spell. Not long ago we witnessed the passion and enthusiasm that Royal Antwerp bought to Kenilworth Road in their pre-season friendly, such positivity from supporters can only bring positivity onto the playing area also.

Luton's starting line-up for this afternoon is; Mark Tyler, Fraser Franks, Steve McNulty, Luke Wilkinson, Michael Harriman, Luke Guttridge, Nathan Doyle, Jonathan Smith, Jake Howells, Paul Benson and Mark Cullen. Along with subs for the day: Alex Lacey, Andy Drury, Scott Griffiths, Luke Rooney, Elliot Justham, Pelly Ruddock Mpanzu and Ricky Miller.

The only change from the Newport cup match, being the return from injury of Fraser Franks. Following a long layoff after his hernia operation in September, replacing Alex Lacey.

Luton Town 1 Tranmere Rovers 0

Yet again the "Hatters" had to work hard to win the three points on offer. I like the fact that we are able to win games under such conditions. To win games too easily week in week out can bring complacency into performances, that for me is, how some sides play well for a few games and then they suddenly dip totally out of form, complacency is difficult to fight back from. I know many will sneer at this, but the fact is that a hard-earned victory gives a side much more self-confidence than one that has not fully extended the players. Also if we are to be promoted at the end of this season, we will be better prepared for League One as that really is not by any realms of the imagination going to be a walk in the park.

Tranmere, as expected from a Micky Adams side, were a well organised side who were at times the better of the two, having more possession and a greater tally of shots on goal. They were denied twice by the agility of Mark Tyler who was forced to make at least two very fine saves. The second of which was in the dying embers of the game when called upon to make an outstanding save getting down to Odejayi's downward header at the far post. Despite Tranmere's upper-hand Luton again took their chances when the opposition failed to do likewise. Another plus this season this season has been the depth of our squad on occasion and it is thanks to that depth that yet again this afternoon a player or players have come off the bench and made the difference. Today Jonathan Smith, Luke Wilkinson and skipper Steve McNulty were the outstanding players. What in reality a quite mundane affair was bought to life in one shining piece of play. Tyler collected the ball from a Tranmere cross, rolling out to Smith who with ball at feet made a purposeful run through the middle, laying a forward pass to substitute Ricky Miller, who had replaced Mark Cullen some minutes prior. Miller produced a neat touch and turn that totally fooled Ihiekwe, looking up briefly and then hitting an early shot which Brezovan, the Rovers' keeper did well to get a hand to, but the ball had enough on it to rollover the line.

There was a moment early in the game, Gnanduillet won a free kick. Despite the fact that right in sight of referee Kettle he blatantly fell over Fraser Franks, rather than bought down. What was strange is the fact that would easily have beaten Franks if deciding to stay on his feet. However, I take the cynical stance that he may have been trying to con the referee into getting Franks a yellow card. Which would take its effect later in the game when having to be more aware of his tackling in the danger of receiving a second, such is the way the game is played these days, no honour between men as it used to be. Luke Wilkinson took exception to the obvious dive and locked heads with Gnanduillet, totally unnecessary from both parties, but the incident caused a certain amount of bad blood for the remainder of the game between both sets of players.

It seems, along with that incident and another where Jennings grabbed Luke Guttridge. Blatantly dragging him to the ground, again in full sight of the gentleman with the whistle between pursed lips. However, ignored, then equally as childish as the head locks, decided to straddle over Guttridge not allowing him to get up with no free kick being given Luton's way, the refereeing standard in League Two is just as terrible as it was last season and those before within the conference.

So strong is Luton's defending these days that it seems we only need that one piece of magic to win games, against even the strongest of sides. It will though be quite interesting once we start hitting real form up front. Nevertheless, hard fought games will place us in good stead for next season if we do manage to win promotion. Be it by the automatic way or through the play-offs, although I am not a great fan of the play-off system in any shape, to me they do not benefit anyone but the Football League and the FA who own the Wembley rights, more end of season revenue in their already bulging pockets. More to do with themselves than the clubs concerned who have already battled through a hard fought season, but then what do those two self-appreciating organisations care about that?

Following this result the "Hatters" return to the top of the table, although the Monday night game between Wycombe Wanderers and our next opponents Burton Albion result in Wycombe returning to the top of the pile if they win.

Results elsewhere today meant that Hartlepool, following their 1-0 defeat at Roots Hall to Southend United remain lodged in bottom place with Tranmere just above them but only on goal difference.

In the derby of the West Country docklands Plymouth beat Portsmouth easily 3-0.

Sunday November 16th 2014
Sifting through the social media sites yet again "Hatters Talk" gets my attention most, however I have to say with a certain amount of happiness that this time I see a more positive view.

One of the members asked the question "Who is the best manager between David Pleat and John Still?"

Well in all honesty one cannot really compare the two, especially at this stage. Football in DP's time was so different to that played today in many ways, Luton played to what I see as the more conventional way, from the flanks, which was synonymous with the Luton Town side of the 1980s. Pleat not only managed, but also built his own team. He bought in players from lower leagues such as Brian Stein, from Edgeware Town, he also bought many players up through the ranks, including Mitchell Thomas of Limbury Boys Club and Marvin Johnson an apprentice player, as was the enigmatic Ricky Hill along with one of the best defenders I have witnessed at Kenilworth Road Tim Breaker. Thomas was taken on by the club through a government employment scheme better known as "YTS", the Youth Training Scheme. Kirk Stephens signed from non-league Nuneaton Borough. To think that all these players played at the top flight of English league football. Both Stein and Hill, representing England with full caps. Many more besides these, one in particular, Mal Donaghy who went on to represent his country, Northern Ireland, at the World Cup whilst a Luton player, great honours as these are rarely bestowed on our so called "small" club, that in our eyes is the most magnificent football club on planet earth. Donaghy was bought over from Northern Ireland by Mr Pleat also from a little known club Larne Town and actual fact was better known in his home country for his exploits at Gaelic football by all accounts. David Pleat had a fantastic eye for a player and employed a superb scouting team in addition.

We have to remember also the big name players at the time who Pleat was able to lure into Kenilworth Road, the likes of Mick Harford, Danny Wilson, the irreplaceable Stevie Foster, maybe the greatest goalkeeper in modern times to have graced Kenilworth Road the irrepressible, late but much lamented Les Sealey.

John Still, is a manager of similar Ilk as David Pleat, he knows the difference between a good player and a player that is good but also has potential and the scope to improve to the required level of football the managers' side may be playing at the time. He proved that at Dagenham and Redbridge and also Dartford a club he assisted in getting better things for in their early days. I think it is much too early to compare the two, hopefully JLS will stay with Luton Town long enough to prove he is at least on an equal par to DP, but time to be honest is not on his side age wise, I am sure he will at least be looking at retirement. David Pleat at the time had age on his side. The job he has done in such a short time has been fantastic though and each and every supporter of Luton Town will never forget the name John Still that is for sure, the man who steered us back into the realms of league football.

However what I will say is this Luton Town as a club of our so called small stature are most fortunate to have experienced two such managers at the helm in a lifetime.

Monday November 17th 2014

It is quite disheartening and upsetting as a football supporter in general to witness what is going on within the game with FIFA. They are for sure covering something up, they have claimed that the English FA have tarnished the name of world football because of the accusations Greg Dyke and his team have thrown around regarding corruption in the choosing of Russia and Qatar to hold the FIFA World Cup in 2018 and 2022 respectively. As much as I am not a great fan of the FA at the moment, for many reasons not just the way they treated Luton Town in the past. For me in all honesty that in itself has to be put to sleep and buried with, we, as fans moving on. I am with The F.A. on this, especially now that an investigational report has yet again attempted to brush the truth away. But now it is not only England, it is UEFA also who are looking to break away from FIFA which is, as each day passes losing any credibility it once had. FIFA and Sep Blatter are losing sight of the real football world and living in their own little bubble that is for sure. Until Blatter is left out in the cold, not re-elected or any other way he happens to leave the post vacant and all his followers etc. disappear with him FIFA for me is a spent cause, all respect gone worldwide. What all of this is going to do in regards to the next two World Cup competitions at the moment is any ones guess, I dare not even begin to comprehend, but creditable they will not be unless someone acts fast.

Tuesday November 18th 2014
At the beginning of Octobers I wrote about the way football supporters within the UK are being shafted by the likes of The Premier League, SKY and BT over the selling of TV rights for football matches in this country and the difference between the tariffs to viewers in other European countries and our own. This morning I am extremely happy to learn that at least there is to be an investigation by OFCOM concerning this matter. Would it not be great if something is finally done to eradicate the despicable charges that have been passed down to us as the viewer?
Apart from that SKY and BT virtually have a hold over the Premier League, themselves determining the days certain fixtures are played and the time of the kick offs. I actually believe when games are played after other games there is a distinct advantage for those playing at a later time or date for that particular weeks fixtures, they know what's to be done to give them advantage and play their game accordingly. To that case I am a traditionalist and feel all games should kick off at the same time on the same day of that weeks' round of fixtures giving no advantage either way. Do what other countries do. They televise every game played that day and the subscriber chooses the game they want to watch, much fairer and sporting all round.

Thursday November 20th 2014
Understandably, following the superb gate figures Luton Town have been experiencing recently and the magnificent away support also, it really does not come as any surprise that fans are beginning to discuss the need for a new stadium at the earliest opportunity possible.
Club chairman Gary Sweet some months ago let it be known that a great deal of his time, now that at last the Luton Town finances are on an even keel, was now being devoted to planning for a new stadium to send the club into the future as bigger and better than ever before. He also admitted though that such a project will not happen overnight, it will take years rather than months to secure. Yes, we do need something sooner rather than later, but how refreshing, after all the shenanigans in recent years of the clubs colourful and sometimes distressing history to at last have a chairman at the helm who has the future of the club at heart rather than his own pocket. When one looks back at the nonsense we have had to endure in the past from self-promoting chairpersons or owners, it is a relief to my footballing heart. Property developer David Kohler and the "Kohler Dome".
Then in 2004 the farce that was John Gurney. His true intentions were hidden behind the façade of a phantom syndicate that he convinced the Football League, for confidential reasons he could not name the members of, they in their almighty wisdom decided to take him at his word, how convenient that was for him as there were no other members in this so called consortium.
Therefore to some extent we have to blame the football authorities for the so near total demise of our great club. Gurney purchased Luton Town Football Club for the princely sum of £4. His only intention was in fact, not to own a football club but to run it down to nothing and develop a retail park on the proceeds of his handy work. However thankfully the fast thinking of the likes of Gary

Sweet, then chairman of the Luton Town supporters group "Loyal Luton" who saw through the plans of the dastardly Mr. Gurney, made sure that Gurney had no close season cash flow from the sale of season tickets by getting supporters to boycott the purchase of such tickets. Seeing a loophole in the clause of the sale of the club to Gurney, Gary and his followers were able to buy shares in the sleeping company that held the debentures of the land owned by Luton Town Football Club, totally scuppering Gurneys plans and sending him on his way tail between his legs. That same saviour, Gary Sweet is now being totally honest and realistic in bringing the good times back to Luton Town, it will not happen overnight, a lot of hard work is still required, but with a true "Hatter" at the helm at least if we do not succeed it will not be for the want of trying. Luton Town are not going to be a force in the top flight of football likened to the late 1980s and early 90s without a stadium of relative capacity to other clubs at the top end of the English football tier. But we have to remember we have after years of great turmoil recovered from the brink of oblivion, so little steps. Yes, it is upsetting to see other clubs such as Shrewsbury Town etc., having new stadia to show off, however we have to learn to walk again within the Football League. Last time the club were too hasty look what happened. I sometimes, not often in all fairness, hear calls for Mr Sweet to put his pen to cheque book or step down. That would in my humble opinion be a step backwards, give the man space to breathe and get on with the task ahead, without the likes of Gary Sweet and the rest of the 2020 consortium we would not have a Luton Town to cheer on each weekend of the football season. For me Gary Sweet deserves a knighthood at the very least for services to Luton Town, simply for his instrumentation in the resurrection of Luton Town Football Club, from being worth the paltry sum of £4 to where we stand today.

Friday November 21st 2014
Back to the footballing side of affairs, it's a trip to Burton Albion for tomorrows League Two fixture. Another town of distant memories for me, having spent some time in latter end of the eighties. I frequently visited the local hostelries in the town, however age has gotten the better of me in recent times so the memory lapses more frequent, but I do recall it was not the most exciting of towns despite being mainly a town of brewers. Also the English home of Pirelli tyres, of whom their new stadium, the Pirelli Stadium yes they have one also, takes its name from, having moved from their previous ground, Eton Park in 2005.
Burton Alboin have not long been a Football League side themselves, being promoted from the Conference Premier following taking the champions spot in the 2008-2009 season under the leadership of initially Nigel Clough who left the club to join Derby County and then ex Derby and England favourite Roy McFarland. The club actually holds the record for the largest away sides following at Old Trafford of 11,000, when they played their FA Cup home replay against Manchester United at the Manchester Stadium in 2006, a game United won 5-0, following the 0-0 draw at Burton.
This will be recently acquired manager Jimmy Floyd Hassalbaink first home game in charge of the side following Gary Rowett's departure to manage Championship side Birmingham City.
For the "Hatters" this will be a most memorable game for goalkeeper Mark Tyler who will be making his 250th senior appearance for the club. One of the most prolific keepers we have seen at Kenilworth Road without a doubt, I would liken him to my favourite Town keeper through the many years I have followed the "Hatters" the late great Les Sealey. "Tiles" has made some amazing stops over the years, many of which, even this season and last we could call match winners. It is quite amazing for me in actual fact that the man has not played at a much higher level during his career, many I am sure will agree that he was the best goalkeeper by a long way in

the Conference Premier over the years and also this season the best seen in League Two. Congratulations on such an amazing feat Mark and may we see much more of you yet at the home of the "Hatters", long may you reign sir.

Saturday November 22nd 2014
Not the nicest of days thus far this season that is a fact.
Luton Town line up as follows: Mark Tyler, Michael Harriman, Steve McNulty, Luke Wilkinson, Scott Griffiths, Shaun Whalley, Jonathan Smith, Nathan Doyle, Jake Howells, Luke Guttridge and Paul Benson. Substitutes: Fraser Franks, Andy Drury, Mark Cullen, Luke Rooney, Elliot Justham, Pelly Ruddock Mpanzu and Ricky Miller.

Burton Albion 1 Luton Town 0
Finally, the unbeaten run comes to an end, well it had to happen sooner or later. The Town played well enough and if the truth known we have played a great deal worse this season and come away victorious. What was unusual was the inability to score, something the "Hatters" have only failed to do in four other games before today.
Burton, a well organised team, play together as a unit, they will almost certainly be in the shake up for the play offs come the end of the season if not automatic promotion.
John Still made two changes from the Tranmere game. Scott Griffiths replacing Fraser Franks and Shaun Whalley for the out of sorts Mark Cullen who had only resumed training the day before the match, so the manager thought it best to allow him some more hours of training before risking him, although placing him on the bench in the case of being needed.
For much of the game the Town had the upper hand, although not causing the home sides defence too many problems.
Half time came and not surprisingly the half was goalless. However, within minutes of the restart Burton took the lead when Palmer's corner kick found the head of Edwards who nodded the ball downwards into the net, 1-0 Burton.
It has been quite a while since the "Hatters" have been looking at a deficit during a game and their character shone through after the goal, their fighting spirit was evident in the attempt to recover the game from Burton's grasp.
When Ruddock Mpanzu replaced a somewhat lack lustre Howells, it could be seen that word had got out about Pelly, it had to happen sooner or later, two players were on him from the moment he stepped onto the field of play.
As the game went on Luton pressed for the equaliser but it was not going to come.
In the final minutes of the game Luke Wilkinson had the red card brandished by referee Adcock, who had in all honesty had a bad game, however on this occasion unfortunately he made the correct decision after the unopposed Palmer was bought down preventing a goal scoring opportunity. That is a one game ban for the Luton player.
Despite the defeat the Luton players enjoyed a fantastic reception from yet another record breaking away contingency of over 2,000 travelling "Hatters", a good sign indeed seeing it was not so long ago the team would have been booed off the pitch after even such a narrow defeat.
With that result Luton were knocked off the top spot being overtaken by both Wycombe and the victorious Burton Albion.

After the game John Still was his usual philosophical self, I enjoy it when a manager can be totally honest about his side when beaten, no excuses just the facts, Luton final passes were not good enough this afternoon.

Sunday November 23rd 2014
It's only a small minority these days, but it does amaze me that some are complaining following yesterday's defeat. That to me is incredible we have just come off an eleven game unbeaten run in the league and still they moan. INCREDIBLE!!

Tuesday November 25th 2014
The dreaded flu has gotten its claws into me over the past few days. So I am late on the draw following the alleged coin throwing incident at Burton on Saturday by someone in the Luton end, I will not call them a supporter because that is not what I call supporting your team, by launching a coin at the opponents goalkeeper. Quite the opposite, especially when it comes to the "Hatters." Although, I am more in the hope of letting the past go when it comes down to the football authorities of this country and Luton Town. I have to say that they will be rubbing their hands with much glee at the opportunity of taking the club to the cleaners yet again, incidents like this do not help matters at all, we will be hit hard that is for certain if the investigation proves that someone did in fact throw a coin, as suggested. I hope if anyone knows who the perpetrator is that they will name and shame them, because the club is going to be dragged across the fires again for this, the stupidity of one total idiot, and that is being diplomatic, could cost the club thousands of pounds or worst. This type of nonsense really does need to be stamped on, if the guilty person is found and I hope that they are sooner rather than later, both Luton and the relevant authorities come down so heavily on their heads.

Thursday November 26th 2014
I wake up, make my first tea of the morning turn on the TV to BBC News, I stop in my tracks as I hear Mike Bushell talking about the passing of Phillip Hughes, the Australian test cricketer who had been hit by a bouncer from his good friend Sean Abbot in a domestic game a couple of days earlier. Stunned yes, surprised not really, the extent of the injuries were always going to be a danger to his life.
How devastating for all concerned that must have been, Sean Abbot and the other participating players must be beside themselves right now, but particularly Abbot who delivered that fatal ball.

Just 25 years of age, so much was in front of this young man, destined for greatness, looked at in the same light as the great Ricky Ponting, a most amazing accolade in itself. Not only an Australian test player but also played on the English County scene, for Worcestershire, Hampshire and Middlesex.
He will surely be missed next summer for the Ashes tour which I would hope the Australians and English alike will dedicate to this so talented young man who has departed this world much too early.
I have just read a most interesting question, "I am wondering if this will turn cricket into a nanny state following this tragic event?" For myself I hope that will not be the case because lets be sensible in reviewing this. Cricket has been with us for nearly 200 years and the number of fatalities, due to wild balls have been minimal to say the least, it would in my honest opinion be somewhat churlish to look too deeply into this, yes there will be an investigation that is for sure,

however it has to be kept real. It is also coming to light, in defence of the helmet manufacturers, that Phil Hughes was wearing an out of date helmet, that was his personal choice, most probably for his own comfort, a very sad but freak accident that must for the sake of cricket be taken as simply that nothing more. Our hearts, thoughts and prayers must be with Philips family, friends and colleagues at this most distressing time.

The injury to Phil Hughes is not unlike that of jockey Brian Toomey who following a most horrific fall in July 2014 at Perth racecourse had similar surgery to Hughes, Brian was one of the fortunate ones and is making a most amazing recovery.

Other news from the Town is that Alex Wall has been sent out on loan to Conference Premier side Bristol Rovers, who were relegated to play non-league football passing the "Hatters" on the way down. Wall has made just the one full appearance for Luton in the League this season away to Cambridge United, plus coming on as a substitute on three occasions and also in the Johnson's Paint Trophy tie against Crawley Town. With one goal to his credit in those games scoring the winning goal away to Stevenage Town. He is capable of so much, however his attitude and work rate has been questioned so far this season. He needs to calm down at times, he tries too hard I front of goal I feel and maybe a period in the Conference, where he made his mark last season with Dartford when on loan will help him to find a more settled footing.

Friday November 27th 2014
This weekend brings Mansfield Town and their supporters to the "Kenny". Not unlike York City we have "history" they are a potential banana skin, we always seem to have a hard time against the "Stags". With the departure of Paul Cox earlier this month they have caretaker Adam Murray in charge for tomorrows' game. Murray a former "Hatter" made seven appearances for Luton in 2010, a two year contract cut short and moved on loan to the Stags before signing permanently in 2011. He had played for several clubs before moving to the "Hatters" from Oxford United, including Derby County and Notts. County.

Having secured promotion from the Conference Premier in 2013 when they won the League, just as Luton twelve months later.

Mansfield boss and former "Hatter" Adam Murray.

Mansfield are having a somewhat indifferent season so far, winning only one game away from home to date, so Luton will be hoping to carry the six home games unbeaten run going tomorrow afternoon.

Saturday November 28th 2014
The damned flu still has its hold on me and therefore not at my best, if of course I have a best, but that's for you to decide I suppose.
The "Hatters" line-up is as follows for this game: Mark Tyler, Michael Harriman, Steve McNulty, Fraser Franks, Scott Griffiths, Shaun Whalley, Jonathan Smith, Nathan Doyle, Andy Drury, Paul Benson and Mark Cullen. With subs: Alex Lace, Jake Howells, Luke Rooney, Elliot Justham, Pelly Ruddock Mpanzu, Ricky Miller and Charlie Walker.
Three changes from last weeks' defeat at Burton Albion, with Andy Drury replacing Luke Guttridge who has suffered an injury setback. Mark Cullen returns and replaces Jake Howells and Fraser Franks for Luke Wilkinson who is on a one game ban following his red card last week.

Luton Town 3 Mansfield Town 0
Mansfield settled into the game faster than Luton and were unfortunate not to take an early lead when Freeman made a fierce cross, which if Oliver had managed to get even the slenderest of touches on would almost certainly have beaten Mark Tyler in the Luton goal.
Luton's first real attempt came from the unlikely source of Nathan Doyle who tried his luck from 35 yards out, almost catching Mansfield's keeper Studler by surprise who just got a touch to the ball and pushed it behind for a corner.
Luton took the lead when Drury made a crisp pass to Mark Cullen, who from the left entered the box with ball at feet. Then squared it to Paul Benson who stabbed at the ball, Beevors blocked, the ball getting away from him, resulting in a melee of players attempting to get the ball away or score, Benson regained possession turned and eased the ball over the line, the "Hatters" were on their way.
Scorer Benson went into a challenge with Mansfield's Riley, as soon as he went down he knew it was an injury he was not going to be able to play on with and was subsequently stretchered off to be replaced by Jake Howells.
Half time came and went, Cullen was unlucky not to give Luton a second when his looping header crashed against the bar following an excellent right sided cross from Michael Harriman.
The "Stags" came into the game a little more, a low driven effort from Brown thwarted by Tyler. Despite this little flourish Luton went two goals ahead. Shaun Whalley destroying any challenge from Beevors, put in a powerful cross towards the far post completely startling the Mansfield keeper. Whether or not it was a cross or a shot, which is solely for Whalley to admit to or keep quiet about. It hit the back of the net to the delights of the Kenilworth Road end and the rest of the ground also, if that was intended what a sublime goal it was, any player in the World of football would have been proud of that. If Lionel Messi had put the same away it would have been spoken

about all weekend, such is the difference between coverage of this level of football and the higher echelons of our beautiful game.

If that was a fluke Whalley's next was definitely no, he again slaughtered Beevors as he surged forward, hitting the ball low and hard into the corner giving the keeper no chance whatsoever of preventing it going over the line. The "Kenny" erupted as the Town went three goals ahead. Another superb display from the marauding "Hatters" The blip that was last week, distantly pushed into the annals of history.

This totally knocked the stuffing out of the visitors, although Heslop could have pulled a goal back, but his strike that had Tyler beaten dipped a fraction too late and went over.

Another resounding win that puts the "Hatters" into the second place berth.

Shaun Whalley had an excellent game and his goals were the icing on the cake. Also, Jonathan Smith has been excellent following his return from a broken leg at Christmas. In other League Two games, next week's FA Cup opponents Bury were well beaten at home by Dagenham & Redbridge by two goals to nil, Wycombe consolidated their first place position when winning by three goals to one at Hartlepool United, which leaves Hartlepool three points adrift of Tranmere Rovers at the bottom of League Two.

Sunday November 30th 2014

Not so good news coming through this morning is the news that Paul Benson may very well have played his final game for Luton, if the rumours are correct, the 35 year old may well have broken his leg during yesterdays' game. If so I for one will be extremely sorry to lose him. There are those for sure that will not agree with me on that issue. But Benson never was going to set the season alight, not at the ripe age of thirty five, his pace is not anywhere as it used to be, his experience however, priceless. Many it seems to me do not appreciate, even when he seems to be having a quiet game, the deft touches to set a player free. His ability to draw defenders away from others. His determination second to none. For me he will be sorely missed if the rumours are true. Let's hope he is able though to make a full recovery and put those rumours to sleep allowing us to yet again witness him in a Luton shirt.

December

Monday December 1st 2014

Maybe I am slow, but more disturbing new comes through the wire that during the Mansfield game within the confines of the main stand, in G Block, some bright spark decided it would be so much fun to let off a fire cracker during the game. What we have to bear in mind here is that the main stand is constructed predominantly of wood so it is not going to take too much to ignite what could have become a most catastrophic occurrence.

Memories of Bradford City Football Club, when on Saturday May 11th 1985, during the course of a match between "The Bantams" and Lincoln City a discarded cigarette butt started a fire I the main stand. I may be wrong but I believe our own Marc North was on loan with Lincoln City at the time and was on the pitch on that fateful day. Fifty six people lost their lives with many more treated for injuries, a total well over two hundred and fifty.

The Bradford Stadium fire

Some may question as to why I add such images, well it is to remind the culprits of such a moronic act exactly what one small ember can cause.

The result of such a fire at Kenilworth Road would have been just as catastrophic, in such a confined area with let's face it limited routes of access from the main stand.

The culprit at the time of writing has still to be dragged forward or pointed out. It is quite obvious there are others who know this morons identity but have not the courage to put forward their name. The club have issued a statement regarding both this and the coin throwing incident at Burton the week prior and have promised that anyone found to have been responsible for each occurrence will be banned for up to six years, personally six years is not adequate and should for both incidents result in life bans. We have had enough of our club being dragged through the mud in recent years.

Let us be brutally honest here. When anything happens at Luton Town, or, that is linked to Luton Town Football Club not only the media but also the Football authority's ears suddenly spring to life. We need to find these, I cannot call them supporters, because they are not supporting the club with their actions, they are sending messages out that nothing has changed for the better at the club, that to me is not support and bring them to justice.

I also hear that during the incident, that we also have to acknowledge how quickly and thankfully, the stewards dealt with it, a young boy was burned slightly, but enough to warrant a hospital visit, my thoughts and I am sure many others also wish the young lad well and it does not put him off coming to more games. If you know these idiots name and shame them please, for the good of Luton Town Football Club and more importantly still the safety of all that come to see our mighty "Hatters" week in week out.

Tuesday December 2nd 2014

After yesterday little rant, yes I love a rant, as you have most probably guessed by now. I thought I would just look out and see what ever happened to the North brothers, who both climbed up through the ranks of the Luton Town squads from youth to first team in the nineteen eighties, it was always going to be difficult for any youngster in those days to make a massive impression, especially with the calibre of player we had at the club during those so heady days. But both brothers managed to do so.

Stacey a decent defender, but as mentioned, was always going to find it difficult to break into what was an already formidable defence at the club. Between 1983 and 1987 he managed a handful of first team appearances, twenty five in all, plus three appearances whilst out on loan to Wolverhampton Wanderers in 1985, before moving to West Bromwich Albion and then Fulham in 1990. Later moving to the United States of America as a coach.

As for his brother Marc, who was a more forward player, he made a total of eighteen first team appearances between 1985 and 1987 scoring three goals in that time, his first in the 2-0 home win against Newcastle United on 7th December 1985 with Mick Harford scoring the other. He again shared the goals with Harford at the Hawthorns on Boxing Day of that year helping the "Hatters" to a 2-1 victory against West Bromwich Albion and two days later picked up his third and final goal for Luton Town at Portman Road, Ipswich to earn the Town a 1-1 draw. During his two years at Luton Town Marc went out on loan to Lincoln City, as already mentioned, Scunthorpe United and Birmingham City. He moved to Grimsby under the management of Alan Buckley in 1987, before moving on to Leicester City. Marc returned for a short spell to Grimsby but never made an impression into the first team apart from one appearance. He moved then to Kettering Town, where during only his fifth appearance for the "Poppies" he injured his back, this bought to an end a somewhat indifferent footballing career, although he did play non-league football for a while from 1998 to 1999 with Bell Green Athletic.

Sadly Marc contracted mild neoplasm cancer in the thoracic region of his spine, which resulted in more tumours gathering in his illumuni muscle. As a result Marc North passed away on 7th February 2001 at the slender age of 34 years.

Wednesday December 3rd 2014

The FA Cup 2nd Round bares down upon us again. This time we travel northwards to Bury. What really upsets me and this is regarding the competition in general, not necessarily to do with Luton Town, the way this great competition is fading away into the distance for many, for want of a better way of putting it.

For my generation at least, The FA Cup has been one of the magical highlights of every season. We used to look forward to the draw every Monday lunchtime on the radio, it was not just about who your team were going to be drawn against, but also those that had the opportunity to play against the best in the country that would not normally have that chance. I used to love it when another great FA Cup fighting club from our county, Bedford Town, The Eagles were involved, before my time as I was only three years old in 1956, they had an amazing two game battle with the mighty Arsenal, taking them to extra-time at the Bedford Eyrie, after a magnificent draw at Highbury. Then there was 1963when they toppled the mighty Magpies, Newcastle United at St James Park. Such moments make the FA Cup something we should cherish for all time. However, sadly I find that is not the case. My own take on it is that with the arrival of so many foreign owners and also management the magic has been lost along the way in their quest for Premiership and European glory, money before tradition, which again sadly seems to be the way of the world. As I see it managers and owners alike of the larger clubs have lost within those quests I just mentioned, the real meaning of what for us older supporters of our great game, the biggest and best club football competition in the world is to us. The problem is for some supporters that lack of respect for the competition is rubbing off onto the new generation of football supporters, which to me is so sad.

Once upon a time the clamour for any FA Cup round ticket would have been enormous home or away, how things have changed, we take 2000 plus to a league game at Burton Albion but only it seems we will take about 600 at the most to Bury on Saturday, how things have changed. I hear people saying "I don't want a good cup run", I would have called anyone, a few years ago, mad if they told me fans would be expressing such feelings. Where has the tradition gone? For me it is heart-breaking as a veteran football supporter, the FA Cup has always had so much to offer in the past, obviously not now. Sad indeed.

Friday December 5th 2014

Unfortunately this flu thing is really getting on my case, angry little varmint is it not!

Saturday December 6th 2014

The Luton line up for the Bury game is as follows; Mark Tyler, Fraser Franks, Steve McNulty, Luke Wilkinson, Michael Harriman, Jonathan Smith, Andy Drury, Nathan Doyle, Scott Griffiths, Charlie Walker and Mark Cullen. Subs: Alex Lacey, Jake Howells, Luke Rooney, Elliot Justham, Ricky Miller, Matt Robinson and Luke Stevenson.

Bury 1 Luton Town 1

Luton took the lead in the 51st minute when Scott Griffiths cross went through the goalkeepers legs to Mark Cullen who had no trouble in tapping the ball into the back of the net.

Daniel Nardiello equalised in injury time to ensure a replay at Kenilworth Road.

A draw it seems was a fair reflection on a hard fought game where both sides had to battle.

I for one will be looking forward to the replay and also the draw for the Third Round in the hope……

Monday December 8th 2014

I remember in my early youth four young guys from Liverpool, they rocked our world back then with the most amazing sounds. I am also writing a book in addition to this one, about the 1960s decade of The Grand National that is run at Aintree Racecourse, Liverpool, at that time these same four guys were making themselves known to us as The Beatles. To many they were four delinquents making a cacophony. A noise not welcoming to their ears. To others they were an integral part of the music revolution that was hitting Britain. A much needed boost to catch up with the American scene that was in all honesty running away from the rest of the world, thanks to The Beatles and other bands such as Freddie and the Dreamers, The Searchers, The Rolling Stones and Gerry and The Pacemakers the Brits were at last hitting back.

Those four lads, George Harrison, Paul McCartney, Richard Starkey (better known to most by his stage name Ringo Starr) and John Winston Lennon became the epitome of the British pop scene. The rest as they say is history.

There have been many conversations over the years, which derive from one question. "Can you remember where you were when the news of John F Kennedy's assassination came through?" However, for myself and many others the question is somewhat the same but the name different, "Can you recall where you were when you learnt of John Lennon's assassination?"

I can actually recall both despite only being 10 years old at the time of the JFK killing. But the one that sticks so firmly in my mind is that morning in 1980, it was about eight in the morning at my parent's home in Kempston. A rural town just west of Bedford. I was recovering from a fall, I was off work and decided to visit Mum and Dad for a few days, the news hit me like a straight punch to the solar plexus, I felt as if a part of my life had been taken from me, strange maybe even weird as I did not know the man personally, he was just another musician to many, to me he was my musical hero, a most talented young man not just through his music and prose but also his humanity, to some of us he was a saint to others a pain in the arse. A peaceful man, outspoken yes, but peace loving. My heart sank that day and it still hurts deeply on this same date every year.

You may well ask what has this to do with Luton Town being back in the Football League. Well today it had the significance of being the one reason I could not get myself excited as many others around the country and the majority of "Hatters" awaiting this evenings FA Cup 3rd round draw, the enthusiasm and expectation I would usually have all day, especially with Luton in the hat has been totally thwarted. This is the one day of the year I play Lennon and the Beatles all day long, it's an integral part of my year these days, sad yes, but also true. So I ask forgiveness for my lack of fervour towards this evenings draw, who do I hope we get? Well, Arsenal away would be nice, maybe only for the fact that my good friend Kenny Cook is also, or was when I knew him better a massive Lennon fan and a Gooner to boot. How fitting in my heart that would be if on this day our two contrasting clubs were drawn against each other, that would for me make the day a better one and something to look forward to.

I have most amazing memories of Kenny and his brother Michael from our early years, such times we had. I used to actually follow Arsenal until I came to my senses, but yes admittedly still a place in my heart for them it has to be said. My friend Alan Hudson, played for them just after I had changed my allegiance and these days I rue the fact that the only times I really saw him play was against the "Hatters" for Stoke City. If I am honest, gave him some abuse from the terraces, but that abuse stemmed from the fact that he was such a magnificent player and he frightened me half to death every time he had the ball at his feet. But that's another story.

Well disappointment is the FA Cup draw, we are drawn away to either Mansfield Town or Cambridge United, yet another encounter with Richard Money hangs in the balance, that will certainly give us something to look forward to if both teams make it through the relevant replays that is for sure. No Arsenal is actually a shame, I have memories of many Arsenal games. There was one particular day I recall quite vividly. We were about 15 years of age at the time, 16th September 1967. Michael, myself and Kenny two years older than us, as I have said I will digress at times away from Luton Town, however I think that can be a good thing, there is let's face more to life than Luton Town, unless of course one is so single minded that it gets to the state of boredom for others. It was in the days of the steam train which used to make train journeys that more enjoyable than now, the carriages comprised of compartments that seated four on either side if I remember correctly with a sliding door into the corridor. Yes travelling was much more fun in those days. We decided a week in advance that we would go to Highbury, pre Emirates Stadium, in case you are not aware, for the North London derby Arsenal v Tottenham. Something we had at that time dreamed of when even younger, with Kenny and myself, happy Gooner's and Michael a lone Spur, cannot really say the Lone Ranger, as Rangers were not in the equation. We envisaged a tight game that afternoon as we travelled from Bedford to St. Pancras, a cold and bleak day I recall. On our arrival in London we had a cup of tea in a café on St Pancras Road and then made our way to Arsenal via the Piccadilly Line, yes Arsenal even have a tube station named after the club. Quite an adventure for us our first game well out of reach of Bedford without a parent or grown up with us, in those days it was not so normal for boys of our age to travel so far alone. The excitement was high, we even managed to get a place right at the front of the famous North Bank and we were on that day in our element. We were witnessing such players as wee Georgie Armstrong, the blonde giant from Scotland Ian Ure in the red shirts of Arsenal Alan Gilzean and Danny Blanchflower for the lilywhite boys of Spurs. As already mentioned we expected a tight game, how wrong we were, Arsenal totally dominated from beginning to the end, it was a total rout, Arsenal winning 4-0. I still remember the Arsenal line up for that afternoon. Jim Furnell, Peter Storey, Peter Simpson, Frank McLintock, Terry Neill and my favourite Gunner of all time George Armstrong included. I used to fashion myself on him when I played, speedy small built winger, not as good as him of course but yes I could do the business at our level. The Arsenal scorers that day were Terry Neill from the penalty spot to open the scoring, with further goals from John Radford, George Graham and Colin Addison. In those days 60,000 plus crowds at Highbury were a normality. I did experience my first ever piece of football violence that day on the North Bank. As Colin Addison turned away from the North Bank faithful after slotting the ball past the stranded Spurs keeper, my best friend Michael firmly buried his fist deep into my stomach after a little taunting on my part it has to be said. So maybe a little insensitive of me, as I saw the tears welling up in his eyes, so maybe a little deserved. The poor fellow had to endure a somewhat tearful journey all the way back to Bedford that evening. I remember a porter at St Pancras asking us the score when noticing the programmes in our hands. Just as myself and Kenny were about to gleefully pronounce to the chap 4-0 to the Arsenal Michael blurted out something to the effect of go forth and multiply, upon which with a feel of diplomacy Kenny and myself looked at each other laughed and kept our lips firmly sealed.

The following week at school, it was difficult not to taunt my poor friend more. However, I did not have to, as he received enough stick from everyone else, we were so cruel in those days, but all in good fun it has to be said, unlike these days, where young lads have to watch everything they say in fear of incrimination, oh how we miss those days of relative innocence.

Wednesday December 10th 2014

The Eric Morecambe Trophy, to be contested between Morecambe and Luton Town.

The next league game is quite a poignant one. Simply for the man that was Eric Morecambe, we shall not only be competing for three much required three points in our endeavour to stay in touch with the leaders of League Two but also we shall be competing in the inaugural match of the newly formed Eric Morecambe Trophy, that will be contested solely by ourselves and Morecambe FC. Readers in general will not need to be reminded as to why this small but significant trophy has come into being, but for those who may not be aware, Morecambe was the hometown of Eric Bartholomew, whom as a young up and coming comedian changed his name to Eric Morecambe, after his hometown as it sounded more appropriate. Eric was in his lifetime a great Luton Town supporter and was for a while a major director of the club he so loved. Following his passing the town of Morecambe erected a life-size statue of the great man on the sea front. Sadly a couple of months ago the statue was attacked and vandalised and quite fittingly after repairs the statue will be returned to its place on the seafront this week, the same week as Luton Town visit for a League Two game. It was decided it would be a massive tribute to the much loved comedian to contest for a trophy as well as the league points, the trophy has been reproduced as a miniature version of the statue. A fantastic idea to bring two sets of fans together.

Saturday December 13th 2014
A multitude of Luton Town fans are today converging upon the small seaside town of Morecambe on the Lancashire coast, some it seems in fancy dress, as the image of Eric Morecambe, large rimmed spectacles, the famous Mackintosh and pipe to add to the look.
Many will be making their way to the re-erected statue to have photographs taken alongside bronze effigy.

Many thanks to my good friend Paul Stanyon for the collection of photographs he most kindly shared with me for this publication.

It will be Luton Town's first appearance at the newly acquired Globe Arena, so a new ground to tick off for those who like to keep a record of such. As mentioned above many thanks indeed for the photographs supplied by my good friend Paul Stanyon, whom himself has now recorded every League ground, all be it not all Luton Town games, however the majority being so.
Morecambe are a most enterprising side and they will not be an easy challenge that is for sure. The Luton Town line up is as follows; Mark Tyler, Luke Wilkinson, Steve McNulty, Fraser Franks, Jake Howells, Jonathon Smith, Nathan Doyle, Andy Drury, Michael Harriman, Shawn Whalley and Mark Cullen. With substitutes; Alex Lacey, Scott Griffiths, Luke Rooney, Elliot Justham, Ross Lafayette, Ricky Miller and Jim Stevenson.

Approaching the Globe Arena, Morecambe.

Morecambe 3 Luton Town 0
As Paul Wright so eloquently put it….
Bring me Sunshine? Morrissey's "Every Day is Like Sunday" would be more appropriate for the town of Morecambe. A cold, cheerless day on the Lancashire coast, with a performance and result to match. We played all the right passes, but not necessarily in the right order. Three goals conceded from set pieces meant we never remotely looked like potting the "Shrimps".
It was a shock to the system, after being spoiled by some wonderful performances over the past year or so. The manner of the goals, the dire first half performance when we were lucky to score nil. Defensively, we were a right old shambles, so unusual for a John Still side. Every game this season apart from Shrewsbury we have competed in whether having won, lost or drawn. An unfortunate flashback to the bad old days when we were a soft touch in the winter.
In all honesty Luton beat themselves, rather than Morecambe. The "Hatters" made errors whereas Morecambe did not, that was the difference throughout the game. They deserved to win on that merit alone.
Morecambe won the game with ease with two first half goals from Ellison and Hughes and their third with about ten minutes remaining from Amond.
Life on the pitch was not made any easier when the "Hatters" skipper Steve McNulty received a second yellow, leaving an already lacklustre Luton to cope with ten men.
A day better forgotten it seems. Such an anti-climax throughout the preceding week. Elsewhere both Burton Albion and Wycombe Wanderers scored four to launch themselves into the top two positions of the table Wycombe at the top of the perch with 41 points followed by Burton on 39 and Shrewsbury in third on 37 points topping Luton in the fourth place berth on goal difference.

Monday December 16th 2014
Tomorrow evenings home replay in the FA Cup third round is as the first game going to be a tight knit affair of that I am certain. I would not be at all surprised if the game was to go all the way to the dreaded penalty shoot-out, which looking back at our recent history of such events we shall be really hoping to avoid at all costs. Definitely not Luton Town's forte. This is a busy time of the year for all of us, with Christmas and New Year just days away. So none will be condemned for not being attend this game I am sure. There are a few games to contend with in the next three weeks so the finances of most are going to be stretched, although I am hearing that the Portsmouth tickets and those for Wycombe away are being grabbed with fervour and the possibility is that Pompey's visit to the "Kenny" could easily be a total sell-out. Golden days indeed.

Tuesday December 17th 2014
The Town line up is as follows for the visit of Bury this evening; Mark Tyler, Michael Harriman, Fraser Franks, Luke Wilkinson, Scott Griffiths, Nathan Doyle, Jonathan Smith, Shaun Whalley, Andy Drury, Luke Rooney and Mark Cullen. Substitutes being; Alex Lacey, Elliot Justham, Ricky Miller, Jim Stevenson, Matt Robinson, Jake Howells and Ross Lafayette.

Luton Town 1 Bury 0
Considering the side John Still put out tonight an excellent win against the stand out footballing side in League One, however for all of Bury's clever pass and move football they really do lack quality in attacking positions it has to be said. Luton deserved the win after an improved second

half performance. Once again the team showed good character after the horror show at Morecambe.

As expected both sides were evenly matched, which has been the case in all three encounters thus far this season.

Luton began the game maybe the more productive of the two, although once Bury managed to get into their stride they dominated the remainder of the first half, although seldom did they really look like actually penetrating our defences enough to make anything count.

The "Hatters" attacked towards the "Kenny" in the first half, most of their attacking movement coming from Shaun Whalley. Half time came with neither side really testing the relevant keepers.

As in the first half Luton started the brighter of the two teams, Rooney taking the ball away from Soares on the left, tried to find Cullen in the box, but the curl took the ball away from Cullen and trickled into the far corner, with Jalal, the Bury keeper barely moving. The breakthrough complete, 1-0, by courtesy of a fluke Rooney goal.

After the goal Luton continued to push forward. Shaun Whalley failed to capitalise when Drury set him free, but his shot ran past the far post, out for a goal kick. But those sides had their chances in the second half, but the Town held on to win 1-0 and secure an away to tie to Cambridge United on January 3rd.

Watch out Dicky here comes Stilly.

Friday December 19th, 2014

Another sad day for football on the whole. A club I have mentioned a couple of times already in earlier parts of this book Hereford United FC were formally wound up at the High Court in London this morning. Despite efforts to save the club, the final nail to the coffin was finally hammered tightly home.

But out of the simmering embers there is hope. I have been dependably informed by my good friend Clive Pritchard that provisions have already been laid into place to rebuild the club under the name of Hereford FC and they have already been affiliated by the FA which means they have also secured the Edgar Street Stadium as their home ground, the local council agreed to this with the provision that they were registered and affiliated with the relevant football authorities. HUST (Hereford United Supporters Trust), are the force behind this move and reliable information is that they are already deeming to return to football pyramid next season. Most probably at a lower tier but all the same they will have a club which is all that matters to the supporters of this famous club, a team to follow at the home they know so well. We wish them all the good fortune they deserve and it will not be too long before they are a major force in non-league football very soon.

Saturday December 20th, 2014

I am not going to be as active over the next week or so, commitments will prevent me from being able to journalise as much as I would truly like to but yes all games will hopefully be covered. Christmas period in the past for me has always been a difficult time to concentrate on football as much as I would have liked. Just as it is for football, horse racing is very busy also, I remember many a Christmas Day, stuck in a crowded horse transporter on the way to race meetings that are peppered all over the country, great days all the same. So these days I do tend to pledge my time to the family more so than before.

Today we host Newport County again, it's only a few weeks since they were here last, in the FA Cup second round tie. A similar result today would be most welcomed. This time round they will be without their prolific striker and former "Hatter" Aaron O'Connor due to suspension.

The Luton line up for today's game: Mark Tyler, Michael Harriman, Steve McNulty, Luke Wilkinson, Scott Griffiths, Nathan Doyle, Jonathan Smith, Shaun Whalley, Andy Drury, Luke Rooney and Mark Cullen. With substitutes on show: Elliot Justham, Jake Howells, Ricky Miller, Ross Lafayette, Jim Stevenson and Paul Connelly.

Luton Town 3 Newport County 0

The Town battled well in the first half, whilst having to withstand an aerial bombardment.

It was Andy Drury's best game so far since he has re-joined the club, not only on the ball but off it as well. Not only his, but the whole team's work rate was excellent throughout. The most impressive factor today was that they kept their heads in the face of some severe provocation and to add some quite lamentable officiating.

There was a comment later in Twitter that summed it up perfectly, "Newport were beaten when their best player, the referee, was replaced at half time through illness".

Newport were very physical opponents, poor, with little pace apart from Jackson at the back, not dissimilar to the earlier cup game. They lacked the quality upfront in that game also. They had plenty of the ball after conceding to Wilkinson's header from Drury's corner leaving the scorer totally unmarked to make it 1-0.

Their only real tactic was to launch the ball forward to that human lamp-post that is Zebroski and also trying to find Francis Jeffers, who if was in a better side would have been more of a danger. There were times when they looked to be a danger from set-pieces, Mark Tyler forced to make three excellent reaction saves, I am wondering how many points in actual fact over the years "Tyles" has won us, to keep County at bay. When they did manage to get balls into the box, we coped well enough, unlike last week at Morecambe.

Newport reacted well to going behind, Luton reverting to their usual tactics of sitting back once in front, something that really does frustrate at times. Sometimes we do seem to lack that killer instinct.

The referee ignored quite a few ragged tackles, including one obvious foul by Zebroski on Scott Griffiths, as play continued Jackson popped up in the area, striking a ferocious shot that fortunately Nathan Doyle was able to block. Sandell's in swinging corners did manage to cause some concern for the "Hatters" defence, particularly as they had so many players of size.

A fine flick by Mark Cullen was met by Whalley, despite his initial hesitation to take on Jackson he passed him with some ease, his shot was not of the best calibre, the ball tamely taken by Jones. Despite their possession Newport were unable to trouble Tyler too much.

For much of the second half Luton produced some excellent football, Luke Rooney getting much more involved than normal made a chipped pass to Whalley in the right channel, unfortunately his shot went ridiculously wide, in fact so wide that it did not go out of play.

The second goal transpired from some good work between Harriman and Drury, the goalkeeper failed to collect the ball, dropping kindly for Rooney, who keeping his calm chested down and slotted the ball into the unguarded net.

From this moment on Luton's play flowed so fluently, good movement off the ball, as the visitors had to press forward which resulted in them leaving gaps not only in midfield but likewise their defence. They sent on Chapman and Howe, but nothing or anyone able to stem the "Hatters" excellent display of football. The team again proving that we can mix it up against physical sides and beat others on occasion.

Whalley sent a pass for Harriman to pick up, he, playing the ball into Cullen, who had to take his shot early with Chapman in close attendance, Stephens palmed the strike away.

Ross Lafayette replaced Rooney, who was in superb form for this game, putting himself about well.

Luton's two substitutes almost combined for a third, a through ball by Howells to Lafayette who elected to turn right rather than left, so Jones could narrow the angle and stop the shot.

Jeffers then had a rare attempt on goal when he sent over a cross towards Zebroski, his touch was well saved by Tyler though.

With three minutes injury time signalled by the fourth official, the "Hatters" wrapped up the victory with the impressive Andy Drury ghosting in along the by-line to find Howells making a good run towards the near post. Howells latched onto the pass and flicked the ball in to the far post to complete another home win, bringing to an abrupt end the visitors' nine match unbeaten run in the league.

Kenilworth Road is beginning to become something of a fortress. It has been a splendid season in that respect.

Elsewhere in League Two Wycombe were being held to a draw at Accrington with Shrewsbury beating Morecambe at home by one goal to nil. At the other end of the table Hartlepool and Oxford shared the spoils in a 1-1 draw. Other contenders at the top of the table Burton Albion had been in a goalless draw at Roots Hall, with Southend the evening prior.

The Hatters climb one place up the table to again enter the automatic promotion zone in third place, two points behind leaders Wycombe Wanderers, and goal difference only separating the third and second place with Shrewsbury having the better ratio by five goals from Luton and nine goals difference from fourth place Burton in fourth also on forty points.

Sunday December 21st 2014

"Hatters" first team coach Hakan Hayrettin, following the Towns capitulation of Newport County yesterday said the "Hatters" were superb in all departments, wrong he was not.

We have much to look forward to for the remainder of this season, maybe we will miss out on promotion, the Town still have a long trek in front of them, but what a journey our first season back will have been that is for sure. Luton Town really are back where we belong. Championship football within the next six years must be a reasonable target to chase and as my old mum used to say "it's do-able if you want it so badly".

Monday December 22nd 2014

Just hearing the news about former chairman of the Professional Footballers Association Clarke Carlisle being hit by a lorry in Bishopsthorpe, North Yorkshire and seriously ill, a life threatening situation. Carlisle actually played five games for Luton in 2007 whilst on loan from Watford. He had been recently working for ITV Sports as a football pundit. Another accolade is the fact that Carlisle was the first footballer to appear on the panel of BBC's "Question Time". We wish himself and wife Gemma good fortune and hope that he, in time, makes a full recovery.

Some marvellous news in contrast this morning is that Paul Benson. Who many of us feared had played his last game for Luton Town when breaking his left leg on November 29th during the 3-0 home win against Mansfield Town, has had his plaster removed and replaced with a boot and hoping to be fit and ready to play for the final push at the end of the season. Never say die

"Hatters" all the way. A superb tonic not only for "Benno" and the rest of the squad but also Luton fans in general.

Four days to Christmas and for myself a hectic time with six children and two grandchildren at home, two more sons in Derby and two more grandchildren up there. I have to admit they have not had as much of my attention as they deserve, but time will change that soon hopefully, just a though as I sit down to look over the season so far. Yes Christmas really is a time we reflect on not only the good things and those around us but also the not so good that we could maybe do more about.

The Development side played Nottingham Forest in a friendly this afternoon at Kenilworth Road, winning by three goals to one, with Luton's goals coming from Ricky Miller, Matt Robinson and Ross Lafayette.

Well that is me away now until Boxing Day, have a great Christmas folks. Enjoy but do not overdo it, big game on Friday COYH!!!

Friday December 26th, 2015

Merry Christmas? We shall know more on that score in a few hours.

The problems of being a footballer or a jockey at Christmas is simple. Eat little drink none and sleep much, unless your name happened to be Jimmy Duggan in the eighties and nineties. But that's for another book entirely, look out for it folks, maybe the perfect Christmas present for next year Jimmy Duggan, a book by Chris Luke, on the exploits of a jockey unequalled by none, stories that will shake your boots off as you read them, a couple of stories worth feature films in their own rights believe me. Hope you are making up for all those missed Christmases young James, sober and eating. Well actually, I know you are, a changed man, one in a million even more so now.

The line-up for the "Hatters against Wycombe goes as such; Mark Tyler, Michael Harriman, Steve McNulty, Luke Wilkinson, Scott Griffiths, Nathan Doyle, Jonathan Smith, Shaun Whalley, Andy Drury, Luke Rooney and Mark Cullen. On the bench; Fraser Franks, Ricky Miller, Elliot Justham, Jim Stevenson, Jake Howells, Ross Lafayette and Paul Connolly.

Wycombe Wanderers 1 Luton Town 1

Wycombe are a well organised side, they play as team, with no stars. Gareth Ainsworth has done a fantastic job there to turn a team on the cusp of relegation into league leaders at the half way stage. Luton attempted put an aggressive marker down in the early stages.

Wycombe took the lead from a Jacobson corner kick to the near post headed down by Cowan-Hall that went across goal and sneaked in to give them an early lead.

The lead did not last too long though after Michael Harriman's low centre was half cleared but only as far as Jonathan Smith who chested the ball down and thumped the ball into the back of Wycombe's net, a shot that gave keeper Ingram no chance of stopping. Quite a poignant moment for the young Smith who, exactly a year to the day, at Barnet, suffered a broken leg.

Two goals in the opening ten minutes was surely the beginning of a Christmas feast in the way of goals, but alas that was not to be, although a decent game on the whole.

Only a short report for today's game, its back to the children and the washing up that seems never ending and the Remy Martin flowing a little too easily again as was the case yesterday evening, hence an elongated period of an aching head today.

Saturday December 27th, 2014

What a strange Saturday, feels like Sunday, but I am constantly being reminded by the kids that no Dad its Saturday, your football mad, that's all you think about. No children you are wrong, is there anything on Sky Sports relating to football? Racing not bad though. But the Remy Martin after effects still linger, yet again, where's that bottle Santa?

Sunday December 28th, 2014

Now I am confused, Saturday was a Sunday and now Sunday becomes a Saturday, bottle please. My body clock is drifting far away, it has deserted me totally, the insanity of it all is too much, apparently it really is Sunday and the "Hatters" are playing Portsmouth today. My mind is a haze, have I gone totally senile overnight, or has it in fact been creeping up on me for months? What's my name again?

The Town are lining up as follows apparently; Mark Tyler, Michael Harriman, Steve McNulty, Luke Wilkinson, Scott Griffiths, Nathan Doyle, Jonathan Smith, Shaun Whalley, Andy Drury, Luke Rooney and Mark Cullen. With the following covered in blankets and freezing in the dugout; Fraser Franks, Elliot Justham, Jake Howells, Ross Lafayette, Ricky Miller, Jim Stevenson and Paul Connolly.

Luton Town 1 Portsmouth 1

The Saturday come Sunday, Sunday being Saturday feeling did not only affect me it seems. After a bright, decent game and performance on Friday, the players struggled to replicate forty eight hours later (whoever arranges two games in three days in late December is a sadist), as Luton gave a rather flat and laboured performance, following the efforts in testing, energy sapping conditions on Friday in High Wycombe. Unlike the Mary Rose, unfortunately, Portsmouth didn't sink. The effort once again for the "Hatters" can never be doubted these days, but we lacked the kind of inspiration and class required to unlock a stubborn Portsmouth team who from the outset showed that they came to stifle and left the point they so blatantly obvious came for. Portsmouth showed little sense of adventure, so not difficult to understand why their away record this season is as abysmal as it reads.

Unlike Friday Luton's creative play lacked verve despite having the boost of an early goal - an assured left footed shot by Rooney, after Whalley had intelligently played the ball into his path by showing good awareness.

The Pompey equaliser came from Wallace's low pass that Wilkinson was unable to clear and Taylor was there to tap the ball over the line.

Yes, the Remy is still in the system, don't worry though by the New year I will be quite used to it again, this is what happens when you leave the serious drinking sessions alone for a couple of years, you become used to being permanently sober, strange as it may be, but yes I have gotten used to it. Start buying Remy Martin shares in the New Year guys, Huey is back with a vengeance. Catch you next year guys….

January

Thursday January 1st, 2015
Welcome then to the year 2015, it has the potential to be a most interesting year for Luton Town Football Club. Leaving behind what was a magnificent year in contrast to those that preceded 2014. For myself, I believe this New Year can be just as fantastic as the one that now passes into history.

Whether or not the club can carry on the momentum that we have witnessed so far this season we can be proud of and delighted with the efforts of not only the playing staff and coaching staff. Also the administration and the board, because we can at last say Luton Town has a financial future, it really has been a good while since we have been able to say yes, for this supporter at least, I am looking forward with expectations of a bright future for our much loved club.

This season the home attendance has been amazing, with the away support second to no other club in League Two. If that in itself is not a reminder to the people of Luton, in general that the club is in need of a new and larger stadium. The club cannot guarantee higher status currently relying on a full stadium of 10,000 each week, until that figure be bettered with a larger capacity stadium League One is the best we can wish for financially and status worth. At the moment despite the superb feeling around the club and within the squad, until we can show higher gates top calibre players are not going to be tempted to sign for Luton Town purely for the fact that at the moment we cannot promise or command an appropriate wage structure for the first team squad.

On that point, it is easy to move on the next topic on the first day of the year, as the transfer window opens again. Speculation over the next month as to who John Still and his immediate staff will be looking at is going to be rife, already the jokes are abundant and its great banter, Thierry Henry is joining Luton not Sky, if only, images being photo-shopped of Lionel Messi in an Orange Luton shirt. As I look through the PFA list of players out of contract, I see a number of players who would fit right in with the Towns set up now, although I will refrain from actually naming names for now. One name on the list that does disappointment me somewhat is Ed. Asafu-Adjaye. To think the young lad to show great promise whilst on the Town's books, until Paul Buckle allowed him to go to Forest Green Rovers after 21 full appearances for the "Hatters" I believe he now plays for Hemel Hempstead Town; it just goes to prove that nothing is guaranteed in football. Let us at least wish the lad well in his quest to find a professional contract again soon.

Friday January 2nd 2015
The FA Cup third round game at Cambridge United's Abbey stadium is upon us tomorrow. The news is that the "Hatters" are struggling with injuries and a flu bug within the squad, of all the games to leave us short of full squad, if there is one manager in the whole of the country that I would like to see given a good tanning by John Still it has to be Richard Money. It is amazing how often this season I have read after his side have been beaten he claims they were the better side on the day but were unlucky on all counts. He must have lost all of his lucky charms many years ago if that is the case, I would love to read or hear a quote from him where he admits to being beaten by a better side on the day, however we will have to wait a long time for him to that I imagine. If they do beat the "Hatters", tomorrow I am already trying to imagine the gloating that will follow.

I have just heard that Clarke Carlisle has been removed from the "critical" listing and is now comfortable, a full recovery is possible but it will be a long road ahead, we wish him well, following his accident on December 22nd, 2014.

Saturday January 3rd, 2014
Cold, wet and totally depressing weather to welcome Luton to Cambridge, typical third Round FA Cup weather from the past to be honest, it all adds to the atmosphere, with over 2,000 "Hatters" set to converge on the Abbey stadium, that seems to be surrounded by more police than one would see at the Reading Festival. The Town's line up for this afternoons tie is as follows; Mark Tyler, Michael Harriman, Fraser Franks, Luke Wilkinson, Paul Connelly, Jim Stevenson, Jonathan Smith, Jake Howells, Andy Drury, Ricky Miller, Mark Cullen. Substitutes; Pelly Ruddock Mpanza, Alex Lacey, Charlie Walker, Luke Rooney, Elliot Justham Matt Robinson and Ross Lafayette.

Cambridge United 2 Luton Town 1
From the moment the team line-ups were announced, with McNulty injured and four other players having flu we realised it was going to be an uphill struggle.
Considering the amount of rainfall this morning, the pitch was not in too bad shape, no standing water, nothing like the Barnet game last season, but it churned up throughout the match and it turned out to be a bit of a slog for both teams.
One problem we may have had was the amount of times Cambridge managed to get a two versus one situation down our right. Harriman was up against Donaldson and Taylor in wide areas, as no-one tracked back to give Harriman cover, so a lot of crosses came from their left, but generally the crossing wasn't great, either Tyler claimed them or Elliott's knock downs fell to a white Luton shirt rather than his own team.
Somewhat against the run of early play, Drury squared the ball into Smith, who was desperately unlucky to see his near perfect drive crash against the post with the Cambridge keeper Dunn slow to move.
Mark Tyler then made a good save from Taylor, a corner played deep by Hughes, from which Coulson nodded the ball across goal, Connolly managed to clear, but only as far as the former "Hatter", whose probing shot Tyler blocked low down, despite probably not seeing it until late on.

Drury made a pass forward to the overlapping Jake Howells, whose decent cross into the box found Harriman popping up alone, his headed effort on target but easily palmed away by Dunn.
It was typical that just at the time when Luton started to settle down and find their feet, Cambridge scored. An excellent through pass from Simpson found Donaldson running through. His first touch took the ball away from goal Tyler making a genuine attempt to reach the ball, clipping Donaldson, who is the type of player who doesn't need asking twice whether he would like to fall over, with his out stretched arm, Tyler did catch him, but couldn't do much about it. Simpson's spot kick was rather tame, Tyler's right palm pushed it onto the post, but the ball went back to Simpson who swept home into the unguarded net. Similar to Mark Cullen's penalty incident in the League game at the Abbey in September, when Dunn saved in similar fashion and Cullen latched onto the rebounding ball to place beyond the keeper.
Half time came with Cambridge leading from Simpson's goal.
The "Hatters" upped their game after the break. Only Drury himself will know how he failed to put us back on equal terms, an excellent burst forward by Harriman, a perfect low teasing centre, just

out of the reach of Miller, with Drury arriving at the far post to take the ball, a splendid opportunity wasted as he fired wide across goal.

A double change brought about the welcome sight of the fit again Pelly Ruddock Mpanzu. Ross Lafayette appeared also for Connolly and Cullen respectively, Howells went to left back in a back four, Drury moved across to the left wing, with Pelly joining up on the right.

Not surprisingly Ruddock Mpanzu struggled to find the pace of the game, but was a threat against Taylor, both subs combined, turning the ball back to Smith squaring it to Stevenson, who tried his luck and whilst a decent effort it was never going to trouble Dunn. The Town were beginning to push forward more. From a Luton attack, Cambridge took hold of the ball and surged forward towards the "Hatters" goal.

Hughes won the ball from substitute Charlie Walker, who had earlier replaced the lacklustre Ricky Miller, in midfield, giving to Champion who laid on a fine pass down the left to Donaldson who ran and ran with the ball before dispatching the ball into the far corner. An effortless and class strike, 2-0.

As ever Luton did not give up the game, that is one of their characteristics this season, whatever the limitations placed through injuries and the like, giving a game up is not something they seem to understand and credit to them for that week in week out.

Harriman and Pelly attacked down the right, a low centre steered away by Coulson.

Smith was starting to get a grip in midfield, with Cambridge conceding acres of ground, a good pass found Lafayette, lovely turn, but a horribly screwed finish.

Stevenson played Harriman into trouble bestowing the ball upon Donaldson, Harriman, did brilliantly to track back and dispossess the Cambridge man.

Drury was found on the left , a low dragged cross, which Nelson simply played back to Drury, a far better centre towards the back post, Harriman taking advantage of some dozy marking by dear old Gregory Taylor, it's nice to see some things in life never change, allowing the defender to score with a header at the back post. 2-1 Luton back in with a shout.

Naturally, Cambridge looked to time waste at every given opportunity. Sadly, it is part of the game these days, but it is a horrible cowardly one and the game suffers from it. It was almost like an attack v defence training session. Cambridge pulled everyone back, clearing the ball to a none existent forward as Elliott was tiring badly at this point and Simpson had dropped back into midfield. Luton had to throw caution to the wind, leaving gaps at the back, therefore vulnerable to a counter attack. Chadwick hassled Smith into making a mistake, Wilkinson injured himself trying to stop he same player going forward, play carried on, Champion shooting low at Tyler who showed good handling as always.

In the circumstances, it was a most valiant effort against competitive opponents up for the game. Therefore, Richard Money and his Cambridge United march into the fourth round draw on Monday evening.

If I am honest I am rather upset that Richard Money made no scything remarks about the game, in fact he nearly made the admission that Luton were worthy of a draw, strange man though.

Elsewhere in the cup, there were no massive shocks on the day, although Gary Brabin's Southport did make a brave attempt at taking Derby County to a replay, but foiled in the fourth minute of added time by a Chris Martin penalty. West Bromwich made sure that new manager Tony Pulis would not be embarrassed in his first game in charge by seeing off Conference side Gateshead 7-0 at the Hawthorns.

Sunday January 4th 2015

With the FA Cup well out of the way, it is time to concentrate on the League campaign full time. Maybe time to sign an accomplished striker, I notice that Andy Johnsons name mentioned in certain quarters; whether he is the right type of player for the "Hatters", I am not sure, we shall have to see and whom John Still decides to move for if anybody.

It is also interesting to hear rumours of Harry Redknapp's interest in former Town striker Andre Gray, with whom we have a sell on clause pending, which would be a welcome boost to the finances of the club for sure.

Wednesday January 7th, 2015

Jayden Stockley has signed on loan initially for a period of one month. Until October he had been on loan to Cambridge United, the loan had meant to be until the transfer window opened, however after scoring in his first game for Richard Money the Cambridge manager decided not to use him as much as Bournemouth had hoped for and they recalled him. What was most frustrating for both the player and his parent club, due to the terms of the loan agreement Stockley has not been allowed to play for the Cherries or go to any other club until the end of the ongoing loan agreement ended at the opening of the transfer window. Cambridge though did allow special dispensation for him to appear in development games and ironically, in November during that period he plundered a well-taken hat trick against Cambridge United. He is a player of height and will be quite an addition if able to link up with and play alongside Mark Cullen in front of goal. I for one am looking forward very much to seeing what this young man may have to offer, I have heard that he does have much potential. Good luck and welcome to Kenilworth Road.

Thursday January 8th, 2015

Match day on a Thursday is not of the normal kind it has to be said, not something we will be experiencing until the inevitable arrives when we have finally qualified for either the Europa or the Champions League, something we wait to happen with baited breathe at the "Kenny". This evening it is because Sky Sports would like to showcase the best two defences in League Two, ourselves and the side I have a serious bet on to win League Two outright, Shrewsbury Town, whom I honestly believe are worthy contenders for that number one spot. Some will scorn me for such, but sometimes our heads have to rule our hearts, especially for me when my bank balance is concerned.

A pleasantly crisp kind of evening, with a most interesting match in prospect.

Will both sides totally cancel each other out, or will it be a spectacle of goals for one of the sides, I cannot see both defences surrendering their superb records, but maybe one. What worries me from the "Hatters" point of view is that Luton do seem to run out of luck when shown live on TV in recent times. Not questions of the lads freezing or anything like that, but just how the run of the green goes and the show of fortune seems to take sides against us. Despite all of that, I am looking forward to a superb game of football.

The "Hatters" team lines up as follows; Mark Tyler, Michael Harriman, Steve McNulty ,Luke Wilkinson, Scott Griffiths, Nathan Doyle, Jonathan Smith, Andy Drury, Luke Rooney, Jake Howells and Jayden Stockley. With on the bench; Ricky Miller, Fraser Franks, Mark Cullen, Elliot Justham, Shaun Whalley, Matt Robinson and Charlie Walker.

Luton Town 0 Shrewsbury Town 0
It must be looked upon as a good point against a side who are for myself favourites at least for automatic promotion. They totally turned us over in the reverse fixture and totally changed the shape of their side tonight, which really is a compliment. So yes, it is a true sign that progress has been made on Luton's part. Shrewsbury showed little adventure and parked their bus in front of Leutwilier's goal. They were rock solid at the back, the centre halves gave little away, apart from a bagful of fouls – but not many penalised, it was a miracle, following all the other ludicrous non decisions when Knight-Percival was shown red for what was a blatant late lunge on Smith, within minutes of another foul on the same player.
Debutant Jayden Stockley showed good promise and there is better to come from him but our other attacking players were not really at the races, apart from a bright and breezy opening twenty minutes.
In the first quarter of the game we looked bright, a good tempo, not allowing Shrewsbury to settle. Jake Howells had an early opportunity to put the Town in front but his shot hit the post, followed then by some superb keeping from Leutwiler making two quick saves from Scott Griffiths and Andy Drury that a lesser keeper would have struggled with one of them least alone both efforts. When Shrewsbury did settle down they were much more superior in possession and were able to retain the ball more securely than Luton, although in the final third they were not that much of a threat to Mark Tyler between the sticks.
Playing one up front was not working for Luton, especially when the service was not particularly good from midfield, but Stockley battled well against three central defenders who kept the Lone Ranger at bay most effectively, but he looks a real live wire with some strength and against lesser defenders than he faced tonight he could prove a handful.
Steve McNulty was in great form, he was blocking everything and his positioning was spot on most of the match, for me Luton's man of the match.
It is obvious that without Pelly Ruddock Mpanzu, Alex Lawless and Luke Guttridge available we are lacking some of the creativity required and against the well-organised defences, we face, as tonight with Shrewsbury and again in our next fixture against another strong defence Plymouth we are going to struggle to breakthrough and make an impression.
With this result the "Hatters" move up one place to fourth two points behind tonight's opponents but a game in hand over them, so that is something to work on.

Friday January 9th, 2015
When I read articles regarding players who think they are bigger more important than anyone else within the club they play for I have to admit I do get a little annoyed. I know the media only surmise a great deal, but the allegations that Lionel Messi is trying to get Lois Enrique fired from his position as manager of Barcelona does ring true for me. Best player in the world or not for me he needs to learn his place. He being contracted to play for the club irrespective of who the manager may or may not be. To start a campaign within the playing ranks to get the manager fired is a disgrace. Yes, granted the club are having a sticky patch results wise, but that cannot be down to only the manager, the players need to take some of the responsibility, that is one of the big problems now for me in top-flight football.
Managers get the sack too often and too easily in football for my liking. It is because of how the system works now that players always have the upper hand. When certain players have a fall out with a manager is much too easy for the other players in the squad to become influenced by others

to drop their commitment. Maybe not enough to be noticed week in week out but enough for results to slide, simply because they know they will still have a job, the manager out of favour with the players is then made the scapegoat, pressure hits him more so than the players and subsequently the board gives the manager his marching orders. It is so obvious in some cases, obviously not all, but yes it does happen, especially when in the next game with or without a new manager the team play their socks off again. The players, who let us face it, spoiled out of this world by clubs and sponsors alike already, again get their own way. In my humble opinion, something has to be done to help eradicate such incidents in football. Too many managers get the brunt of the board and also the supporters too much, more blame should be thrown upon the players, why can the board not look at the playing squad as well as the manager, that is why such happenings as at Barcelona are allowed to develop. I hear that Neymar was to be substituted in a game recently and he refused to listen to the manager and told him straight that he is not coming off, that should have been a matter for a disciplinary, but no because he is who he is that's fine. Disgraceful, does not teach the youngsters that idolise these players much of a lesson in respect does it. For me players hold too much power in their hands these days. Could you imagine Martin O'Neill, John Robinson or Archie Gemmell for example, doing such to Brian Clough? No, because players in those days had respect for their manager. Players today think they are more important than anyone is, some even think they are bigger than the club they represent, that should never be allowed. As much as I did not have much time for Sir Alex Ferguson one thing I had to admire about him was exactly what should happen within a club, if one did not like the way he managed the club they were shown where the door is. The example was more prominent for me, when David Moyes took over from Fergie, certain players did not like him from day one, I am sure we all know who that was and his influence was enough to sway others to his way of thinking. The proof was there to be seen for me because no team of United's calibre drop to the level, they began playing at, as they did overnight. Some say the factor was that Fergie purposefully left a team of old men and has-beens, which is a part of it, however not to the extent of how playing standards dropped so rapidly. Moyes was also to blame for not being strong enough to nip it in the bud and get axe players that were causing the discourse.
For me Lionel Messi and others like him should remember when they are no more there will still be a club, the mighty can fall as quickly as they rise in football, despite how talented they may be.

Saturday January 10th 2015
Apart from Luton and Shrewsbury obviously, there was a full League Two programme this afternoon. Both Burton and Wycombe kept up their winning ways, Burton winning at home 2-1 against Mansfield and Wycombe also recording a victory at Home to York City one goal to nil. Hartlepool United now under the control of seasoned campaigning manager Ronnie Moore, picked up three much needed points against Cheltenham Town, now managed by former Luton boss Paul Buckle, who since his return from the United States has been having a torrid time of it in his new managerial position, nothing changes there then.
Wycombe remain in top place followed a point behind by Burton Albion in second, who are three points ahead of Newport County in third. Shrewsbury in fourth place on 45 points with the "Hatters" sitting in fifth place two points behind Shrewsbury but with a game in hand over the clubs above them and seven points adrift of the leaders. I have a feeling that the table will begin to take a more stable shape now that the New Year is upon us and the game of "Snakes and Ladders" will dissipate at least where the top seven or eight teams are concerned now.
Luton's next game is away on Saturday at Plymouth Argyle, another difficult game.

I read somewhere earlier today that some are saying that after the Plymouth game we can expect to forge ahead with some easy games to come. I beg to differ, this is not the Conference League any longer, no game is easy, this is the Football League now and all teams are worthy of beating each other on the day irrespective of their league placing. Never take a game or a team for granted, that is my look on it.

Monday January 12th, 2015
Interesting piece of news I have just been reading, the move of former "Hatters" defender Kevin Foley from Wolverhampton Wanderers to Danish club FC Copenhagen. Foley moved from Luton to Wolves at the beginning of the 2007/2008 season after making 166 appearances for the "Hatters". At thirty years of age, Foley would have been a massive coup if maybe John Still had made a bold move for him, truth is we would never have been able to match the wage deal he would have wanted, but one can dream in moments like this. The Copenhagen side are sitting in second place in the Danish Superliga, so not a bad move at all, even the chance of European football next season, good luck to you KF.

Another piece of transfer news that will disappoint many including myself is the loan agreement made today between Richard Money the Cambridge United manager and last season "Kenny favourite" Cameron McGeehan; although I am reliably informed, JLS did make an enquiry, the player today signed for Money. I am sure that will give the man of dosh something to gloat about, especially if McGeehan is as successful there as he was for the "Hatters" last season. Nevertheless, as my good friend Mike Thomas reminded me at the time, how could he possibly turn down the chance of maybe facing Manchester United? It could even be that was the big draw for him at the end of the day and to be fair who could blame him for that?
In the Final Third Development league, the "Hatters", so called second string have played out a goalless draw at Kenilworth Road against a strong looking Brighton and Hove Albion side. Alex Lawless playing for the first time since November because of injury, he played for the first 45 minutes where the Town had plenty of chances to go ahead. At half time, Ricky Miller replaced Lawless and the chances again came and went with one rasping effort from Alex Wall that the "Seagulls" keeper Harry Doherty somehow managed to turn round the post.
It is particularly good news for the Town that Alex Lawless is at last, it has to be said though again, following his second long term injury of a fractured foot bone which he sustained I the wake of from his earlier return from a hamstring problem. Let us hope that this is the end of his injury woes and he can battle back into a first team place for the final push for promotion this season.
Andy Parry has returned to Southport on loan for a month, Southport managed by former Luton Town manager Gary Brabin. Parry has recently returned from a loan move to AFC Telford where he managed to score on three occasions on his thirteen appearances for them.
Over the weekend it was good to see also the return in the Under 18s side of Luke Trotman, following his leg break in September, the Under 18s lost 1-3 to MK Dons under 18 side, the Towns single goal coming from Alex Watkinson. The Alex's are taking over Kenilworth Road it seems.

January 16th 2015

What a man this John Leonard Still surely is, a few years back he was given the freedom of the town in Dagenham in the wake of his services when leading Dagenham and Redbridge FC into the Football League for the first time in their history. Now today he has picked up the equivalent in Luton, from the Borough Council, following the euphoria of last season when guiding the "Hatters" back where we belong. Therefore, Mr Still, free taxi rides within the town, as the great man himself said "Let all the taxi drivers of Luton remember this face" Many congratulations sir, yet another job well done. As already written, what a man.

With the transfer window now well and truly open there is more to write about for a while. Solomon Taiwo has been released by the club, unfortunately only a bit player since signing in March 2013, making just sixteen appearances for Luton in that time, he also went on loan for a short while with Conference side Dover Athletic earlier this season. In addition, winger Dave Martin is available for transfer.

Ross Lafayette has gone on loan to Vanarama, damn that gets the tongue twisted when trying to spurt out, so glad for that alone we are back in the league, Conference side Woking Town. For myself I sincerely hope he gets some games under his belt and comes back so much more match fit. To date this season, since signing from Welling United, he really has not been able to win a regular first team spot. Which from watching him quite a few times last season when at Welling, I know full well he is more than capable of commanding if given a real opportunity, however injury again has marred his progress, like so many other players in the squad this season. It does rile me when I read and hear in certain quarters some Luton supporters today saying such things a "good riddance" or "good, fuck off and don't bother coming back". Because, as I so mentioned the lad has a lot to offer this club given a good run out. When he has played he has only been given a short term to shine and let's face it in all honesty, not just with Ross but other forwards in the squad, the service has not always been the greatest, especially with such players as Lawless, Guttridge, Benson and Ruddock Mpanzu all side-lined through injury. I will stand by my convictions that I have maintained all season when we keep hearing the call for a new striker. "We have plenty of strikers adequate, but without the good service that was available to the team last season it has never been easy, especially when we play with one up front so often. The truth is if I have one criticism of our superb leader, it is that he uses that formation so much, however at the same time the man knows the job he has to do and for me overall he has worked wonders at Luton Town over the two seasons he has thus far been at the helm. Lafayette is in safe hands then at Woking under the Woking manager Garry Hill who is in the same managerial mould as our own leader of men. Some more fantastic news today is that Michael Harriman has been the go ahead by QPR boss Harry Redknapp to stay for the remainder of the season on loan. Harriman has been a terrific addition to the side so far this season it has to be agreed.

It is also interesting to realise that John Still has been in touch with the secretary of referees regarding the abysmal level of refereeing at this level that the Town have had to endure this season. One referee in particular he has pointed out is James Adcock who has in two games so far this season denied the "Hatters" three obvious penalties in two different games, the first time a few weeks ago at Burton Albion and again in our last match against Shrewsbury Town. It has to be said the sensible Mr Still does do things the correct way on occasion, instead of ranting and raving at the time, goes away first and watches the incidents and reflects on what to do before making any rash decisions or comments which could get his little footsie's dangling in the proverbial bowl of hot steamy water. A mark of a diligent man.

Saturday January 17th, 2015

With a total of just over seven hundred away tickets sold for this afternoons clash at Plymouth Argyle and the added bonus that there is also a pay on the day policy, again the Town can be sure of a bumper away contingent to support the boys.

Luke Rooney being quite doubtful to travel because of a groin injury to add to the list of players of that ilk that are injured right now. John Still yesterday explained brilliantly why it is such a hard decision for him to bring more players into the squad whilst the transfer window is open. It would have to be a player who can walk straight into the side, as Jayden Stockley was able to do with great effect last Thursday against Shrewsbury, unfortunately he was not given much protection by referee Adcock when getting kicked and shoved all over the park that evening and his will to fight did wain a little. The manager explains that having so many players of the same type injured now is a worry. Nevertheless, would it be a sensible ploy long term to bring yet another player in to saturate those positions further, it all depends if or not those players already battling their injuries are yet ready for return in the coming weeks, he will continue to assess the situation through the coming days. Mr Still also explained something for some of the more critical supporters who are making comments about all the players bought in this season so far and then sent away on loan or just not getting games as of yet. He tells us that he has two grades of players at the club, grade A, those that are ready and able to make the first team regularly right now. Followed by grade B players who have been bought in for development to play for the club in the future, those more inclined obviously to go out on loan for the time being to get first team experience elsewhere. For a bystander like myself that seems the perfect way to run a full squad. Look not just for the now, but the future also. We have a great future with all the youth players we have coming up through the ranks in Paul Drivers youth squad and of course those that JLS has bought in and subsequently loaned out. The future yes looks reasonably settled for Luton Town Football Club.

Much rain has been reported in the Plymouth area over the past couple of days, but the game is certain to go ahead Plymouth Argyle have announced.

Despite their decent position in the League the "Pilgrims" have not had a great time of it, they have not found the net in their previous four games and their last win was on December 20th when beating Dagenham and Redbridge 3-0 at Home Park. The last two matches have both ended in goalless draws, both away fixtures at York City and Southend United respectively.

Luton line up as follows; Mark Tyler, Michael Harriman, Steve McNulty, Luke Wilkinson, Scott Griffiths, Jonathan Smith, Nathan Doyle, Shaun Whalley, Andy Drury, Jake Howells and Jayden Stockley. With on the subs bench today; Alex Lacey, Alex Wall, Mark Cullen, Elliot Justham, Matt Robinson, Paul Connolly and Charlie Walker.

Jake Howells becomes the youngest player in the history of Luton Town Football Club to reach the 300 appearances milestone. To achieve this record at such an age is an amazing feat for anybody. Jake has been a massive player in his time since his debut in 2008 away to Huddersfield Town, which the Town narrowly lost 0-1. Apparently whilst playing for Luton youth he actually turned down the opportunity to sign for then Premier League clubs Fulham and Portsmouth to stay at the "Hatters", good move. Jake plays both at the back and on the wing, a natural left footed player. He can also command a central midfield position with ease, a versatile player. In addition to his three hundred appearances, he has worn the England "C" shirt on four occasions scoring his only England goal against Estonia U23s on October 12th, 2010. Because the England C appearances were only in a semi-professional context Jake was able in to turn out for Wales U21 side, as one of his grandfather's is Welsh, making his debut on August 10th, 2011 against Hungary U21s the

Welsh losing 1-2. Between 2011 and 2012, Jake made five appearances for the Welsh side. His first goal for the "Hatters" came at the Abbey Stadium in that most enthralling of games under Mick Harford when the "Hatters" came back from behind to beat Cambridge United 4-3. Let us hope we are able to witness another three hundred notched up as quickly Jake, thank you.

Plymouth Argyle 0 Luton Town 1

An almost perfect away performance, everyone contributed and performed the roles they were required. Another fantastic day for our away support considering a 500-mile roundtrip in the middle of January, particularly as the team had lost their way slightly in the last few games. It is bizarre we have a larger away support now than we ever did during our glory days in the First Division, which says something about how the club has progressed since 2008 when sent to the back of the class like scolded schoolboys.

It says lot about the performance that there no substitutions throughout the ninety minutes today, not even to run the clock down. Once Reid's goal was chalked out Drury finished with a classy controlled finish from the edge of the box we were in complete control, the longer the game went on, the less chance the hosts looked like scoring.

The Home Park pitch was in excellent condition. Luton looked very sharp from the first whistle, looking stronger and quicker on the ball from the very outset of the game.

The most eye catching aspect of the performance, was how superbly the whole team retained the ball, outstandingly well with little use of the long ball either which rarely benefits at the best of times. Admittedly Plymouth are not one of those teams who get in your face, but the "Hatters" used the ball intelligently and did not' give away cheap possession. Which was the major let down during the previous game against Shrewsbury.

Following Drury's goal Luton sat back, keeping shape. Rarely can a 1-0 away victory been achieved so comfortably, without much pressure. Plymouth looked devoid of confidence to begin with. Slowly but surely got worse and even the Seagulls perched up on the roof of the Grandstand had given up long before the end, flying away far into the afternoon and looking for a fishy or two to feast on.

As has been the case for a great deal of the season so far the "Hatter's" back four were outstanding to a man, Wilkinson had a magnificent game and he had Alessandro, a decent player it has to said, safely tucked away in his back pocket. Tyler only called up for the odd pot shot and collecting corners, when his handling was immaculate.

Doyle had total command of the midfield; Stockley linked the play well considering he was again up against three centre halves, much the same as the Shrewsbury game. It is worth mentioning that he has done pretty well against two very good defensives and is proving the reasons for Mr Stills signing him on loan. It was good to see both Whalley and Howells contribute more to the team, coming inside off the line more than they have maybe done in previous games, giving Stockley more support, they also tracked back to prevent Plymouth's wing backs getting forward.

It did make a nice change to see a game not ruined by time wasting. Neither team went out to kick the other one off the park. Although Doyle's tackle that went through Alessandro with extensive force was not his finest hour and the chances are, maybe that another referee on the day would have dispatched him with a red card.

Whalley for Rooney the only change from the Shrewsbury stalemate. It was the usual set up. The back four sitting behind, with Smith and Doyle enforcing the midfield. Drury playing behind Stockley with Whalley and Howells on the wings.

Plymouth played a system of wingbacks, tried to pass their way through us, but apart from Lee, they lacked creativity and relied on the speed of Alessandro, who looked far more dangerous in wide areas than when trying to run through the middle.

Their only ploy to score was trying to isolate Alessandro against McNulty, although with Harriman never far away, McNulty would hold him up with Harriman then sweeping the danger away.

The problem Plymouth had was that both forwards played too far apart and rarely got enough men in the box.

Stockley struggled to hold the ball up against three centre halves. They had obviously took note of Shrewsbury's tactics against him. He did find the net following a pass from Whalley and his finish was crisp clipping the ball into the top corner with a side foot finish but the offside flag was up long before the ball left his foot. Encouraging though.

After the break, Plymouth brought on Harvey another attacker and went to a 4-4-2 formation. Whilst it is normally, a risky decision to sit back on a 1-0 lead but such was the Town's defensive superiority Plymouth could have played until Pancake Day and still not scored, or probably even tested Tyler with a serious effort. Such was there play throughout the afternoon. In fact it was until the final five minutes that Plymouth built up a little spell of pressure, Reid, who for most of the game looking completely out of sorts, for one of the better forwards in this division, drove through Harriman and McNulty, Wilkinson cleared against McNulty and the ball went behind. Then Alessandro's pass found Purrington who made a beeline for the by-line, Doyle always in the right place at the right time, cleared at the expense of a corner.

With only two minutes of stoppage time added, which is a good reflection of a game, which was devoid of time wasting, and a sign of a game that has been allowed to flow, Plymouth's last chance came as Mellor won a corner against Griffiths. Thomas' in swinging corner towards the near post flicked over by McHugh.

The final whistle sounded not too long following that miss and three more points away from home secured nicely.

With Wycombe and Bury sharing the points, Shrewsbury having beaten hapless Hartlepool 3-0 and Cambridge totally smashing Newport County away 4-0, a shock result in contrast to Newport's recent form. Luton's win moved them one place up the table to fourth with Newport slipping back to fifth but only on goal difference of five in the "Hatters" favour. Shrewsbury climbed from fourth to third, two points more than the Town, Burton stayed in second following a 1-1 draw at Fratton Park against Portsmouth, with Wycombe un moved also in top spot with 51 points. Luton now five points short of top place with one game in hand, the away tie at Mansfield Town being the one that matters. At the bottom Hartlepool are already in dire trouble nine points adrift of Dagenham and Redbridge who drop into the bottom two allowing Tranmere and Carlisle to move up one place each.

Monday 19th January 2015
Six days to the game at Cheltenham and already the Town allocation of 995 seats have all but 80, been sold. With Cheltenham prepared to allocate more if those remaining tickets go. One cannot say that Luton does not have a great following of fans. In the past whilst in the old First Division, it was a standing joke for many clubs up and down the country regarding the so-called minute fan base of Luton Town. However, these days without a doubt we can boast some of the best away

following figures in the country throughout the football league and even equalling many Premier matches away ticket sales. The Town really have come a long way in such a short time since 2008 when we were dumped out of the Football League, whether it was legal or not so legal, we have risen from the embers that they tried so hard to dampen to nothing. Luton will never again be the victims of such scorn. The club and fans alike have proved that Luton Town is a club that will fight to the end and it will take more than a bunch of self-righteous hypocrites to cut the heart out of our great club and ebb the flow of the "Hatters" blood that runs so deeply in our veins. Some cannot be there week in week out because other commitments prevent it. This does not mean that one has more commitment to the club than another does, the blood runs as strongly as those who are there most weeks. We are a family; Luton Town Football Club is stronger now than ever before, long may that reign so. COYH!

Only an hour after writing the above regarding the Cheltenham game it has been announced that Cheltenham will later this week grant the "Hatters" a further 400 seats, that will make a possible away contingency of 1,395, if only the Town could fill all those seats for Saturday, what an accomplishment that would be and yes they are capable. Paul Buckle, yes finally had to mention him, must be wondering what has transformed since his departure. That is easy to answer; his name is John Leonard Still.

After his loan debut for Woking Town on Saturday, Ross Lafayette was given the thumbs up from their manager Garry Hill on his contribution to the game, nice to see him getting some good plaudits. It was great also to realise that Luton have a youth player on loan at the club I played for in my youth AFC Kempston Rovers, young Lee Hawkes making his debut for them in their 2-1 defeat at Deeping Rangers in the United Counties Premier League. Other loaned out players that made their mark at the weekend included Mark Onyemah who scored for Hampton and Richmond in their win against Harrow Borough in the Ryman Premier League.

Staying with players on loan, another member of the first team squad, Jim Stevenson, begins a loan period with Conference side Aldershot Town, the initial loan deal being for one month up to and including February 21st. Last season Jim was on loan at Dartford where he had a reasonably productive time, so here is hoping that this will be as successful for him. He has scored one goal in his two full appearances this season the goal coming away at Hartlepool United.

Thursday January 22nd 2015

Nothing has bored and irritated more this week when it comes to Luton Town and football in general than all the talk about Andy Johnson meeting with JLS that they cancelled from Monday until today. It seems that Johnson has suddenly become the only topic regarding the "Hatters" this week. Each posting on media sites I have read have questioned if he will or will not sign, if one post is not enough. Some of the comments we have endured are to be fair funny and entertaining, however, overall the repetitiveness from some is more tedious than listening to the drivel dished out on PM questions at the House of Commons, when David Cameron opens his mouth. The fact is the parties involved could not make the Monday meeting for whatever reasons, both sides, nothing sinister regarding AJ maybe signing for MK Dons or anyone else. The transfer news that interests me more is that of JLS looking at young West Ham striker Elliot Lee, son of former West Ham, Newcastle, Charlton and England player Rob Lee. Someone to look to the future with not a quick fix. Yes, for a while, Johnson may bring a little experience into the front line for the "Hatters" but the future for myself at least is much more of paramount importance. Sorry people, just my opinion. In JLS I trust, so whatever he does and whoever he decides to bring into the side is fine, however if Johnson decides the Town is not for him, I will not lose any sleep or be overly upset and in my humble opinion youth is the key to the future. In addition, I have a gut feeling that the Town will benefit more in the long term by spending another season in League Two. Boy could I become the victim of a public lynching for saying that. The younger players are still feeling their feet, a disastrous season in League One, if it did not work out would maybe blunt their confidence and the club again going backwards, when we need to move forward gradually and steadily in an upwards mode.

On a controversial note, I have been visiting a few forums not to join but solely for an insight to other clubs. I have to say that I cannot find another club that has so many negative and complaining supporters. They have differing opinions yes, but there is no disrespect and insults thrown about it all seems to be good banter, then I come back to the Luton pages/forums, and how distressing to see the negativity, the complaining, the disrespect aimed at fellow Luton supporters who may have different opinions. If I am also very honest, I have not seen other forums where one individual inserts a post and rather than make comments on that post, someone will make the same post a couple of hours later rather than make a comment on the original post. I have desisted from posting this season; it seems like a waste of my time and energy. Because what is the point, the post ignored for maybe someone else to open a similar thread rather than comment on the original of which someone else has taken the time to think up. Maybe a little plagiarism there somewhere maybe, I am not egoistical to the fact that I would command a response, but it just makes no sense in repetitive posts to outdo the previous post, it really does get rather boring and puts me off visiting the page too often. Just my thoughts but I am sure others also feel the same way, hence it seems the same posting members day in day out. At the same time, please do not misinterpret what I am saying and get the opinion that I do not find all posts interesting and worth taking note of. Some amazing posts from the past and present capture the imagination and the memories so perfectly. The trouble is some days the banal often outweighs the thought and memory provoking. How good to see that Scott Griffiths has signed for another twelve months at the "Hatters" this week, good news for a superb and dependable defender. He is obviously hoping to add more promotion credits to his CV from League Two after a winner's medal in 2010/2011 with Chesterfield.

Team wise the news is also rather uplifting, with both Luke Guttridge and Alex Lawless almost ready to resume following injuries that as far as I, at least, am concerned is superb news both have been missed for me. Whether they will start is doubtful but on the bench maybe a possibility, to rush back now would be a massive risk. Then just as I think things are going to get better we here Luke Rooney goes in for a Hernia operation on Monday, two steps forward two steps back I suppose, wish the Rooney a rapid recovery and we see him back soonest.

The end of the world as we know it is one minute closer today than yesterday on what scientists call the Doomsday clock, all amounting from the recent atrocities in the middle east that have escalated to Europe in recent weeks. They believe it is all surmounting to something quite catastrophic, I hope I am able to see the "Hatters" in the Championship at least; Jimmy D. and I get the biography out to appease those shouting out for its release. If those war mongers want to destroy each other let them go ahead but please do it on their own doorstep not ours. Just because they will never win the World Cup like as we have, they need not go to such extremes. I thought North Korea were bad enough to change the news. Apparently their mighty leader, yes he is on the heavy side isn't he, Kim Jong-Un, told his countrymen that North Korea won the World Cup and not West Germany as we were so cruelly led to believe by our lying media, damn we were so duped by FIFA and Brazil. Maybe this Saturday it is really Chel…….sea not Chel…...tenham.

Saturday 24th January 2015

I find it difficult to believe the first month of the year is near its end already. How rapidly time passes in these the latter days of life, when I wanted them to speed by they tended to drag out endlessly, nowadays when I beg them to take as long as possible and allow me to do more than physically possible I curse every minute that passes.

Cheltenham is choked to the limit today with a thousand "Hatters" and another few thousand race goers also, the forces that be really do know how to mix it up do they not. The two loves of my sporting and working life clash within a couple of miles of each other, if only today's game was an early evening or morning kick off, it would be personally the most exciting day of the year thus far.

As much as many of us dislike Richard Money and his Cambridge United at times, we cannot take away their fantastic performance against Manchester United last night in the goalless draw. If "Fergie" had still been in charge at United he would most probably have fielded a much weaker side, something I always found quite disrespectful towards their opponents, but respect to Louis Van Gaal for fielding such a strong starting eleven and an even stronger finishing eleven. The fact that the likes of Di Maria, Falcao, Van Persie and De Gea was testament to how serious he has to take the FA Cup now that there are no other trophies to chase. Cambridge along with two former "Hatters" and a former "Hatter" manager were superb in the way they defended and at times pushed forward, especially in the latter stages of the game where they could so easily have pinched the game. Cannot fault Greg Taylors defending, a few loose passes but then that would not be Greg Taylor if he did not give a few balls away. My only disappointment was that Ryan Donaldson and not Michael Nelson at the conclusion of the game awarded Man of the Match, Nelson was influential in much of the Cambridge defending, for myself a much more deserving candidate. It will be a much harder time in the replay for them, Old Trafford much more open than the Abbey Stadium, not so compact and the partisan crowd will be a massive difference to last night. However I sincerely wish them luck, this is all that I love about this our magnificent FA Cup competition.

I am though quite astonished that Louis Van Gaal can be today complaining about the refereeing last night, the ref allowed the game to flow, making the game quite entertaining. Then in the next breathe is also complaining about the Abbey Stadium pitch, his players are supposed to be some of the best footballers in Europe if not the world, so for me they should be able to handle any pitch put their way to contend with, the pitch was the same for both sides, live with it. Stop looking for excuses and accept in a dignified manner the fact that a lower placed club equalled you. Shameful!

A crisp spring like day at Cheltenham today, perfect racing and football weather.

The Hatters line up is as it was last week at Plymouth so; Mark Tyler, Michael Harriman, Scott Griffiths, Steve McNulty, Luke Wilkinson, Nathan Doyle, Jonathan Smith, Andy Drury, Jake Howells, Shaun Whalley and Jayden Stockley. With the following keeping the bench warm; Elliot Justham, Alex Lawless, Alex Lacey, Alex Wall, Mark Cullen, Matt Robinson and Ricky Miller

It is great to see Alex Lawless back in the fray albeit on the bench.

Cheltenham Town 1 Luton Town 1

For a side from the home of National Hunt racing the tactics that Cheltenham employed were quite apt with the up and over game. They were obviously happy with a point and showed zero ambition to try to win the game. As for Luton they were on the day not good enough in the final third, rarely looking like a goal would materialise in the second half. Stockley showed some promise but it is plain to see that he requires company up front for him to be successful. There seemed to be a lack of urgency in the "Hatters" play although to be fair opponents playing with such negativity did not make it easy.

Jonathan Smith was outstanding and Scott Griffiths got forward well at times. When Cullen was introduced from the bench he was maybe trying too hard I was admittedly rather upset that Richard Money made no scything remarks about the game, in fact he nearly made the admission that Luton were worthy of a draw, strange man though, but it is good to see Alex Lawless get some minutes following his lengthy lay-off.

Cheltenham were unable to retain possession for long periods, most of the time hitting long balls to Dunn, on loan from Liverpool. They did look dangerous at times though especially when on rare occasion they played the ball to the feet and able to reach Kotwica.

It was not a day to remember for the usually un-nerved McNulty. Who knows, maybe the fact he was playing against the man who gave him a lifeline by getting him to sign for Luton Town at a time he was losing faith in the game was on his mind. Football can be strange like that at times, it's not all about the physical hard man that he portrays, the mental strains are sometimes more difficult to overcome in any situation. He was making uncharacteristically for him a number of unforced errors.

Cheltenham's best move evolved when Kotwica made a powerful run down the left side, finding Dunn who in turn passed the ball through to Ferdinand, his low pass to the advancing Braham-Barrett, fortunately for the Town Griffiths managed to intercept and play into touch.

The home side took the lead when Stewart moved in from the right with the ball his low centre played into Kotwica who turned it past Tyler.

With the cheers of the home fans still ringing around the ground Scott Griffiths throw in found Andy Drury who sent a superb curling shot towards the goal. Carson the Cheltenham keeper managed to palm the ball away but only as far as Shaun Whalley who slotted home to silence the Cheltenham faithful before they had really had time to celebrate the fact they were a goal to the good.

Cheltenham began to wobble following Whalley's goal and Luton were experiencing their best spell of the game so far, but that crucial last touch was missing and they were unable to capitalise gainfully.

Luton were dominant in possession with Jonathan Smith beginning to run the show, but despite the majority of possession was unable to test Carson to the extreme.

In all the game was an abysmal affair, one that will not linger in the memories of the Luton following. Apart maybe for one instant when Steve McNulty forgot the fact was playing football, but more likely Rugby Union when he exacted a full-length rugby style diving tackle to bring Dunn crashing to the ground, arms wrapped so effectively around the lower waist. Cliff Morgan would have been proud of such a tackle if made at Cardiff Arms Park against a marauding Englishman.

Elsewhere results fortunately went the way of Luton allowing them to retain their fourth place in the table.

As for the FA Cup, today has certainly been one for the history books to mull over in years to come that is for sure, at least Jose Mourinho was gracious in defeat and to be fair he had no other choice though, unlike others we could mention. Chelsea losing at home to League One side Bradford City.

Sunday January 25th 2015

Following what has been a tremendous weekend the giant killing FA Cup victories for Bradford City against Chelsea at Stamford Bridge. Middlesbrough defeating Manchester City and Cambridge holding Manchester United to a goalless draw also; it brings back childhood memories of going to watch my then home team Bedford Town "The Eagles" at the "Ford End Road Eyrie". I, with brothers Kenny and Michael Cook, pocket money secured would walk the near to two miles from our homes in Kempston over the Queens Park footbridge, crossing the River Ouse to what was football's dream factory for us in those days. Yes, the memories come streaming back. From the age of eight, we used to look forward through the week to seeing our heroes. Such players as Mick Benning, Dave Sturrock, Steve Miles and goalkeeper Alan Collier to name but a few.

I recall from memory the ground covered on three sides, for a non-league side a formidable main stand. A covered end, which sat over the club offices and the dressing room. The players would emerge from a small tunnel from behind the goal. I remember we used to cram ourselves as close to that entrance for many of the matches we frequented before wandering around the ground as a game went on. In those days, we could move about freely from one end of the pitch to the other. The side opposite the main stand was also covered. Then at the other goal end, the slipe end, so called because of the rivers slipe beyond the wall, this end was fully open, and was on some great cup days fully packed, when the "Eyrie" was packed it was a most fantastic atmosphere that makes the goose bumps on my arms rise as I recall those fond memories now. The ground overlooked by two massive gasholders, not unlike the Kennington Oval, which always when there for cricket happens to evoke such memories as now.

"The Eagles" played in the Southern League. One of the more famous of England's non-league clubs. Well known initially for their FA Cup feat in the 1955-56 season when following victories against Biggleswade Town at home 4-0, Away to Dunstable Town winning again by four goals to nil, another away win at Eynesbury Rovers this time 4-1 and thumping Walthamstow Avenue in a 4th Qualifying Round home tie 6-0. They were drawn in the 1st Round proper at home to Leyton and winning quite majestically against league opposition 3-0, the second round bought them up against Watford again at home who they duly beat 3 goals to 2 . The third round draw, as it does now, saw the introduction of the top two divisions of the Football League and Bedford found themselves drawn away to the Mighty Arsenal at Highbury.

Arsenal were the team of the decade at the time, managed by Tom Whitaker. Bedford took a support of over 10,000 to Highbury on a cold murky afternoon and a crowd of 55,178 witnessed a pulsating and evenly matched game. Arsenal took the lead through Tapscott after just five minutes and that was how it was at the half time whistle. Arsenal went two goals ahead; again, five minutes into the half with a perfect volley that goalkeeper Terry Pope had no chance of stopping. Bedford were not going to allow that to phase them, Ronnie Steel made a pulsating run down the right wing ending with a shot across the Arsenal goal that caught the Gunners keeper, Sullivan, standing in for the legendary Jack Kelsey, off guard and hit the back of the net to give Bedford a glimmer of hope at 2-1. With six minutes remaining Bedford battled on gamely. There was no hint at all at the massive difference between the two clubs in terms of football stature. A move started by Felix "Starry" Staroscik, who played the ball inside to Arthur Adey, a pass to Harry Yates who slipped the ball between defenders for Bernard Moore to latch onto and hit the ball home for a Bedford equaliser from close distance, with time ticking down. However, Bedford were not going to sit back and wait for the final whistle. They pushed forward again and with only seconds remaining Yates sent the ball goal bound. It looked certain to being a winning goal for the underdogs of the day until a defiant outstretched leg of an Arsenal defender just managed to reach the ball and put it wide of the goal denying what would have been one of the most famous FA Cup upsets of all time. The game finished 2-2 and The Eagles wings spanned out with pride, they had held the mighty Arsenal on their own turf.

The team line-ups were:

Arsenal: Con Sullivan, Stan Charlton, Dennis Evans, Peter Goring, Jim Fotheringham, Cliff Holton, Derek Tapscott, Vic Groves, Jimmy Bloomfield and Mike Tiddy.

Bedford Town: Terry pope, Billy Cooke, Des Quinn, Douglas Farquhar, Bob Craig, Len Garwood, Ronnie Steel, Harry Yates, Bernard Moore, Arthur Adey and Felix Staroscik.

The replay played five days later at the Bedford Eyrie, a crowd of 15,306 managed to squeeze into the Ford End Road ground, which today would put a few grounds to shame if still standing, where the Eyrie once stood is now the Charles Wells brewery where such ales as Bombardier and Eagle Pale Ale are brewed.

The replay was again a lively affair, Jack Kelsey was back between the sticks for the Gunners, Bedford certainly had the better of the first half and both teams got to the half way stage without conceding. Then, virtually from the kick off every house in the whole of Bedfordshire must have shook to the rafters with the noise from the crowd who went wild with delight and expectation, the sound barriers near to breaking point, when Yates hit the ball home. Not long after it looked as though Yates had scored a second only to be ruled offside. Groves equalised for Arsenal with a diving header to spare Arsenal's blushes. Can you imagine in those days with the ball as heavy as it must have been on that dank cold and wet Thursday afternoon? Those leather balls when wet became so heavy and when headed it felt more like taking ones head to a eighteenth century cannonball with the added danger of having ones skin ripped by the laces that held the balls rubber air bag in place. I once cutting my forehead when heading one of those old-fashioned balls and not only having a cut on my head but also a blinding headache after heading the balls of the day. My style of play would have resembled that of David Beckham now if I had become a professional footballer, no, not for untold skills, but because I as Beckham shied away from having to head a ball if able. Nevertheless, getting back to the game, those guys of that era have my total respect when it comes to heading one of those lumps of leather like rocks at any time let alone when soaked through.

Bedford had taken Arsenal to extra-time, even if they lose now they would certainly come out winners in many ways. Tapscott put Arsenal ahead two minutes into extra time, but again Bedford town refused to lay down and die, they were not going to allow their eagle wings to be clipped without a fight. As the game came to its climax Bedford it seemed that Bedford had equalised through Staroscik, but was disallowed and Arsenal held on to win the replay 2-1. Bedford Town though had put up the fight of their lives.

Bedford Town: Terry Pope, Billy Cooke, Des Quinn, Douglas Farquhar, Bob Craig, Len Garwood, Ronnie Steel, Harry Yates, Bernard Moore, Arthur Adey and Felix Staroscik.

Arsenal: Jack Kelsey, Stan Charlton, Dennis Evans, Peter Goring, Jim Fotheringham, Cliff Holton, Vic Groves, Derek Tapscott, Don Roper Jimmy Bloomfield and Mike Tiddy.

When in later years one looks back it is only now that I realise the enormity of what that Bedford side achieved.

Going through the Arsenal side at that time…

Although at best, their reserve keeper Con Sullivan was a much-respected member of the team. Limited to only thirty-two appearances in a seven-season career, simply because he was overshadowed by the great Jack Kelsey, in that period keeping twenty two clean sheets and conceding only nine goals, what a record in itself, something any top class keeper today would be more than satisfied with. Jack Kelsey the man who kept him from what would most certainly been a much more illustrious career, the Welsh goalkeeper of world renowned, even in those days, rated as being one of the very best goalkeepers around during the fifties. He made forty eight appearances for wales, but what has to be remembered the amount of Internationals played in a year is much less than the games played in today's era.

Peter Goring who spent the whole of his playing time at Highbury, a total of nine seasons.

Vic Groves who made appearances for England although not at the senior level.

Jimmy Bloomfield, a superb player of his time, played for West Ham also and made appearances for the England under 23 side.

Maybe at first glance you would not think these players amounted to much but you have to look deep into their playing careers to realise their stature, I have done so but this would be turned into a book of its own maybe and not just a short chapter as I initially planned.

Obviously all of that was before our time, but the stories of that day have never died, we were bought up on such stories by our relatives and older family friends and it was such stories that would sit in our minds and hope that one day we would be able to witness similar. In 1966, we nearly got it.

However, before that there was another famous cup run to grace "The Eyrie" in the 1963-64 season.

By this time we were going to a handful of games, Bedford had former West Bromwich Albion keeper Jock Wallace along with Vernon Avis, Ron Heckman, David Skinn, Dave Sturrock and Stevie Miles. These are now legendary names in the History of Bedford Town. Jock Wallace went on to manage Glasgow Rangers in the seventies, and heralded as one of the greatest Scottish managers of recent times.

Bedford Town's later FA Cup adventures I will leave for another time.

Tuesday January 27th 2015

Yes, I know that I may yet again be repeating myself right now, but I am continually amazed at the mentality that some Luton supporters seem to portray. It genuinely is for me quite irritating and tedious constantly hearing when things go a little pear shaped in a game and results do not go the way of the "Hatters". There are it seems those within the ranks of supporters that really believe that Luton Town have a divine right to win every game and when as I say things to do not go as they seem to think it should week in week out, their heads rear from the depths. If it is not the players who are at fault it is the manager, but yes the team do have off days, it is upsetting for all of us but come on they are not robots, sometimes it may be the conditions, it may be a number of factors. I get the distinct feeling that some people seem to wish a bad game on the team sometimes just to give them an opportunity to moan.

I am sure both players and management are fully aware of what may have gone wrong on the pitch in any particular game and work on eradicating it, let's face it they want success just as much as the supporters, although some supporters maybe get it into their heads that is not the case. Now Luton have what can be described as a very happy squad in my opinion, I just hope the minority of so called fans do not allow that level to drop, because the players do see these comments.

We have quite a few injuries to key players at this time; those that are taking their places are not all experienced at this level of football some are youngsters still finding their way. I for one have to applaud John Still for not jumping in with two feet now that the transfer window is open, that has in the past, not worked and quite honestly, in my very humble opinion it would not work now.

They also seem to forget where for the past five years Luton Town were, their memory span must be so limited at times, this time last season most of us would have given anything if promised fourth place at the end of January in the Football League. Some it seems are never satisfied this is not my happy chappie mode this is the head of realism. Most of us are grateful that we shall not be in a fight to stave off relegation. That for now is enough for me.

Later this evening a strong side from the Development squad will turn out in the second round tie of The Bedfordshire Senior Cup against Stotfold at their Roker Park home, I went to Roker Park many moons ago, but that was not in Stotfold. Great name for a stadium though. Stotfold ply their trade in the Premier division of the Spartan South Midland League, which these days carries the name of Molten at the front of it for the sake of sponsorship. I do hope the moaners are ready with talons sharpened in case the Town manage to slip up tonight. Now that would give them something to harp about would it not.

Wednesday January 28th 2015

Last night Luton came out easy winners at Stotfold with a 5-0 score-line. The side, captained by Alex Lacey, dominated throughout, Charlie Walker recording a brace, other goals coming from Alex Wall, who slotted home from the penalty spot for the opener. The second coming from a Wall cross that Charlie Walker headed home. Walker's second and Luton third came from a superb long ball that he then lobbed quite clinically over the head of the Stotfold keeper. Mark Onyemah made it four with an angled shot that had the keeper well beaten. The fifth goal was one to savour, back from injury and having a most outstanding game Luke Guttridge curled the ball into the back of the net to finish the scoring, although he could have easily netted a second right on fulltime when a rasping long range shot slammed onto the post, just denying the Town a sixth. Gutts' and of course John Still will be happy that he was able to get a game under his belt and maybe even put him in contention for a place, at the very least on the bench, in Saturdays home league game against Cambridge United.

It is also good to see youngster Luke Trotman make a substitute's appearance in his comeback from his broken leg sustained in August. Taking the place of the as always dependable Alex Lacey, who for me is unlucky not to be getting a decent run in the first team, however not because he is not worthy, simply because the back four we have at the moment are having such a superb season. For Trotman to play alongside the likes of Franks, Robinson and Guttridge can be looked upon as good experience for him, another player of whom I myself have expectations of being a great asset to the Town in the coming years if he continues to develop as he has done.

With only days left before the end of the January transfer window, for me it gets more like the New Year sales on the high street each year, however I am happy that JLS is not running around like a headless chicken looking for basement bargains as some managers have done in years gone by. There is talk thought that he is still very much on the trail of Norwich City youngster Cameron McGeehan, who many of us would love to get back on a more permanent basis.

The temperature here has been plummeting over the past couple of days, and to be honest I am starting to feel quite under the weather, the old chest just not what it used to be, but that's life, at least we still have breathe I say, at least we still have breathe.

I am going to for a while, yes again folks, so please just go with it and humour me, reminisce about the days of our youth. A time when kids of fourteen years of age knew how to go out into the local parks and fields and make our own fun, no X-Box's, laptops, tablets or PlayStation to keep us locked up in our bedrooms. No danger of gun toting, knife wielding sociopathic gangs making us look over our shoulders instead of enjoying the moment. No mobile phones to distract us at any given moment, if only our kids today could experience a youthful time such as we did in our day, how much happier they would be I am sure. We had a life that is for sure.

Facebook is one of those media happenings that one either loathes or loves. Believe me, at times I am torn between the two. But one if its many pluses that helps dissipate the negatives is that without it I would not have reconnected with some great guys from my youth, especially loving so far away from Kempston these days on the banks of the Thames Estuary down here on the border with Kent and Greater London. I have mentioned Kenny Cook a few times before already and yes he is again most prominent in this little memory also along with Michael his brother. What really assisted those hidden memories to come churning back recently was linking up with one particular face from the past, Peter Parker, what a memory that man and his father seem to possess, despite his father being in his nineties. We both joined in a discussion on page for people that used to live in Kempston. Yes I may be waffling, but please be patient with me. Remember I am of that time in one's life where I should have tea cup in hand, a slight glazed over look and as I speak the shadowy mist billows in front of me as I look back and the words echo gently into submission to a picture of long ago. Sorry that is not going to happen here, you will have to put up with my scribbling instead. No Peter Parker is not Spiderman, he is Peter Parker but has a superb memory it seems. Along with Pete I also quite recently on Facebook came upon another guy, Michael "Mick" Lock who now not unlike Pete as it happens resides a million or so light years away in the Far East of our ever expanding global set of friends, his name really set the ball running for me about this particular set of memoires.

As I was saying, we were quite innovative in those days. Kempston was then known as a village but for a village it covered a large area. As I said there were no gangs like as we have today in different areas. Well not gangs in the way known as now. Our gangs were clusters of lads who loved to play football in the park from sunrise to sunset. It mattered not if the rain hammering down or snow was falling, the ground rock hard from a heavy frost, there we would be every possible moment, whether it be with proper or makeshift goalposts, coats and jumpers to substitute for posts if nothing else.

We lived in the Balliol Park area, so we named ourselves The Balliol Park Rangers, other nearby areas formed other teams and there were the Owen Close Rovers, Chantry United to name just a couple. Mick Lock was a member of Chantry United and we had some right royal clashes with them.

Balliol Park Rangers, we had some players, apart from the effigy of Arsenal's "wee" Georgie Armstrong, that being myself, I use to be quite a nifty little fellow on the wing I can tell you. I could knock over a mean cross with either foot. We had three lads who could play equally well between the sticks in Mick Cook, Lester Holly and Ray Thomas although Lester was the better of the three. Ray Thomas, that boy he had a hammer for a right foot, powerful was an understatement. Nevertheless, he should at times have also had a compass fitted because accuracy was not his forte. I once felt the power that he possessed face first; having one of his more wayward efforts slam into my face at full strength. Leaving a bruise on my face for many days. After a little tear, was up and running again without the assistance of the "magic" sponge or spray, no physio coming on to see how many of his three fingers I could or could not see, we just picked ourselves up, dusted ourselves down and started all over again, the histrionics of today's professional game nowhere to be seen. Ken Cook, a superb right foot a head of concrete and a look so menacing as he ran toward you with ball it sometimes seemed the wiser decision to just allow him through, although in all honesty a gentle soul unless of course one needled him. His brother Mick also had a good right foot, but more of a defensive punch bag rather than the puncher. There was Pete Parker as mentioned. Little red headed Jan Smith, not so little now, who was equally as speedy as myself and maybe more talented than I was, though despite being younger by a few years. He was one of our younger members along with Lester's brother Richard also, the Huckle brothers, great lads Chris and Trevor there was Mick "hacker" Panter and Mick Butcher to name but a few, must not forget Clive "Monty" Milton either, I wonder where the latter mentioned are now, we were a formidable bunch that is for sure.

Between the teams, we formed a little league between ourselves and a cup competition, great games and rivalry we had. The memories that really come to mind are that we always seemed to have tight games against Chantry and invariably Mick Lock and I would come to blows after some really quiet innocuous challenges, it was like Peter Storey and Norman Hunter clashing together, neither of us were large in build but boy could we mix it. However, you knew that despite it all there was a mutual respect that seems to be there even to this day over the miles. Can you imagine that now in these days of violence and demand of respect without earning such? These days if such happens in the local parks, the masses would come searching for you, not just with fist but also with gun, knife, machete or even sword it seems. How times have changed for the worse. Times if innocence so long forgotten, I can cry so easily cry for the youth of the day now, no realisation of freedom of movement, too much peer pressure in all they do, if only the times could return to how we used to play.

Friday January 30th 2015
Apparently, there is a threat of snow around the area of Bedfordshire today. Fingers crossed that the home game will go as planned tomorrow against last season's promotion rivals Cambridge United, whose thoughts must to a certain point be elsewhere, what with their upcoming FA Cup replay at Old Trafford looming next Tuesday. Some are saying they hope our opponents thoughts will be distracted towards that game. I am not thinking along those lines because if we are as some many hope us to do, going to gain promotion this season, we have to beat sides when they are at their best in order to think ourselves as worthy contenders. Just in case this reads as though I do not want the Town to win promotion, that is not the case, but if we are to be promoted it has to be on merit not because of our opponents mind set being elsewhere other than on playing us. For me that's like being a jockey sitting in second place of a race going to the final fence and wishing the horse in front to fall or something similar. Winning a game in such a manner is for me a false victory, I know, a win is a win however gained, but surely, it feels better when won on total merit other than any other way.

Something else that makes me smile in total bemusement is noticing people saying, "It could have been us" that are looking forward to a replay at Old Trafford. Well yes we could have beaten Cambridge in the previous round and been in the draw, but would in fact the scenario worked out in the same way had it been ourselves in the bag rather than the "U's"? The possibilities are, no. Firstly, Luton would have most likely been a different ball number; therefore not necessarily been drawn against Manchester United, so I have my doubts simply on that reason. In all honesty unless one of those glory hunters who only seem to be "true Hatters" when the Town play massive cup games. I am one of those who would rather the chance of picking up three valuable league points rather than going into a game with a cup replay to follow of such magnitude as Cambridge have and look at another fixture concern. When otherwise able to concentrate on our league campaign, as much as I love the tradition of the FA Cup, in our position as it is today I would rather the league points. Simple as that for me anyway. At the same time I would never take away the exciting prospect for the Cambridge players and supporters of the chance of again upsetting Van Gall and companies plans and dreams, I wish Cambridge genuine good fortune on Tuesday evening.

It will be yet another superb gate tomorrow with the game a sell out as far as home fans seats are concerned, I doubt thought that Cambridge will use up their full quota a trip to Old Trafford is not a cheap outing these days.

Saturday January 31st 2015

The most pleasant of days it was not by all accounts, I myself am in bed, not by choice one may add, with what can only be described as more than what they tend to call man flu. I feel like I have fallen at the first fence in the Grand National and then trampled over by each other runner of a maximum field of forty. Therefore my coverage may be even less enjoyable than those before me, simply because the strength has been sapped from me even too much to read Paul Wright's so amusing report that he has so kindly forwarded to me as always.

The Hatters lined up as follows: Mark Tyler, Michael Harriman, Steve McNulty, Luke Wilkinson, Scott Griffiths, Nathan Doyle, Jonathan Smith, Andy Drury, Shaun Whalley, Jake Howells and Jayden Stockley. Subs available were Fraser Franks, Mark Cullen, Alex Lawless, Alex Wall, Elliot Justham, Luke Guttridge and Matt Robinson.

Luton Town 3 Cambridge United 2

Luton totally controlled most first forty-five minutes with intelligent use of the ball and making Cambridge chase shadows once Drury had fired home the opening goal following goalkeeper Dunn's save from Jake Howells solo effort from a great run. Luton soon went further ahead when Drury's right sided corner found the head of Luke Wilkinson who powered the ball past the hapless Dunn to make it 2-0 to the "Hatters". The third came just before halftime when Jonathan Smith drove home a fierce shot past Dunn who was completely unsighted. The Town left the field to a rapturous reception, not a foot. put wrong during a fantastic first half that found them three goals to the good and cruising, or they were at that point.

With nothing to lose Cambridge came out fighting in the second half, maters thought were not helped after losing Luke Wilkinson to a hamstring injury and then Scott Griffiths who picked up an injury also.

Cam McGeehan had a good game, as did the rest of the Cambridge side. Following the break, they looked more organised and they took the game to the Town. One difference was the replacement of Kaikai, who had a nightmare of a first half, with Hunt, a good move on Richard Money's part. Hunt and McGeehan combined down their left which resulted in Cambridge's first goal when Hunt flicked the ball past Tyler to make it 3-1.

Cambridge found the back of the Luton net again, when a long ball from Greg Taylor which found Simpson who with a crisp finish placed the ball into the far corner, 3-2. The Luton hearts were starting to flutter as their team started to stutter a little, but without such we could not truly be Luton supporters because we have been bought up on heart attack style football and would we have it any other way. In all honesty, I doubt it. We are Luton Town, a certain style of uniqueness that we seem to thrive.

The boys held on and another three points slotted safely into the bag, thank you kindly see you next week.

Following the game, the Hatters still sit in fourth place in the league.

It was interesting whilst watching Sky Sports Special that Paul Merson made a mention of our on loan youngster Lee Angol who is at Borehamwood right now, saying that he would be a superb asset for any Championship club, for myself I hope he stays at Luton and next season JLS begins to give him some serious first team minutes. However, it will be difficult to keep a player of his calibre at Luton I believe, unless promoted at the end of this campaign.

February

Sunday February 1st 2015
Where has January gone? Passed me by that I am sure about.
Ryan Hall, formerly of Rotherham United is set to sign for Luton, an attacking midfielder by all accounts who has a good eye for goal.
Sorry, back to bed feel like the back end of a Frozen Forecast…

Monday February 2nd 2015
This damned flu is really getting to me. However, I have just had to drag myself away from the pillow to mention the signing of young Nathan Oduwa on loan for the rest of the season from Tottenham Hotspur. Nathan was capped for England at Under 18 level. JSL believes he will along with Ryan Hall; bring some much-needed speed into the Luton squad. If these two youngsters blend in as Still hopes, these could prove to be an exciting final three months to the season. Especially with Guttridge, Lawless and Mpanza returning to near match fitness, Jayden Stockley upfront does need some good service that is without saying. Which will allow him to play the style of football he thrives on. With him now staying at the club on loan until March 3rd, hopefully enough time to prove his full worth. Who knows maybe even an even longer stay, it is a fact that not many players, if at any at all, who come to Luton on loan wish to leave, such is the fantastic atmosphere and family spirit held at Luton Town.
One player who has walked through the Kenilworth Road doors as a Luton player for the final time is a guy local to where I now live Dave Martin. I was in all honesty always in the hope that he would make a bigger impression to the side, but unfortunately that was not to be, I for one wish him luck for the future.

Thursday February 5th 2015
Unfortunately, nothing has changed, but I will soldier on best I can for now. So brave and sturdy, such a tart, more like.

Friday February 6th 2015
How good to see former Luton Town loanee, albeit only a handful of appearances, Clark Carlisle being discharged from hospital following his failed suicide attempt a few days before the Christmas period. Quite miraculous considering the horrendous injuries reportedly sustained.
What really upsets me after such incidents and particularly this one, I have been reading on various social media websites individuals commenting about how irresponsible he was to walk in front of the said vehicle with no thought for the driver who was unfortunate to be in the right place at maybe the wrong time. I admit freely that the poor driver has suffered a most disturbing and horrific experience himself, that nobody should have to go through, but to totally condemn Carlisle is showing the ignorance many people still possess when it comes to depression as deep as the former footballer must have been experiencing at the time.
I am not going to try to look clever and attempt to give intelligent reasoning and statistics; anybody can sit down at their laptop and do that by reading through medical journals and the like. I will just be myself as always I do my best to be and tell how it is from another individual perceptive.

When Clark Carlisle walked from his home on that December morning, leaving behind his family, what could really have been going through that young man's thoughts is anyone's guess. Only he alone will ever really know that, whether he can recall is another matter entirely, depression is a terrible illness, in some ways it is more dangerous and terrible than cancer, but only because it is like a cancer itself, not of the physical kind but the mental. It slowly but surely eats away at you, without being fully aware. One does not even know it is there lurking in the shadows waiting to pounce, sneaky and extremely evil, relentless in its quest to win the battle that is brewing within the mind. It is the invisible enemy, not the sufferer or their closest of friends and family can detect it until too late it has the sufferer totally within its grasp. Once it has taken hold it just digs its claws deep into the mind. It plays with you like a cat may play with a mouse once it has caught it, gives the impression it has let you go and allowing normality to return until crunch there it is again, yet now more determined to take you to new lows than ever before.

I am talking from experience believe me, it strangles your mind from within, saps all good thoughts from your being, where the laughter was only moments ago rapidly taken over by a darkness that one cannot imagine if not experienced.

However, also remember, no two depressed souls are the same.

Not many years ago, I was accused whilst suffering from this devilish disease, not only by a work colleague but close family members of being lazy and no good to man or beast, I was told to my face, get a grip and get to work there is nothing wrong with you. Physically that was true, I looked as fit as I ever had done, maybe heavier set yes, but fit all the same. How could I explain what was happening to me? I could not, simply because I did not know, my energy levels would just crash within me, my levels of tolerance to anything became non-existent. I would hide away and cry, in exactly the same way that the illness was hiding away in my head at times, I was powerless, totally powerless to it. I found it so difficult to cope with anything one day, but the next everything seemed to fit into place again, for a while at least.

Some days I would just lay there and sleep all day in contrast there were other days I would be a livewire could not sleep or rest for days on end. It was a vicious circle never seeming to stop running around within my head.

One comment that sticks in my mind repeatedly was instrumental for me to write this. "Those that attempt or in fact successfully commit suicide are selfish they think not of those left to clear up the mess they leave in their wake, no thought for the poor lorry driver or train driver they have walked or jumped out in front of in their quest of selfishness."

The comment in itself is true that no one does not think of those consequences that result from the act of suicide, however selfishness has nothing to do with it, at that moment there is no rhyme, no reason the thought process of such things are tucked so far back that they are buried from one consciousness. Some things I do not believe are planned. One can be sitting at home, something clicks inside the mind, the evil that is within takes hold without warning. It can be so strong that one cannot fight it off. The thought process can be so rapid, you do not have the time or the reasoning at that moment to fight back. It can all happen in a split second, with some there is no going back, the determination; maybe the whole pain of nothingness takes you on a helter skelter ride, falling deeper and deeper, each step you take nearer to the desired goal that the evil sickness has placed in your mind.

I had that feeling on one occasion, it was not strength of mind that saved me, I was one of the fortunate ones, who not so much fought it off, but in fact did not have and could not find the strength to move for that final moment. There was no thought process telling me it was wrong, no pang of guilt, the feeling just suddenly dissipated, that was not my strength that was more like the disease wanting to see how far it could take me, this time I was lucky. Who knows what is still lurking in those dark hidden depths, if it is there believe me I am not aware of it, what will trigger a new assault on my mental being? No one knows, I do not know, for now I am free of its clutches, but I say for now, because it is the sneakiest of devils that will play with your mind and your body for year upon year before deciding the time is right again.

So please as much as, yes one should think of the consequences and the turmoil that is left in the wake of such an act, others should also understand the turmoil that has erupted like the most violent of volcanoes in ones thoughts. The human mind is a complex and most fragile element of our being.

Also, look out for the signs…. The problem there is that there are no set signs.

My young daughter asked the scariest question following a religious knowledge class at school a few days ago, "Dad, do you believe in the Devil?" I wanted to say "Yes, because I have met him." However, how can I give such a reply to a sweet dear seven-year-old girl, full of innocence? Simple I cannot, so I said if there is a God then there must be a Devil.

Oxford United are our next obstacle a side we have already beaten this season at home, beating them two goals to nil on that occasion with goals from Luke Wilkinson and Jake Howells in front of a solid 9,100 gate, there will not be so many tomorrow, although I do predict some fun before and maybe after the game. The Oxford lot fancy themselves when the "Hatters" come to town, calm it lads (laughing cynically).

Oxfords new signing Irishman Patrick Hoban is adamant in their local press that he will score his first goal for the club against the "Hatters" tomorrow. Good news on that front, defensive matters, is that Luke Wilkinson has been deemed fit by manager John Still following his hamstring scare last weekend and is likely to start alongside Steve McNulty in an effort to keep the bragging striker at bay.

Another new signing hoping to make a mark in the game tomorrow will be the Towns loaned Nathan Oduwa from Spurs. Who admitted that despite loan offers earlier in the season that he turned down, he was waiting for the right contract for him rather than rush into anything and claiming this is the right move at the right time for him, a very level headed young man by the sound of it. Looking forward very much to seeing what he may have to offer the "Hatters".

Fifty-seven years to the day at six minutes past the fifteenth hour, Munich airport, a plane carrying the Manchester United team home from a European Cup game crashed on take-off, it was without doubt one of the bleakest days in the history of British football. The club was all but wiped out on that fateful day and we must remember them with grief. I do not care that we may not be great lovers of the club these days. However, if you have a heart and a true soul one should for a moment think of those lost, England lost a young man who could so easily have turned out to be one of the greatest players to ever don the white shirt and the three lions badge in Duncan Edwards, taken much too young. Along with Duncan who lost his fight for life fifteen days after the crash, those players that perished were, Roger Byrne, Mark Jones, Tommy Taylor, Eddie Coleman, Liam Whelan, David Pegg, and Geoff Bent. In addition, chief coach Bert Whalley, along with fourteen other souls, including one of Manchester City's greatest ever goalkeepers Frank Swift who was travelling with the club in the capacity of journalist.

Those that miraculously survived were the players, Bill Foulkes, goalkeeper Harry Gregg was cited later for continuously returning to the plane's fuselage area to assist with trying to save others, John Berry, Jackie Blanchflower, Bobby Charlton, Ken Morgans, Albert Scanlon, Dennis Violet, Ray Wood and manager Matt Busby, along with another ten persons.

Saturday February 7th 2015

For Luton Town supporters an away day to Oxford is always something of a nightmare for some, the local authorities always seem to go totally over the top when the "Hatters" come to town. The referee in his infinite wisdom decided that an eleven thirty pitch inspection was required. Maybe this was a tactical ploy in the hope of a mid-morning invasion of the city by the marauding Luton masses, over two thousand expected to travel the short distance to see their club, we shall never know the true reasoning but that is just one from my own conspirator's point of view.

For this game, with myself still well and truly poleaxed, my good friend Mike Thomas offered to give his short but sweet insight into the match and the pre match build up on the way to the ground.

So take it away Lord T., that's what I tend to call him at times ever since he realised I was a Surrey CCC fan and his name for me Sir Percy, of Percy Fender fame. I have on occasion attempted to educate the man, the chances of seeing better cricket at the Oval rather than the Northants County ground. However, all to no avail, I thought I was stubborn, but if nothing else, the man is loyal to the cause and not a man for mincing his words I have given up any hope of him ever reconsidering.

The day did not begin as brightly as the boys could have wished. Despite parking in a local village a good two miles adrift of the Kassam Stadium, attempts to enter the village pub were instantly diverted with Ivan the giant guarding the door with the look of a menacing Cossack. Who, without a hint of emotion in his voice advised them that Luton supporters were not to be allowed into the pub on the orders from the local constabulary. I have to wonder sometimes how for a few hours each Saturday this wonderful democratic country suddenly becomes a police state, civil liberties totally discarded like a partially eaten Pukka Pie. Mike is at an age in all fairness that, well he is not actually looking like Ray Winston out for a spot of bovver down New Cross Gate. More your professor of human habits, and his best mate Chris, yes there are a lot of us it seems apparently older and more reserved looking than Mike. So where the threat of a pool cue stuck down the trouser leg came into effect and two middle age gentleman obstructed in their quest of a pint and a sandwich I fathom to comprehend. Most probably Ivan himself was more menacing to the locals than ever Mike and Chris could ever have been, but that is how it seems to be when Luton travel away to certain towns and cities it appears.

With that plan of action totally thwarted, they moved on, most probably a little bemused at the way things had panned out so far.

With no hope it seemed of getting that pint and sandwich in the near future, our hapless pair ventured into a burger bar to sample what could only be described as an overcharged strip of so-called meat, resembling something like a carpet remnant placed between two pieces of breaded bun. Appetising not, but it sufficed, despite the fact they had to munch their so-called burgers on the street with a certain lack of decorum. Yet another kick in the teeth from the City of Oxford, it is no wonder that Mike plums for the sofa on a cold Saturday afternoon rather than spend pound upon pound just to be treated like a miscreant of dubious being. Entering the local vicinity of Oxford United's new stadium, they sauntered over to towards the bowling alley come sports bar, where yet again they were stopped in their tracks as if they were more like Kublai Khan attempting to ransack a Chinese city. No away fans being permitted to enter this establishment either. They stayed at the door chatting and having some friendly banter with the two door persons, we must be courteous and after some fine conversation, the door attendants came to their senses. They realising, it was not Ronnie and Reggie Kray with snooker ball filled socks and a baseball bat under the arm with intent to cause damage to the bar and locals alike and allowed our two intrepid travellers to pass through the doors of what must have been a salubrious drinking palace the way it was being so closely guarded. Mike thought to himself. "What if it was seventeen Accrington Stanley supporters that had travelled down from Lancashire, would they also have been such welcoming behaviour?" Doubtful at best.

After a much welcomed and deserved pint and watching the conclusion of Spurs versus Arsenal on the big screen they made their way to the Kassam Stadium, where again they were thrown back in time to mid-seventies to late eighties where regardless of age or gender each and every "Hatter" was being searched. So much for progress, it seems.

Mike observes on entering the ground that it does not stand in good stead for any Luton supporter who is hoping and waiting for the Town to build and move to a new stadium. Especially, when one enters the Kassam, the fact that the place is miles from anywhere and then the shattering realisation that it is at best a three-sided affair. I wonder if big Bob Maxwell squandered part of the funds from beyond the grave to halt proceedings at any time.

Luton line up as follows: Mark Tyler, Michael Harriman, Steve McNulty, Luke Wilkinson, Jake Howells, Nathan Doyle, Jonathan Smith, Andy Drury, Shaun Whalley, Ryan Hall and Jayden Stockley. With those watching from the dug-out: Alex Lacey, Elliott Justham, Luke Guttridge, Matt Robinson, Mark Cullen, Nathan Oduwa and Alex Wall.

With Scott Griffiths, injured, new signing Ryan Hall took over.

Oxford United 1 Luton Town 1

Well Mike has the same thoughts as myself regarding this, 4-5-1 or as some will see it 4-2-3-1 is not the way we have been bought up on football, the old ways are still the best a traditional 4-4-2 much more enjoyable and palatable to watch. Mikes observation is that only one team can carry such a formation off and have success, but only because they are graced with such players as Eden Hazard, Oscar and the likes, not Whalley and Drury. Luton are not the greatest of exponents of such a formation. Not helped, by having some thirty to forty yard gap, between the midfield trio and lone striker Jayden Stockley. Whom just five weeks into his tenure at Kenilworth Road must have already shortened his life span by a few years due to his non-stop running after more often than not lost causes, one can only assume Luton failed in their bid to sign Haile Gebrselassie to play as the lone marathon runner up front role.

Despite what can only be described a pretty lacklustre opening thirty five minutes with Luton looking defensively solid but totally ineffective going forward, a quick break, a deflection and the ball falls to Stockley who in a slow motion effect lunge pokes the ball over the line to put Luton a goal in front.

Here we go, or better to the point, here we don't go, Andy Drury who had a mare of a game, pondering where to send the ball next gifts the ball to Oxford and following a scramble the ball crosses the line with seconds remaining to the half time break, 1-1.

Oxford tails are bristling after the break; they have several chances but fortunately, for the "Hatters" squandered away to nothing. Luton aimlessly hoofing the ball forward hopeful on finding Stockley, I hear that is closer to the Manchester United tactics these days also. John Still finally awakes from his slumber, realising that a change is required with the way Luton are playing. As ineffective as it has been thus far and introduces new loan signing Nathan Oduwa into the fray, tall dark and lightning fast, within five minutes of being on the pitch he shows more attacking intent with a couple of runs than the rest of the team in the past sixty five minutes. Cullen and Wall also come into play, Stockley is replaced by Wall most probably needed to be administered oxygen and a session on the defibrillator.

Suddenly the game comes alive. end to end stuff, both sides see chances go begging, Alex Walls takes a free kick with only minutes remaining from twenty five yards out that the keeper does exceptionally well to keep out, parries it to Cullen who somehow totally misses the target, although he was flagged offside by a linesman who maybe had Luton down a draw on his fixed odds coupon with Paddy Power.

On the leaving the ground it seems most Luton fans walked away happy to come out with a draw, but if like so many supporters they haver aspirations of a back to back promotion this was a game they should have been looking to win. The negative tactics are surprising when the Town definitely have players capable of much better, but at times seem shackled by the 4-5-1 format. If Oduwa is not in the starting line-up for Tuesdays home game against York City there is something very wrong, York are a side we should be taking the game to from the outset.

Leaving the ground, the large Luton contingency was met with what appeared to be every member of the Thames Valley police force. Maybe they decided on having an outing to enable a glimpse of the best away support in the country. Or, more likely maximum overtime being employed and enjoyed, there were horses, riot police and although maybe there in the wings but not actually seen a fleet of helicopters ready to swarm up and down like Aussie sheep farmers herding their sheep from the skies. Football fans are being treated no better than the eighties when pushed and shoved about like condemned cattle rather than treated like human beings, or is it just because it is Luton Town, are we really deserving of such a poor reputation?

As for Mike whom I thank for this superb insight to a day out with the "Hatter" It is back to the sofa and the next book for him, realising that he is not really missing a great deal.

Luton remain in fourth place. Nevertheless, it really is a question of how long we can stay there unless points are picked up, yes we are again eight games without a defeat in the league, but six of those games have been draws.

Monday February 9th 2015

As much as I am a great fan of what John Still has achieved in such a short while, this does not mean I am rapidly having a change of heart regarding him. I sometimes believe he needs to go back to the drawing board, return to the basic 4-4-2, allow players to play to their strengths, not as my friend Mike Thomas so perfectly puts it, shackle them to a formation that is clearly not bringing dividends. I have always made it clear that I am a great fan of the old style football, allow players to get out there, play to their individual strengths, back to the sixties and seventies era when the likes of Best, Law, Charlton, Osgood, Hudson and others were not shackled but given total licence to express themselves. For me too much emphasis is made these days on coaches trying to run the game from the touchline with diagrams and orders that tend to totally bamboozle players, yes, it may be likened to a game of chess rather than football at times. I would love to see players allowed to run at defences both down the flanks and through the centre, how I long for the dazzling twist and turns of Best, the strength and ability to run at players of Greaves, the ingenuity of Hudson and Baldwin. The game run from the middle of the pitch by generals such as the best in the game Bobby Moore and Ian Ure, not from the side-lines, orchestrated and choreographed from the tablet or note pad of Mourinho and Pellegrini. Some say football is better now than ever before, sorry guys but I disagree, the excitement of old has gone, for me everything gets clogged up in midfield with this tactic and that, the magic and the excitement has long gone. We knocked him as a manager, but Keegan had the right idea, let the players do their thing allow the game to flow, exciting attacking football, okay the defensive side was a shambles at times but all the more exciting I say.

Back to Luton, JLS has been quoted that he was looking to inject some pace into the squad and hopefully he has done so by bringing in Nathan Oduwa. Surely then this is the time to revert back to a 4-4-2 stance us the likes of Oduwa and Whalley, their pace on the flanks and Ruddock Mpanzu's strength in the middle there to support a front pairing of Stockley and Cullen who would in my opinion complement each other, Stockley's strength able to assist Cullen. Maybe, I am very wrong but that is how I see it. At least it's a positive move not the negativity we have been seeing recently, granted with all the injuries the managers hand have been tied somewhat but surely this is the time now to gamble and see if it will work, because the 4-5-1 mode is definitely not doing it for me at the moment.

Tuesday February 10th 2015

I was having a word with Mike Thomas again regarding Saturday's game. He bought up a most valid point within his observations. That it is very typical of Luton this season to play the game like a war of attrition, whereas we attempt to grind down the opposition for the first seventy minutes and then rely on them getting tired and we then pounce on them, a very risky game to play, although effective at times. But, seriously he has a point and that is worrying, it is not going to always work, we should be attacking from the off, this negative approach of recent games is definitely not effective. I just wonder what tactics will be employed this evening against York City. We need a more positive game plan, last season we were glutinous in front of goal. I cannot think it has been because we no longer have the likes of Andre Gray because in reality we do have players capable of scoring goals, maybe we should be questioning the lack of service providers at the moment rather than the lack of strikers. I hear and read day in day out that the strikers are not doing their jobs, but a striker can only be effective if given the adequate service.

It is actually very strange how vociferous I seem to be when in the writing mode, however when face to face I seem to say little, I often sit watch and listen rather than open my mouth. This also said before some years ago. I recall one day at the racing stables I was based at Himley, just west of Wolverhampton and a little North of Dudley in the Black Country. I had that day worked a horse that used to win a chase or two for us when I was with trainer Sally Oliver, the owner a quite glamorous if not older woman had come to watch her horse, Hope End, do some work in preparation for a race that coming weekend. After the work session, I was riding back into the yard on her horse and she enquired how he was. Usually the lads would make a bee line to talk with this owner who was quite charming as well as glamorous. However, I just told her enough, with no waffle just enough to let her know that the horse was right. Ready and in good shape and how he had worked that morning, the ins and outs I can no longer recall, but Hope End was always a perfect horse to ride, genuine and honest throughout, so most probably just a straight forward piece of had been done. From the look on her face I believe she expected more, but said nothing, a smile and a pat of the horses' neck and she was on her way. It was only later that evening when down the local pub that Jacqui, the trainers step daughter mentioned to me. Jacqui a most talented lady jockey of her era it has to be mentioned, said Huey you were bought up in conversation in the house earlier by Hope Ends owner, she says you are a strange one, do not say much and questioning your evaluation of her horse this morning. I was surprised; I have to say, because I always thought I was quite concise in my reports after riding work to all owners. Jacqui continued then to say, well Dad, Henry, was straight to your defence, saying that you are of a quiet nature yes, but strange you are not, just straight to the point, you get no waffle just the facts, if Huey says your horse worked well, believe me your horse worked well. If there was a problem, you would have known, he is not one to bullshit to owners who are told what they want to hear, Huey will not do that he will tell you exactly how it is, when done, he is done. The horse being his concern, not the owner. That was so true. I always thought, although I had known Henry for many years that he did not really understand me either. However, he understood me totally. If I have nothing to say I say nothing, I do not talk for the sake of it to please others, I say what is on my mind, what I have observed, if others do not like what I say that's fine, but at least it is my true thoughts and opinions not anyone else's my own. The same goes now. Actually, I seem to say more when writing than I would ever say with my mouth. So, anything I say may not be agreeable to some or even many nut at least I say it as how I see it and it is my true opinion. Sometimes within this book I may totally contradict what I may have said at an earlier date, but that is simply because like that horse one day what seems right may on another occasion be totally different and relative to that moment. Just for the record, Hope End ran a couple of days later and won by a distance at Stratford.

Now, York City are our opponents this evening, they are second from the bottom in the league, however for me that means nothing, it does not mean they are going to be easy pickings, an easy three points despite what many are expecting. To be honest I do not look upon any side as easy pickings. We as supporters, yes do at times kid ourselves that Luton can beat anyone. Yes sometimes we do play to that vein and yes we can beat the best of them. However, we are also so very unpredictable. As unfortunately, has been the case all season. Injuries and the like have not helped matters. Continuity within the starting line ups has not been something the management team has been able to rely on this season. Hence, sometimes having to play formations that many of us including myself, are not happy with. Yet again, we have two new additions to the side who are going to take time to get used to the Luton set up. No player is expected to just slot in naturally and work wonders from day one, sometimes it happens but let us be realistic that is not very often, there have been too many upheavals and forced changes this season to be able to honestly boast a settled side. That said there have been games where we have not played well enough and that lies, not only with management, but the players also. One factor alone, cannot be blamed, it is up to them to get it right, how perfect it would be though for the opposition to conform to any best-laid plan, no opposing team is the same as the last one or the next one and things are not always going to go to plan. In all honesty, I believe the Luton are fortunate to be in the position they still find themselves in the league table. When we did have a stable side we had one heck of a superb winning run so it proves when the side is balanced and we have a semblance of continuity the Town do get the results. However, we have in recent weeks been hampered by long term and small niggled injuries alike, since the club suffered that flu breakout things have been not as good, maybe players have been affected by that, flu is not something that shakes off easily, it can sap a great deal of strength from any individual and not even be noticed. Since he had flu, for instance, Mark Cullen has been virtually keeping the bench warm, one does not become a bad player overnight, therefore is there actually an underlying situation that they are trying to work out? Only the management and the player can know that for sure, all I do know is if he was totally right he would be in the starting side. Some are trying to assume that maybe he has upset the manager, if that was so would he be even on the bench, would he have been loaned out? For me I believe once the squad is more settled and an element of continuity is back in the team the results will start to come again, patience is something we all need at this time and get behind the players totally not on their backs. As I say that is my opinion not as a happy chappy but as a realist.

The Luton line up for tonight's game is: Mark Tyler, Michael Harriman, Steve McNulty, Luke Wilkinson, Jake Howells, Nathan Doyle, Jonathan Smith, Andy Drury, Ryan Hall, Jayden Stockley and Nathan Oduwa. Viewing from the confines of the subs bench are: Alex Wall, Elliot Justham, Mark Cullen, Luke Guttridge, Matt Robinson, Alex Lacey and Shaun Whalley.

Luton Town 2 York City 2

Just one change from Saturday's drawn game at Oxford. Nathan Oduwa, replacing Shaun Whalley, who reverts to the bench.

Although they looked the better side on the ball York were rarely a threat to Mark Tyler's goal in the first half.

Luton's build ups were patient, but with the Minsters defending in numbers it was difficult to break through. At times the "Hatters" wasted opportunity in trying the long ball forward approach instead of looking to the pace of both Ryan Hall and Oduwa who had a good game, some good linking up between the two at times, but York dealt with anything thrown at them quite comfortably.

As halftime approached, both sides produced a couple of good chances. A fierce effort by Carson that Doyle was able to block effectively and Tyler forced to make a decent from Carson who again sent a powerful shot on target. Jayden Stockley was unlucky to see a fine header cleared off the line from a Drury set piece, so half time arrived to find both sides lacking too much in the final third of the field.

After the break, York took the initiative, placing the Town defence under increased pressure. Luke Wilkinson was definitely having problems with an injury that he had picked up and replaced by Alex Lacey. Lacey who was apparently also not in the best of health carrying some kind of illness it was learnt later, such it seems is the struggle that John Still is faced with to find a fully fit side to field at the moment.

The York keeper Olejnik sent a long ball forward to Hyde who was able to beat Lacey with some ease, a pass to Coulson on the right who floated his centre towards Carson, who got the better of Michael Harriman to nod the ball past Mark Tyler to score and take a deserved lead, 0-1.

Mark Cullen replaced the yet again ineffective Drury who I am surprised to be having a torrid past couple of games so soon after being nominated for the league's player of the month, a player does not become bad overnight which really makes me wonder if even he is fully fit. Others will disagree and say he is just useless as I keep reading, but I for some reason cannot totally agree with that, he produces some superb crosses at times and last month played some superb football.

Immediately following the substitution York went further ahead to stun the Luton fans, the ever dangerous Coulson receiving the ball from Sinclair and placed the ball perfectly across and out of Tyler's reach into the far corner, a two goal lead and looking quite comfortable and deserving of it.

Hyde what was adjudged to be a dangerous high challenge on Nathan Doyle which the referee did not hesitate in bringing out the red card, York down to ten men, although a little harsh maybe.

Before Hyde's sending off, Luton looked a very poor second best, their passing was quite abysmal it has to be said and York read Luton with ease and foiling any attacking movement.

Ryan Hall who it has to mentioned seem to have a more settled game than that of his debut at Oxford was substituted for Shaun Whalley.

The tide of the game turned drastically Luton suddenly came to life, the two subs Cullen and Whalley the difference.

Whalley and Jonathan Smith attacked down the right flank forcing Benning to give away a corner that was taken by Whalley who sent a low ball in that was intercepted by Cullen to score a well-taken goal, the "Hatters" were fighting back and the deficit now just the one goal.

Nathan Oduwa was being blatantly man-handled by Lowe but incredibly the referee ended up talking to the Luton player rather than Lowe.

Mark Tyler was asked to make a quite superb save to down to his left to deny Coulson and York a third goal which would have all but killed the game.

The "Hatters" equalizer came from Whalley's run, going past two light blue shirted defenders and placing an inch perfect pass for Cullen to get to and drive the ball well out of the reach of Olejnik. 2-2, Kenilworth Road erupted. They were obviously envisaging more of the same and maybe even stealing the game from York completely.

Steve McNulty can on occasion make some rash decisions, he certainly did this evening, went in rather high and could also be interpreted as showing his studs and the referee for the second time in the game did not hesitate in bringing out the red card, both sides now down to ten men. Could there be another twist in the tale, the second half a totally different game to the first.

Following McNulty's red card the "Hatters" found themselves on the back foot again and put under increasing pressure at the back, fortunately able to hold off their opponents and settle for a 2-2 draw, a totally different result than expected before kick-off, but happy in the end to come away with a point in the end.

The main concern following the game now is that two more players are injured, both Luke Wilkinson and Nathan Doyle and to add to that Steve McNulty is looking at a lengthy suspension. We can only hope that players like Ruddock Mpanzu, Guttridge and Lawless are close enough to fitness in time for Saturday's home game against Carlisle United. It will be most interesting to see who will be called up for the central defenders roles.

The "Hatters", following this draw slip one place to fifth, being leapfrogged by Southend United.

Friday February 13th 2015
It transpires that Nathan Doyle could be out for anything up to six weeks with a knee injury and Luke Wilkinson is also quite doubtful.

As for Steve McNulty, after appealing against his red card on Tuesday night and losing he now faces a four match ban, which is crippling for the "Hatters" right now.

It never just rains at Kenilworth Road does it, it simply pours.

The writing was on the wall for a few days really and after only thirteen games in charge at Cheltenham, former town boss Paul Buckle has been given his marching orders following a truly torrid time. To be honest I feel for any manager that is sacked so quickly, patience though is something totally lacking in football worldwide these days sadly.

I was actually stunned earlier this week to read the back page headlines that Leicester were to sack Nigel Pearson, although they did not in the end it riles me when I see these clubs get promoted to the Premier league and from day one it is on the cards that they are going to struggle against the big boys. After the miracle, Pearson orchestrated last season to get the "Foxes" promoted into the top flight, the revenue he won them, it would be criminal to sack him. We always hear how clubs up and down the country ask for loyalty from their employees, but surely, that should be a two-way affair, loyalty from the employers also. Too many clubs are too quick to look at the manager rather than the players on the park not doing the jobs some are paid ridiculously immoral amounts for. In this instance I cannot say that about the Leicester players this season though, they have played their socks off but some results have just not gone their way, management and players at that club this season should be applauded for their concerted efforts and they are still determined to fight what looks at times to be a lost cause. I for one wish them well.

Another back page that really got my goat earlier this week was that discussing the fact that Raheem Sterling despite being given a 100% pay rise of sorts that will bring him to £11m is still not entirely happy. This same player not too long ago was crying at how tired he was. I get extremely pissed off when I hear these players asking for more money when already on ridiculous telephone number salaries. The papers and fans call them heroes at times, I have to ask and if I offend anyone one so be it, but what do they really and truly do that is so heroic? For me nothing, nothing whatsoever.

There are heroic sportsmen but not in many lines of sport, I will call snowboarders not heroic, just damned crazy, although I do admire them immensely. Many will question why I name National Hunt, jump, jockeys as heroic. Not because I was in the game myself no, but simply because they are, they do not for a moment think or ask for stupid amounts of money to do the sport they love, because let's face it jump jockeys do not get that great remuneration for the jobs they do, that's why yes it is done purely for love. I cringe when I see footballers get a knock and go rolling around the floor as if their leg is about to amputated. Watch a jump jockey after taking a crashing fall, at first it sometimes looks as if poleaxed, they are motionless on the ground, they catch their breath and eighty per cent get up and shake whatever injury they may off. No big fuss, just get back to the weighing room and prepare for the next ride, sometimes in pain, but despite that pain go out and do the job again. Yes, there are sometimes horrific injuries in football, but let us be honest, and fair most of those on field histrionics are pathetic at best.

I know jockeys who work every day of the year, in the morning they will go to the stables ride as many as eight horses. Sometimes even more, riding on the gallops and schooling is no walk in the park either. They do not then go and put their feet up and their every whim pampered for, they majority of them then have to get behind the wheel and drive for hours to get to the racecourse they are booked at, some in the longer days of the year will do two racecourses, one in the afternoon another in the evening. For example, after a 7am start, no real break before driving to the races. Let us say for instance riding four or five races on an average day. Believe me race riding is a strenuous affair, some sap every ounce of strength from your body and you will have if riding in the next race also, what with having to sort yourself out for the next, weigh out walk to the paddock, giving about on average about a five minute break between races. Then after racing one still has to again drive home, sometimes not arriving home until late evening. A few hours' sleep and it all begins again. No complaints about being tired no tantrums, just get on with it. Be honest could anyone see the majority of our highly paid pampered footballers being able to keep that up for a month let alone all year? I doubt that very much, so yes when I hear these guys complaining and demanding more money I do cringe and get totally pissed off.

Oh boy yes I do love a good rant and rave sometimes, it helps the blood flow faster and keeps the warmth in (laughing).

Saturday February 14th 2015

Carlisle at home, a game some are relishing as they look forward to what they hope will be a re-enactment of the "Valentine's Day Massacre." In relation to the score line, I though, have my reservations on that front, looking back to Tuesday evening when if not for the time added on at the end of the ninety minutes at home to Shrewsbury they could well have beaten the high flying Shrews. But, as it was in the six added on minutes following Charlie Wyke's sixty sixth minute goal, Mickey Demetriou and James Collins respectively broke the Cumbrian sides hearts with two quick fire goals in added time. Sending the Shrews to the top of the table following Burton Albion's goalless draw at home to AFC Wimbledon and Wycombe Wanderers falling prey at home 0-2 against another club vying for automatic promotion or the play offs Plymouth Argyle. The top of League two really hotting up now.

As already mentioned the "Hatters" are experiencing selection problems at the moment for all the wrong reasons. With so many players out on loan already and the injury list mounting up daily and to add to it all McNulty's four games ban I do not envy John Still and his coaching team at all, it is going to be difficult finding a good balance out there this afternoon.

However after what must have been a most harrowing time the guys came up with a line-up that should suffice in winning three points later, they have selected as follows, to face Carlisle United: Mark Tyler, Michael Harriman, Fraser Franks, Luke Wilkinson, Scott Griffiths, Andy Drury, Jonathan Smith, Matt Robinson, Nathan Oduwa, Jayden Stockley and Mark Cullen. Keeping John Still company on the subs bench. Alex Lacey, Jake Howells, Elliot Justham, Shaun Whalley, Pelly Ruddock Mpanzu, Luke Guttridge and Ryan Hall.

Luton Town 1 Carlisle United 0

A crowd of 8,502 witnessed a Luton Town gain a most professional and well-deserved three points, although maybe not the envisaged "Valentine's Day Massacre" but a superb performance all the same, from what seemed a rejuvenated "Hatters" following the performance experienced on Tuesday evening against York City.

Despite missing skipper Steve McNulty, the defence was in superb form, I myself happy to see Fraser Franks getting the opportunity to prove himself again, for me he is under estimated by some of the Luton support. I sincerely hope he proves me right over the next few games and is able to cement his place in the side. Luke Wilkinson deemed fit to play following his groin injury scare, but to be fair did not look very comfortable at times. I was though surprised to see following recent performances Shaun Whalley on the bench again. Robinson and Franks at the back certainly played well to subdue any aerial bombardment from Carlisle's long ball tactics. Mark Cullen looks to have won his confidence back and again had a very good match.

Keith Curles' side were well organised at the back but their prowess up front was their let down if anything. It did seem though that time wasting was paramount in The Northern clubs agenda. Even from early in the first half, although referee James Linington said or did nothing to stop them doing so throughout the game. Something that is too rife in League Two this season and continually allowed to be carried on. Something needs to be done, no wonder then that some clubs attendances are falling weekly, not what they pay their money for, to see their sides blatantly wasting time week in week out, thank you "Hatters" for not employing such tactics on a regular basis at least.

Jayden Stockley's work rate was again second to none the lad certainly knows how to put in a shift.

Oduwa is finding it difficult to accept that he is not playing alongside those with the same ability as what used to at Tottenham and sometimes his frustration shows, but what a player.

Hanford, the Carlisle keeper, was not the best keeper that Luton have come up against this season that is fact and he was very suspect whenever the ball was crossed towards his goal.

The only goal of the game came out from a good angled pass from Matt Robinson that found Mark Cullen who calmly toe poked the ball into the near post on the thirty-eighth minute.

The second half resulted in some chances for both sides. Drury unlucky not to double the lead when his powered effort crashed against the bar, Cullen put the rebound home but deemed offside. With a quarter of an hour remaining Pelly Ruddock Mpanzu replaced Matt Robinson in midfield, but he never really got going, he looked quite subdued a shadow of his normal self, however after such a long lay-off through injury and clearly still not fully match fit one could not expect more. In the sixty-sixth minute Luke Wilkinson became the second Luton player to see red in five days after bringing down Antony Sweeney. So another player to miss matches through suspension, it really does not just rain at Kenilworth Road does it.

The game came to a close and another three points to add to the "Hatters" tally for the season. Games elsewhere have gone in the Towns favour, apart from Burton beating Oxford two goals to nil, Wycombe lost for the second successive game at home to Newport County and a surprising victory at Roots Hall for Accrington meant that the Town regained fourth place AFC Wimbledon. At the bottom Hartlepool lost more ground from those above them losing at home 1-3 to Stevenage, whose opening goal was scored by recently released "Hatter" Dave Martin, sods law really, but I have to admit that I was disappointed when hearing that he had put pen to paper for them.

Great news though that Cameron McGeehan has re-joined the Town on loan until the end of the season with the possibility of a permanent move from Norwich City, which if his tweets on Twitter are anything to go by the deal already done, as he was thanking the Canaries for his time there and the opportunities they gave him. Unfortunately, again because of suspension, following a red card whilst on loan to Cambridge United he also will not be available for selection until the Accrington game. As I said, it never just rains.

Sunday February 15th 2015
The only entry I am going to make today is a sad one.
Yesterday on the M1 motorway in Bedfordshire, three West Ham supporters lost their lives in an accident when their car was involved in an accident with a coach on their way to West Bromwich for the clubs FA Cup tie at The Hawthorns. Our thoughts, heart and prayers are with their families this morning. A very sad day indeed, such happenings bring it all into perspective at times like this. May they Rest in Peace.

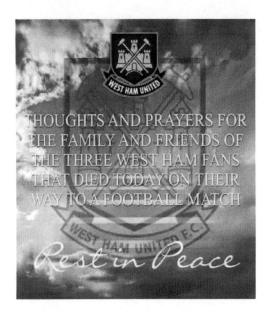

There are no rivalries at times such as this, the football family comes together as one and remembers.

Monday February 16th 2015
A midweek game to look forward to, this time a trip to Nottinghamshire, Sherwood Forest, Robin Hood and all that.
Not one of our more joyous of away grounds, Luton never seem to fare well at Mill Field the home of Mansfield Town.
Mill field is in fact the oldest football ground in the world still playing professional football, with games played there since 1862, which obviously makes it the oldest ground in existence in the Football League. Two other firsts for Field Mill include the first stadium to play a match under artificial lighting in 1930 when the North Notts. League Senior Cup Final played, also the first game played with a yellow fluorescent ball took place at the ground in 1998.
On the player's contract front, Town keeper Mark Tyler automatically triggered a new one-year extension to his contract after making 30 league appearances this season. Which include the fantastic tally of 14 clean sheets in that time, this in itself means that "Tyles" will more likely than not end his playing career with the "Hatters", but hopefully not too early. Looking forward to many more appearances before he finally decided to hang up the gloves, a most valued and respected member of the Town squad.
I have just been advised by a neighbour of mine who supports Welling that Jim Stevenson scored against his club for Aldershot on Saturday in the 2-1 defeat of my local side. Something to smile about regarding our players out on loan, I actually recall him scoring against Welling last season also when on loan at Dartford.

Tuesday February 17th 2015
Match day or night whichever way you would want to look at it.
As the Kings Ferry coach glides up the M1 motorway towards Nottinghamshire with the squad all but totally prepared for this evening's game, I sit here and contemplate over the expectations of

many "Hatters" who think this evening will be another game that Luton should win with ease. If only it was that simple. Gone are the days of the Conference where we would more or less be guaranteed three points against those sides at the bottom end of the table, games are going to be tightly contested affairs despite the fact we are fourth in the table and our opponents languishing in the zone reserved for relegation candidates. I keep saying this but will repeat myself yet again, this is not the Vanarama Conference league, teams from the bottom club to the top club are far more organised, they have the experience that was lacking in many sides faced last season, it is more difficult. We have overall a young experienced squad, some very shallow minded supporters need to understand that, as soon as a good run comes to fruition they expect every game, to win with ease, naivety and delusional at times that Luton can win just about every game. Yes, we have to go into each game with hope and positive vibes, but when it does not go to plan not throw abuse and start getting on the backs of players that they do not like. I keep saying it, a good deal of this seasons younger signings have not been bought in for the quick fix, they are the future, something we are fortunate to have at our fingertips after the tumultuous years of recent history. Luton need a settled side until that happens we will be inconsistent. Patience my friends.

With all the problems within the squad now, John Still and his staff are in all honesty going to struggle to find a well-balanced side with plenty of experience. Risks and gambles will have to be taken. A precarious game to look forward to tonight. Mansfield though, are also struggling through injuries. Which will make it a most interesting game, it could even result in stalemate, there will undoubtedly be some young nervous players out there hoping to please their relevant managers but also scared witless that they will embarrass themselves their club and rile the paying fans, it's a no win situation for some of them.

The Town line up has just been called and as I wrote earlier, it does not look the most experienced or confident sides that will take the field in a few minutes time: Mark Tyler, Michael Harriman, Fraser Franks, Alex Lacey, Scott Griffiths, Andy Drury, Jonathan Smith, Matt Robinson, Jake Howells, Jayden Stockley and Mark Cullen. Bench mates this evening being: Andy Parry, Elliot Justham, Ross Lafayette, Ryan Hall, Nathan Oduwa, Shaun Whalley and Luke Guttridge.

Mansfield Town 1 Luton Town 0

A game played on one of the most atrocious fields of play recently. The ploughed field that used to be prominent in the centre of Fakenham racecourse in my racing days comes to mind. A reasonable likeness, that field used to stop a loose horse dead in its tracks, much can be said of the same regarding the pitch Mansfield, most apt that Mans field, that was mistaken for a football pitch, disgraceful in this day and age especially for a football league club I would have thought. Fans are complaining about the hoof forward tactics that the "Hatters" used, but in reality what more could they do on such a surface? Not really, the ideal field of play for the ground passing we are used to being treated to. So one does have to a semblance of sympathy with the players; however, the performance was still one of a low par that should and must not be tolerated. The fact is Luton just were not good enough in any department, Mansfield had the greater desire throughout the game. There is the possibility that on such a surface Luton players knew they were not going to be able to compete the way they know best by playing proper football. However, the problem being the pitch was the same for both sets of players so they should have learnt to adapt and match their opponents at least in the desire to play and win the game. Maybe they have been spoilt in recent games when things have gone their way despite not so impressive performances, a touch of complacency on their part. Whatever the reasons they were just not at the races at all. If maybe our opponents from nearby Sherwood Forest had pinched the game in Robin Hood fashion maybe then it would not have been so bad, but to be rolled over from start to finish is not the Luton Town way usually.

The only goal of the game came from a counter attacking break away an outstanding pass from Thomas finding Bingham in space who was able to slot the ball past Mark Tyler.

In the second half the Town who made two changes after the break Oduwa for Howells and Whalley for Robinson, it made some difference but not enough.

The "Stags" nearly pinched a second, again from a break-away when Heslop found Thomas an optimistic lob over Tyler that bounced off the bar.

Luton could and should have levelled the game when Oduwa flicked the ball on from Griffiths thrown in, to Cullen who, although at an awkward angle admittedly, missed abysmally, his effort rolling wide of the far post.

There was a weak shout for a Luton penalty in added time when Guttridge was tripped in the box, it was ignored by the referee, the loose ball did come to Smith who was unable to squeeze past the post from again an awkward angle it has to be said and ended up in the side netting.

Luton seem to have lost their way a little in recent games, the trouble being are they capable of picking themselves up allowing them to push on for automatic promotion? Because let us be realistic, our history when it comes to play offs is not the most alluring to recall.

With tonight's defeat the "Hatters" missed out on the opportunity to overtake the flailing Wycombe Wanderers who themselves have dropped a few points recently and be back in the automatic promotion zone.

Wednesday February 18th 2015

Admittedly, I expected such, the moaners and groaners out in their dozens. It amazes me that they are so quiet when there is a good run of games in place but as soon as we fall at the latest hurdle they seem to show up from nowhere, but that is cool, gives me more fodder to work on and a few more pages to include. I know I am most probably boring many of you to tears by now, but it is not all my doing I promise you.

There are, this morning, some moronic individuals calling many of the players uncalled for names. Abusing each other, for me I keep well out of it. Let them get on with it, because when the winning ways are back the same people will be there on the bandwagon singing those same players, they are today abusing, praises and adulating about them, pathetic and fickle some are when it comes to supporting, is that what they really call it, their football club.

Do not misunderstand, criticism is good but please in the correct context and for the right reasons, abuse though is not good and quite uncalled for.

I did actually make a rare post on "Hatters Talk" just a while ago, as follows. For me it sums it up. "One defeat in ten games, admittedly not playing as well as would really like, injuries and suspensions, newly bought in players, it all mounts up. Players have been asked to step up, who, like it or not have limited league experience, the opposition wilier, maybe even less naive than those in the Conference. Yes, maybe we should, looking at our league position be beating sides such as York, Oxford and Mansfield given their recent form but hey fourth in the league this side of the new year we would have snatched with both hands after five or six games at the start of the season. A young side, building for the future, it was not so long ago we thought Luton had no future. The manager asked for patience saying it will take three seasons to get where he wanted us to be, who would have thought eighteen months ago we would be now knocking on the door for automatic promotion to league one? Too much too soon could be a disaster waiting to happen. Little steps, bigger aspirations."

The response was reasonable and a couple of guys made some superb points in agreement with myself and likewise I agreed with much that they had to contribute also, if only people sat back and thought before posting there, sometimes they post before their brains have had time to function correctly, that is of course if….. Sorry that was below the belt.

With Cameron McGeehan available to play against Wimbledon this coming weekend, I hope there are some people who will have some patience and not expect too much too soon. Something we have to remember is last season has gone, also gone is Andre Gray with whom he linked up with so well.

Also missing are the likes of Paul Benson and Alex Lawless, so please if he does not fit in as easily this time round, I beg that we do not hear all the sounds after a couple of games that he is not trying or he has lost it.

Remember he is also match rusty and will be coming into a side different to that one of last season. A player does not necessarily fit into a new side just like that, so when if forbid it does, go a little off key at first, show your patience, there has been for me too much abuse to certain players already this season.

Because from what I have seen this season there are some that love to jump on a players back when it is not going as expected, but are just as quick to jump on the bandwagon again when things are going perfectly. Just saying guys…. I thought I would have some extra fun and added this little piece as a post on "Hatters Talk" also, always a glutton for a bit of controversial slamming.

Thursday February 19th 2015

Can you imagine, if those Chelsea morons that were responsible for those disgraceful scenes shown on TV when physically pushing a French black man from a metro train in Paris and shouting racial abuse, were actually Luton supporters on a jolly boys day out? The uproar and noise from the F.A. would have been heard over the world, however because it is Chelski it will be a slap on the wrist for the club and bans for any of those recognised from the video clip. For Luton it would have meant possible expulsion from the league a massive fine and a ban of Luton supporters travelling away for five years, yes guys I am going over the top somewhat admittedly, but I think you get my gist. One rule for them another for us syndrome.

Something much closer to home, a sad affair was the passing on February 3rd. I know a couple of weeks ago now but I have been trying to find out as much as possible before covering this, of former Luton Town player Ken Hawkes, one of the members of the 1959 FA Cup final side that were beaten by Nottingham Forest under the twin towers.

Ken was born on 6th May 1933 in Easington, County Durham. He signed for Luton Town in 1957 from a local club Shotton Colliery Welfare, as did his brother Barry a couple of years later in 1959, but only making a handful of appearances. Ken made a total of 102 appearances for the "Hatters", which included 90 league, and 10 FA Cup games. His debut was at home on December 14th 1957 in the 5-1 capitulation of West Bromwich Albion in front of a healthy attendance of 15,365. His solitary Luton goal came his way on October 25th 1958 at Fratton Park in a 2-2 draw. His final game was on 3rd April 1961 away at Vetch Field to Swansea City where the "Hatters" were beaten 1-3.

Not long after that Ken signed for Peterborough United but was limited to only three appearances for them before moving to Bedford Town. Again he only made one Southern League appearances Dartford away, and two appearances in the Southern League Cup in both kegs against Cambridge United in the preliminary round that Bedford won eventually on the away goals rule after a 6-6 aggregate score. Ken last move as far as can be found was to St. Neots Town who played in the United Counties League. Farewell to one of our legendary Cup finalist, R.I.P. sir.

I am having a small battle with my conscience at the moment, being a true "Hatter" I am tempted to deny my second eldest daughter the opportunity she has been waiting for. A couple of days ago she approached me to advise that she has been scouted and asked to train with the option of signing if she likes the set up for Millwall Ladies, as much as I do not want to stand in her way of something she dearly wants to do I am in two minds. The thought of Millwall shirts, track suits, bags and all the other paraphernalia that comes with it is testing my resilience, also I would, as she is under the age of 16, just, for the time being at least have to accompany her not only to training but the matches also when chosen to play. I have a lot deal of deciding over the next few days. It was not so bad when my oldest daughter Surya, who actually played for my ladies team, was scouted by both Arsenal and Charlton Athletic. We have no real history with either, in any case she was eventually turned down by both, but just the fact that the two top Ladies teams in the country at the time took interest in her was enough to be so proud of her. However, Millwall, a different kettle of the proverbial fishes. Let me think it over, trouble is though how can I, in all honesty so no. Decisions, decisions.

Friday February 20th 2015

I have to admit that I am, not unlike many others now, getting quite frustrated at the long ball tactics that have been employed recently, in general that has never been the Luton Town way as long as I can remember.

It's just a thought. I am not trying to defend anyone. However, the indifferent run of late coincidentally seems to have come about since the spate of bad weather experienced throughout the country. It brings me to wonder if the state of the pitches has something to contribute for the sudden change of the up and over games we have been subject to from the "Hatters" of late, the pitches not conducive with the way we like to play the game. Because some of the playing surfaces have not been of the vest quality that is for sure, it just seems somewhat coincidental to me that is all.

I am not attempting to find excuses or defend anyone, just a personal observation.

Has John Still tried, maybe not successfully though, to combat the situation and it has backfired somewhat?

John Still finally got his man, in addition to Cameron McGeehan the "boss" has also been chasing, as mentioned last month, he was looking at West Ham striker Elliot Lee, once his loan agreement was over Lee became available and JLS swooped in to get him until mid-March.

At the same time another player went out on loan, Charlie walker headed to Borehamwood to join fellow "Hatter" Lee Angol.

Tomorrow the Town travel to Wimbledon, wombling in mid table they will be a formidable opponent, many too often see them as a non-entity, however they have a strong forward line lead by the big fella Akinfenwa, how sad there will be no battle of the giants again this time round with Steve McNulty still serving his suspension. I have a distinct feeling Luton are going to face a very tough afternoon, as much as I like Fraser Franks and Alex Lacey I would be much happier with "Sumo" in the centre controlling things, we lack his experience, that was so evident against Mansfield.

Saturday February 22nd 2015

Bloody hell the sun is out, shame I am not at my best though. If the game had not already been sold out for Town supporters I may have ventured my way to Thornton Heath, had some banter with some Wombles I know and then moved on to the "Cherry Red Records" Stadium, has a weird but somewhat likeable sound. Instead I am stuck at home and as I mentioned not in the greatest of modes, but hopefully Jeff Stelling will ease that as he continuously over the period of 105 minutes, pours out goal after goal produced by the mighty "hatters". I am allowed to dream you know, I clearly need something to snap me out of this feeling of sitting on the doomed deck of Titanic as she slips piece by broken piece down into the depths of the North Atlantic, with Celine Dion giving me severe ear ache in the background.

Mark Tyler is a no go today due to a knee injury I have been reliably informed. I cannot help but feel a little sorry for young Elliot Justham being thrown into the deep end, somewhat like Titanic, with a makeshift defence to welcome him into league football with the sight of the tank that is Akinfenwa there ready to charge at him like one of those steam breathing ferocious black bulls at a Madrid bullfight. I wish him all the best; at least it will be an afternoon to remember for the young debutant.

So, the Hatters line up reads as this: Elliot Justham, Michael Harriman, Fraser Franks, Alex Lacey, Scott Griffiths, Andy Drury, Jonathan Smith, Cameron McGeehan, Nathan Oduwa, Luke

Guttridge and Jayden Stockley. With a substitutes bench that was squashed from end to end with: Elliot Lee, Jake Howells, Andy Parry, Alex Wall, Alex Lawless, Shaun Whalley and Liam Gooch. It is good to see Luke Guttridge starting again and Alex Lawless on the bench. It would be great if his plague of injuries has at last done a Lord Lucan and disappeared without trace. Once fully fit he will be a very valuable addition on the run in to the end of the season, with Pelly fit again as soon as possible we shall then again have a most formidable midfield, all I ask is we revert back to the 4-4-2 formation, two up front and an attack minded midfield.

AFC Wimbledon 3 Luton Town 2
It is amazing that even before a ball is kicked some moronic so-called supporter is shouting abuse at Jayden Stockley, who has whilst here done nothing but work tirelessly in all games. No wonder some players seem to give up at Luton when we have such dummies following the club and shouting utter shit, pardon my language at times throughout this, but some Luton fans really make the blood boil to the extreme of a volcanic eruption. If one does not like the players on show, don't bother going to the games. If you want to shout abuse instead of getting behind the players why not go to either that place in the vicinity of a vicarage, or to the a stadium more renowned for its hockey in the early days other than football, your abuse will be much welcomed by fellow Luton fans if you were to that.
An absolute nightmare of a game in the first half, typically lack lustre, Wimbledon could and should have had a hat full in reality. Akinfenwa hit the upright on no less than three occasions. Fraser Franks, as much as I like the guy was totally out of his depth this afternoon, he is not in all honesty cut out for this level of football against the stronger sides in the division, good against the lesser sides admittedly but up against an opponent of Akinfenwa's ilk totally out of place sadly. Justham, fortunately showing what a good keeper he will be as he develops, he proved his right to be number two to Tyler, it will be a blessing if he is able to stay patient until "Tyles" decided enough is enough and hangs up his gloves for good, can I personally see hi hanging around that long? I honestly doubt it.
Wimbledon took a deserved lead following Akinfenwa's nicely placed pass to Reeves who had a poke at goal, Justham was only able to push the ball out which found the unmarked Alfie Potter, despite at an angle, had only a gaping net to hit for his first goal as a Wimbledon player.
It was only a matter of time, before they were deservedly two goals to the good. From a Reeves corner Elliot Justham punched the ball clear but only as far as the foot of Bulman, franks too slow in closing him down, allowing him a second touch from which he powered a shot that smashed into the back of the net at speed, 2-0. The "Hatters" looked finished before half time.
However, such has been the case at times this season, credit to the town for that, they refused to lay down and be slaughtered like a "Lamb on Broadway", they hit back just before half time a shot from Luke Guttridge came back off the post to the foot of Jayden Stockley to poke over the line, 2-1. If I was, Stockley my patience would have slipped at that moment and I would have run over to the vicinity of the abusive moron and gave him a mouthful of the same, however thankfully he obviously has more control than I ever have had in such a situation. I once did exactly that whilst representing my regiment in an Army cup match. I had been earlier slated for missing what was never an easy chance by the team manager, an officer from the public school crowd, who had never played football in his life apparently, so because it was a sporting event there was no rank as such so I sauntered over to where he stood, stuck two fingers virtually up his snobbish nose and went on to score the winner some minutes later. He wanted me charged with insubordination and

verbal assault, however our commanding officer put him right on that one, although I was reprimanded after the said captain of the regiment had been dismissed from the office. As I say, good work Jayden for not doing likewise.

So half time we went in flattered at only being two goals to one down.

The second half was a total turn around, Luton starting to look the more superior, Guttridge was making some good runs, a couple of chances falling to Stockley, but unable to convert into goals. Stockley was working hard and deemed to have dived, a clear-cut foul. It should have resulted in a penalty to the "Hatters." But, for reasons only he can give, not that he will, the referee decided Stockley deserved a yellow card. Last week Wayne Rooney won a penalty after diving at least eight inches clear of a defenders foot, a clear dive make no mistake, but then this is Luton Town, League Two, the refereeing abysmal at best all round, Rooney is Rooney therefore he must have been fouled, such of his like never dive do they.

Stockley replaced by Alex Wall, late in the game, John Still giving him a reassuring hug following the abuse received.

Alex Lawless came on to replace Nathan Oduwa who had a reasonably quiet game and newcomer Elliot Lee came on to take the place of Andy Drury, who yet again had a disappointing afternoon. Guttridge was instrumental in Luton's second and equalising goal, a sweet pass to Lee who finished with ease, a goal on his debut, not a bad start for the young fellow.

As the game run to its close Wimbledon put the Town under some pressure, but it was poor defending that cost all three points right at the death when Franks poor defending allowed Connolly to round Justham and place the ball in the net.

Disappointing, following the tenacious comeback. However, at least the "Hatters" proved their character in the second half even if it was Forty-five minutes too late.

Thank you to Paul Wright as usual whom has been generous enough to allow me to use his match report to work from. It is appreciated.

With results elsewhere in Luton's favour allowing them to stay in fourth place, following Southend's defeat at Stevenage.

Shrewsbury's surprise 1-2 defeat at Prenton Park allowed Burton to go to the top again following their 3-1 defeat of Dagenham and Redbridge. Luton are now still four points adrift of the automatic promotion places, with Wycombe who won 3-2 at Carlisle.

Before today Portsmouth had scored a total of six away goals all season, at Cambridge United they doubled that tally with a 6-2 away victory against Dicky Dosh's side, I did manage a wee smile at that I have to admit.

Sunday February 22nd 2015

I find it amazing how certain people on learning that Mark Cullen has asked to leave the club have reacted. He has been head hunted by Peterborough United of League One, if I was in his shoes I would want to move also. There are a few factors as to why I say that. Firstly, the opportunity to play at a higher level. Secondly he has to look at the wage rise, a young man with a family to support, thirdly, let's face it despite his work ethics which are it has to be said exemplary for the "Hatters" he is in and of the side more times than David Pleat in the Oak Road car park late at night. When he plays, the majority of times he scores and yet there are still those within the Town's fan-base that give him abuse and get on his back, nothing ever changes there unfortunately. It saps the strength from a player mentally and emotionally. He then most probably has an agent who is turning his head, because we have to understand all an agent see's in front of his eyes are massive pound signs, they in reality do not have the players best interest at heart, only their own bank balance. If the lads head was all over the place because of this, one cannot blame John Still for not playing him yesterday. Some are blaming Cullen for not wanting to play. From what I have heard that is not the case. The reason was, John Still needed players whose minds were totally on the job. Would an agent be advising the player to take it easy, not get injured and mess up the forthcoming medical, we shall never know that, but please I wish some people would accept the fact that the lad has been offered a great opportunity in his eyes and as far as I am concerned fair play to him.

As it is the deal may well fall through following this morning news that Peterborough have dismissed Darren Ferguson, as manager after eight long years at the helm and that deal must be up in the air now. Time will tell.

Monday February 23rd 2015

I am not so sure I am in total agreement with John Still's comments yesterday regarding want-away striker Mark Cullen not playing for Luton Town again following his revelations that he wants to leave Kenilworth Road.

Cully reasons for wanting a move are also understandable, it must be quite frustrating for the young striker when there are so many additional strikers being bought in on loan, soul destroying and confidence sapping.

It also saddens me greatly to find the usual boo boys coming out of their holes and being quite offensive towards Mark, I can never understand such nonsensical behaviour. The guy wants to better himself, what is so wrong with that? Just as we all do throughout our working lives, it is human nature especially when having a young family to support and tend to. Such behaviour really does sicken me at times like this. However, this is a universal trait amongst football supporters, not just Luton Town; it is going to happen regardless to what anyone says against it in reality.

I just hope for the sake of all involved this situation is resolved as soon as possible as it cannot be the greatest morale booster in the dressing room at the moment. Whatever transpires in the next few days let us just hope that it will be the best decision for all parties involved.

Tuesday February 24th 2015

Cullen's future is still uncertain, but I feel enough said on the matter for now until anything more transpires.

Today the Development squad were away to Leyton Orient, recording a decent 3-2 victory.

It was good to see Paul Benson back in the fray and managing a full ninety minutes, that is most encouraging news for all "Hatters" following the broken leg received in the home game against Mansfield. Many feared, as I did also, could have meant the end of his career and consequently his final appearance for the Town and even the end of his playing career at the age of thirty-five. It just goes to prove the strength and resilience of the man, also his determination to wear the Luton shirt again.

Also playing a full ninety minutes in this game after injury were Alex Lawless and Luke Rooney. Goals from Alex Wall, Ross Lafayette and a superb Jake Howells spot kick in the final minutes of the game secured the win after having to come back from being a goal down.

Youth goalkeeper Liam Gooch gave a superb performance between the sticks. Gooch had graced the first team bench for the first time in a football league game last weekend at Wimbledon. We certainly have some good back up for Mark Tyler.

There was on the "Hatter Talk" Facebook page this morning a marvellous post by Luton fan Brian Anley regarding FIFA's plans to play the 2022 Qatar World Cup in the winter months. Brian quoted the FA's Chief Executive Richard Scudamore, who was complaining that such a decision would ruin the English football tradition of the Christmas and New Year programme. That in itself being quite something when coming from the man who has been instrumental in allowing both Sky and BT Sports channels in dictating the kick off times of many games on Monday nights, Sunday lunchtimes and from next season, Friday nights also, which to me has ruined football for myself. If I am totally honest with myself I would actually say that the expectation I once had of watching a game on TV has waned somewhat these days with there being too much televised football these days, it has taken the enjoyment away from it, I may get lynched for saying that but that is my honest and personal opinion. I have mentioned in an earlier chapter how I have become quite disillusioned with the road in which football has continued to go down in recent years; this for me just adds fuel to the fire.

Therefore, for Richard Scudamore to be worrying about the football traditions of our great game he has already let the horse out of the stable and allowed it to go on its merry journey.

I have the solution for these plans during a winter World Cup that will apparently be played throughout the Christmas and New Year period according to the FIFA tyrant Sep Blatter. I suggest that the Premier and football league programmes should continue as normal. Allow those foreign players go toddling off to Qatar and run themselves ragged in the searing heat of the Arabian sun. Let them compete in a World Cup which in my opinion should never be anyway, this competition is no longer about football it is all about money, it was illegally and fraudulently voted on and the pockets of a few filled to the brim. The Premier league clubs have an ample array of young English players that could step into the absent players roles and do the job. It would also give those players an opportunity to showcase themselves and prove their worth. Much over the past months having been bandied about regarding the "B team" players getting more opportunities to play at a more suitable level, well here is one possibility for them to do so, or is it that the bigger clubs are so afraid they will not draw in the attendances they are normally used to having.

I did love a quote from Gary Neville earlier today on Sky Sports News though, mentioning when interviewed that a World Cup played in the winter months would be the perfect opportunity for England to win the World Cup again. My stomach still aches from the laughter that bought to me. I am sure I was not the only one totally amused at such a ludicrous comment; the man was obviously deluded at the time. I do though Mr Neville thank you from my heart for making my day so much better, having experienced such a good laugh.

Wednesday February 25th 2015
Despite what I happened to mention yesterday regarding too much football on TV at times, here I am this evening sitting comfortably in my favourite chair with a plate of Cumberland sausage, a jar of Colman's English Mustard, waffles and the coffee machine at arm's length waiting for Arsenal versus Monaco to commence. The perfect remedy for what is here in Kent one hell of a cold evening.

I have to revert to the old-fashioned way, as my laptop is in hospital having keyboard surgery therefore having to produce much of this week and next week's entries by longhand with pen in hand. This provokes thoughts of how such past authors such as Tolkien, D H Lawrence, Ernest Hemmingway and John Steinbeck were able to write so many riveting pages in this way, very tiring on the hands and the wrists it has to be said. I am already suffering from writer's cramp, I said "WRITERS" by the way, just in case anyone may have misread.

Well that was a very dismal effort from Mr Wenger's side, completely outplayed by the so-called underdog side from his native France, somewhat of an anti-climax for yours truly.

Thursday February 26th 2015
"A likeable character and one of the most respected managers in the entirety of English football." That is how the Luton Town manager John Still is described in the "Elite Soccer Coaching Magazine.
The "boss" celebrates two years at the helm of Luton Town today, a feat in itself these days. The longest reining manager at Kenilworth Road since Mike Newell who was in charge for a few months under four years, from June 2003 until his demise in March 2007.
Mr. Stills has a winning ratio of just over 50% as present; the only other managers that can boast such a record have not done so in such an elongated period.
Once the Town revert to their fast flowing, free football that record will stay as it is and finds us back to our winning ways.

Friday February 27th 2015
Early team news regarding tomorrow's home game against Accrington Stanley, who were instrumental in bringing to an end Burton Albion's unbeaten league run suggests that Luke Wilkinson will return from suspension and walk straight back into the line-up. Skipper Steve McNulty still has one game remaining of his four-match ban. Mark Tyler is also a doubt; therefore, Elliot Justham will be prepared to stand in again following his impressive debut, despite the "Hatters" losing to a last minute goal.
On the Mark Cullen front, it has been reported that there have been a number of bids for the striker, but none having closely matched the valuation placed on the players head. It does seem doubtful that he will be in contention for a place, expecting manager John Still to stick by his guns and not play him again.
As for the Towns opponents, they have no ensuing injury worries before travelling south.
To be honest I am getting myself geared up for two weeks from now and the Cheltenham Festival, four days of the best National Hunt racing in the world. What makes it more special this year is that it will be the master himself final festival before retiring. AP McCoy I shall miss your wit but most importantly your undying wish to succeed in every race you compete in, be it a £750 seller at Kelso or The Cheltenham Gold Cup itself. I will miss you mate.

Saturday February 28th 2015
At last, following much speculation regarding Mark Cullen the misunderstanding between himself and the manager now cleared up. Cullen admits that his head was turned by reports of higher league clubs being interested in him. However, contrary to reports that he wanted to leave Luton Town were grossly misread. At no time had he ever actually said that although he may be guilty of not explaining himself correctly and his words were misconstrued. He has apologised to the fact that he may had unsettled some people, again that was never his intention. As far as Cullen is concerned, he is still a Luton Town player and looking forward to getting back into the side and assisting in the push for promotion.
Cullen's statement been clarified by management with inclusion on the substitutes bench this for the home game against Accrington Stanley.

The team line-up then is as follows: Elliot Justham, Michael Harriman, Fraser Franks, Luke Wilkinson, Scott Griffiths, Luke Guttridge, Jonathan Smith, Cameron McGeehan, Jake Howells, Elliot Lee and Jayden Stockley. With the bench consisting of: Alex Lawless, Andy Drury, Mark Cullen, Andy Parry, Shaun Whalley, Nathan Oduwa and Craig King.

Luton Town 2 Accrington Stanley 0
On the whole a satisfactory performance from the "Hatters".
Three changes from the Wimbledon game a week ago. Wilkinson, back from suspension. Howells and Lee replacing Lacey, Oduwa and Drury respectively.
I have to admit an element of surprise on my part to find the Tottenham lad only on the bench this afternoon. The Town commenced the game using a diamond formation, but they rarely looked comfortable with it. Full credit to the manager, for picking it up and not being too bull-headed, changing it around.
Stanley were at times the better footballing side, however fortunately for the "Hatters" their firepower was lacking in comparison.
When John still realised the mistake and rectified it accordingly, switching the formation Luton began to show some positive shape. With Lee on the right flank and Jake Howells to the left the Town began to stretch Accrington, this new formation also allowed Luke Guttridge to see more of the ball resulting in the "Hatters" beginning to threaten the Accrington defence more.
It seems that Jayden Stockley is much too often used in a role that really does not suit his talents. For myself he would be comfortable receiving balls to his feet rather than the long high balls from midfield when he looks much too isolated. Sadly, there are some Luton supporters who obviously have no real knowledge or understanding of football, otherwise they would not be constantly moaning and getting on the lads back unnecessarily.
Stanley were gifted an early chance when Gornell made a weak effort to beat Justham, but the Luton keeper stood his ground and the effort wasted as the ball was directed straight to the young stand in keeper of whom it has to be said has coped magnificently to date.
At the other end, Elliot Lee had an opportunity to open the scoring for Luton. However, his somehow his curling shot was blocked successfully by the defending Winnard.
Luton's main threat came from the left when Griffiths and Howells linked up well down the left. Pressure was mounting on Stanley.
The "Hatters" won a corner that Luke Guttridge placed towards the far post, the Accrington keeper seemed hesitant as how to deal with the cross, which in turn allowed Stockley to twist and latch on to the ball with a well-placed header over for the opening goal. A much-needed break, as far as Luton were concerned, to give them a much needed confidence boost following recent disappointing results.
Despite what was in reality a rather drab first half the Town went in at the break with a one-goal advantage.
The second half started much better for the "Hatters". Cameron McGeehan missed a super opportunity to double their lead but totally misjudged his effort.
Mark Cullen replaced the hard working Jayden Stockley and despite the recent problems looked as if he were serious to get himself back in full favour.
Luton Town's second goal came about from a Scott Griffiths throw-in looking for Stockley down the line, who was able to head the ball on to Lee who gathered the ball and unselfishly played the ball into Guttridge who just had the job of tapping over the line to make it 2-0.

The game fizzled out a little following the second goal and that was how the game eventually finished up, Luton the two goal victors.

With this much welcomed victory Luton were able to gain some ground on the leading three clubs, leaders Burton yet again faltered, losing at home to Newport County by the single goal of the game, however because Shrewsbury also lost their unbeaten home record to Northampton nothing changed at the top. Wycombe shared the points with Stevenage in a 2-2 draw. This means that Luton are now only two points off Wycombe in third place and six points adrift of leaders Burton Albion.

At the bottom Hartlepool are certainly trying to make a fight of it after their 1-0 home win over AFC Wimbledon, although still six points adrift of safety as the table stands at the moment.

March

Sunday March 1st 2015

Marching forward into another month, hopefully better than the one just passed. Maybe with that some change in weather and fortunes for Luton. We need something to spur us on again that is for sure. Despite the cold we have been enduring of late, it is most encouraging, at least down here in Kent, to see some blossom on the trees and the spring buds coming through. Spring in the air and maybe even a spring in the feet for the "Hatters" However, the next game is not going to be any easy affair on Tuesday evening when the Town and our merry band of followers travel northwards to Bury. I know their ground is now named after that famous footwear conglomerate that we all seem to frequent on our high streets and malls for their overpriced trainers and more. Nevertheless, I like to keep things simple and for me it is still Gigg Lane, same it has been for the past fifty-two years of my following our so unpredictable game. Anyway despite my joy at the arrival of spring blooming here I have been reliably informed from my friend who loves in Manchester that it is not likewise in their neck of the woods, in fact as they so eloquently put it "the cold wind is ripping the skin off my butt!"

The plan was originally to follow in stages the fortunes of the England cricket team, who are currently down-under for the one day World Cup that is happening jointly in Australia and New Zealand. However, you know what; the way things are going is definitely not to plan. They had a very shaky start both Australia and New Zealand, did I really say shaky? More like shudderingly awful. They notched up a win against Scotland, the news hounds were shouting about how England has turned it around, and they can now focus with a valuable win under their belts. Excuse me but am I missing something? I see no turning around, more likely a small deviation towards the middle of the road; it was Scotland for pity's sake, no lack of disrespect indicated towards Scotland, but come on. Humiliated by Australia, slaughtered by New Zealand, and now at this moment, after what seemed a decent enough start, being totally blown away by Messrs. Thirimanne and Dilshan. One hundred for no loss right now. As I write that, our illustrious captain Eion Morgan catches Dilshan and a wicket falls on a century score. Not exactly encouraging though, with Sangakkara making his way to the crease. Now there is something to relish, the opportunity to enjoy his batting prowess throughout the summer following the mighty Surrey. I cannot help but frown at the fact that England has a one-day master in Kevin Pietersen at their disposal and refuse to use him, ludicrous. Nevertheless, that is England mentality through and through, reminds me of the early seventies with the England football team when Don Revie, one of the biggest mistakes in the history of England, was manager and refused to play the likes of Peter Osgood and Alan Hudson. The pair of them would have ripped apart any international defence. However, because Revie did not like them for the fact that they were Chelsea players and had beaten his beloved Leeds at Wembley despite the Yorkshire side attempting to kick them off the park at the time; he refused to allow them a place in the squad, again ludicrous. Also in the Ramsey years, the same Alan Hudson banned for three years from playing for England because he refused to travel with the under twenty-three side on tour, not because as they say now, being tired, but because he was experiencing a niggling knee injury. These days he would have had the protection of club doctors and specialists, but at that time players were not afforded that luxury. So incorrectly accused of malingering the stuffed white shirts in their perfectly pressed Saville row blazers stood by their yes man Ramsey and barred Huddy from playing for those three years. That same injury came back to haunt him and cost him dearly later. So yes, that is still the mentality of the England set up, not only in football but cricket also. KP just is not liked full stop, but boy, what a cricketer. Their loss.

Sri Lanka is ripping shreds out of the English bowlers.

Turned it around? I do not think so.

In addition, Afghanistan and Bangladesh are most probably rubbing the palms of their hands in sweet anticipation at facing the whipping boys, England. Because let us be honest this time around they are no more than that. Unfortunately, that is how it will stay until as Mike Thomas so rightly pointed out to me during a discussion a day or so ago. Not until the committee is no longer parading members who are renowned in their careers as non-winners, for a better phrase, will England be a major force again. As in football, a major overhaul required at the top. Former players who had a reputation for winning, because for myself winners breed winners, no different in any sport. We need footballers running football, not stuffed shirts who sit behind their oak desks and know nothing, have no experience of what it is like to be out there. Some will ask "What about Trevor Brooking?" and I will ask back "What about Trevor Brooking?" A token gesture by the authorities at best, with that making sure that token gesture is a "yes" man to their cause at the same time. As much as I admired Brooking as a player, he does not show the same mettle shown on the pitch. Football needs people that will stand up to the arrogant masters. Serfdom at its best. Superb, the tide has turned back to normal, humiliated yet again. Sri Lanka surpassing the England total with ease, losing only the one wicket and centuries for both Thirimanne and Sangakkara. So there we have it, Morgan and his boys will soon be singing, "We're leaving on a jet plane, don't know when we will win again…"

Time to put the head on pillow me thinks.

Monday March 2nd 2015

Having nicely recovered from yesterday's exertions of watching that dismal display of cricket. But now back to the daily drudgery.

Although at least have something to look forward to, a lunchtime soirée with Huddy tomorrow down the pub in Putney, more enthralling stories from the golden age of football, when football was football, not ballerinas in drag.

Just hearing that the Under 18s were beaten on Saturday in their home meeting with their Plymouth Argyle counterparts. Their first defeat of the season recorded at Creasey Park. The boys actually took the lead through Leeroy Maguraushe but allowed Plymouth two goals before half time. The score staying that way in the second half.

Mark Tyler is doubtful for the game at Bury tomorrow, John Still saying that he will have a fitness test later today. Therefore, Elliot Justham cameo run in the league continues, that is no worry though; the lad is a more than capable replacement for the veteran Tyler.

Sumo will be available again following his four-match ban, it will be interesting to see if he walks straight back into the side, for me despite the results the stand in boys have not done too badly. Despite what many are saying I will reiterate what I have said before Alex Lacey has the potential to become a fine player given a decent run in the side.

Tuesday March 3rd 2015

A distressing morning, for sure. As mentioned yesterday I was looking forward to meeting Huddy for a lunchtime drink. However at three this morning I was woken by my phone, to be honest I was not really sleeping, I had been reading jockey Graham Bradley's autobiography "The Wayward

Lad", if you like that sort of thing please get, a damned good read, a little earlier. Therefore, not yet properly sleeping. I was devastated to hear that Al. had been rushed to Chelsea and Westminster Hospital earlier in the evening. As you will have read earlier in the book he had been diagnosed with prostate cancer last year. However, even though obviously not well the resilience of the man shone through in his text message telling me that he was disappointed we would not meet today. However, we shall reroute for another day soon. We certainly shall my friend; we certainly shall, whenever you are ready.

No doubt had we met up today one of the first articles of the day would have been to toast a great player of the past who sadly passed away yesterday. The former Tottenham and Scotland defender Dave McKay. I know as I did also, that Alan had so much admiration for McKay. Not only as a player but also as a person, by all accounts a most wonderful human being, football today lost a true legend, a word that I do not usually like when it comes to football, however McKay is one of the few men I can so easily afford to label as such.

I was fortunate to see the man play on quite a few occasions when with my good friends the Cook brothers. We would venture to see not only Arsenal on occasion but also Tottenham, we were all fair to each other in that respect, it was not just about the team one supported, we would allow for each other to see our teams play.

With not going to meet Huddy I will I suppose at least be sober to listen to the "Hatters" game from Gigg Lane. Sober is not something that comes to mind on days, as today though, I will need a bottle of something at least by my side.

Bury are for myself one of the better sides in this division of the Football League. Although not far off the top, their position is a false one, I truly think they will be by the end of the season very dangerous contenders for promotion, they did lose their way for a while but they are now back to form, as seen earlier in the season. This will be the fourth meeting between the "Hatters" and the "Shakers". All have been close affairs, goal wise at least.

I have just come off the phone with Paul Stanyon who is up in Bury for this evening's game and he informs me that it is damned cold up there. Good luck, as I have just read rain also forecast for later in the evening.

The Luton team named online and as expected Tyler is again out with that knee injury and Skipper Steve McNulty returns from suspension.

The "Hatters" side as follows: Elliot Justham, Michael Harriman, Luke Wilkinson, Steve McNulty, Scott Griffiths, Jonathan Smith, Luke Guttridge, Cameron McGeehan, Jake Howells, Jayden Stockley and Elliot Lee. With blankets ordered for a cold night on the bench: Fraser Franks, Alex Lawless Andy Drury, Mark Cullen, Shaun Whalley, Nathan Oduwa and Craig King.

Bury 1 Luton Town 0
Again as often has been the case this season Luton were slow in coming out of the traps.

The home side dominated from kick off, the absence of Nathan Doyle is prominent that is easy for anyone to see. Bury dominated not only the field but total possession also, not allowing the "Hatters" to even get the ball let alone hold on to it. If not for better finishing from the home side, they would have been out of sight by half time. Luton were nowhere to be seen at times. Adams put the ball in the net for Bury, but fortunately for Luton, caught offside.

The only goal of the game was a simple affair Hussey and Mayor combining well down the left, Scott Griffiths exposed by his lack of height, a pin point cross for Soares to head home.

The second half Luton made a more concerted effort in fact unlucky not to find an equaliser, with chances for Guttridge and McGeehan.

Luton most fortunate to travel back to Bedfordshire with only a one-goal deficit.

There was a full programme tonight so in other league two games. Shrewsbury overtook Burton at the top following their win at Accrington and Wycombe marched further away from Luton stretching the point difference between third and fourth places to five points. Winning at Prenton Park. Beating Tranmere 2-1. The play-off places becoming very tightly bunched now with Luton, Bury and Southend all on fifty-eight points. The other remaining position held by Newport County who are a further five points adrift on fifty-three. In all honesty, unless Luton start finding some form they will be fortunate to be contending for a play-off place come the last couple of games of the season. They have three difficult games approaching, Morecambe, who made a mockery of us when besting us 3-0 at their place. Portsmouth, away, who are starting to show reasonable form, also play-off contenders Newport another away fixture. March could well be a very tough month for the "Hatters".

Wednesday March 4ᵗʰ 2015

Well as expected the moaners are out in their millions following last night's result. Some to be fair feasible comments. Nevertheless, there were those also that just seem to moan and get on the players, or at least certain players backs for the sake of it. I have not said this before but it is not all down to the players, John Still, Terry Harris and Hakan Hayrettin have to shoulder some of the blame; the formations are at best questionable at times. However, I know the injury situation does not help matters. Nevertheless, we have enough front men to be playing 4-4-2 and even against some sides at home probably 3-5-3, we need to take the game to the opposition more often than we are. That is when the "Hatters" look to be at their strongest. We have players capable of providing the service from the midfield, so why not revert to what is without doubt our best style of play. However, it is so easy for us to criticise from our comfortable armchairs, we are not the ones under pressure, which falls directly on the men just mentioned. I am sure they are doing what in their minds what is best for the club. Therefore, they obviously have their reasons for using the formations they are. At least JLS admits when he has it wrong, which he be should be commended for, in the past that has been one of the things lacking from other managers and coaches. Whatever happens let us remember though, that this has not been a disastrous season in away. In fact, it is for many players within the squad a learning curve. The future should be taken into consideration as much as the present.

Thursday March 5ᵗʰ 2015

Knocked out of the Bedfordshire Senior Cup on penalties to Biggleswade Town, is not the news one would want to read this morning, but it is fact. Not the most illustrious of trophies admittedly. Nevertheless, with players such as Alex Wall, Charlie Walker, Alex Lawless, Alex Lacey and Ross Lafayette on show, one would have thought…

I had to laugh though after watching a short interview with John Still earlier, regarding the club analyst who could not produce a disc to the manager to evaluate the Bury defeat. The man is a "plank" don't you hold back from telling I told you that, with a wry smile on his face. Classic! Mark Tyler is still struggling with a knee injury and has been booked to have a scan on it later this week. Elliot Justham will therefore be between the Kenilworth Road posts on Saturday against Morecambe then.

Friday March 6th 2015.
It confirmed that Jayden Stockley's loan from AFC Bournemouth be extended for a third month. Personally, I would personally not be sorry to see the lad get a permanent move to the "Hatters", for me he has shown he can do a job for us,
I am a little subdued learning that Keith Keane has gone on loan to Graham Westley's Stevenage Town. I wonder though if he was to return to Luton, would he still be the force he was when here before? I actually have my reservations.
Morecambe are at the "Kenny" tomorrow, it hoped that we should give a much better showing than we did on December 13th at their Globe Arena.
In their most recent game on Tuesday evening, they left Oxford with a 1-1 draw. They sit in a reasonably safe thirteenth position in the table. They will again, come to Luton hoping to give a good account of themselves under the management of Jim Bentley.

Saturday March 7th 2015
A beautiful spring like day, the sun is shining down on us, we can hope that the rays of fortune also shine favourably on our mighty "Hatters".
Today I have much to do building my new website, sometimes we have to prioritise.
However, thanks to Paul Wright, his eyes and thoughts will assist this afternoon.
I am a little peeved though as will a few fellow supporters, with the news that Kenilworth Road will change to a new name later in the month. Obviously, the club have sent out tenders I would imagine for what I see as stadium sponsorship. To me it will always be my beloved "Kenny" no sweat. I dread to think what Kenilworth Road could be called. I am not going to hazard a guess right now.
Just received the team news via the "Hatters" web site and there are two changes from Tuesdays defeat at Bury, with both Mark Cullen and Shaun Whalley being promoted from the bench.
The starting line up as follows: Elliot Justham, Michael Harriman, Scott Griffiths, Steve McNulty, Luke Wilkinson, Jonathan Smith, Cameron McGeehan, Shaun Whalley, Jake Howells, Luke Guttridge and Mark Cullen. Those that will be bleaching it on the bench today are as follows: Craig King, Fraser Franks, Elliot Lee, Andy Drury, Jayden Stockley, Alex Lawless and Nathan Oduwa.
I am again quite stunned to keep seeing the name Oduwa in the list of substitutes instead of the starting line-up. His pace would be perfect in what one would hope will be an attacking formation, especially being at home.

Luton Town 2 Morecambe 3
Yet again, it seems a game of two halves. Against Wimbledon, sucker punched in the dying embers of the game. This afternoon a somewhat cruel reminder, that inexperience is no substitute for the experience of Mark Tyler. Having said that one honestly cannot fault Elliot Justham. Maybe he should have been verbal allowing Wilkinson to leave a ball that the keeper had covered. When things are going wrong, they truly go wrong. Luton are at the moment experiencing such a period. However, Luton were poor there are no two ways about that. What the problem is can be anyone's guess at the moment, but no getting away from it; it needs sorting. In addition, it is obvious that throughout the season results have tended to paint over the cracks that have been there throughout. Nevertheless, I will continue to see this season as a learning curve rather than a disaster. Disaster is a little strong anyway. I know also that I am forever repeating myself when expressing my view that we have to remember the position we were in two years ago before the

coming of JLS and company and I will stick by that. We lost two very influential players between last and this season in Andre Gray and Ronnie Henry, players of their kind are difficult to replace. Their absence plain to see, some will not agree regarding Henry, however, he had a way of organising the defence perfectly, something unfortunately that is blatantly lacking this season. Also yes I will bore some with the fact that we have so many key players injured it is a miracle we are still in a fight for a play-off place. Our position flatters us somewhat in reality. As much as I admire and rate John Still highly, I do question some of his formations and starting line ups. That is though very easy for me to comment sitting here now. The manager is a seasoned campaigner, whatever moves he makes he will be having his reasons, at best he is not going to please every individual Luton supporter. This is not as much a criticism as a wish on my own behalf, which he would start with Nathan Oduwa. When he runs at defenders they panic, he can be a little unsophisticated, for want of a better word, at times, but he has been having the desired effect when coming into the game.

Today Luton were run ragged by a player who will not be playing at this level too long, Jack Redshaw looked a cut above every other player on the park. On Tuesday evening, the same said about Bury's Danny Mayor. We are lacking this season a player that can run a game as Andre used to accomplish last season.

Opposing sides this season are not so naïve as many of the Conference sides we were meeting last season. They are more seasoned, they will close down any threats we offer up quicker, they have the skill for taking players out of the game legally. Tis season we are coming up against sides who know how to manipulate our weaknesses more. We find ourselves coming up against more accomplished players and coaches, experienced campaigners.

The officiating today was extremely poor at best; the referee was weak, not just in regards to Luton Town, but both sides. Handing out cards as if he was advertising his wares on the High Street. If we are all honest, Cameron McGeehan most fortunate to still be on the pitch after only three minutes following his attack on Morecambe's Wilson.

Mark Cullen looked like a little boy lost, up there alone against three defenders. Good to see him back though, I have to say.

Morecambe took the lead when Redshaw left Wilkinson for dead and blasted the ball out of Justham's reach low past the far post.

It was not long before the "Shrimps" doubled their lead, Redshaw who initially looked to be offside, later replay proves different, pulled the ball back to Wilson, a great strike that any keeper would have been troubled by, placing the ball into the top corner, a most sublime strike.

Alex Lawless replaced Griffiths, who most uncharacteristically seemed to be elsewhere just after the half hour mark.

Ellison and Redshaw were running the game; repeatedly they pushed forward, putting the "Hatters" defence to the limits.

Not long before the break Luton pulled a goal back. Some good play by Jonathan Smith, playing the ball to Harriman who played a superb cross into the centre for McGeehan to head home from distance.

Luton seemed to suddenly come alive, why does it always seem to be this way?

The second half was not unlike many we have experienced from the "Hatters" this season. Morecambe pinned in at the back for periods. The addition of Lawless made a marked difference, his sense of urgency there to most to see. Cullen and Whalley began to play off each other. Harriman also pushing forward on occasion and looking to get Luton back into the game.

Lawless had a good effort pass just wide of the post, the "Hatters" seemed rejuvenated.

There was an incident where Wilkinson manhandled quite blatantly in the box by Edwards, but no penalty awarded, story of Luton's season.

Lawless saw his shot deflected just over when Wilson just got himself in the way of it in time.

John Still made the second substitution of the afternoon replacing the lack lustre Smith with Lee.

Luton changed their formation to 4-3-3, why did we not start with such, especially at home.

Edwards tripped Lee on the edge of the box and received a yellow card for his actions. Guttridge dummied the free kick for Lee to place the ball sweetly over the wall bringing a good save from Arestidou, Morecambe's keeper.

Luton's third substitution saw Oduwa replace Whalley, who put in a decent shift eventually, quite underestimated in my humble opinion. The Tottenham loanee soon had the visitor's defence shaking.

Luton scored an equaliser, this coming from a Guttridge corner kick that found the head of skipper Steve McNulty, his effort coming off the crossbar, running loose to Alex Lawless who placed his shot sweetly from the edge of the box. Level scores and seemingly the "Hatter" on the ascendance.

Edwards who had already been booked made a most horrendous high tackle on McGeehan, this resulting in a fracas between a handful of players, the referee, not that he had any in the first place, seemed to have lost all control of the game. Even if he had not been booked previously the foul would have merited a straight red anyway, as it is the ref. waved first a yellow and then a red, it was so long Edwards, your carriage awaits.

Cameron McGeehan had a fine chance to put the Town ahead, but totally fluffed it with a lazy effort. Lawless had another fine effort denied by the busier keeper in the second half Arestidou.

Morecambe went up the other end and against the run of play in the second half scored what turned out to be the winning goal, the ball coming in from the left, no real danger it seemed, but somehow Wilkinson got a stab at the ball and played it into his own goal.

Again, the Town managed to push forward, an unmarked McGeehan from Harriman's cross heading over.

The fourth official held up his board stating that there would be six minutes of added time, an ironic cheer echoing around the ground.

Oduwa received a yellow after catching Hughes, who made a meal of the fact and rolled around as if shot. Reminds me some of what I wrote earlier regarding the difference between footballers and Jockeys, men and well, let us leave it there shall we.

McGeehan had one more opportunity to square the game up just prior to the final whistle, after Oduwa effort turned out for a corner by Hughes. Guttridge's ensuing corner dropped nicely for McGeehan denied by Hughes, who did well to get in the way to block.

Shrewsbury saw a late Equaliser from Cambridge United's Kaikai assist in moving them from top spot, in what was another dent in their home form following last week's first home defeat of the season. Burton Albion taking over that top mantle with a 1-0 away win at Hartlepool's Victoria Park, which leaves the North East club in a crisis as far as the relegation battle at the bottom goes.

Wycombe and Southend drew 2-2 at Roots Hall, which allowed Wycombe to stay five points clear from play-off positions and sitting comfortably for now at least in the automatic promotion zone. With Southend climbing above Luton, who now drop down one place to fifth with Bury on the same points, but the "Hatters" having a better goal difference. It is certainly getting tight just below Luton.

As a Luton supporter of many years indeed, I am disgusted, whoever the Morons were that confronted both Steve McNulty and John Still; they also need to be disgusted with themselves. The truth is though, they will not be and they will be in the pub as I write this boasting at how they told John and Steve what they thought of this afternoon's performance. Okay, granted the team is not playing good enough. Nevertheless, such behaviour cannot be accepted anywhere in football, least of all Luton Town Football Club. Therefore, whomever you are if you cannot behave and show some respect to players, management and other supporters of our great club, I have one solution to the problems you seem to so dislike, fuck off and do not come back, you are not wanted and not worthy of calling yourselves true supporters.

Steve McNulty later offered any supporter that feels angered at the side's recent drop in form to meet up at the training ground and discuss matters. I wonder if in reality there will be any takers.

Sunday March 8th 2015

I am going to begin with a word about a Watford supporter. It is not the done thing, usually to sympathise with the club and their supporters, being as we are avid "Hatters". Today different, today we have to rise above our prejudices and join as one, as a football family. Following their 2-2 away draw at Wolverhampton, forty four year old Nick Cruwys along with some other fans were walking back towards the railway station from the Molineux Stadium. On their way, a gang that outnumbered them accosted them. This gang of men savagely attacked Nick and his friends. As a result, Mr Cruwys is now in hospital fighting for his life after receiving brutal head injuries.

Our thoughts and prayers must be with Nick Cruwys family and friends this morning and we wish all concerned well, and a good outcome transpires.

Let us hope also that the West Midlands constabulary are able to find catch and jail these despicable individuals as soon as possible, football or the world in general does not need such thugs on our streets.

Following yesterday's game and the incident that followed regarding the verbal attack on John Still, social media has been rumbling. Condemnations of the culprit on the whole, a few moronic individuals have joined the cause; I made a mistake there sorry, calling them supporters. Supporters the most certainly are not.

One Luton fan Paul Stillwell went as far as to write a short story on the incident and with Paul's kind permission, I have added below.

Here is a little story for you...

There was a football team stuck in the conference for 5 years. A new manager comes in and wins the league in his first year (hard to believe but stick with it...).

But, in their first season in league two they lose a striker called Gray who was as important to them as Suarez was to Liverpool, but sadly this team weren't given 75 million to replace him. They had virtually nothing. Their manager had to beg, borrow and steal reserve players with no first team experience.

Two months into the season, their two next best strikers called Benson and Lawless get serious injuries and will be out for 4 months. But the manager searches for more reserve players, because that's all they can afford.

He throws them in the team, with no time to teach them anything. Incredibly, the team climb the table.

Then... Their two best midfielders called Ruddock and Guttridge get injured and are out for 3 months, but they hold their position. But three months later Ruddock comes back and is injured in his first game, out for another month. Their next best midfielder called Doyle gets injured, out for 2 months. The manager hurriedly tries to train and teach the new young reserve players and yet

keeps the team in their position!
No this is not Roy of the Rovers.
But then...they lose their best goalkeeper, out for a month!
Now my friends, with only 11 games left, reading this story, where do you suppose our fictional team is in the league?
Bottom half?
Relegation zone?
Well my friends they are 5th and only 6 points off promotion!
What's that I hear you cry? "Don't be silly that's impossible!"
Well it's true!
What's that you say?
"Only Mourinho could pull that off"
Well my friends they don't have Mourinho, but here is the funny part, some fans of this club want the manager sacked! One fan even ran down from the stands to the edge of the pitch and insulted the manager for what he has done to the club.
Stop laughing folks!
This is a true story!
I tell you its true!
Paul, Luton born, has been watching the "Hatters" since 1976 and was match day mascot on the opening game of the 1978-1979 season on August 18th against Oldham Athletic, which the "Hatters" duly came away 6-1 victors, with a brace from Bob Hatton (2), David Moss (2), Brian Stein and a Lil Fuccillo penalty. So a most memorable day all round for the young Mascot.

Paul leading out the "Hatters" on his memorable day as match day mascot.

Another of his array of Luton claims to fame, as he puts it, is the fact that his Mothers cousin is Luton Town 1959 FA Cup finalist Tony Gregory.
When Paul moved to Bournemouth in 2005, unfortunately having to miss a couple of seasons. However, he now drives, along with his father, a "Hatter" since 1946 himself, to every game home

and away. Until recently, Paul was a professional artist and some of us may recall his amazing portrait painting of Mick Harford with the Johnson's Paint Trophy, which in fact now hangs on the wall at Mick's home.

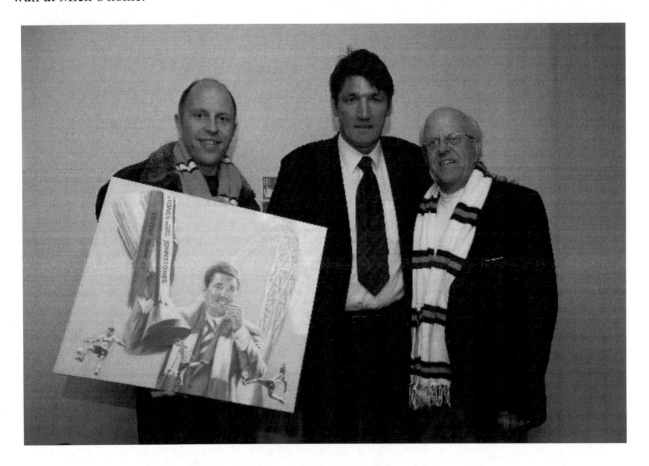

Paul Stillwell's painting of Mick Harford with the Johnson's Paint Trophy, circa. 2009.

Better news from the Under 18s side who recorded a resounding victory against their Southend United counterparts on Saturday morning, goals from Daril Ngwala and Osamu Allman, with goals in each half.

Monday March 9th 2015
I am usually at my desk bright and early most mornings, but today I was intrigued to see how England would fare in a game they had to win to qualify for the Quarter finals of the Cricket World Cup against Bangladesh. Instead, it would have been better if I had stayed within the confines of my warm bed or just went directly to work at the desk. Humiliation is not a word I use lightly, but to depart from the competition in the way England have, in the five games they have played so far out of the scheduled six is humiliating, without doubt. Out of the five games one win, that being against Scotland, I cannot wait to see how they manage against Afghanistan that will be interesting indeed. However, best not to dwell on such things. Have to get back to business. Either here or my other books that have I will admit been neglected unfairly of late, mainly yes due to the cricket going on. What makes it even more worrying work wise is that tomorrow the Cheltenham festival commences. Not much gambling will be going on from here, but I cannot wait for the racing to start. Some amazing battles are awaiting us. Tomorrow for instance, The Stan James Champion Hurdle, only eight runners this year but eight of the very best. It could turn out to be a true battle royal. My heart is hoping that the mighty Hurricane Fly will continue what has been a most amazing career. In addition, the chance maybe of AP McCoy winning what is to be his final ride in this so prestigious race on Jezki. However, my head is telling me, despite not coming to form as of yet this season, Hurricane Fly's stablemate Faugheen, both trained by Willie Mullins in Ireland. It is too tough a call for me to have a right royal bet, that means I will be able to sit back relax and enjoy what will almost certainly be e most sensational and memorable race.

I have just finished watching the Manchester United v Arsenal FA Cup Quarter Final on BBC. The conclusion I have come to is that, Manchester United are their own worst enemies, they fall over when tackled, they beg opponents get cards. If they were to play football and stop the histrionics as they used to do then maybe they would be a little more successful again. I have noticed since Van Gaal took charge the number of dives in and around the box have multiplied drastically. It is shameful. Di Maria should get a long ban for his actions this evening. Welbeck must be laughing all the way to the bank, despite being a Manchester United fan; he must be thinking "thank-you Mr Van Gaal for releasing me from the theatre of misguided dreams. I now play football where not expected to fall over at every little tackle that I lose the ball. I am allowed to stand and show what I can do; I left you a little something to remind you of me tonight, a goal for you to chew on." From the same game how refreshing to see a referee officiating a game where he took no crap from so-called influential players. Bravely done. I will sign off tonight by saying, how good to see Mr Pat Rice in the stands watching the game at Old Trafford. Top man. We wish the man well.

Tuesday March 10th 2015

One of the major talking points throughout the Luton town fan base right now is concerning the announcement made by club Chairman Nick Owen last week. The board are considering or in fact even done so already, agreed to a stadium sponsorship, which will in effect, mean our home will change from Kenilworth Road. Instead, to something similar to the "Reebok" or the "Etihad" stadium. Obviously, Luton Town are not going to be associated with the likes of those, nevertheless, it looks like it is going to happen within the month. I think most supporters are a little upset at the prospect, including myself. However, in all fairness to those making the decision they are solely concerned with the financial benefits to keep the club in the stable financial position they are able to boast now, in comparison to our slippery past.

We as supporters have to accept football has progressed worldwide and it is inevitable for such a day to arrive eventually.

If the "Hatters" wish to compete with the bigger club's in the future the board obviously have to look down every avenue available to give the club that financial push it so sorely needs.

It is common sense that Luton are not going to get a massively life changing sponsorship, there will be nothing comparative to the £400m sponsorship that Manchester City have with Etihad Airways, but we can only hope that it will be a substantial deal.

Most of us realise that Luton Town needs a new stadium in order to go forward, maybe this is even the stepping-stone to that requirement, only the board knows that for now. A substantial injection of funds can only be a good move for Luton town right now of that I am certain. In addition, there are those supporters who want the board to dip into the coffers to purchase players that are more experienced. Something not possible if the money is not there to implement such purchases. The money has to come from somewhere.

One reason I believe, that it is the correct time to go down this path. We at last have board members that have the club at heart. If it had been a few years ago I would have been most dubious about such a decision.

The most dangerous risk I can foresee is if the sponsoring company was to go into bankruptcy during such a deal. Where would that leave Luton Town both legally and financially?

However, I am sure that both the board and its consultants have looked very deeply into all those implications before making their decision.

In not only John Still and his team do I trust, but also those that run the club on our behalf. Personally, I believe Luton Town Football Club is at its most secure footing very many years. Therefore, this can only be a good move. Let us face it, as fans we shall know the place we make our weekly pilgrimage to as our beloved "Kenny" despite any other name that it is given. The new name known only as that by the media and those not associated with the "Hatters" Onwards we strive.

Moving on, what an afternoon of racing we had today from Cheltenham, how glad I am I decided not to have wagers all over the place, because I would most certainly have had Annie Power as my banker. How she must have broken many a punters heart yesterday. There was though that amazing powerhouse Faugheen winning The Stan James Champion Hurdle, he was formidable from the starting tape to the finishing line, he bossed the race throughout.

Looking at the way he is put together. He will go on to be an even better chasing prospect than he ever has been as a hurdler. However, in racing, one can never be certain of course. Nevertheless, for me personally he will be a champion chaser if taken down that road by his trainer Willie Mullins.

Wednesday March 11th 2015

Something I have been holding off from making any comment about until now is the next phase of attempting to get Premiership clubs B teams integrated into the third and fourth tiers if the football league. This time it is a proposal that they be to compete in the Johnsons Paint Trophy or whatever names it will play under in future season.

Earlier in the season it had been suggested that "B teams" be injected into the Conference and League Two, fortunately that plan as at least been put on hold.

Initially, last week word was that there had been a vote by all seventy-two league clubs to allow the introduction into the JPS and that AFC Wimbledon had been the only club to vote against the idea. However, later on the same day, Luton Town along with other clubs including AFC Wimbledon put out statements that no such vote took place. Although the clubs were notified that the proposals were being considered.

The problem for myself with this is the conditions that would ensure that the Premier clubs do not abuse the idea using senior players within the competition. It would only work for me if certain limitations of which players they could play were put in place. The fear being that what was supposed to be a completion to give the lower league clubs the opportunity to play at Wembley in a cup final, would in time be dominated by sides from Premier clubs.

There is the other side of the argument though. Quite interestingly pointed out to me by Mike Thomas as we discussed this, that would it not be more financially beneficial to the lower league clubs to playing the likes of Arsenal, Tottenham and Manchester United sides rather than maybe Port Vale and Rochdale, no disrespect intended to either clubs, generating larger attendances and therefore more revenue also. Mike quite rightly indicated that many would rather leave home to sit in the cold in a half empty stadium to watch Arsenal rather than one of the lower clubs. A good point of fact. It would work I suppose, as long, as I mentioned earlier, certain conditions were implemented that would not allow players with Premier League appearances to take part. In addition, because it suggested that one of the major reasons for the proposals was to get young English players the opportunity to get competitive match experience, maybe it should be made open to only home-grown players of a certain age grouping, then maybe it would be acceptable. If that was not the case, I cannot honestly see the relevance of the proposals going ahead. This is just my personal take on the situation. As with "B teams" in the lower leagues, I have my misgivings.

Thursday March 12th 2015

Rory McCrohan RIP

Luton Town website today announced the sad news that former "Hatters" head coach and assistant manager Rory McCrohan passed away on March 3rd 2015.
Rory was head coach and assistant manager in the 1960s alongside one of the Towns legendary managers' Harry Haslam.
His playing career included 426 first team appearances for Norwich City in the mid to late fifties and early sixties. Added to the Norwich City Hall of Fame in 2003 was stated as being a true Canaries legend who was able to slot in to most positions if required at any given time.
He was in the Norwich side of the 1958-59 season that despite being in what was then Division Three reached the FA Cup Semi-Final, their run halted by losing finalists Luton Town, of which the player noted being the most disappointing day of his playing career.
In 1962, he was a member of the Canaries 1962 League Cup winning side, having beaten Rochdale 4-0 on aggregate, when the trophy decided on a two legged home and away basis. The second leg at Carrow Road was to be his final appearance for the club. Whereupon he moved to Colchester United. Following a brief spell at Colchester, he moved again to Bristol Rovers, making a minimal number of appearances.
In his coaching career before moving to Luton, he was working alongside the Bobby Robson at Fulham.
After his tenure with Harry Haslam at the "Hatters" he moved across the pond to America, joining Detroit Express as assistant coach for the NSL side.
Later he was named as Head Coach for Minnesota Kickers in 1978.
Rory passed away following a long illness in a West Country hospital at the age of 84. He leaves his wife Mary, son Andy and daughter Sue. RIP sir.

It may be that Pelly Ruddock Mpanzu may have played his final game for the season. Having been plagued with injury for a majority of the season, Pelly scheduled to see a specialist regarding his ongoing hamstring injury has no timeline set for his return, as of yet. This is a devastating blow to the "Hatters" as they try to bring to a halt what has become a four-match run of successive defeats. The ripples in the aftermath of last Saturday's verbal attack on both John Still and Steve McNulty at Kenilworth Road have not yet died down.

Yesterday the club released a video with JLS giving a very emotional statement in the wake of the uncalled for scenes.

John explained how, as the teams were leaving the Kenilworth Road pitch at the end of the gutting 2-3 defeat by Morecambe, that in fairness the "Hatters" had done well to claw back to 2-2 after being 0-2 down. Thwarted of a point in the last minutes of the game by a luckless own goal by Luke Wilkinson. In the corner of his eye, he had noticed an altercation between a group of fans and two other individuals. He heard clearly the comments thrown at him, which were at the very least quite disgraceful especially in front of women and young children. Stopping he replied "How dare you, how dare you!"

Mr Still quite correctly states that on his arrival at Luton Town just two years ago, not at any time has he promised a quick fix or immediate success. However, he states, we were quite fortunate enough to win the Skrill Premier at the first attempt in his role at the club. He continued to express that one of the main reasons for the unexpected success was down primarily to the fact that the whole squad came together as a team not only on the playing field but also off. This is not unlike the side that David Pleat had in the eighties when having that superb First Division side of the 1980s. He also went on to confess that the success would not be having such a successful time without the amazing backing of the majority of our supporters during his time here so far. He then went on to ask the question, "What if we did gain promotion to League One at the conclusion of this season, and it got to the point we are at now this season and we hit a bad patch, losing a few games. Would those same fans be moaning then? What if the next season we followed up with a third promotion, this time into the Championship and a similar scenario was to come about. Would those same supporters yet again be moaning?"

That is one very good question.

I myself have often thought that what would happen if John Still were to become perplexed with all the unnecessary complaining aimed towards the team and himself the past few weeks and decide enough is enough. Where would that leave the club then?

The minority that are causing all these ripples should honestly sit back and have a thought to the past.

I realise that I am continually throughout this book stressing the same thing repeatedly, but at times such as this, I find myself unable to hold back.

Look back to the past five years prior to this season. Can people really forget so easily the disrespect and contempt shown towards the supporters by the man who should have been thrown at times a straightjacket rather than a lifejacket, Richard Money?

We now have a manager at the helm who has not only bought success and league football to the club, but also shows great respect towards the fans, appreciates the part we play.

These people that seem intent on throwing away what we have in our midst honestly need to take a step back and realise what we have now, is a manager that has the future of this club in his heart not just the here and now. Immediate success may be good for some. However, I know the majority would rather have a more moderate success now and allow building for the future and enjoying more continued success in seasons to come. How many sides do we see grab success by the balls and then once those players of that period are too old and slow the success dissipates into a cyclone of despair and bad results? Quite a few! Let us please not allow that to happen to Luton

Town Football Club. We may not totally deserve, but we want it, so let us have it, we are worthy and our time will come, but please not at the price of the clubs future.

In the same context, these people need to stop and think fully at what those that cry "Still Out" and yes unfortunately there are a handful and I do not include those that I know sometimes say it in a sarcastically styled manner, taking the piss out of those that do. I mean those that really say it with venom, I will repeat, yes there are some. I ask those this, what will be the outcome when you get your wish?

Because when that day comes remember what you were pushing for. We will not get another like John Still that is for sure. We will most probably get the likes of Kevin "let us sign has been's and fill their pockets with silver" Blackwell. Their heart not in the club but only their bank balance.

We may get someone who has the passion but not the means, unlike JLS who it is so obvious to the majority of us has both. Yes, admittedly, we all question his selections and formations at times, but it is long-term not short term that matters. When that day comes do not expect the bright picture we are experiencing now.

Believe me it will come to the point where news will get out. If not already done so of course, that Luton Town supporters can be ungrateful, it may be the minority, however as word gets around the rumours bring the numbers up from person to person, those young and talented managers will look at our past record and ask the question as to why anyone would want to go there. What will go through their minds is that even if they do bring success to the club they will all the same be berated by supporters, crap thrown in their faces at the slightest hiccup in form, irrelevant of how much success they have bought the club. Therefore one look at the vacancy whenever it may come about and all they will think is "No thank you, goodbye to that."

So please you people, seriously, stop, think and only then speak. For most, that is not so difficult apparently, so they tell me anyway.

After all that he has witnessed, at the end of his statement, John still went on to praise the support in general this season. Quite remarkable considering, do you not think.

Friday March 13th 2015

It was not until I commenced writing, this evening that I realised "damn its Friday 13th, watch out for the Krugerman."

Despite all I was forced to write yesterday about supporters, one could not help but marvel at the number of supporters this evening already travelling or preparing to travel to Portsmouth for tomorrow's game at Fratton Park. So amazing. Not many clubs at the top of the football tier can boast such. Leave alone a League Two side. Over 2,600 tickets sold.

Portsmouth, I recall from experiences of the past not the most friendly of places for away supporters.

Saturday March 14th 2015

Exactly thirty years ago today at Kenilworth Road football witnessed one of the most horrendous scenes at an English football stadium for many years.

Thousands of Millwall fans descended on Luton for a FA Cup sixth round tie between Luton Town and Millwall at Kenilworth Road. In the afternoon there had already been isolated incidents within the town centre, but nothing too have the people of Luton or the relevant authorities to show too much concern over.

However, in the aftermath it was to become known to many in the media as "The day football died" at the time.

It was not by any means of the imagination one the most attractive of games, with a Brian Stein goal in the thirty-third minute being enough to seal Millwall's fate and send Luton to Villa Park on Saturday 13th April for a semi-final tie against team of the moment Everton.

With only fifteen minutes into the game, a large contingent of Millwall supporters surged onto the pitch. The police had to use Alsatian dogs to assist in getting the crowd back under control, during this time referee David Hutchinson ordered both sets of players off the pitch for their safety and to allow the police to get the pitch cleared of the mob. Before the game was able to restart both the referee and Millwall's then manager George Graham pleaded with the Millwall supporters for calm to allow the game to continue.

Eventually, the game continuing, but the players obviously affected by the volatile atmosphere that polluted the stadium air. Not as already mentioned, the best of games.

As the final whistle approached, again, the Millwall supporters were trying persistently to get onto the pitch, but by now the police attendance had grown enough to foil any attempt for them successfully to enter upon the field of play, in their attempt to get the match abandoned and so the game replayed.

When the final whistle sounded the wall of police succumbed to the mass of supporters who charged on to the pitch attempting to get at the Luton supporters who were still trying to leave the Bobbers stand and the Oak road end. A sea of South London invaders rushed the Bobber's stand and began ripping out the seats from their holdings, the seats thrown at the now retreating police who had lost all control of the situation, totally out numbered.

It later reported that over a thousand Millwall supporters, following a broken turnstile at the Kenilworth Road entrance, managed to get into the ground without paying.

For myself and many other "Hatters" it was one of the most frightening sights at a football game having witnessed and not wanting to do so again. Although I have to admit I was totally as scared when caught up in the 2013 riots in Peckham, that was more terrorising than one could imagine, as one was walking home from work a throng of marauding, drink and drug driven lunatics, eyes bulging out of their heads running at speed towards you. I am still to this day not sure how I came through the experience both times without injury of some kind. Shaken up on both occasions greatly yes but injured no. That second time in Peckham I was more concerned for my children as I noticed bellows of smoke coming from the vicinity of their home. Fortunately, no one injured that time also. Nevertheless, yes, March 14th 1985 was worse than anything I had witnessed before anywhere. A sad night for the game of football.

Back to today, a glum old day on the south coast, but hopes are high for the "Hatters" fans, the atmosphere is already electric, although a Weatherspoon's pub has requested all day police protection because of Luton fans being in town, totally over the top.

The "Hatters" will line-up as follows: Elliot Justham, Michael Harriman, Steve McNulty, Luke Wilkinson, Jake Howells, Shaun Whalley, Andy Drury, Cameron McGeehan, Alex Lawless, Luke Guttridge and Mark Cullen. With those waiting with anticipation to bought into the battle fray: Fraser Franks, Nathan Oduwa, Paul Benson, Matt Robinson, Jayden Stockley, Elliot Lee and Craig King.

Portsmouth 2 Luton Town 0
In front of a crowd of 17,149 at Fratton Park and an atmosphere, that any Championship or even Premier league game would be content with, Luton dealt harshly as far as the score line is concerned. Marginally the better side it some will agree in footballing terms. If anything, as has been the case on more than one occasion recently beaten in effect by sucker punch type goals. The "Hatters" fighting back with a certain determination but not reaping the deserved rewards for their efforts.
Although as is again the case in recent weeks gone by I am inclined to question the team selection and also the formation used, as yet again just the one up front player despite the number of strikers we have available within the squad, not forgetting good attacking midfielders also that are not continuously used. I am not criticising as much as just questioning. No doubt the manager has his reasons and ideas and let us face it he knows the job much better than I ever will, so be it.
The last time Luton visited Fratton Park was December 16th 1995, on that occasion Portsmouth won 4-0.
Before today's game, the head to head both home and away was:

Played 45 Won 21 Drawn 12 Lost 12 GF 74 GA 67 (including all cup games).

The game three minutes old, when Matt Tubbs netted the first superbly taken. Wallace hit the ball towards the near post, Tubbs latching on to it perfectly. Justham was able to get a finger or maybe two onto it but never enough to prevent the ball from hitting the back of the net. I have heard some comments recently that some will be glad to see Tyler back, but looking back, in my humble opinion, all but maybe one of the goals conceded whilst the young lad has been keeping goal, Mark Tyler would have had to excel himself to stop them. Therefore comments such of the like very much un-called for.
McNulty suffered a cut to the head and after treatment, returned to the field of battle looking more Steve Foster like, if only as effective, although that is an unfair comment, I will leave it in for good measure.
Luton battled to level the score but in all honesty the fire power was not equal to that of Portsmouth, who had the one player up front that many Luton supporters were for a second time hoping to secure the signature of earlier in the season, that of the scorer Matt Tubbs.
At the half-time break captain Steve McNulty, headband and all, replaced by Fraser Franks, someone I believe has had a raw deal from a section of the fans this season.
Luton went for the jugular but the firepower was still lacking.
Despite Luton pressing forward at every chance, they could not penetrate the Pompey goal.
Portsmouth virtually killed the game in the sixty-second minute when another superb strike beat Elliot Justham without trouble, another no chance to reach effort, From Tubbs miskick and Taylor latched onto the ball and blasted the ball into the net.
Luton have to be commended on their will to fight despite the two-goal deficit, something they have never been lacking most of the season, a will to fight. Cullen had a shot kicked off the line.
One good piece of news in the match was his return to the first team; when Paul Benson came on to replace Mark Cullen, his first league appearance since breaking his leg against Mansfield at Kenilworth road in October of last year. Luton to the end battled on, but it was as the time went on a losing battle.

The support for the afternoon was again amazing, with over 2,600 "Hatters", making the journey and supporting the team with fervour from start to finish. I get the feeling this season has not slipped by from Luton yet, as some are predicting. Nevertheless, if it does it will not be for the want of trying.

With that loss Luton dropped one place to fifth, but still time to pick up the pieces and battle for a play-off place, although with our history in the seasonal play-offs is that a good thing or not?

Sunday March 15th 2015
The next day inquests were of a mixed bunch, some seeing the Town as poor and others questioning those that followed that course by saying one of the better performances of the season despite losing 2-0.
I would be inclined to agree with the latter.
To be honest I am not sure if I am angered, amused or just bewildered at the injustice being thrown the way of Elliot Justham. The lad has proved his worth there is no getting away from it.
Nevertheless, I hear some crying out for the return of Mark Tyler. They are saying that since "Tyles" sustained his injury the results have faltered. I suppose there is an element of truth in that, but that is coincidental nothing more. Looking back again at the goals conceded whilst Justham has been between the posts I have concluded that most would have given "Tyles" problems in stopping also. I find the criticism way out of order, the lad has done a fantastic job whilst standing in for our regular keeper.
Back to yesterday and the senseless actions of a few have yet again marred what was on the whole a most fantastic atmosphere at Fratton Park. I have been told that during the game another flare was thrown from the area at where the Town support was situated. However, some are saying they do not know from which direction it was directed from. There are others that say it was from our own fans and others that it was directed at the Luton fans by a Portsmouth fan. To me it does not matter who threw it, whoever it is they are morons of the highest calibre. It was not too far back that I sent a reminder of Bradford City's disaster. Apparently again, as like before, a young lad was slightly injured because of those morons actions. How long before there is a more serious injury.
Following the game and whilst walking back to their relevant modes of transport home, some "Hatters" fans complained that groups of Portsmouth thugs were trying to goad Luton fans into fights. However, there are also conflicting reports regarding trouble before the game, where police horses were bought in to stave off trouble flaring up between two rival sets of fans. This report was made by the Thames Valley police apparently, however my question is a simple one. Why would Thames Valley police be at a Portsmouth game? I think there was some wind-up going on here. The news was broken by journalist student's blog, aptly named Luton Blog. I have a feeling myself that a touch of journalistic sensationalism was to blame on this occasion. Maybe looking for some National coverage. Luton Town support has already been handed bad name when it comes to football journalism recently and not all has been justifiable. Such reports when bestowed upon us only adds fuel to a fire that some would love to see stoked up.
I sometimes wonder if there are too many conspiracy theories running around at the moment relating to Luton Town. Some trying to invoke that the FA and its official have it in for Luton Town. Hence the decisions made in games against us or just simply other incidents on the field of play overlooked because it is Luton Town. Sorry I for one do hold with all that nonsense. I am hearing from the Premiership down to the lower non-leagues regarding the incompetence of match officials over the past couple of years. The truth of the matter is, the standard of match officiating

has dropped to an all-time low. Too many referees seem to be more inclined to not allow a game to flow, which in turn brings out frustrations within the players, they in turn bring that frustration in their game. Many referees have no control of players these days. Some of the antics that go down would not have been tolerated by the likes of the old school referees such as Clive Thomas and even the happy go lucky Roger Kirkpatrick, although a joker, could also become quite rigid in his decisions.

What also troubles me is that some not all players of today do not have the same element of respect for the match officials as was the case in the past. It was up until a few years ago a rare occurrence to see players waving hands in the air to get an opponent either booked or sent-off, maybe I am completely wrong, but that is my view. Not long ago I was interviewing former National Hunt jockey Ron Hyett, who stressed similar is now happening at race meetings where Jockeys of today do not respect the race starters as much as was so in the past. Respect across the whole spectrum of our society has plummeted rapidly in recent years. That is one of the fundamental problems for factions throughout Britain at the moment, respect for authority is dying, that being a very sad state to be in.

Nice to see the Youth side reversing the scores though against the Pompey Academy, a deserved 2-0 victory. It was Portsmouth first defeat of the season in the Merit League One. A penalty from Daril Ngwala and a second well taken goal ensured Luton the spoils, also an impressive show from Liam Gooch in the Luton goal kept any efforts that Portsmouth had, at bay.

Monday March 16th 2015
The focus is now on tomorrow night's game at Newport, where the "Hatters" must look for all three points. News is that Paul Benson may be on the return and a possible appearance on the bench would be a welcome sight to most "Hatters" out there.

John Still post game thoughts following a Sunday to sit back and reflect, were for me just about spot-on. His feelings were that the Town played as well as anytime during the season so far. My adage to that is one of agreement. I spoke with a Pompey fan yesterday, who quoted to me his thoughts that the "Hatter" were for him, the best side seen at Fratton Park, this season.

The manager went on to say that there were times in the game where Luton's movement was very good, including a number, in his words, very clever moves. His feeling was that until Portsmouth scored their second, completely against the run of play, albeit a very good goal from Taylor, the "Hatters" were taking the game to Portsmouth and on the ascendance, which despite the goal they continued to do so straight from the restart. If there was to be any criticism, maybe the fact that we did not make use of the ball for the amount of possession we had. However, at the same time credit must be afforded to the way Portsmouth defended in and around their goal. Luton had a couple of shots kicked off the line, obstructing the Town from getting back into the game.

In terms of their overall performance, the boss was absolutely delighted with the way the players went about the job. I would tend to agree, again, with that comment. The problem is that it is a known fact, that it does matter who the team is, be it, Arsenal, Manchester United, Luton Town or lowly Kempston Rovers, when a team is going through a bad run, at times it seems that everything goes against them. It is just how the game runs and nothing can be done about that but stick to the job, persevere and wait with patience for it to come together again. Because let us face it the side is not a bad side. We have won games this season where we have played much worse than some of the recent defeats that have been witnessed. When such a bleak period is being experienced it is a matter of battling on, because the frustration does come into play, the doubts do creep in, a good manager worth his salt, will dispel any of these within a squad. The frustration does not only rub off on the fans, the players must be feeling it even more than we are, that is why I always try to get behind them and give that support, because despondency only brings a lack in confidences. I believe that is one of JLS's major strengths, he stands by his players when things are not going according to plan.

As the season slowly descends upon it climax, yes, I am reaching just a little deeper getting more involved. Too little too late, who knows, maybe I should have been more alert from day one. But anyhow let us roll on regardless. I am listening to and taking more notice of the management comments, I will admit to that.

Although, one thing that I do continue to find somewhat baffling is, despite having signed two obviously extremely talented young guys on loan, Nathan Oduwa and Elliot Lee from Tottenham and West Ham respectively, why are they not getting, for want of a better phrasing maybe, more air time on the pitch? Even more so maybe. Why are they not in the starting line-ups?

Back to the interview. I am listening to a segment at a time which is in turn allowing me to stop and think about what has been said.

John Still admits wholeheartedly that our that our lack of returning to winning ways since the New Year has not only been frustrating but mystifying also. The fact is he says it is not good enough, that we need to start winning games again.

One of the manager and the rest of the staff also main frustrations, apart from those already mentioned, are based maybe on the eve of games. When after all the formations and game plans have been worked out on the training field, along comes either the club doctor or physio with the news that another player has been forced out of an ensuing game. Some will say some games more important than the other, so some they should be able to deal with. For myself I do not hold court with that. We are back in the Football League, therefore every game is important as the previous or the one following. No opponent is a lesser threat than another these days. Despite some peoples thoughts to the contrary. Therefore, when it is realised on the eve of a game that a player has to be overlooked because of injury, illness or any other relevant factor, it must make life difficult. The consistency and continuity of the team is greatly affected. Any side has to have a reasonable semblance of both those elements throughout a season. As far as I am concerned they are two of the most important ingredients of a successful team, along with morale and unity. Without them the team is far ever in a state of disruption. Unfortunately that has been one of the compelling problems for John Still throughout this season. Some I hear say we should not be using the excuse of all the injuries we have been having, especially with the size of the squad as it is. The problem is not so much the injuries in themselves, but the disruption caused by their presence. If I sound patronising, I do not care, because some really need to look at the bigger picture rather than what is in front of them. Players link together more effectively when able to get minutes and successive games under their belts alongside each other. I will say again, Luton have missed those settled partnerships too much this season.

This is why a manager cannot just look at the players to find the solutions to what is going wrong, but also look straight into the mirror at himself, that is what makes the difference from a good manager and a not so good one. The ones that can look in that mirror and come out with an answer are the ones that will prosper long term.

It is so easy for us the supporters, I feel, to sit back in our armchair and criticise week after week, game after game. We have the right as fans to criticise, yes of course we do. However, there are certain factors we should understand before making unnecessary and unhelpful comments regarding any given situation. As I have said before, before casting our stones at the accused, we must stop think and determine whether we are correct before condemning.

Let us be absolutely honest with ourselves though. Luton Town are without doubt some of the worst for that. However, who can really blame us for that. Even John Still recognises the tribulations, heartache and grief that we as supporters of the Town have had to endure. Something the likes Of Richard Money are too gormless or just plain ignorant to accept and take into account. At least John realises that and accepts us mostly for who we are. The problems we have had to face and endure as Luton Town fans would prove too much for many weaker band of supporters. Our strength, our passion, our endurance and our bloody minded doggedness in the face of adversity has shown through on more than one too many occasion. We are a hardy bunch it has to be said. My heart really goes out to those other clubs supporters when I read in the media that certain clubs have a crisis, when, having just been eliminated from a European competition, despite the fact they have received umpteen millions in revenue along the way. It seriously does have me rolling in laughter and feeling sorry for them. Crisis? They would not know what a real crisis was. I often say to a moaning Manchester City or especially Liverpool fan who is having a right whinge and saying the club is in trouble as they will not get into Europe next season or something to the like. I always say one thing, come to Kenilworth Road and become a Luton Town supporter for just a few seasons, only then you will know what it is like to "really" support a football club. Their response, "Why would I want to support a no chance side like Luton?" My reply "Exactly the reason you would not fit in, you are a fucking glory hunter, nothing more than that, you would not know what it is to support a real football club, people like you want it all on a plate. You don't like football you like winning. There is a massive difference." Believe me I have got into many close scrapes with certain people whilst I lived in Peckham, South-East London. I also asked three Liverpool supporters in a pub one night who were attempting to take the piss out of me for supporting Luton when the Luton v Liverpool cup game was on TV. What was most intriguing, the silence that hovered over their heads when Luton were two goals up. But once they were level they began their mouths. One thing that really upset them was when asked if they had been to Anfield as many times as I have. None of the three had ever set foot in Liverpool city centre leave alone been to Anfield. Again my reply. "That my friends says it all for me, when you have been to Anfield as many times as I have, then you can talk to me about supporting Liverpool, I have been over six times, I lost count." On that note, they were left totally speechless and a Millwall supporter, came up to me and said perfectly done mate, not an air of malice in your voice as you told them, just plain matter of fact truth. So as I was saying, no one can deny us our say, as long as it is worthy, because our passion comes direct from the heart. Many of us, if unfortunate to have open heart surgery during our lifetime, upon opening us up, the surgeon will find "HATTERS" tattooed on the blood filled, pumping muscle.

John admits that losing both Luke Wilkinson and Steve McNulty through suspension and also the addition of Nathan Doyle's injury has been a massive blow. The defence has since then been a little shaky at times with players being bought in and asked to step up to the mark. Fraser Franks, himself returning from a Hernia operation, has looked rusty and not completely ready, so that was in itself a big ask for him, that is my point of view not the managers. I believe Franks, when fully fit is up to the job, I know there are many out there who will totally disagree with me on that count, but that is my opinion.

Following my questioning regarding the use of Oduwa and Lee earlier, it is really a coincidence that I am now listening to John Still's pre Newport interview on "Hatters player" and he produces the very answer I for one wanted to hear. It all begins to make some kind of sense now, to me anyway.

He stressed that Nathan Oduwa's situation has been discussed with Tottenham and they are in agreement with the manager. Apparently Nathan has been struggling to fully comprehend the role that the guvnor wants him to play within the side. Having done some extensive work with the youngster on the training ground, the lad has a much better understanding of what is required of him and the chances are he will in future games be more prominent. I wonder how many managers would actually sit down talk to a loanee and coach him to his way of thinking, instead sending a player back to his parent club as not what was expected. It shows the stamp of the manager we have, patient and willing to talk rather than blindly condemn. How can certain individuals want to be rid of such a manager as astute and commanding as the man we have? As is said again and again and not just by yours truly, the quick fix is no longer the way to go. Gradual better than instantaneous success.

With Elliot Lee he also had an answer to. Before coming to Kenilworth Road Lee had not played a great deal of football in recent months, therefore, time has been spent in training to get him to a reasonable and required state of fitness to allow him to get more consecutive games under his belt. Again no rush, what would be the point of overdoing it and he is out again. Questions answered, appreciated and noted. This again proves my point, it is better that we as a collective attempt to find out what is going on behind the scenes before casting aspersions and condemning without thinking. Something to chew the cud on for sure.

One thing I have noticed with the Town this season, the amount of hernia injuries that seem to have emerged. As far as I know there is nothing one can do to prevent such injuries, I myself have suffered two hernia operations. Just a part of life unfortunately for most of us.

Pelly has a defect that a specialist has discovered, that may be cause of his ever recurring hamstring problem. Apparently one leg being slightly shorter than the other, which in turn contributes to one leg taking more pressure than the other. I have my thoughts as to the extent of the damage this may effectively cause long term, which brings the question to mind, where does this leave the young man football career wise. It must be a very troubling time for him. Let us hope that something can be done to allow him to continue in career that has looked so promising up to this point.

Tomorrow evening the "Hatters" are at Newport County, who have a new manager following the departure of Justin Edinburgh to Gillingham. His replacement being his former assistant at County Jimmy Dack. I can imagine he will be hoping to get a scalp such as Luton Town onto his pole as soon as possible.

Newport are knocking on the door of the play off places, so it is going to be a difficult prospect. They will be difficult to break down. Nevertheless, if the "Hatters" play in the same vein as Saturday at Portsmouth, the chances are that they could just pinch, what will likely be a very tight game, despite the previous two results this season. They look to be going through a period of rejuvenation right now.

Tuesday March 17th 2015
Another match day, more hopes and dreams for some.

 Before that I am on a high this morning. The launch of my new website approaches later this afternoon "Chris Luke Sporting Lives'." Initially it will be a little basic, however as I get into a certain work schedule each day it will become easier to update on maybe even an hourly basis in time. The aim is to eventually, have sports news flashes as they happen, a results page, a cricket scorecard page for chosen games be it Test Match, ODI or County games. That though is in the future, I have no intention of running before I can walk. Other possibilities include a sports memorabilia page whereupon I will buy and sell items if interest across the sporting spectrum. One page that is ready for the launch is news and progress reports of the books I am or will be in the progress of writing. Also a page dedicated to not only my own articles but also guest writers and bloggers.

However, with much to do let us proceed. This evening Luton travel to Newport County. A good display will not be enough this evening, three points desperately, yes desperately required if some fans dream are to be made a reality. We do need to get back to winning ways that is for sure.

However, despite recent results this season against Newport must be forgotten, they are in the past, form has turned around for both clubs in recent weeks.

A dour evening in the suburbs of South Wales, unfortunately not the most welcoming of places for the "Hatters" fan to be rolling into on a cold Tuesday March evening.

The "Hatters" starting line-up follows as this: Elliot Justham, Michael Harriman, Steve McNulty, Luke Wilkinson, Jake Howells, Alex Lawless, Andy Drury, Cameron McGeehan, Luke Guttridge, Mark Cullen and Elliot Lee. With those hugging each other to keep the cold out: Craig King, Fraser Franks, Ryan Hall, Paul Benson, Jayden Stockley, Paul Benson and Matt Robinson.

Newport County 1 Luton Town 0
If anything at all was proved tonight, it has to be the fact, which despite all my previous protestations regarding Luton's formations, actually playing 4-4-2 when they finally decide to implement it, is not the way to go. As Paul Wright has indicated. Not with the squad of players we have at the moment at least.

One change from Saturdays defeat at Fratton Park, Elliot Lee replacing Shaun Whalley.

The line-up therefore reads, Justham between the sticks. A back four of Harriman McNulty, headband and all, Wilkinson and Howells. A midfield consisting of Lawless, McGeehan, Drury and Guttridge. With Cullen and Lee leading the attack upfront.

The only goal of the game coming in the twenty first minute, resulting from Jackson's long throw, Minshull flicking the ball into the path of Aaron O'Connor, who on the turn completely wrong footed Justham and netting easily.

Most of the first half was marred by misplaced passes and aimless long balls, both sides guilty of such.

Apart from a couple of neat exchanges between Guttridge and Lee there was not much to shout home about. Newport having marginally the better of the midfield battles.

Cameron McGeehan picked up another yellow to add to his collection, kleptomaniac comes to mind. Resulting from yet another of his miss-timed tackles. Maybe due to the exuberance of youthfulness, of which one is hopeful of him growing out of as he continues to develop.

Yet again this season the whole of the Luton contingency, players, coaching staff and fans together, were left baffled and bewildered. Totally bemused in fact, when a shot from Elliot Lee, in clear view of the referee, hit the outstretched hand of Newport's defender Darren Jones and yet incredibly looked away and waved play on. Something now though that we as "Hatters" are beginning to accept as an everyday part of life. I earlier mentioned that I am not one for those conspiracy theories being bandied around the homes of social media. But sometimes one is forced to sit up, think and maybe re-address previous thoughts. It really is getting too much of a coincidence, since the New Year festivities we are not far from averaging one incident of the like, per match. It is quite ludicrous. The problem being now, when and if we awarded one of those very rare commodities, the penalty kick, will anyone really remember what they have to do, when one is placed at their feet? At this rate we shall be recording a strike rate of denied penalties to equal that of the England ODI teams strike rates put together. Especially during the period of their recent world cup flop. Now where have those words been heard before in recent years? One would not just be able to write a book about, more likely a complete set of volumes.

The half time break was a short one for the Town in comparison to that of the home side. Maybe it was a sign of even the usual cool, calm and collected Mr Still showing that he is after all human and prone to uncontrolled rage. Only the players and he himself will truly know that. Because they were out extremely early for the second half, I can imagine them running out onto the pitch for safety sake, away from the galloping Stillman. Newport's presence less of a threat man for man. In contrast a very calm and relaxed Newport, having read the recent form books and realising that Luton just do not come back to win again when conceding an early first half goal I recent months. Then the ever present huddle, maybe a view shuddering voices asking what they do next, do they confront the Stillman face to face smile quietly and get on with the job? Or most probably more content in agreeing the only way to appease the raging bull was to play their socks off for the remaining forty-five minutes and have his faith in them restored to a positive effect. Whatever it was it worked. Work wise at least. Although the final touch still a little on the nervy side.

However with the turn-around Newport gained and extra defender, namely goalpost, as well of course as that very helpful and most generous referee, Brendan Malone, certainly was not a dead eyed dick that is for sure, there being a pun of sorts somewhere within all of that, I promise you all.

Elliot Lee was unfortunate when his effort crashed against the post, the first of a couple of shots crashing against said upright. Feely making a superb, it has to be said, diving header to clear the ball and turn it round that same post for a "Hatters" corner.

The manager made an early second half change when replacing Michael Harriman with Fraser Franks. Franks contribution this evening bringing a little smile to my face. Because, the stick he has been receiving of late has not been that fair on certain social media sites. His distribution and presence was noticeable, both equal to what I know him to be capable of, reminiscent to his times at Welling United, obviously being one of the reason he was bought to Kenilworth Road by the manager in the first place.

Nathan Oduwa replaced Alex Lawless, who coming back from injury, was not considered worth risking for a full ninety minutes obviously.

There was a rare opportunity in the second half for Newport to put the game firmly out of Luton's reach. However, Elliot Justham, who recently has been given some unfair criticism, as with Franks, from certain poor sighted individuals, was able to shut them up with an excellent save stop from Aaron O'Connor's well placed drive.

The fourth officials' board read four minutes of stoppage time. Justham given another opportunity to silence those critics and prove his worth, which he did superbly, saving Zebroski's effort.

But true to form, the form although not pleasing, getting as consistent as that of Champion Hurdler, Faugheen, Wilkinson was bundled unceremoniously to ground by Feely. The referee again completely ignoring any protestation from the Luton camp. His whistle yet again proving elusive when it came to the crunch for the "Hatters."

The full time whistle was though not as elusive as other times during this evenings match and Newport left the field gathering all three points into their caps as they left the field of play.

Leaving John Still much to think about and try to work out what the heck is happening, because in recent games one cannot deny it is not for the lack of effort on the player's part.

Another defeat, fortunes cannot continue to go against us, or can they? AS the manager has quoted, "he doesn't believe in luck." We do thought need something to crack.

It was a full league programme tonight and in other games, Shrewsbury showed Morecambe that not all sides in the top ten are as easy to put away as Luton, with Shrewsbury knocking them out of sight at the Globe Arena 1-4. They move up to second place, removing Wycombe on goal difference, who could only muster up a 2-2 draw at home to Accrington. Bury winning at Bootham Crescent, York 1-0. The battle for play off positions is really hotting up with a cluster of sides waiting for the teams above them, including Luton Town to drop points.

Saturday Luton will be without a game as they host Wycombe Wanderers at Kenilworth Road in a televised game on Sky Sports a week from today. Therefore, a week's break and an opportunity to do something in training to try and get the club back to much required winning ways.

Wednesday March 18th 2015

The aftermath of last night's game is secondary today, following the surprising announcement made today regarding the change of name for Kenilworth Road. Following all the speculation, the inquests, questions and thoughts the hour of truth emerged. It has to be said with a most amazing turnaround of support from the fans and quite rightly. Nick Owen announced that Kenilworth Road would change its name for one match only, the match in question next weeks televised game against Wycombe.

This much welcomed deal ensures that yet again the "Hatters" board lead the way with yet another ground breaking announcement. Earlier in the season the Town were also one of the first if not the first to make the pledge that all staff within the club, form the programme sellers up were to be awarded the minimum wage. Putting therefore many of the bigger British clubs to shame. Some who even now have not followed Luton's example. Comparing their annual budget to the "Hatters" that to me is quite despicable. They have no excuse, I myself find it incredible and they should be named and shamed by the government if not doing so.

Now the Town board have yet again paved the way for other clubs to follow in their footsteps. By changing the grounds name to a very prominent and important charity Prostate Cancer UK. The charity are already a partner of the Football League and in fact every Football League player's shirt carries the Men United logo for the charity organisation on their shirts this season.

Therefore the ground will for just one day be known as the Prostate Cancer UK Stadium, to coincide with the televised home game on Tuesday March 24th against promotion and local rivals Wycombe Wanderers. This is a most generous gesture by the club, especially in an age when usually clubs up and down the country are prostituting their stadiums name out for financial gain. Our Faith in Luton town and our pride never wavers.

This in fact will be the first time in the history of the Football League whereupon a clubs stadium will be renamed in support of a charity. I will say it again as before, we as a collective have every right to be proud of our ever forward moving football club. A credit to the cause.

The decision has been backed by many, especially I would imagine former "Hatters" youth scout from the Lennie Lawrence managerial teams era. Erroll McKellar was diagnosed with prostate cancer in 2010.

I myself was a year later in 2011 having a similar scare, but I am one of the few fortunate ones. It was found after a number of tests that I was not suffering from this terrible illness, but something much less dangerous and easily treated. For that I am and always will be eternally grateful.

A few months back within this journalised book I mentioned the shock when my friend former football legend Alan Hudson informed me via email that he himself had been diagnosed with this despicable and horrifying illness. With that I have come to the decision that I will donate on pound to Prostate Cancer UK for each copy I am fortunate enough to sell of this book. No different to my upcoming book The Nineteen Sixties Grand National book that I am also working on at the moment, where a similar donation will be made to the Injured Jockeys Fund, which in the past I was very fortunate to have had some assistance from. I therefore make this pledge in conjunction with the Luton Town deal. To ensure all is done correctly I will be looking to an independent body to keep an exact count of all books sold and pay all donations on my behalf accordingly. Raising no doubts that my pledge will be carried through, without question.

Saturday March 21st 2015
A much needed rest from the keyboards. However, I am disgusted with a certain individual today, not anyone who is connected with Luton Town or even a supporter, who when learning of my decision to donate an amount of money for copies sold, saying it is a well-timed and planned gimmick to sell copies. I am appalled that someone whom I thought knew me much better than that could say such. To be totally honest I was not going to even advertise the fact, but such was the rage within me this morning I had to let this person know publicly my thoughts of his accusations. In fact in my introduction to the book at the very beginning, as I have mentioned at many people already, I am not doing this to sell copies, it is more of something that started out as a bit of fun and grew from there. In fact if it was not for a couple of friends, one being Luton supporter Mike Thomas the other an Arsenal fan in fact I doubt I would have even kept it going. Having been inspired and pushed on by others I then decided to make it a book. Anyway, with a saddened heart I carry on regardless, yes I am upset, but life moves on and better friends less cynical are a welcome commodity within my life.

Apart from the "Hatters" versus Wycombe game taking place it has been another full programme of League Two football. To be honest a little weird all the other games being covered by the ever excitable Jeff Stelling and we not even participating.

Former young "Hatter" Cauley Woodrow, now at Fulham, certainly got some air time this afternoon at Huddersfield. Apparently he was sent off for handball on the goal line, preventing a goal for the home team. It is reported that he has taken his shirt off on the pitch and refused to leave the field of play. It seems he is also in tears at the referee's decision. Jeff Stelling now explaining that it is a definite case of mistaken identity and incredulously he has now had the red card rescinded and the Fulham captain now dismissed instead. Cannot remember such scenes like that happening before. I wonder if some refs would actually have the balls to admit an incorrect decision, although it should not have happened in the first place fair play to the official for that. To cap it all Stelling who saw the incident on his screen says it was not even handball. The players definitely chested the ball away. So a double calamity there. The story doesn't end there, Huddersfield actually miss the penalty. I thought only such incidents happened at Luton Town.

League Two was Luton friendly it seems results wise, although the top two Burton and Shrewsbury won and strengthened their positions at the top, Burton on seventy-six points followed by Shrewsbury with seventy-one, Tuesdays opponents who obviously as Luton did not play a further three points behind on sixty-eight. Then in the play-off places Bury sit in fourth, Southend United in fifth with Luton just holding onto the sixth position with teams below them dropping points today. But now with fifty-eight points, a massive eighteen points behind the leaders and ten points adrift of Wycombe, if they are to find themselves winning promotion it seems now highly unlikely to come from an automatic promotion place. Behind them, Newport Plymouth and Stevenage all waiting for the "Hatters" to continue their slump, ready to leap above them. It is going to be a tense end to the season that is for certain.

These will indeed be a stress ridden few weeks for some, up to the last game on Saturday May 2nd, when the final game of the season is played at Kenilworth Road against Stevenage. It could become a real tasty affair if both sides are battling each other for a play-off place. Still and McNulty versus Westley and Henry, a thriller in the making.

Sunday March 22nd 2015
It seems Louis Suarez has a copycat fan, in the guise of Dagenham & Redbridge's Joss Labadie. It alleged that the midfielder took a bite out of Former "Hatters" captain and now Stevenage skipper Ronnie Henry, in their game at Broadhall Way yesterday, followed by obviously the usual handbags at fifty paces scenario after. The police are apparently looking into the situation. Maybe they will ask for Labadie's dental records to fit the bite marks on Ronnie's arm. Dagenham really should remember to feed the players before a game. It is not even a long coach journey from Essex to the Hertfordshire village of Stevenage. Take-away anyone?

The Luton town youth side, carried on their winning ways yesterday with their third successive win, beating Swindon Town 2-0. Two goals in the first thirty minutes from Geo Craig and Alex Atkinson, yes we another Alex, to seal the game.

Monday March 23rd 2015
It was the Town's development sides turn to win, is it not a shame the first eleven cannot do as the other two sides are, winning. They proved too good for AFC Wimbledon on the day. A resounding 3-0 victory, which ensures the "Hatters" remain in first place the Final Third Development League South Division. A somewhat rejuvenated Ricky Miller scored a goal in each half and Leeroy Magaurasle scoring the third with a thirty yard screamer. Andy Parry, helped carry on the trend, a player injured in every game, the story of Luton's season unfortunately. The physio team are certainly earning their crust this season, relentless injuries throughout. Luke Rooney, having the captain's armband for the evening. Liam Gooch the

development teams keeper, showed yet another valuable performance, making some good saves to thwart the Wimbledon attack.

Tuesday March 24th 2015
Here we are, it is the televised match of Luton Town v Wycombe Wanderers, at the Prostate Cancer UK Stadium.

The build-up for the day has not really been football orientated for myself, with the release this morning of my first book, "Memories from the Green Carpet." An exciting day indeed, today, released in digital form for the Kindle and tomorrow it will go out in printed form. Let us hope it can be an added celebration, with a win for Luton included.

The Town must begin to pick up some points, if only to boost both morale and confidence within the club. The longer this run of defeats goes on the harder it will become to change the trend.

It is an important game for both sides, Luton, in sixth place will be hoping to keep in touch, points wise with the three sides in the automatic promotion places, which includes Wycombe. They will also be hoping for all three points to consolidate their third place position.

The "Hatters" line up for tonight is, Elliot Justham, Michael Harriman, Fraser Franks, Steve McNulty, Luke Wilkinson, Jake Howells, Andy Drury, Cameron McGeehan, Luke Guttridge, Paul Benson and Elliot Lee. With on the subs bench, Alex Lacey, Alex Lawless, Matt Robinson, Jayden Stockley, Nathan Oduwa, Mark Cullen and Craig King.

Luton Town 2 Wycombe Wanderers 3

Some good points can be taken away taken from this evening's game, not unlike other recent games also. Some good attacking football displayed by Luton. However, again though as has been the case for much of the season, too many unforced errors. To counteract that we proved also at Portsmouth that we are capable of to cause even the better sides problems in front of goal.

It pains me greatly to say this but it has been quite pitiful to watch Drury at times this season. Not a touch on the player he was during his first term at Kenilworth Road. Having said before, now I will say again, I am not in favour of former players returning to a club for a second spell, the expectation is it seems, always too much to have on ones shoulders. For myself, they had certain players they moulded with and it is difficult to recoup those kinds of partnerships again with another set of players. In addition, if the style of football does not suit second time around then that is another problem, not being able to get into similar mind-set. It seems we all like to bash Drury these days, but should we not sometimes sit back and think, yes I am guilty as charged also at times. One of the saddest sights on the field of play for me in recent seasons at Luton was the return of Kevin Nicholls, for Kevin he was admittedly Lee shadow of what he used to be. Sad times they were.

Returning to the present, Wycombe opened the scoring in the second minute, another case of going behind so early on. From Jacobsen's in-swinging corner, McNulty made a poor headed clearance straight into the path of Sam Saunders, on loan from Brentford, his wayward effort hitting Fraser Franks, ricocheting across the line with Harriman unable to get a good enough touch to prevent the ball crossing the line.

The "Hatters" responded well, not taking long in drawing level again, a Jake Howells corner finding Guttridge whose drive was spilled away by Wycombe's keeper Ingram, only as far as Elliott Lee who blasted the ball into the net to bring the Town level again.

Luton playing with a good tempo, Benson and Lee combining well, something we have been lacking for much of this season. Lee looked a hungry player, ready to battle for the ball and put himself about, a constant nuisance for the Wycombe defenders to contend.

However, it should be said that such is Luton's defence at times coupled with the tenacity of Wycombe's attacking prowess they looked the more dangerous each time they pressed forward. Sure enough despite the Town's surges forward, Wycombe regained their advantage, following what can only be described at best, a clumsy attempt by Wilkinson to take the ball off Bloomfield on the edge of the eighteen-yard box, bringing the attacking player to the ground. The referee had no hesitation in pointing to the spot, have to agree a simple decision for him to make.

Hayes stepped up, a cool finish, despite Justham being able to get a fingertip to it, unable to prevent Wycombe regaining their lead, 1-2.

Drury played an awful pass to Franks, leaving him in all kinds of trouble, allowing Woods to dispossess him easily of the ball, fortunately for the "Hatters" Saunders only able to put the ball over Justham's goal.

The visitor's third goal was a superb take, a good run and the final delivery brilliant. The problem there though, that it could easily been avoided had the defence made some concerted effort to challenge the run of Mawson instead of admiring the view. Mawson, picking up the ball on the halfway line and running directly through the centre at the Town defence, exchanged a quick one-two with Hayes and then placed the ball perfectly past Justham, who had no chance of stopping.

At this point, I am going to mention something that has bugged me for a few weeks now. There has been some unnecessary chat about Justham being partly to blame for the clubs demise recently. How easy it is for some to find a scapegoat to pick on. It has been said that the run of losses have coincided with the loss of Mark Tyler to his knee injury. Yes, maybe it is coincidental, but that is all it is an unfortunate coincidence. One agrees he could be more commanding at times, however, he is still learning at this level, in time that will come. We have to be thankful it is whilst we are not in any danger of being relegated. We should be giving thanks for that. But, to blame Justham entirely is ludicrous at best. A goalkeeper, even the best at times can only be as good as the defence he has in front of him, let us be quite honest, our defence has been anything but solid of late, many of the goals scored against us, in fact the majority, Tyler would have been well pushed to prevent also.

Following the third goal, I noticed something of interest and quite concerning, the manager looked bemused, he gave the impression of a man who had no idea how to stop the rot we are experiencing. Not all his fault it has to be agreed, but at the same time most worrying.

A lifeline for Luton just before half time, a high cross from Jake Howells, wonderfully played into the box by Michael Harriman for Elliot Lee to latch on to and calmly knock in for his second goal of the game.

During the break Fraser Franks was given a fitness test at the side of the pitch for a knock he received halfway thought he first half. Again, I have to comment on some of the tripe heard after the game that Franks had been taken off because he was unhappy with Franks commitment and so forth. I find it quite incredulous that people do not see what is right there in front of them. It was plain for all that the defender was struggling for much of the game with an injury. I would be the first to agree that he is not having the best of seasons, but please get the facts correct before making such comments. In fact, my opinion is that this evening his delivery of the ball was quite good and he also putting himself about.

With Franks injured it was Matty Robinson who was to replace him, not sure about that hair though.

With Wycombe's obvious midfield superiority, there for all to see in the first half, I was surprised to see Robinson rather than Lawless replacing the defender.

Luton started the livelier, throwing more men forward than had done before the break. The visitors were pinned in their own half more. Lee had a good effort blocked by Mawson.

Nathan Oduwa replaced Cameron McGeehan. Then an incredulous foul on Lee, he had just beaten Saunders in a tackle alongside the touchline, as he went away with the ball Sam Saunders must have chased back at least fifteen yards and quite blatantly scythed Lee down from behind. The Wycombe man was intent on getting his man before the ball. It was so plain for everyone to see, however, the referee decided a yellow card was sufficient punishment along with a free kick to the "Hatters" One has to ponder over the fact that had the roles been reversed, would Lee have been walking across to the changing rooms for an early bath, one fears so. Such have things gone for us this season at times. Lee, was later taken off as he struggled with an injury caused by that innocuous challenge from Saunders, to be replaced by out of sorts Mark Cullen.

That in itself put paid to any Luton comeback, the fire taken out of the Luton hearts. Some will say Saunders had completed exactly what he set out to do. With Lee now out of the equation, the attacking flair fizzled out of existence.

Another defeat, the alarm bells clearly ringing in many a pair of ears.

Thursday March 26th 2015

Luke Rooney has departed from Kenilworth Road, by mutual consent, within an hour has signed for Ebbsfleet United, which was rather quick, one has to say.

Rooney made twelve first team appearances this season on seven occasions. In addition, bought on as substitute on another seven occasions. In that period, he netted seven goals.

To be honest talking myself, a little disappointed that he has gone, although I am aware there are many here amongst us that will not necessarily agree with me, but we all entitled to our own thoughts and opinions.

Surprise, surprise, the injuries continue to rise. Following the cynical scything down of Elliot Lee on Tuesday evening, he being ruled out of Saturday's game against Northampton. Although, John Still is hopeful that he will recover in time for the Easter programme of games.

Another casualty from Tuesday's game is Fraser Franks, one can hear the cynical cheers coming up from a few Luton supporters. He will be out for a month, so the chances are that he will be out for the remainder of the season.

With defensive injuries again mounting up for the manager, he has gone into the loan market yet again, are loans really the answer? I have to keep asking myself this same question. Why not cut our losses this season, bring in some young hungry blood from the youth squad and get them asserted for next season instead of bringing in a player who will again walk away back to his parent club. All the talk about building for the future and yet the youth players not being given a chance to prove themselves. Granted the young lad we have taken on for the remaining games of the season by all accounts is a talented player, Lewis Kinsella, from Aston Villa. He has been on the bench a couple of occasions this season in Premier League games.

Friday March 27th 2015
Tomorrow I can only envisage another tough game coming Luton's way. They travel to to Sixfields Stadium for an encounter with Northampton Town, managed by Chris Wilder.
John Still's selection will be an interesting one. I cannot help but wonder again if he will persist with Andy Drury, or will he at last look to other faces. Somehow, though it is doubtful.

Saturday March 28th 2015
There will not be the usual mass of coaches, cars and orange shirts on trains travelling northwards today, as Northampton have decided to offer a small amount of tickets to the "Hatters." One must wonder if that is because they are concerned that our normally large away support will influence the game some, however, it is most more likely to be the Northamptonshire Police making the noises and advising against. Despite such, we often told to believe that Britain is not a police state, only when it suits.
The "Hatters" are definitely going to miss the hunger, energy of Elliot Lee up front. One does get the nagging feeling that today could be a long one for players and supporters, both.
The Town line up as follows: Elliot Justham, Michael Harriman, Steve McNulty, Luke Wilkinson, Lewis Kinsella, Andy Drury, Nathan Doyle, Jonathan Smith, Alex Lawless, Paul Benson and Mark Cullen. With those sitting in hope: Luke Guttridge, Jayden Stockley, Alex Lacey, Cameron McGeehan, Ricky Miller, Ryan Hall and Liam Gooch.

Northampton Town 2 Luton Town 1
Following some decent displays of late, this one has to go down as one of the more lamentable of performances. If not for the goalkeeping of Elliot Justham, the margin may have been much wider. A poor performance against what one can at best call an average side. They, on a not so good run also.
On a grey, miserable and blustery March afternoon, one would expect seasoned professional footballers to know better, than attempt to play long high balls up the pitch. However, we have to remember this is Luton Town and to learn from previous games is not one of their better traits this season.
Nathan Doyle, his first game back after a six-week layoff was noticeably game rusty. Having been installed into the side without having a development game under his belt was not for this fan the best of moves. Again, Drury picked in front of other more deserving players is questionable. As the reader, you must have noticed that until now I have always done my utmost to not criticise team selections, however, I feel inclined to do so this evening, not in hindsight after knowing the result, but because on seeing the team sheet I was having the thoughts that are being expressed now. Jonathan Smith and Nathan Doyle so clearly lacking match fitness. Surely, John has other

players capable of playing in league games, without playing half-fit players, or is it that we really do have an even longer injury list than we know about.

The first half was at best a miserable affair. Luton defending in numbers, maybe this tactic adopted to give Doyle as much cover as possible. If Doyle was not ready, why not give Alex Lacey the chance he needs to get some much-needed experience, because he has the potential to be a good player, but he has to have the opportunity to play to get that experience.

Northampton although beginning well soon changed to t hoofing the ball towards their lone man up front, Gray, outnumbered by both McNulty and Wilkinson combined.

Benson and Cullen both found themselves stranded up front due to a lack of service from the midfield that if honest has been missing at times this season. Benson worked hard at times, but mostly chasing lost causes.

A difficult debut for the young lad from Aston Villa, Lewis Kinsella, Lawless not tracking back against Holmes was not much help. Kinsella, booked for dragging down Holmes, was most probably more out of frustration rather than any malice involved.

Luton did have one opportunity when Wilkinson's powerful header found Mark Cullen. He did well to hold off Cresswell, however, his low drive that lacked any real power was never going to test Duke in the Cobblers goal.

The first half thankfully ended, time for a well needed hot cup of Bovril and maybe a Pukka Pie. Maybe not a great advert for league two football that is for sure.

The second half produced something of a rarity where Luton is concerned of late. The "Hatters" taking the lead. Maybe at lasts the glut was over.

Drury played the ball into Benson, Lawless picking the ball up on the left edge of the box, Duke came off his line, Lawless seeing this craftily chipped the ball into the top corner, a superbly taken goal.

Luton, now in front started to rise in confidence, with some decent moves being implemented.

The game changer was when Luton lost skipper Steve McNulty, a pulled muscle. Yes another one for the ever-growing list. It would be nice to see a few more coming off the list, rather than added.

Alex Lacey bought on to replace him, Lacey one of the young players I would dearly like to have seen get more opportunities this season. A decent run in the side would boost his confidence enormously, instead of the nervous wreck he portrayed this afternoon.

The "Cobblers" started to push forward more. A right wing cross from Moloney, D'ath looked to push |Harriman forward into the ball on the goal line, there was no kind of appeal from the Northampton players, however, the referee pointed to the spot. Obviously thinking it would be the courteous thing to do and award the home side a penalty. Harriman sitting in the muddy goalmouth, looking bewildered to the fact that adjudged to have handled the ball off the line. The accused looking rather discombobulated by the whole affair that was transpiring in front of him. Holmes drove the ensuing penalty kick low, beating Justham to his right.

Northampton, began to turn the screw, it became an onslaught. McGeehan replaced Lawless. Justham was continually tested he had definitely earned his salt ration this afternoon.

The winning goal was unlucky on Justham's part, twice repelling shots from Holmes before Gray was able to turn the ball over the line.

There was never any real threat of an equaliser, a comfortable win for Northampton.

Another dismal day in the life of a "Hatter" one could write a book on the season so far.

Other results from around the world meant that the "Hatters" dropped out of the play-off places, it had to happen eventually, one supposes. Let us not kid ourselves, a little fortunate to be in that position in the first place. We have not actually set the world alight with our football this season.

Sunday March 29th 2015
As expected the moaners and groaners out in force. The armchair managers also, ones' own self included recently it has to be admitted.
I am not sure whether I should in fact laugh or cry. When Mike and myself agreed it would be a bit of fun to turn the initial scribblings into a book. It was at the time pleasing to be doing something to keep my interest moving along throughout the season. Well, it has certainly done that, one cannot deny. I never though, thought I would find myself begging for the season end to arrive, and long for the peaceful serenity of the cricket season in comparison. I hope that some cheer to bring my effervescent smile back to a much-bedraggled face.

April

Wednesday April 1st 2015

I would have had the perfect April fools. However, it will be at least two months out of date by the time it reaches you.

Maybe John Still should look at the development side that thumped Portsmouth at Kenilworth Road yesterday. Because they showed, character and resilience in addition scored a few goals also. Luton's Final Third Development side fought back from a goal deficit to beat their Portsmouth rivals 5-2. Scott Griffiths, despite his hernia problem, Nathan Doyle, Shaun Whalley, Matt Robinson, Ricky Miller, Alex Wall all featured, with the inclusion also of Curtley Williams, side-lined for three months with a shoulder injury managed 85 minutes before suffering from cramp, it is allowed following such a lengthy lay off. The "Hatters" goal scorers, Alex Wall 2, Ryan Hall, Scott Griffiths and Shaun Whalley.

Thursday April 2nd 2015

The injury crisis continues, it is unlikely that either skipper Steve McNulty or Elliot Lee will be in contention for Friday's home match against Exeter City, not the best of starts for the Easter programme.

There are rumours developing that the manager is looking to sign out former West Ham United and Ipswich midfielder Jack Collinson, a Welsh international, gaining 17 caps. Collinson is currently without a club after his release by the Tractormen in December.

After Greg Dyke we have Colin Graves, crickets answer to the crown prince of football fools. First, it was Greg Dyke, attempting to change the face of English domestic football, with the inclusion of Premier League clubs "B teams" into the lower tiers of the football league.

Now it seems the incoming ECB chairperson, let us be politically correct, is drawing up plans to change the length of test matches, from five to four days. What is it with these people, meddling what has worked quite well enough for over a century. Is it a case, in fact of their ego's, wanting to make their own mark in the history of sport, despite never kicking, bowling or hitting a ball in anger. I believe so.

Mr Graves believes that such changes will invigorate our game, along with other reasons also. However, hidden sweetly and carefully in the middle of the list, although if the truth known the real and only reason, it will make cricket more financially viable. As so eloquently put, to place the game more in tune with the culture of our times. What he is really saying, between the lines of what he believes hidden within is this, bank balance before tradition, the new age of sport.

Over the years football and horseracing has become more leaning towards corporate rather than the everyday average person. Now it seems, cricket is following in the same direction. The common man on the street, those that keep this country going with their hard toil, are being priced out of many of our national events. Money before those that really matter yet again.

When the ECB changed the county championship format to four day rather than three, one was in favour of that, the impression being that it allowed a fairer result and more allotted time for a result when a game is prone to interruption by inclement weather, which is unfortunately a trait in English cricket we have to endure. However, as they say that is cricket.

Test matches named so, because they are a test of endurance, at one time a game would be played out to its conclusion, regardless of how long it may take. Obviously, that is taking it a little far these days. However, how would we be able to continue to call it a test match if the length of the match was no different to an everyday county match?

Is it going to be another case then of "sod" the real cricket people?

Ensuring the banks appeased first, with the likes of the ECB and TCB filling their pockets accordingly. Not so different then from FIFA, UEFA the FA and others, and let those that patronise the game and understand the game, obviously more than some of those running it, fall in line with what we say and be damned with them.

It may be again for the sporting fans of this country, others also, to stand up and be counted, as with earlier this year when the peoples voice beat the FA and Football league hands down to prevent Mr Dyke getting his way.

Friday April 3rd 2015

Good Friday, with the question on many lips today must be is it going to be a good Friday for Luton Town as the fight for a return to winning ways continues. Seven consecutive defeats is a little heart breaking. However, one may have to contradict oneself at times and maybe this could be one of those moments. Because, with one hand I have to condemn the management team for not looking at their selections in recent weeks, but then on the other one has to understand the predicament they are in and to be fair have been for a great deal of this season. Do they select players who are not fully match fit, which speaks for itself not the best of ideas. Otherwise, should they select those that are either are not experienced enough or equally so not cut out for league football at this. Let us be fair they have not had an easy time of it in that respect this season. Again though, saying that, it is all well and good having a forty plus squad, but no amount of players can be a substitute for experience. I know I have written earlier in this publication that John is taking the club the right way and to a point, I still think that. However, when we have accumulated the injuries we have to the more experienced players, surely, if a player is bought in as a loan replacement, it should be one of at least similar experience. For fans and management alike, though this season has to be a learning curve. Firstly, for the fans, some have to realise that a quick fix is not the way to go. I have said this before and I will say it again. Suppose Luton did win promotion this season, what would be the odds on us doing as well again next season? Not good I would think. Some supporters seem to want Luton Town to run before they can walk. Despite the fact that many of our earlier successes this season took us into the automatic promotion placings, let us be honest with ourselves, despite the victories the performances were not that convincing. Equally, we were able to stay in the play-off places not because we played well enough to be in such heady positions, but because other sides around us were not getting consistent results either. The plain truth is Luton have been fortunate to be in the position they are even now. That is how unpredictable league two has been this season.

I am not defending anyone, neither am I condemning, the fact is, now Luton Town are rebuilding, no one knew how good this side we have was, or was not when we set out for Carlisle. I think winning at Carlisle gave too many people false hope from the very first day. Some were saying we can win this league easily, from that very day, when we sat in eighteenth place, most realised with sensibility that it was not going to be as easy as first thought. The problem arose again when we had that fantastic run of wins. Hopes built up, dreams of promotion took over. False hope is a dangerous thing in football, because when reality sets in it brings the worst out in some. They build their hopes up to such a crescendo that when shattered they cannot handle the situation. From the outset of the season, I have at least attempted to be as realistic as I possibly could. John Still is a bloody nice man, he is honest, he has integrity and most of all something we have lacked at Luton Town in management is one who is genuine, has a feeling for the club. Whatever the man has done, he has truly believed it is for the good of Luton Town. I have spoken with others from former clubs that he has been in charge of and all have said the same, the man's passion for his work is second to none.

To be honest I do not think we have a side that is good enough. The manager earlier this week made the decision that in the next few weeks there is going to be a massive clear out. It will be most interesting to see who goes and who stays. I have my own thoughts on that. However, with prudence I will keep those thoughts totally to myself. I would though be ecstatic if John could talk Michael Harriman to sign for us permanently, if of course he is affordable, for myself the most consistent player this season and I do like the way he makes his forward runs.

Today, on a damp Good Friday, we are hosting Exeter City. They are having a fantastic season in contrast to their recent history. In Paul Tisdale, they now have a manger who likes to play football the way it should be played. I believe today will be a difficult game for the "Hatters" however I do expect us to win a very tough contest.

The Town lines up as follows: Elliot Justham, Michael Harriman, Steve McNulty, Luke Wilkinson, Lewis Kinsella, Mark Cullen, Nathan Doyle, Jonathan Smith, Alex Lawless, Luke Guttridge and Paul Benson. With substitutes: Ricky Miller, Jayden Stockley, Ryan Hall, Nathan Oduwa, Cameron McGeehan, Alex Lacey and Craig King.

Luton Town 2 Exeter City 3

To be honest I have no idea now where the "Hatters" next win will emerge from, ordinarily I would be thinking three points at Tranmere on Easter Monday would be likely, however I would think right now the Prenton Park faithful could be rubbing their hands in anticipation.

As wrote earlier this morning, John Still is in that catch-22 situation, either he plays experienced players who are not fully fit or play squad players who are not up to league standard.

Problems compounded with the fact they had to chase Exeter around the pitch and playing six players barely eighty per cent fit was never going to help the cause. McNulty coped well enough although his hamstring appeared to be giving him some discomfort. What was most disconcerting was his constant barrage of abuse aimed at goalkeeper Elliot Justham, which cannot be doing the young keeper very much good in the way of confidence. Nathan Doyle did the best he could considering he could barely move, but he did contribute with some good tackles, at least.

The Grecians were much the better side in all departments, even when two goals down they "urned" their victory. Yes, I know leave the comedy to the comedians.

It was noticeable that both the Town goals came from passing moves, but despite that still deciding to hoof the ball forward to Benson at times, who at times was the lone attacker and having to do a great deal of running and chasing balls, not the most sensible tactics taken his age. In the second half Luton were crying out for some pace to be injected into the side and with Hall, Oduwa and Miller available to bring on the chances were there, however what does the manager do? He decides that Jayden Stockley be the answer, playing him on the wing. Not the best-made decision he has made during the season with Stockley being a striker, however he is the boss and he knows what he is doing.

Well played Exeter, with only Bury being able to equal their excellent passing game this season, much credit has to go to their manager, Paul Tisdale.

Luton began much brighter than normal in the opening minutes of a game. At times showing intensity in their game, not allowing City to settle. However, once Exeter settled into their game they took full control of the situation.

The "Hatters" went in front against the run of play. However, saying that it was a good move. Jonathan Smith found Mark Cullen to his right, a neat pass to Guttridge who found the bottom corner. For a squad that is apparently in good spirits it does seem strange that, as mentioned earlier McNulty was verbally abusing Justham on a regular basis and also there looked to be a war of words between McNulty and Guttridge before the game restarted following the goal. Despite Luton's lead, Exeter were winning the second ball.

Just before the break, Cullen doubled the "Hatters" lead with a cool finish. Picking up the ball, after Kinsella had been fortunate not to be pulled up for a foul on Holmes.

The teams came out after the break, kept waiting for a good three minutes or so by the match officials. As with the start of the first half Luton began on the front foot, but again that did not last too long.

Exeter got themselves back into the game, courtesy of non-existent pressing on Luton's behalf. Oakley clipped the ball into the box. Harley turned and finished most expertly from a difficult position with the ball arriving over his head.

Luton's response was to defend deeper, not the best of choices. The passing was, for use of a better phrase, damned abysmal. In comparison, Exeter's passing and movement sublime. Whenever the ball cleared from defence, it would land at the feet of an Exeter player. The visitors were peppering Justham's goal.

Another player replaced by injury in a game, this time it was Jonathan Smith, clearly limping from the field of play. Cameron McGeehan taking his place, a rather strange substitution given the way the game was going.

Exeter deservedly equalised from Davies' free kick, the much-travelled Clinton Morrison knocked the ball down and slipped over the line by Moore-Taylor.

It was one-way traffic and any sign of that changing was not to be found by Luton.

Despite the odd break Luton were unable to capitalise.

With just a minute left of the five added, Ribeiro, who had not been picked up by anyone was handed a free header which hit the post, however, Wheeler was given the space to slide in and put the ball over the line for a last-gasp winner.

Game over and more importantly, it seems season over.

Questions to be answered, but we have to wait and see what the manager has to say now.

Saturday April 4th 2015
The Town have now slipped down to ninth place following the home defeat by Exeter.

Leapfrogged, by Stevenage of all the clubs to choose from, that is a bitter pill to swallow.

John Still has admitted that the "Hatters" ran out of steam. Too many players out there, not fully match fit, does not make his job any easier. However, having such a large squad surely it is time to allow those others a break, or does he realise that some are just not up to the task in hand.

It will be interesting to see which of those out of contract he will decide to offload. I have a feeling it may be the majority rather than the minority, the likeliness of a new look Luton Town first team squad next season.

The guys do not have much time to prepare for the next game, two days in fact. Together with a long journey up the motorways to Merseyside not the best of preparations for a team with so many tired legs out there.

Monday April 6th 2015

Another day in the saga that we know as Luton Town Football Club. For us pain and torture is not exclusive for the Spanish inquisition, these days it reflects on life as a Luton Town supporter. I repeat what I have written before, "Never a Dull moment, when one is a "Hatter" that is for sure" Tranmere, despite being second from bottom, with only Cheltenham to hold them up, are not going to be an easy pushover. Especially the way the Town squad stands at this moment.

Rovers, under the management of seasoned campaigner Mickey Adams are going to fight to the final whistle. Not only today's game, but also for the remainder of this season. For what will be a massive battle to remain within the bounds of the Football League.

Easter Monday, the most glorious of mornings, fresh, lively and invigorating. If only the Town can come out onto the pitch in the same vein, later this afternoon.

The main interest will be which side John Still will send out. He has his work cut out there.

No suppositions from this "Hatter" that is for sure.

Something that I have found rather tiresome throughout the season through social media largely, are the comments regarding our strike force. One thing that upsets a little is the comment that keeps coming up, "If Andre Gray was still with us, we would not be in this predicament." One cannot help but laugh when seen. Andre was a most prolific goal scorer in the Conference last season for Luton with thirty goals. This season following his move to Brentford in the summer has also reaped rewards, up to today scoring fifteen goals so far for the Bees this season, fourteen in the league.

My question is, would he be having such a prolific season in League Two if he had decided to stay another season with the Town?

I very much doubt it, not because he would not be up to it, but because in league two, the way games are played, especially against Luton, he would have had four players around him, not unlike Jayden Stockley when he played the lone striker. That also applies to Pelly.

The possibilities are that with teams having knowledge of his pace, they would have kicked him off the park, as some did with Ruddock Mpanzu early on and as happened to Elliot Lee also recently against Wycombe. I doubt if Gray would have got through the season without injury.

His step up two divisions was for him a good move, if anything I believe Luton undervalued him when letting him go, half a million should perhaps have read a million. I do not say that in hindsight either; I have thought that since the day he signed for Warburton. When the Brentford manager made the comment that Gray was not the finished article on joining them from Luton but is so now, he did Luton and John Still a most disrespectful injustice, that however, is most likely his excuse for not wanting to pay over the half million he spent. Gray for me was already the finished article. However, some may argue that point.

Just one point before moving back to this afternoon's game, I am aware of the bottle throwing incident when Exeter scored their winner on Friday, but I am inclined not to give the perpetrator too much coverage.

The "Hatters" line up of crocks and the like for today being: Elliot Justham, Michael Harriman, Scott Griffiths, Steve McNulty, Luke Wilkinson, Jonathan Smith, Nathan Doyle, Cameron McGeehan, Ryan Hall, Paul Benson and Mark Cullen. With the subs supporting from the dugout:

Alex Lacey, Alex Lawless, Jake Howells, Luke Guttridge, Matt Robinson, Jayden Stockley and Craig King.

We must send best wishes to Cameron McGeehan in his birthday today and the lads can make it a double celebration tonight by bringing home three very precious points.

Tranmere Rovers 0 Luton Town 1

Not one of those games that will live long and prosper in the memory banks of most. Apart of course from the fact that it is our first win since February.

Luton looked a more balanced side than the one that lost to Exeter on Friday. Having players that are mobile at least, helps somewhat. Scott Griffiths and Cameron McGeehan made the difference. Griffiths it seems back to the Scott we admire most, impressed greatly the way kept Myrie-Williams at bay. Easily McGeehan's best game following his return, making some surging runs forward.

There was a lack of belief in both sides following their similar barren runs of late.

Rovers had an early chance, when Doyle's poor pass gifted Jennings, his through ball allowing Myrie-Williams to steal a chance from Wilkinson. Justham managed to stop the ensuing shot with his legs, then getting up to push the ball away for a corner kick.

The "Hatters" first opportunity was instigated by a driving run from McGeehan, who found Jonathan Smith, in turn passing to Harriman. However, when the ball put through to Nathan Doyle, he managed to send his effort skywards, not the best of shots.

Elliot Justham had a good game, his handling consistently good throughout, apart from one scare, making a hash of a cross from Myrie-Williams, which Odejayi jumped for with Justham and the goalkeeper awarded a free kick as a result.

The second half was barely under way when Power went down in a heap, off the ball and no players in close proximity. Following lengthy treatment, which included the use of oxygen, he was stretchered off to standing ovation from both set s of supporters. It later transpired that he was suffering from dehydration and recovering well.

Tranmere made more of an effort after the break, although in all honesty that would not have taken much to do.

Luton's goal came about, against the run of play. Paul Benson jumped high to flick on a clearance up field from Justham. Cullen picked up the ball, ran into the box and upended by Brezovan's outstretched arm. The referee pointed to the spot without hesitation, not even a yellow card for the keeper, strange decision then. Cullen took the spot kick, a poor effort. Brezovan parried away, McGeehan's poacher instinct came into play, following up to score.

The Town saw out the remainder of the game with some comfort. A win at last, but in all honesty nothing to get too excited about.

What is amazing, despite a run of defeats such as Luton have experienced, it is quite incredulous that they are still only one point off the play off places. Exeter beat Newport County, Northampton beaten at home by Cambridge United may also have done us a small favour and Portsmouth beating Plymouth which also assisted in keeping the Town in striking distance.

Tuesday April 7th 2015

To wake up this morning was a pleasure, the sun beating into the bedroom a third consecutive glorious spring morning, a little chilly on the bare toes, but that is fine.

It is quite amazing when one see's the comments after yesterday afternoons victory on Merseyside. To some it was a show of relief, following what has really been a most harrowing period.

Nevertheless, from some, you would think Luton Town had just beaten Bayern Munich and the playoffs now a certainty. Is one stunned? Yes, indeed that is so.

Dear me, it was lowly, out of sorts Tranmere Rovers and let us be fair not the most convincing of wins.

The reality is, we have five games remaining and three of those games are against sides fighting for play off places also. It certainly is not going to be any picnic on the beach at Southend. The beer and tyre making Albion are going to want to send us for a Burton also. That brings us to the final game of the season, Stevenage at home, Graham Westley and the gang.

What a prospect that game holds. I cannot begin to imagine the furore following that match, if it is a fight to the death for both sides. Maybe one should take with them a moneybag to collect the coinage afterwards.

Wednesday April 8th 2015

The squad is slowly diminishing with the departure of Paul Connelly. Thirty one year old Connelly parted company by mutual consent. Paul only managed five first team appearances, his final game in a "Hatters" shirt in January when playing Cambridge United in the FA Cup defeat at the Abbey Stadium.

The development side travelled to Gillingham yesterday and in emphatic style clinched the Final Third Development Southern Region League Championship. A 6-1 trouncing of the Kent side was enough to secure top spot. Shaun Whalley grabbed himself a hat-trick, other goals coming from Ricky Miller and two headed goals from corners from central defender Alex Lacey. An excellent performance, as has been the case throughout the season from all players concerned during the competition was coach Hakan Hayrettin's remarks following the win. It has to be acknowledged that at least something, as is the case with the youth side also, is obviously going right. It is now time for that success to be generated into the first team. Maybe youth is the answer, nothing is going to happen overnight of course, but both sides have proved that we have something to look forward to. Is it time to start looking at who we already have rather than loaning out all the time? I have asked this question before this season which seems more beneficial long term to taking players from other clubs, or do we look at those we already have in our grasp. Maybe the one real decent loan signing of the season being Michael Harriman, who has excelled throughout the season. I know Elliot Lee has also impressed whilst wearing a Luton shirt, however the fact is, we shall not be able to hold on to him, especially as having recently signed an extension to his West Ham United contract. Surely we have to start building from what we already have.

However, one has to ask the question, why have so many players been asked to play out of position all season, surely the manager should be allowing players to play to their natural strengths rather than playing out of position. Something I have come to realise in the latter parts of the season we have been guilty of. Is that one of the reasons McGeehan has not been the player we were hoping him to be on his return? Also to be fair to Andy Drury, he has been playing in unfamiliar roles all season, which may answer some questions about him, but he has lost some of his pace and flair from his original time at the club. Again, it comes to a fact I have made before, they are never the same player second time around.

Getting back to the youth side, they travelled to AFC Bournemouth last Saturday, recording a superb victory. Liam Gooch making some fantastic stops to keep the "Cherries" at bay. Isaac Galliford opened the scoring with Geo Craig netting the second, his third goal in as many games. The final score AFC Bournemouth 0 Luton Town 2. Well done lads.

Scott Griffiths has decided to have his hernia operation and will be out for the majority of remaining games, but insists he will be ready to face Stevenage in the final game of the season if required to do so.

Thursday April 9th 2015

What a fantastic weekend we have lined up. Today witnesses the first day of the US Masters from Augusta. Expectations are high for Rory McIlroy to take the green jacket on Sunday evening. But there will be tough opposition from reigning champion Bubba Watson and also Tiger Woods will be hoping to find some of his old form and turn a few heads after a two month layoff in which time he has been working hard on his play, following a lean spell over the past months and a back operation.

Saturday is one of the biggest days of the racing calendar when all eyes will again be upon Aintree for the Grand National Meeting held over three days starting today. Pineau de ra will be looking to emulate last year's win when Leighton Aspell rode him to victory.

On Sunday it is the opening day of the county cricket campaign, where Kevin Pietersen will be hoping to make his mark with Surrey to impress the new to hierarchy within the ECB following the dismissal of Paul Downton, which was a long time in coming. For myself, I believe Michael Vaughan or Alec Stewart would be the perfect choices. Although quite selfishly hoping that it would be Vaughan out of the two as Stewart is better off at the Oval leading Surrey.

At first, I have to admit to have been a little bemused when today I am reading some comments made by manager John Still, concerning youngster on loan from Tottenham Hotspur, Nathan Oduwa. Still, claiming that the young lad could be Luton's secret weapon if we were to qualify for the play-offs and reach the final at Wembley. I thought to myself, is this man serious? Because up until now although the lad most certainly has talent, that is not an issue. Nevertheless at the same time apart from a couple of good runs, the lad had nowhere impressed to that extent. Seven of his ten appearances have been as substitute and for me looks at times a player who lacks confidence, also he does seems a little lost at times. Maybe I am completely wrong, maybe it is just the fact that he used to playing alongside players of a higher quality at Tottenham, who knows.

However, having sat back and read the article a second time and more slowly, I do actually begin to see where JLS may be coming from. At Wembley a bigger playing area, a well-kept playing surface, maybe allowed more time on the ball and able to run with the ball at his feet. Room also to run at defences, unlike the compact field of play being encountered in the league games, freedom to run with the ball. Yes, maybe the manager does have a point. However, again, I doubt that will happen, I am sorry but the dream is over for this season as far as I am concerned, for me reality kicked in months ago, Luton are just not good enough for promotion this season, to go up now with this squad as it is, would be a train crash waiting to happen, sorry but that is my true and honest opinion. This squad needs time, especially with the injuries incurred this season. That is not being used as an excuse by the way, it is being used in the context that players have not had the time to play together. Get to know each other, it is all well and good on the training field but in battle not at all long enough, too many interruptions, different personnel coming in and out of the side for me. Again I will repeat myself, continuity is not only needed in the management departments but also out there on the field of play. Until we get that, we will not be successful.

The first day of the US Masters at Augusta, drew to a close a few minutes ago. Heading the leader board is American Jordan Speith, looking down at the rest of the field with a three shot lead from, South African Ernie Els. Fellow American, Charley Hoffman, Briton Justin Rose and Australian Jason Day all tying for second place on five under par.

With the likes of Tiger Woods, returning today from a two-month layoff in hope of finding his former glories, with a world rating of 111, something we would have laughed at a couple of years ago if suggested to us, to world number one, Irishman Rory McIlroy.

The day was tee'd off by Jack Nicklaus, before the game got off proper, with reigning champion Bubba Watson grouping with Justin Rose and Korean Gunn Yang.

Following his lengthy lay off Tiger Woods experienced a steady round, not trail blazing at all by his high standards of the past. Many of his shots were veering to the left. Is this a sign of more back problems, or just a touch of ring rustiness? The next couple of days will tell. Woods eventually returning to the club house on one over par.

Veteran America player Ben Crenshaw had the most torrid first round. The pine tree lined course was not found to be as caring and tranquil as he would have hoped. From the outset he was always chasing his opponents. A double bogey at the first hole, not the most ideal of starts. Crenshaw went on to record seven double bogeys in all, as his round, that can only be described as horrendous totalling 91. 19 shots over the par 72.

Further up the leader board at the completion of day one, in tied 41st placing is Tiger Woods. Tiger also had a shaky start to the tournament, with bogies at the first, fourth, ninth and twelfth holes not doing him any favours. However, he did redeem himself with three birdies at the second, eighth and thirteenth holes, to record a total seventy-three round of one over the course par.

World number one Rory McIlroy returned to the bar for a much required orange juice, no doubt. It was a most sedate start for the young Irishman, only managing to par the first five holes and bogeying the sixth. However, he managed to pull the lost shot back at the very next green, to level par again. Another bogey at the eleventh, returned him to one over the par, before his blushes were spared with two birdies at the thirteenth and fifteenth holes, the final three holes being level parred. He finished the day with a 71, one under par round. Rory will most definitely be looking for a redeeming round tomorrow.

But the day belonged without doubt to twenty-one year old Texan Jordan Speith, showing no fear he went out and blazed the trail with a near faultless Sixty-four round. Which included eight birdies and just the one bogey to spoil what would have otherwise been a near perfect round. The only bogey being at the fifteenth, where following a most uncharacteristic wayward second shot, was forced to play cautiously towards the green following that shot, with the water just yard the other side of the green. Otherwise a tremendous first round for the young American.

Tomorrow, the second day of four, promises to be a most fantastic day of golf.

Friday April 10th 2015

Well two first team squad members have really shown their dedication to the cause, one cannot fault them for that, for sure. Scott Griffiths has announced that he is calling off his hernia operation and wants to play against leaders Burton Albion tomorrow. Also against the wishes of his parent club West Ham, Elliot Lee has also expressed his wish to play despite his injury of which West Ham argue that he needs another few days to be match fit. It will be a most interesting decision for both that John still has to make. One cannot doubt their commitment to the "Hatters" but in all honesty would it be a sensible call to play both of them or even one of them? I really do have my reservations on that one.

Two players today signed a one year extension to their contracts, especially happy to learn that one of the few outstanding players of the season Nathan Doyle has signed and also young striker Zane Banton who has been on loan throughout the majority of the season with both Hemel Hempstead and Biggleswade Town. Many are hoping, I know, that sometime in the near future the youngster will break into the Luton first team.

John Still has today admitted that he has made mistakes throughout the season in the way of selection at times, lack of balance being one of the flaws. At least he is man enough to admit. We must give the manager credit for that, but at the same time we have been saying it ourselves all along, so he could not really dodge away from the issue in reality. It would be a little worrying if the supporters were noticing it, along with comments made by Gary Sweet in his programme notes earlier. So he could not really run away from the fact either.

Tomorrow's game at home to leaders Burton Albion is going to be a tough cookie, on what will be the Towns 130th birthday. A celebratory three points would be most welcomed, however I have already had my little wager with the Powers of Paddy, and unfortunately I will upset may by saying my head has had to rule my heart and go for a 0-2 Burton win, sorry guys, but that is the way I see it. Maybe I shall also be wasting my money on a few bob on some poor horse that will be weighted with my hopes and desires which will prevent it competing the course at Aintree tomorrow afternoon. Poor thing!

It has also been reported that the manager explained to journalists that he does not believe that the "hatters" playing squad of forty professionals is too large, not allowing it to be operated properly. He admits though that during a normal season that could be a fair reflection. He was quoted as saying "If I look at players that have been injured, I don't know what we would have done if we'd have been operating with a small squad"

He continues to say and I have to agree with him somewhat, that it takes a good two to three years to get a system working in normal circumstances. So, in fairness injury wise and other factors this has not been a normal season for the veteran manager, r would it have been for any other manager either. That for myself is reason enough to stick with John Still for at least another year and see where it takes us and keep faith with the man who made it happen for us to be received back into the bosom of league football.

The trouble though at Luton Town an ongoing one, once we get a good run in a season, supporters lose their sense of reality, their heads go off into the clouds, common sense often dissipates into fluffy white balls. They smell success, it is like a drug. It eats away at them. This follows with the expectancy of instant success, they want it now, no room for patience and the understanding of what is happening around them. The other problem when it comes to Luton Town supporters, but I will add, only the minority, they appear again from under their carpets when that smell of success gets into their nostrils. However, when things go pear shaped they are there moaning, belittling the players and the management team at every opportunity. But when the good times are waning, eventually they crawl back under their carpets, never to be seen again until another successful run appears. They are the ones that leave a sour taste around Kenilworth Road, the ones that run onto the pitch, throw flares, coins and soft drink bottles onto the playing areas. The same ones that besmirch the good name of Luton Town.

Of course we are not content to sit and watch our side game after game getting beaten, of course we want answers. But there is a right way and a wrong way to show our feelings of dissatisfaction, not with downright stupidity that makes each and every Luton Town supporter look as if we are nothing but brainless morons seeking out trouble, because unfortunately that is how recently we have been looked down upon by other clubs around the country. Some of those morons honestly need pointing out, gotten rid of, before the clubs name is dragged down yet again because of a mindless few.

Things have gone wrong and we have that right to make our point heard, but in the correct manner please. As John Still has pointed out it has not been an easy season to operate even a large squad, let us try to understand that also. Just for the record guys in case some of you pounce on me as a happy clapper living in those fluffy white clouds, oblivious to the problems the Town is going through. No I am not, however there is a right way and a wrong way to go about things. Oops I did it again! Britney spears, I blame you entirely.

So this evening is now for the sofa, a bottle of the red fermented grape juice and an evening in Augusta and some golfing lessons.

And I was not disappointed, following his first round score of 64. Jordan Spieth wrote himself into golfing history and the record books today with a faultless 66. Breaking the 36 hole aggregate record held by Ray Floyd set in 1976. Following dropping just one shot yesterday he bettered that by not dropping a single shot throughout.

Who can see the young Texan being caught over the next couple of days? It will take a very brave person indeed to take high stakes against him. He has so far taken the 2015 US Masters by storm with his lightning play. He goes into the third day with a five shot lead over fellow American Charley Hoffman, with nine under par score.

World number one Rory McIlroy was again spared his blushes. If only just, with birdies recorded at each of the final two holes to go into the clubhouse with a score of two under. It could have though, been so much different. Following a double bogey at the ninth McIlroy was actually staring a premature departure from the tournament face on. Being three shots over par and the likelihood of not making the cut a very realistic prospect.

Tiger Woods, who is on the comeback trail in many ways ended with a steady two under par for the tournament so far. Under the circumstances and looking back over the past eighteen months or so, he may be looking at the past two days in a positive light. Having begun the day on one over. Reigning champion Bubba Watson also finished the day on two under, adding just the one shot to his overnight score.

At the other end of the leader board, 63 year old Ben Crenshaw followed up with another disastrous round of twelve over to add to his first round score of nineteen over. However for a man his age, he still put many a young man to shame who may be a third of his age.

Saturday April 11th 2015
Good morning and HAPPY 130th BIRTHDAY, to Luton Town Football Club.
I have recently come upon a magnificent website that explains how Luton Town Football Club came about, it is a most interesting and very illuminating set of pages put together by a gentleman by the name of Brian Webb. Brian has put many hours of research into the formation of the club including history before and after the famous meeting at Luton Town Hall on Saturday April 11th 1885. It would have been too easy for me to have copied much of what Brian has researched, however that would not have been at all ethical or the right and correct way to write any book. Therefore the only correct way is to put you as the reader on that path towards viewing the website for yourselves. I have placed a direct link on my website for anyone interested. As I mentioned it is

most illuminating and original and much of the contents and there are many pages, are of material not printed in any prior books.

So, onto today's proceedings at Kenilworth Road.

A nice day for football, so I was so reliably informed anyway.

The "Hatters" line up for this afternoon's little jolly at Kenilworth Road as follows: Elliot Justham, Michael Harriman, Steve McNulty, Luke Wilkinson, Scott Griffiths, Alex Lawless, Nathan Doyle, Cameron McGeehan, Jake Howells, Paul Benson and Elliott Lee. With the picnicker's on the bench: Nathan Oduwa, Alex Lacey, Ryan Hall, Luke Guttridge, Lewis Kinsella, Mark Cullen and Craig King.

Three changes from the Tranmere game then, Lee, Howells and Lawless returning to the side at the expense of Cullen, Hall and Smith.

Luton Town 0 Burton Albion 1

Coaching rule number one, play to the whistle, watch the ball and the opponents who are in the vicinity rather the man in black just the other side of the lines with the pretty coloured flag in his hand, that way you may just and I say just, have prevented a goal against yourself.

A very similar game to the one at the Pirelli Stadium last November, the Town for most of the game looking the more likely to score, without actually doing so, however to hit the net at the back of the post's it is a fair comment I think to say that one first has to place a shot that is on target the hit the said netting.

The day a nice sunny one, typical spring weather, with a hint of wind, the "Hatters" attacked the Kenilworth Road end in the first half. We started well enough, some very direct football. Lee, lacking fitness, maybe the West Ham medical staff's wishes should have been adhered to. It's all well and fine the player wanting to do his part, however for me the manager picks the side not the player's. Too many players seem to be starting games not fully fit, not the greatest of starts for any game. But, to be fair times are not normal for Luton Town when it comes down to the fitness of players this season. Lawless also looks to be struggling with fitness recently also.

Burton took their time settling into the game, Luton always looking the more likely to produce something although never finding that final touch of magic.

Albion's goal came about from an Edward's pass that found Naylor, who the Luton defence thought was offside, however, the man dressed in black with the pretty kerchief on the end of a stick though otherwise and kept his hand, and the stick motionless. The "Hatters" defensive line stood still, waving their hands, Naylor fed the ball into Palmer whose strike took a deflection and beat Justham. The cast was set from then on, Luton having to throw men forward in an attempt to get the game back on an even keel. However that allowing Burton the luxury of taking their time on the ball. They saw the game out and collected another three points to edge them closer to automatic promotion and for Luton Town ever closer to another season in League Two without even the opportunity to play another three games on top of those already scheduled, in an attempt to win a playoff situation.

I may be sounding a little cynical but, I think it really is time to sit back reflect on this season, forget about the dream, face reality, Luton in all fairness are not ready. A better, smaller but stronger squad is required before we set our sights on league one, for me. I may be tempting some of you to come looking for me, Fatwah's signed, but the truth is the players are already on their last legs with still four scheduled games to cover. Another three games on top of that, maybe this time round not what the doctor ordered. I personally feel three extra games on touch and highly pressured games at that may be just three games too far.

How many times in the past, not only from the "Hatters" point of view but the whole of the English football league spectrum, and beyond, have we seen sides get to their respective playoffs lose even their semi-final matches, or even worst lose the final. Then the following season, totally crumble, the stuffing knocked out of them.

My other argument is, with the promise from John Still that there has to be a clear out at the end of this season, the squad will have to go through the process of getting to know each other, playing together, understanding each other. For me better to get that out of the way in league two than in league one where the opposition will be that much tougher. If it does not work out we get relegated. Then yet again the knives are out for the head of players and management, a vicious circle that never ends. I have always thought it better to work from the bottom than attempt to work higher up and fall even lower down. Something John Still needs to do this close season maybe is make sure he finds a strong back four before anything else. Then slowly work forwards into midfield and then up front. Building from the defence forward, if you have a strong defence that is the major half of the battle won, because less goals conceded less goals against. For me also this long ball nonsense is not for us. The goalkeeper launching the ball up to the forward line is a gamble at best. I do not think we have a goalkeeping problem, despite what some are inferring. If the captain instead of yelling abuse at a young goalkeeper, encouraged him instead maybe things would be different also. Justham, will in time become the finished article given time. He has proved his worth and the experience he has gathered during this run of appearances can only be beneficial long term. However, what he does not need and this goes for the other youngsters also, are the frustrated supporters making every little mistake they may make a bigger one by getting on their backs. More pressure builds more errors, sadly at Luton Town patience is not something the majority of supporters are blessed with. Therefore hand on heart I really do think that the playoffs, fitness wise, are a disaster waiting to happen and promotion this season, the way things have panned out, would be not a disaster but downright suicidal. However, that is just my own personal opinion.

So now, following publication, I must await the consequences. I honestly feel it is time to say hold on to the dream yes, but please let's face the realities. Tomorrow is another day. A quick fix this season could be next season's bigger mess. Just saying…

Sunday April 12th 2015

I am not going to dwell on yesterday's result too long, however, I am quite bemused to be honest. I check the stats for yesterday's game Luton had at best one shot on target. However, I read I read some saying, the Burton keeper was beaten on three separate occasions. So, please if the keeper was beaten three times, how come we had one shot on target and no goals scored. I am not the only one to say this, but some Luton fans seem to see a different game that actually took place, there wishful minds totally taking over from the realities of the day, sorry but it really does beggar belief at times.

On that note I feel it best, sit back watch the golf and chill.

Monday April 13th 2015

Jason Stockley has returned back to his parent club, AFC Bournemouth, for myself he did okay, especially as asked to play up-front in a lone role at times, also out of position. So thank you for that. Wish you all the best for the future.

More injury/sickness troubles with Alex Lawless most probably out for the remainder of the season with shingles, if that is so I just wonder if the Welshman has made his final appearance in a Luton Town shirt with all the changes being promised by the manager once the season has closed for the summer.

What a fantastic days golf we enjoyed from the US Masters at Augusta. As for Saturday's Grand National, a superb result.

The sun decided to eventually come alive and to greet the bumper 72,000 sell-out crowd that had gathered to witness this year's Grand National race at Aintree.

There had been much pre-race hype this year, speculation regarding the imminent retirement of champion jockey for the past nineteen years, AP "Tony" McCoy. Who having already announced that this would indeed be his final season as a jockey, but had added to the equation the fact that if he was to win this afternoon's race he would announce his immediate retirement following the race, so for that reason alone speculation was rife. McCoy was to be aboard pre-race favourite shutthefrontdoor, so all attention was on them today. One can only imagine the reception horse and rider would return to the enclosure to if that was to happen. The noise at Anfield when Liverpool scored a winner would be nothing in relation to the eruption of noise if this was to happen. Romantics, cynics and realists alike, the hardest men bought to tears, of that most could be certain. There were a number of well fancied runners, including as mentioned, shutthefrontdoor, Soll, Rocky Creek, Balthazar King and the fourteen year old Oscar Time would also be a popular winner. Long

The thirty nine runners and their designated jockeys paraded in front of the stand and then cantered the long journey out to the first fence, to allow both horse and jockey a good look at the first of the thirty obstacles and four miles 770 yards in front of them once they were under way.

The race itself was all it had been built up to be over the preceding days. The usual cavalry like charge to the first, although it seemed not as fast as in recent years, but still a good clip was set. The first fence claimed three casualties but all thankfully unscathed. At the canal turn on the first circuit a most horrific fall for Balthazar King, after falling was run into by another horse and sent literally into the air again and looked stricken as he tried to get up. Many were fearing the worse. On the second circuit the fence was missed out by the remaining runners as the stricken horse was being tended to, it was later made clear that the horse had survived the fall but had fractured ribs, but now being treated accordingly and very much alive.

The race was eventually won by the Oliver Sherwood trained Many Clouds and ridden by the previous year's winning jockey Leighton Aspell. Emulating jockey Brian Fletcher who had also won two consecutive Grand Nationals some forty years earlier. Many Clouds holding off the challenge of Saint Are, to record a very popular victory. Champion jockey Tony McCoy and shutthefrontdoor finished a very creditable fifth and ran a superb race, sitting just behind the leaders until fading from the pace two fences from home.

A fantastic race as expected with the good news that all horses survived. It will be interesting to know who Leighton Aspell will be booked to ride next season the way things are after two wins under his belt now in consecutive years.

The US Masters came to its conclusion earlier this morning with victory going to twenty one year old Texan Jordan Spieth, who in winning became only the fifth player in the history of the tournament to lead from wire to wire throughout the four days, a most fantastic feat for such a young player. Although, young he may be, he has the head and heart of one much older. Over the four days he played with what from the exterior looked like nerves of steel, with a certain panache.

Much of his green play was sublime to watch. He has now amassed over $4million in prize money over the past few weeks.

Spieth won with an overall score of eighteen under par and his score for the final round two under par. Somewhat sedate in comparison to the first three days.

In second place followed fellow American Phil Mickelson, the left handed player who seems to have an affinity with the Augusta course finished the tournament four shots adrift of the winner and three under for the day.

Britain's Justin Rose and world number one Rory McIlroy finished third and fourth respectively, ensuring their invitation to next year's Masters.

A most enjoyable four days golf, now looking forward to St. Andrews and the British 144th Open which is to be held at the beautiful Scottish course from July 12th to 19th. The 29th time it will have been held at St Andrews. Last year won by Rory McIlroy at Royal Liverpool course.

A return to Dagenham and Redbridge FC tomorrow for John Still and Terry Harris. I do hope they receive a warm welcome from their supporters, after all they achieved a great deal whilst at the Essex club.

Tuesday April 14th 2015

It is going to be rather a wet day today I fear, inside at least, as I am meeting me good mate Paul Stanyon for a day in South London. Something we have not done this season as of yet. It will be interesting on many counts that is for sure. Not least the football, although the chances are if past experiences like those expected today, will one even get to see the game, but that is another story for another time for now. Off we go, Stratford, Barking and Dagenham beware we are on our way. Because of my day out the report will be left until Wednesday and hopefully the hangover will have dissipated enough.

Enjoy your day guys and girls, a win would be perfect, but the hopes and our dreams that we build each match day are more often than not splashed against the walls these days, not unlike pebbledash.

Wednesday April 15th 2015

Yesterday, what can I say, a good day for drinking that is for sure, the ale flowed like the canal that runs alongside the micro-brewery pub we located at the back end of an industrial estate in Hackney Wick. Quite surreal to find a pub in such surrounds, industrial units' one side and the canal on the other. As for the beer, despite expensive, most enjoyable but worth the extra paid. The sun came out and was most obliging, which allowed us to sit outside on the canal bank, a couple of barges moored alongside, one of which housed one very luscious young lady for the eyes to peruse over as the beer was enjoyed. Most relaxing, I must say. Not another football shirt in sight bar my own glowing orange "Hatters" shirt, which did get some looks at first, maybe the up-market patrons were not used to such riff raff invading their space, but unlike earlier years I was extremely well behaved, I promise. Paul and I had already started much earlier, myself in Peckham before moving eastwards to Stratford, for Paul I cannot talk though. But we did enjoy a couple of glasses in the real ale pub in Westfield Shopping Centre at Stratford. We embarked on a leisurely but thirst quenching walk around the Olympic Park, I for one was silently tempted to make a move and enjoy the British Swimming Championships for a couple of hours, but the call of ale was forever in the back of my mind. We met and had a good chat with one of the London Lions basketball starts who was having a quiet break outside the copper box as we strolled past on our sojourn towards Hackney. Not only could he spin a ball but could quote the odd poem also, nice guy. We moved on our prey awaiting, namely Case Brewery, as I have mentioned, in such surreal surroundings. Time moved on and so did we, on to Barking, mad or what? There we met and again enjoyed a talk with Elliot Justham's father, who was quite forward in telling us some interesting facts, however for the sake of not being thrown some libel suits, I think it best that I hold my tongue for now. I was beginning to feel of poorer quality as the afternoon wore on, firstly thinking I was just on the verge of inebriation, maybe I was that also. I met one of my Facebook buddies of whom I had not before had the pleasure of meeting, a great guy and fellow music lover and of course "Hatter" Paul Hugh Gallagher. We had a short chat, a picture taken, I could insert here I suppose but the way I was beginning to look, not such a good idea as I learnt this morning when coming upon it on Facebook, oh the shame. After meeting Paul I did begin to feel rather unwell and made the brave but necessary choice to travel home, even before reaching Dagenham East. It was a good move as I later found out that I was suffering from not only the effects of the days supping but also a touch of extreme high blood pressure, so, a good move on my part in hindsight. So I was to miss out on the game, but fortunately along with his £1.50 expenses for half a cup of tea Paul Wright was on hand as always if needed to do the honours.

Therefore here we jolly well go.

The "Hatters" line-up was: Elliot Justham, Michael Harriman, Steve McNulty, Luke Wilkinson, Scott Griffiths, Jonathan Smith, Nathan Doyle, Cameron McGeehan, Ryan Hall, Paul Benson and Elliot Lee. With those in suspended animation: Alex Lacey, Jake Howells, Shaun Whalley, Mark Cullen, Luke Guttridge, Lewis Kinsella and Craig King.

Dagenham & Redbridge 0 Luton Town 0

It has to be said, thank heaven for small mercies, including the fact that the season is coming to a much welcomed end.

Under the circumstances of late, an excellent point gained rather than two lost, at least the floodgates have closed for a while at least, in respect of goals against in recent games. However, following Paul Benson's dismissal we ncither looked as if we would end the stalemate with a goal. But if the truth was known, it was in fact no different when we were playing eleven against eleven, either.

It was good to see John Still receiving a good reception from both sets of supporters. Let's face it, when one thinks of their nearby neighbours West Ham hogging most of the support from the surrounding areas, a good job done when instrumental in building them to where they sit now.

Apart from Benson's sending off, the first half was relatively free of incident. Being held back by Widdowson, which surprise, not, the officials so conveniently failed to see, his kick was high up and in this day and age was always going to be a red card. Why Luton decided to appeal and waste £400, of which they could have easily given to my team, as we need sponsorship desperately for the next book we are soon to undertake, is a mystery. Especially after McNulty's red card for a similar offence, although his foot not half as high was rejected on appeal, there was not ever going to be much chance of Benno's being rescinded.

More injury woe with Doyle having to go off. Then a spot of lunacy, but then we have to keep on reminding ourselves this is actually Luton Town, therefore anything is possible, Cameron McGeehan decided he would leave the field of play during a break in the hostilities for a much required, it seems, toilet break. Something that we shall be more used to come the end of the month for the World Snooker championships in Sheffield.

Elliot Lee looked sharper, the game on Saturday was much needed, so maybe come this weekend against Hartlepool he will be back to a level that will be needed against a Ronnie Moore side fighting to stay in the football league. Elliot Justham made some fine saves and again proved to the doubters amongst us, not me may I add, that he will if we can keep hold of him be a perfect replacement for Tyler, his confidence starting to grow now the goal rout has dissipated from view, at least for the time being.

Although as you know by now I had to flee from Dagenham in disgrace, it was later justified, my thoughts are that the season end will, despite no play off place, be welcomed. The squad so needs to regroup, a shuffling of the cards and the chaff thrown out of the buckets. Which if we are all honest is a very large pile of chaff to be swept clean. New blood is essential and as much as in the past I have lauded the intake of youth to build upon, we do desperately need some experience, but not too long in the tooth to be walked over by the young whippersnappers of pace and endurance. The worrying fact though is, where does one look for such experience would. The long hoof to the lone forward is not for want of a better phrasing, the way forward. Any Luton side for myself, throughout the past has been more successful when building from the back via midfield, not via an overhead EasyJet airplane. The word is that John Still's orders all through the season have been to knock the ball high to the forwards or in our case forward, sorry John but most of us will say, not next season please sir.

I wrote just a moment ago "despite no play off place", although still mathematically possible, let us be honest with each other, the dream was in all fairness over and gone weeks ago. We are not good enough, my fear is if by some miracle we were to reach the gates, well these days the ramp of Wembley, we would be made mince pies of, especially by the likes of Southend United, of whom will undoubtedly give us a very difficult time in ten days or so. Although, having said that if we are out of the running by then, just maybe worth the pressure off and the lads relaxing more, maybe just maybe we will give a much better show of ourselves. Whatever the case I firmly believe we can be pleased on the whole how the season has gone. We were not embedded in a fight to stave off relegation and most of us at the beginning of the season could not have envisaged a fight to get into the playoffs. We have endured in fact a very long hard and strenuous season, maybe not with full honours, nevertheless, able to say Luton town really and truly are back where we belong. We are here to stay.

The club have issued a statement regarding the moron, yes I again use that word, however, only because in a state of calmness I am being extremely forgiving, there are many worse handles I could quite easily produce, but hey respect for the younger generation, including my daughters and yours who may just pick up and say what is all this drivel about and take a sneaky peak at some time or other.

To be honest in the match report against Burton I had tried not to mention the incident, only because the perpetrator was not worthy of being given more publicity, we can do without such acts in football generally, however, even more so at Luton Town. Although I will still to this day dismiss any vendetta against us by the footballing authorities as utter rubbish, this will not assist matters for the club in any way shape or form. It really is a case of bringing such scum and vermin that lie within us to justice, they are not needed not wanted and most definitely must not be tolerated at any time.

Fortunately on this occasion the villain of the peace was apprehended and arrested, at least that is something. However, the fact that he was intent on attacking a football league official is most alarming and obviously an investigation will be made into the incident and not only will the cretin concerned be punished, but no doubt the club. That is going to weigh heavy on many minds and shoulders over the coming weeks as to the extent of the punishment. This person has not just tarnished the reputation of the club and its supporters, they could also cost us financially also, which no club, especially Luton Town can afford, even more so at this end of the league tiers, money being scarce enough already. I do hope the Town decide to ban him for life home and away, and also the courts hit him heavily and the football league allowed to hit him hard rather than the club itself.

On a lighter note, I read that Aviva bus group have named some of their buses after local heroes, one named John in celebration of John Still steering the "Hatters" back to the football league. I actually argue the point that it is really, but quietly, so as not to upset other such deserving "Hatters" fans, in salutation to stalwart Luton Town supporter, a legend in his own right, John "COME ON LUTON" Pyper. The voice of Luton Town, because damn when that mouth opens and he is sitting a metre away from ones unguarded ears, not the most easily on the ear moments, one can be assured.

Thursday April 16th 2015
It's my party and I will drink if I want to…..
Yep, another year passes into the wilderness of time, it is my birthday. The wine will no doubt flow later this afternoon, therefore let me say good day before the festivities ring around Erith, Dartford and Barnehurst in no particular order, watch out Tony Botta, I know where you live and I do know you enjoy a decent slurp now and again of the fermented red grape juice.

Before I disappear I have received many good wishes today from fellow hatters, former racing colleagues and other great friends also, much too many to mention. So, in a sentence, thank you one and all it has been humbling at times and I am so very grateful and thankful. Bless you all. Now let me do what I seem to do best these days. Get totally slaughtered and later in the evening no doubt cry like a baby and thank all my friends and family through tainted tears of happiness and drunkenness. See you all on the morrow.

Friday April 17th 2015
So there we have it another year gone, another year has commenced, is that what this life is all about, from one birthday to the next? Damn, age is catching up on me for real. Never thought of it that way before, not until now. Tranquilisers at the ready.

Hartlepool and Ronnie Moore the next in line wanting to ruin the dreams of those still hoping for a miracle. It's not a case of giving up on that one, more of a resigned notion that we are now chasing our dream rather than actually living it. However, this one has to remind one's self is Luton Town and since when have the "Hatters" done things the easy way, maybe last season being the exception to the rule, John Still had not read the Luton Town management handbook until Boxing Day of last year. Now he realises this is the Luton Town way, so let's give the fans what they are used to a real good and true football roller coaster of a year in 2015. Well he is certainly doing that. Somehow despite such a desperate run of results we are still in within shouting distance of reaching them, I suppose that in itself is quite miraculous.

But Ronnie Moore and co. will certainly have their own agenda, which is a fact. They are wobbling and swaying quite precariously on the edge of an abyss at present. A drop that will cost them dearly if they are to finally succumb to the power that is relegation to non-league football.

Someone has to go I suppose, at least we are safe from that little scenario, therefore, with that in mind we should be thankful.

I am actually going to stick my neck on the line for this one and predict Luton Town 5 Hartlepool United 1. That's us done then.

Saturday April 18th 2015

Another sunny day, it does seem we play better when the sun shines.

It really was a waste of the £400 deposit paid to the football League in advance of Paul Benson's appeal against his red card, having said that the ruling body obviously need the money more than Luton town do. Maybe that is why there are so many red cards this season, more than normal. They could not keep us out of the league one way so they decided let us give them numerous red cards, they will be soft enough to appeal, we charge them £400 a time, they go bust, we win. Now then you lot out there do not please take me seriously though. We have enough conspiracy theories floating about without any more to contend with. One of the most stupid ones I read today. They are making it so that Watford get promotion to the Premiership, giving them millions whilst Luton scrimp and save in the lower tier, that will really piss them off so let's do that. I ask you, as if. Now those theorists have even gotten their claws into me, I am actually thinking, could that be so. The white coats are on their way.

Back to sanity.

The "Hatters" line-up is a hopeful one at least: Elliot Justham, Michael Harriman, Steve McNulty, Luke Wilkinson, Scott Griffiths, Shaun Whalley, Jonathan Smith, Cameron McGeehan, Jake Howells, Elliot Lee and Mark Cullen. With the magnificent seven backing up: Alex Lacey, Alex Wall, Ricky Miller Luke Guttridge Lewis Kinsella, Ryan Hall and Craig King.

Luton Town 3 Hartlepool United 0

Poor Jeff Stelling must have been having palpitations throughout the afternoon. Rather him than us, I say.

A home win, combined with a clean sheet, somethings never cease to amaze, however, this afternoon it does not stop there. Luton Town were awarded a penalty. It gets even better, for the first time this season if I am not wrong, converted from the spot, not from the rebound. Smelling salts please.

A comfortable win, something else I thought I would not be writing this end of the season.

We could, so easily have been four or five goals to the good by half time. A shot cleared off the line from Shaun Whalley, Cullen had a goal disallowed.

To be fair to Ronnie Moore and his merry men, they have done exceptionally well over recent weeks to be in with a shout of avoiding the dreaded drop.

Luton began well, not allowing Hartlepool time to settle, showing good width to our play and stretching the visitors. Howells and Griffiths playing together and working well.

The opening goal was a soft one in all honesty. McGeehan always a threat from set-pieces, headed home at the far post from Jake Howell's right sided corner.

The penalty, shock overcoming most of the Luton faithful, was this a mirage, had we all fallen under the spell of some strange invisible airborne substance? No, the referee really had blown his little pea whistle and pointed to that big white spot half way between the eighteen and six yard boxes. So that it what it is for, some of us had been questioning the reason for its being for a number of weeks now. However, at this point I feel one must have a little sympathy for Mansfield Town, we think we have been hard done by, apparently they have not been awarded a penalty for seventy seven consecutive games. We thought we had problems. Harriman rolled the ball to Whalley, turning infield catching out Tshibola, ran with the ball into the box. Austin leant into him, it was clearly a foul but Whalley making doubly sure of the referee noticing by throwing himself to the floor with some ease. The boy that is Jake Howell's although celebrating his twenty fourth birthday today, it seems has been playing for Luton since he left the warmth of his Mother's womb stepped up, no second thoughts this was his day and he'll score if he wants to. His shot sent keeper Flinders completely the wrong way, neatly ticking into the corner of the goal. Luton town had not only been awarded a penalty, they had actually scored direct from the kick and surely this will be a day to recall in our twilight years.

Hartlepool credit to them tried to play football rather than kicking Town players all over the park. Justham did all he was asked to do, Franks having a number of efforts but not anything to really trouble the young man too much. He really is beginning to find his confidence and at a crucial time too, fair play to the lad.

In the second half, that old Luton Town problem reared its head. They thought it would be good fun to piss the supporters off by electing to sit back rather than attempt to kill the game off properly. A Trait that has been their downfall this season, a rather worrying tactic therefore. The lummox that is Harewood was starting to hold the ball up and Featherstone being allowed too much space.

Harewood played the ball wide to Duckworth, whose centre found Franks, fortunately Howells had dropped back and was able to deal with the situation.

The game was finally wrapped up when from Howells' corner, finding the head of McGeehan who played the ball down to Griffiths who was able to turn and push the ball over the line, confirming a Luton win.

The game was played out with Hartlepool having a couple of chances but nothing to trouble the now very confident and able young keeper that Justham is becoming.

Scores elsewhere have been kind yet again to Luton this season with Stevenage only managing to draw against ten man Accrington who had a man sent off only two minutes into the game, but still managed to lead for most of it. Plymouth were beaten quite resoundingly at Carlisle 2-0, so they only head Luton now by a superior goal difference in the fight for a play-off place. Our next opponents Southend United sealed their play-off place with a 1-0 win at Exeter. So Luton now have it all to play for at Roots Hall, but will be reliant on Plymouth losing at home to Tranmere. What I have noticed there is that there is a great deal of unrest amongst some Argyle supporters who are angry that they have not consolidated their play-off position and some berating manager John Sheridan. It seems that it is not only Luton town that have inpatient supporters this season. I met Sheridan one evening after racing at Doncaster in an Indian restaurant in the town, quite a decent guy to be honest, he was playing for Leeds at the time. We did have quite a lengthy chat. Faff knows what about though, it was a long time ago, no doubt I mentioned Luton town more than Leeds united though. What that has to do with the price of petrol though is anyone's guess. Good win today fella's, kids time now so laptop off, TV on and watch the Scottish Grand National I recorded earlier, yes must get the children educated the right way.

Sunday April 19th 2015

I am laughing, I am sorry but it cannot be helped, those that have been slagging off John still so vehemently in recent weeks are suddenly singing his praises. It really does cease to amaze me. I am not slagging him down but I am not going to shower him in loving kisses either. Feet firmly set on the ground, a good win yesterday without doubt and yes, we have a realistic, well mathematical chance of getting to the play-offs.

Some are saying it is on the cards. It is great to see such positivity, I do like to see that. However, if Plymouth beat Tranmere next Saturday and things do not go well for us at Southend I will be very upset if those same people are slagging John still off at the end of it all. We have done what we set out to do in my opinion, we will have finished in the top ten. I do not like to see people's dreams shattered, I do not like to have my own dreams shattered that is why I do my utmost to be as realistic as possible, what will be, will be. Let us enjoy what we have and celebrate the fact that we have league football next season.

I was going to leave it there today, but some people are amazing aren't they.

I have just read some guy saying that if Mark Tyler is fit enough to play the final two games, he should play instead of Elliot Justham. My question is what more has the young keeper to do for some people, there have been a number of times he has kept us in games recently. If Tyler comes back now, is he going to be match ready? I doubt that very much, the last two games that are so crucial are not the games I personally would want any player returning back to the side if not a hundred per cent ready. Tyler has not even played a reserve type game, there is no way whatsoever he could be match ready. Some people just annoy me with such nonsense. Leave all that talk for another time. If the young lad was to read such stuff it is not going to do his confidence much good is it. Such comments are doing more harm than good, and yet if the lack of confidence shows up they will not gladly take the blame for putting such into the young man's head will they, no of course not. I have said it before and here I go again, people need to engage brain before mouth opens too wide.

Monday April 20th 2015

Gary Sweet has been talking about relocation plans for the club in regards to a new stadium and has hinted that before the start of next season the location for the stadium will be announced. Unlike the previous times I actually have faith in what the club are saying. At last we have a group of people at the helm who really are true "Hatters" and for me that is the difference between previous boards that have made such announcements, for me they were telling us what we wanted to hear, planting false security into our heads, lying for their own corrupt and personal money making schemes. This time, for myself at least, there is a passion there, but also showing a sense of patience, not jumping the gun and making any noise until the substance is there to show. At last I for one have faith in a Luton town board, believe me it has been a long wait.

Tuesday April 23rd 2015

This past Saturday the Under 18s side, following a 2-0 victory over Stevenage Town ensured themselves of the runners-up position in the Youth Alliance Merit League 1. Unbeaten in their last eight games. A most superb season for the club in many ways, this added to the winning of the Final third Development Southern Section Trophy. Now all that is required is for the first team to finish the season with some panache, even if not getting to the play-offs they can hold their heads high with good performances again Southend United and Stevenage Town. It will by all accounts be a most satisfying for Luton Town with all that has been achieved this season. One has to look further than just the first team results and final positioning to see the results that have culminated from the efforts put in by both the coaching and playing staff combined. Great steps forward have been made despite the obvious room for improvement allowing the club to go even further forward next season.

For myself there has been too much pressure put on the players this season in regards to some fans insisting on back to back promotions. That in my opinion has not helped matters at all. All too often in recent years such pressure has resulted in players getting nervous. One of the downfalls of playing for Luton town is that some supporters expect their side to win week in week out, regardless of the fact that we bare building for the clubs future as much as for the here and now. I have to admit though that performances have at the same time been below par and there has to be changes within the playing squad during the close season. It is a thankless job at the best of times, one bad result can change fickle minds. What is encouraging though is the youth that is coming through. Something Luton Town has always been renowned for, a superb youth policy is shining through yet again. The problem over the years has been one of not being able to hold on to talented players for our own benefit. Recently we only have to look as far back to see the likes of Curtis Davies in a Luton shirt and also Cauley Woodrow. Both now plying their wares in the top flight last season, Woodrow now making a mark in the Championship since his club Fulham were relegated from the Premiership. Who knows, maybe we already have players within the youth scheme ready to emulate such players as Davies, Upson and Hartson, who all started their trade here with Luton Town, it is all a matter of time. Personally, I cannot wait to see young Lee Angol given the opportunity in a Luton shirt, if he is as good as I have though all through his time at Borehamwood on loan, we have another gem in our midst. I ask the same question though year after year, can we as a club afford to keep players such as the aforementioned for longer terms in the future, because only then will we become a better and stronger side. The years are drifting away from the likes of myself who have witnessed the great times as well as the lean. That is why many of our time are more patient, because we value the good times and accept the not so good. All I and my kind can hope for is that we are still around to see Luton at the heights we commanded some thirty years ago, would that not be the most amazing feat again.

Wednesday April 22nd 2015

Well, Southend dented many a dream last evening when Southend won at Bury with a goal from former Bury player David Worrall, this now means that Southend and Bury have already cemented their places in the play-offs, both can also mathematically claim automatic promotion if results go their way in the final two games, therefore Southend will be playing all out to clinch that place against Luton on Saturday, which makes it all the more harder for the Town. So, therefore I find it strange that some individuals on media sites are saying that Southend may ease their foot on the pedal a little in their game against Luton as they have already clinched the a play-off place. Guys, do not take this too hard but, do you who are thinking such really look further than your own noses? I seriously doubt it. My point being that you are maybe too busy checking to see what Luton are trying to achieve, which is fair enough. However, one must look at the bigger picture. Luton in all honesty are really going to have their work cut out this weekend to gain even a draw at Root's Hall.

Last weekend we beat in all honesty a mediocre side when victorious over relegation candidates Hartlepool. I hear people saying this is our turning point. Do not misunderstand me thought please, no one would be more happy if that what the case than myself, the truth is though, we are going to

have one hell of a fight on our hands Saturday. I have to look at this situation realistically. I fear there will be many after Saturday's game, who whilst now shouting the odds about Luton making the play-offs, will if the "Hatters" are beaten do a complete U-turn and shout for heads to roll. Some may say I am exaggerating, but no, we have all witnessed such behaviour of late. Being realistic is a better let down when it does not work out, than the heavy fall one can experience when dropping from the heady heights of sitting on white fluffy clouds. Too many expect the Town to walk Saturday's game. That is not just me noticing that. It is fact. All I am saying is I hope certain people are prepared as much for a loss as the walk in the park, or in Saturday's case a stroll on the beach. The other touch of reality is Plymouth are playing Tranmere, not the better of the sides we ourselves have met this season. It could be a rough ride indeed on Saturday, in more ways than one. I for one, am well prepared for the worst case scenario, I hope others are also.
I have just come off the phone with a very old friend of mine, who has sadly seen better days, Jan Van Den Worner, who lives in Zeist, Holland. He reminded me of a week back in 1995, must have been early season about September or October. We had just had two weeks of debauchery in Utrecht and Amsterdam, Jan a massive Ajax fan, was able to get me tickets at times, and believe me in those days that was an extremely difficult thing to do, they apparently had waiting lists for season tickets, leave alone random games. I was supposed to have returned back to London on the Friday evening, however due to unforeseen circumstances, it was decided best not to travel that evening. With that in mind we continued our jolly jaunt throughout the night in Amsterdam, the decision made to find an early flight and get back in time to go to the Luton match, they were home to Charlton that weekend, I remember it well. At that time I was a ticket holder and the twins, Dave and Paul Stanyon. I was the noisy one, if anyone of you cares to remember back then, used to pee a few around us off as I recall. Well Jan reminds me that it was a rather successful evening and we sauntered back to the hotel room at around four in the morning. On awaking I was in no reasonable state to travel if the truth was known. I had recently left horse racing and therefore out on a limb, no real job nut enjoying my days. I made it to Schiphol with minutes to spare for my flight, I was questioned regarding my sobriety, I stunk of beer and brandy apparently. But was after discussion allowed on the Transavia flight back to blighty, much to Jan's amazement at the time. The forty five minute flight to Gatwick was not one of my better flight journeys I recall, not in the best frame of mind that is for sure. But Luton were at home that afternoon to Charlton and I did not want to miss the game. Arriving in Gatwick, I ran down, well ran not actually the correct word considering the state I was in, the hangover really now kicking in, the escalators case bouncing behind me. I actually felt more like my head was bouncing off the escalator to be honest. The train I needed to catch to have time to get myself sorted out and have some food had just trundled along the line, gone, out of sight. Desperation set in, I am not missing this game I thought, if I had been totally well I think to be honest I would have sat back and said, no I will not bother. However, it was make or break, outside to the taxi rank, but for that I had to get to the other terminal. Dash to the little monorail and then the taxi rank. If only my case had have been like the box in Terry Pratchett's "Colour of Magic" life would have been so much easier that day. I commandeered a cab eventually, begged him to take me to Luton, money up front was demanded and given. We must have pulled over to the side of the motorway at least four times, however with the stories I was telling the driver about my latest adventure it do not seem to worry him too much. At least it was not in his car, but windows were totally wound down, and it was not the warmest of days I can tell you. Time was running away from me getting to Luton, dumping my case and getting to the Kenny. I rumbled through my case in the hope my season ticket was with me. In those days it seemed to follow me everywhere. Found it eventually and as we approached

Luton it was around 2.45 and kick off was imminent. Guided the cab to the Wheelwrights pub threw my case in the door, I think a guy called Alex was the landlord then, he used to have the Nelson's Flagship, beforehand, well his father did anyway. As I said threw the case just inside the door, shouting will collect after the game mate and was gone again. Strange how we would not get away with such antics these days, sad really, such fun we used to have. Got to my seat just as the coin was being flipped. Can I recall the game? Not really no! Cannot actually remember but it may have been the only game I actually fell asleep during rather than one of the twins. Apparently we lost anyway, I retrieved my case, got home to an absolute earful I recall for the stench of brewery left over. But damn they were fantastic days. Thank you Jan, brilliant memories, however details of that adventure really are not for the delicate ears of |Luton supporters. He says with a little cheeky grin from times gone by. Luton lost that day by the way and the indignity of relegation to division two.

Thursday April 23rd 2015
Despite the failures of some players this season I am reading that John Still is again looking to the lower leagues for potential signings. As much as I do respect and trust his judgement regarding players of such ilk, in some ways this being instrumental the downfall of this season. Surely we should be looking at some experienced players to steady the ship. It is all well and good but we seriously need some experience in the ranks rather than inexperience. Apparently the three players are from Paulton Rovers, Buxton Town and Concord Rangers, all played as trialists in the final development game of the season against Gillingham that the Town won with some ease 3-0. One of the trialists, Shaun Tuton from Buxton, scored Luton Town's second goal in between two fantastic long range strikes from Isaac Galliford.
Elliot Justham has signed an extension to his contract for the "Hatters" that will keep him at the club until 2017. Therefore, quashing any rumours altogether that he is on the move in the close season.
Sky Sports have compiled what they call an "Ultimate League" the positions of each club calculated from their league positioning's over the past fifty years. Obviously Liverpool claimed the top spot followed by Manchester United, Arsenal, Everton and Tottenham. As for Luton, they have been allocated thirty eighth position. I would like to have been able to say that Watford were below us, however, because of our recent history that was always going to be a tall order, and they finished five places above the Town in thirty third place. Some but little consolation maybe being that we are above one Premier league side, that being, Hull City. Maybe with those five years being out of the football league being different we would have maybe been a little better placed at least.

Friday April 24th 2015
Many Luton supporters are already making their way to Southend for tomorrow's crucial game. Making a weekend of the fact it is on the coast. Crucial being an understatement even. The club have sold well over 2,000 tickets for the clash with the "Shrimpers".
The last time I visited Roots Hall was in fact with my friends from Hereford and Brecon, for a Friday night match. We also made quite a weekend of it. Quite a wet one inside. But for November not bad weather. In fact some strolls along the seafront quite enjoyable, not many about so no crowds to push through. Before the game we were allowed into the "Shrimpers" club bar. Not so sure that will be the same tomorrow however, Hereford only took about sixty away for the game.

The match was a walkover for Southend strolling themselves to a 4-0 victory on the night. But we did not allow that to dampen the weekend, the real dampening was of the alcoholic kind. Strange watching a side other than the "Hatters" but a most enjoyable time all the same.

I have always said I will not allow politics into my works, but today I cannot help myself. David Cameron, what a muppet, as if his policies and his treatment of the common man are not enough to make one cringe, today he, for me, committed the cardinal sin. In recent times, despite his obvious like for things more rural and universitified, that's a word I have just invented by the way, like fox hunting and the boat race, he has been trying so hard to convince us that he is in fact a lover of football and a staunch supporter of Aston Villa, I can think of much worse teams to say one supports, but let us be honest, unlike Cameron. He is no football buff when all said and done, but to bring himself "closer" to the people that really matter when it comes to a general election her has to at least pretend he likes the game. Apparently he was caught completely out when claiming that he is a West Ham supporter. Obviously the colours caught him out. But who in their right mind and an individual who claims to support his club, can get mixed up whom he supports. Just goes to prove more and more what a total liar and fantasist the man really and truly is. Just one more thing, what is this thing about only facing one reporter for interviews on the road and the others have to rely on what he says to relay universally by that one allowed reporter? Well the answer is quite simple really. He is so worried that being bombarded from every corner of a room he will forget his planned lines and maybe blurt out one thing that totally contradicts what he may have said earlier. The man is definitely on his last legs. If the country votes this man in again next month, we are so in for a very rough ride over the next five years. Especially those of us normal people that have to work for our breakfast, dinner and tea. Oops, I forgot they it supper. Enough now sir.

Tomorrow will there could be a great deal of relegation and promotion issues answered, one we must all be dreading is that of our yellow shirted neighbours down the muddy lanes of Hertfordshire. Will we ever hear the last of it if they get where they are threatening to go and receive multi-millions of pounds for their sins. Such taunts we shall have to persevere if they do actually succeed. Also those in the new city, even more shameful, considering their history and birth-right, what birth-right?

Saturday April 25th 2015
Its D-Day for many clubs around the country, often the week before the final games tends to be the bigger issue. Next week will be more about saying farewell to a season or marching on to more money spinning capers for the football authorities rather than the clubs involved. To be honest I do not hold with play-offs. If a club cannot win promotion the automatic way, then they should accept and prepare for the season ahead. Let us be honest, they were never bought about for the clubs, more so the Football League and FA's coffers. Good Luck though to all those clubs fighting relegation, it is not a pleasant place to be and I envy you all not.

A damp start to the morning in Southend, but the forecast is friendlier as the morning wears on. Southend does not know what has hit it, with orange and white everywhere, the pubs must be doing a booming trade for this time of the year, the holiday makers yet to really show their faces. Well in a few short hours we may well know our fate, will it be the dreaded play-offs or the prospect of Saturdays languishing in front of the TV watching cricket for most.

For myself today is going to be an emotional one on two counts, obviously Luton town and the ensuing battle at Roots Hall, but also the very last chance to see one of our greatest bravest and humble down to earth champions of all time. Mr Anthony Peter McCoy, probably the best jockey to ever grace the shores of Britain will at 4.20 this afternoon, climb aboard a horse in the racing colours of JP McManus for the very last time on board the aptly named Box Office for trainer Jonjo O'Neill, a lovely fellow himself whom had many a laugh with some years past. But today it will be scenes never before witnessed at a British racecourse just for one man. However, more about that later, maybe.

Luton Town have named their line-up for this afternoon's battle: Elliot Justham, Michael Harriman, Steve McNulty, Luke Wilkinson, Scott Griffiths, Cameron McGeehan, Jonathan Smith, Nathan Doyle, Jake Howells, Elliot Lee and Mark Cullen. With the bench jockeys: Mark Tyler, Alex Lacey, Luke Guttridge, Shaun Whalley, Alex Wall, Lewis Kinsella and Ryan Hall.

Southend United1 Luton Town 0

Well, what slim chances Luton were hanging onto of winning a play-off place are now all but dead and buried. To be honest a blessing in disguise, as I have been saying for some weeks now.

On the whole a good defensive performance against a team that are really playing well at present and knocking on the door of automatic promotion.

Before the game, as with games across the country, one minute silence being held for those souls lost in the Bradford fire that I had written about earlier in the book. However totally spoiled and disrespected from a minority from both sets of supporters. Shameful to the extreme. Also the moronic action of one or a couple of Southend so called supporters who decided it would amazingly fantastic fun to throw flares around. The brains that some people have in their skull shell not worth a drop of stagnated water, surely.

There was just the one change from the Hartlepool victory last weekend, Nathan Doyle for Shaun Whalley who reverted to the bench.

A fast moving first half, Vin Diesel would have been proud of the games speed and ferocity.

The first chance of the game dropping to Luton, McGeehan pressing forward, rolling the ball to Lee, who tended to rush his shot and hit the ball wide of the post.

Southend on the whole held the ball longer. Justham's kick had been at best erratic and when he did manage to send a good ball forward, the Southend defence were caught off guard, allowing Cullen to pick up the ball, his shot on target but Bolger managed to get himself in the way, promptly clearing the lines.

An awkward slip resulted in McGeehan falling heavily on his arm, this left the Town for a while with just eight players on the field of play as he received treatment. In addition both Wilkinson and Howells decided it would be a good idea to go shopping for new boots, changing their old for new. Why they would have to do this at such a time during the games totally boggles the mind. They had all the warm up session pre match to decide on their choice of footwear surely.

McGeehan's arm continued to trouble him and he was eventually forced to leave the pitch and was replaced by Shaun Whalley.

Half time came and went, however Luton seemed to take an age to come out for the restart.

Despite the length of time taken to return to the field here were no changes for Luton, although, Southend's two wingers reversed flanks they began the half looking more livelier of the two sides having upped the tempo. Luton defended well to keep the scores level. They used the flanks to their advantage, attempting to spread the play, however Luton made it difficult at times, not allowing them to get into the box.

Coker was a constant threat down their left side, both their full backs also playing advanced roles.

Luton's best move of the game came when the ball was being passed along the ground, how many times have I had to say that this season? Griffiths playing the ball to Lee who sent Howells down the line, producing a teasing cross into the centre, unfortunately it seems Barrett wanted the ball much more than Cullen ever did.

Guttridge replaced a tired Lee, whom John still had explained pre match would probably not last the full ninety minutes.

Southend although making changes managed to keep their shape, which resulted in Luton's chances of scoring minimal at best.

The only goal of the game came from almost nothing, Tomlin electing to shoot, the effort looking to be no danger at all, but somehow managed to squeeze under the body of Justham and over the line. The young goalkeeper was quite distraught.

Alex Wall replaced Griffiths but it was too little too late. One of the problems this season has been the fact players have not been allowed to play to their strengths and again using Wall as a battering ram is not really going to bring the best out of the man. I sometimes actually wonder if Wall's attitude problem is something to do with the fact that frustration sets in when things are not going right, using him in unfamiliar roles also cannot be too much help for him.

So the final whistle and Luton Towns season all but over apart from the non-entity game at Kenilworth Road next Saturday against Stevenage. The fact that they have reached the play-offs in itself is going to be a very nut to contend with. Could get a little naughty in Luton Next weekend. Let us hope I am very wrong on that count though.

One must feel for Elliot Justham after the game, unfortunately with all those brain dead followers we seem to have within our ranks, the poor lad is going to be the target of their anger. However, the truth of the matter is the failure to take the season further is a damned lot deeper than his allowing the ball to roll underneath him this afternoon, however, no doubt he will be made the target of abuse over the remainder of the weekend and sadly, even during the course of the close season. Let us hope he is thick skinned and able to ride the tsunami of abuse that threatens.

So, with the "Hatters" loss and Plymouth holding on to beat Carlisle at home, the play-off places are all but completed. It is the matter now of who will go up with Burton and Shrewsbury, will it be Wycombe, Bury or todays winning opponents Southend United. For that we shall have to wait and see next week. For Luton Town the pressure is off, at least next weekend they will be able to go out onto the pitch with the pressure off and try and enjoy a game. However, saying that there will also be certain players out there playing for their Luton Town lives. Although having said that I am sure John still already knows those that are out of the reckoning for next season and those that will be staying to fight another season in the shirts of Orange.

Two sides we shall not be playing unless we get drawn in the FA Cup will be Tranmere Rovers, over ninety years in the league they will next season along with Cheltenham Town be languishing in the Conference. One must congratulate Ronnie Moore who successfully steered Hartlepool United clear of relegation, something that seemed an impossible task to achieve just after Christmas.

Next season battle will recommence against Barnet who successfully won promotion back to the Football League for next season, from the Conference, yet another short journey for the fans to enjoy next season.

As I mentioned earlier, now the euphoria of the Roots Hall game has died down, one of my most emotional days during my lifetime association with horse racing. There have been times when the loss of a horse has knocked me for six, even sent me into short bouts of depression. This evening though it is a different type of emotion, one of pride, happiness and sadness and more besides, all rolled into one massive emotional medicine ball. The pride comes from realising a fellow professional from my chosen sporting career, a man who deserves every accolade thrown his way. Show me another sportsman of our time who can and has generated so much attention over the years and none of it negative. A man who has overcome injury over injury to bounce back each time more determined succeed and carry on where he had left off, even to work on following injury. How many footballer's can any of you name that could take a battering such as any jockey takes to be fair, then get up shake the dust, wash the mud and blood from their faces and carry on, not many. I have known Anthony Peter to ride with a broken clavicle, saying nothing to the authorities with the fear that they will stand him down. I know of jockey's that will eat a can of tinned tomatoes to get at least some intake of food and nothing more other than a sip of water, to ensure they can do the subscribed weight for a horse in a particular race. The feeling of happiness deriving from the fact that through the euphoria of the day the man was able to not allow it to make him lose focus, something that could so easily have happened and he loses concentration, resulting in a fall. The happiness that he ended on a high, leaving Sandown Race course free of injury to enjoy retirement from day one. Happiness that he retires as he should have as reigning champion, that trophy forever his own, no one can take it from him. The sadness is the most simple to explain, the fact that we shall never see his like again, at least not in our lifetime. I salute you Anthony Peter McCoy with pride in my heart for you and our sport, happiness that you, Chanelle, Eve and the so loveable little Archie will be able to enjoy life to the full, no more worried moments as you set out on a bad one, the only sadness being it's all over for the remainder of us. What a man, what a jockey and sincerely what a job we all shared over the years of our lives.

Sunday April 26th 2015

If it comes over at times that I like to rubbish off Luton supporters, I am sorry. That is not how I wanted this book to be, but boy, some really do make one need to bite the biscuit deep between the teeth.

One must feel sorry for the crap being shunted out last night and today regarding Justham Elliot. It is not the lad's fault we are not in the play-offs, it goes so much further than that. Also a season has passed over us virtually and to keep hearing, that we miss Andre Gray is really getting tedious. He has gone, get over it and move on.

It was never going to be easy to find a replacement with the click of the fingers. These days we would have to fork out a great deal more than Luton Town can afford to pay out to find an immediate replacement. If the service had not been from long humps up field instead of working from the back, I am sure Cullen would have scored a great deal more goals this season. Lafayette would have been more effective also Wall and Benson. The fact is we were lacking all over the pitch not in one certain position. Please move on, get over it and please give the young lad Justham a chance. One mistake does not make him a bad keeper, remember also if it was not for some fantastic saves over the past weeks, we would, I doubt have been playing for what was being played for yesterday. Some people really need to wake up, open their eyes and think. It hurts having to write in this frame of mind, but it simply needs to be said. Sadly more often than not it has had to be done.

Monday April 27th 2015

The final week of the season has commenced. It honestly, does not seem a few days ago that I began this book with my introduction and sent to Mike Thomas and asked what he thinks, along with Alan Hudson and Ken Cook. Their responses alone the tools that prompted me to carry on. It has been a slog at times, especially when the depression sat in for a while and the dreaded flu that grabbed me by the balls and just would not let go. However, here we are nearly in the month of May, and my publishing deadline looming. However, still one more to sign off on and I have the distinct feeling it could be a game of incidents to keep us going.

A shock to the system is always a good start to the week and we certainly received that. England cricketers winning away from England shores for the first time in nearly three years is most definitely a shock, however, I am going to a little brave and say that it a game being played out by two very ordinary international sides. I may get lynched, I may even be agreed with. But as with Luton town Football Club, I think for many players it is time to go. There was a moment during England's first innings that beleaguered Jonathan Trott, with whom I do wish well and sympathise with a great deal, even relate to, looked as if he had been able to put all of his recent troubles behind him. Unfortunately, his second innings showing reverted him back to his earlier form yet another waddling duck back to the pavilion. I wonder if his days are numbered or will the hierarchy keep faith and assist in building the man's confidence up again. I suppose this is one decision that is a difficult one all round.

To see Steve McNulty in the League Two team of the year chosen by the PFA caused a seismic shock wave for quite a few I am sure. However, one must remember the superb run earlier in the season that resulted in a minimal amount of goals being scored against and obviously that would have been a very large factor in his selection. Well done to him.

Reading the reasoning for their choice it looked more than just this seasons performances though, because they mentioned his time at Barrow and Fleetwood also, so maybe that was taken into consideration also. I am surprised Michael Harriman or Nathan Doyle were not in the side though.

Last night was the Player of the year awards, as voted by the Luton Town Supporters Club and Trust in Luton. A most popular being midfielder Nathan Doyle. But without doubt it was Jonathan Smith who stole all the accolades otherwise. A player who has been saying he has been playing his heart out to be offered a new contract for next season picked up the following. Players' player of the year. Also young members of the supporters club player of the year and to cap the night for him website player of the year also, one thinks his immediate future at Luton has been sealed somehow, if not, what has a young man to do?

Youth player Luke Trotman was voted young player of the year by the Luton town coaching staff. Alex Lawless goal against Southend United in October was voted as goal of the season. Mark Cullen and Luke Guttridge share the Ian Pearce memorial trophy, in memory of one of the fans most loved and respected broadcasters who passed away in March 2011 aged just 56 years of age. There has been no one to replace his magical and witty tones since, a man greatly missed by us all. Finally Nigel Martin was awarded fan of the year for his continued support and contribution to Luton Town.

Ever since the season began I have been not so much raving, but at the very least watching a young player we have had on loan for the season at Borehamwood. Lee Angol, whom I recall Arsene Wenger praising and keeping a close look on. This weekend he stole the show at Borehamwood's end of season awards. Taking the following awards for the club. Players' Player of the Year, Supporters Player of the Year, Young Player of the Year and Top goal scorer of the season with a most impressive twenty five goals. As I correctly predicted at the time of his initial signing at the beginning of the season one player to definitely watch for the future. The problem now for us as Luton town supporters is one we have had to struggle with for many years. How long will Luton be able to keep him?

It has been a busy day reading about Luton to find some material for the final week, one interesting matter being Steve McNulty's response to Elliot Justham's bloomer against Southend. Quite rightly so Steve said all players make mistakes, we will all get our arms around him and we are all as a team for him" that is comforting despite the abuse he has been seen to throw at the young keeper during a game, but again that is football, heat of the moment to behind him. One mistake does not determine a season, it is a culmination of mistakes and mishaps, and not singularly by the playing squad, with the reasoning going so much deeper.

We must congratulate the phenomena that is Ian Feuer who over the weekend celebrated his marriage to Lindsey Havens in Los Angeles CA. Ian is one of the most likeable players we have at Luton Town over the years, in his latter days as a goalkeeper playing alongside David Beckham for LA Galaxy and now a renowned coach in the United States. I recall his first game for the "Hatters" at the New Den, Millwall. When the team was announced over the tannoy, there was a crescendo of "Who the F**k is this Feuer?" We did not have long to wait, during that game making an array of stops, I cannot in all honesty remember the final result though. From that day in 1995 to 1998 he made 14 appearances for the Town on loan from West Ham before signing permanently in 1996 where he went on to make a further 83 appearances before moving back to the States to sign for New England Revolution. In 1992 he played for the United States Olympic side at the Barcelona Olympics. Yes we had an Olympian on our books. The only other I can think of being former fitness coach the great Daley Thompson. Another interesting fact regarding the "gentle giant", because Ian really was and still is and all credit to him one of the most approachable players known to wear a Luton shirt, is that his Father played keyboard alongside such great performers as Elvis Presley and Diana Ross whilst his Mother sang with two legends in Frank Sinatra and Sammy Davis Jnr. So maybe the man we all came to look upon as a true legend in the late nineties was destined for greatness from the moment he was born.

We wish Ian and Lindsey a long life and many happy times.

Ian and Lindsey Feuer, newlyweds, a guard of honour. Re-produced with kind permission of Ian and Lindsey Feuer.

Cameroon has made his final appearance as a loan player for the "Hatters". Following his arm injury in last Saturday's defeat at Southend it has been discovered that he has in actual fact fractured his elbow. Now, a break such as that is very painful as is a broken collar bone. Do not envy anyone those injuries. It surely has been one of those seasons when it comes to player's collecting injuries. However, I still refuse to use the injury problems as an excuse for the Town's poor spell since New Year.

One more mention but I refuse point blankly to get drawn into it and say too much. Striker Ricky Miller was arrested in the early hours of this morning following an alleged assault on a taxi driver returning home from a certain night spot in Milton Keynes. He has been bailed whilst investigations carry on and the club has suspended him until further notice.

Tuesday April 28th 2015

One has to congratulate AFC Bournemouth's promotion to the Premier League. If there is single club that deserves such from the Championship it surely is the "Cherries" their young manager Eddie Howe working wonders, with some awesome results along the way. His team playing the game the way it should be played throughout. In 2008 the club were apparently only minutes from liquidation, they had staff and volunteers collecting donations with buckets on match days to help them get through tough times. The same season that Luton were deducted 30 points for irregular financial dealings, Bournemouth also in League Two were also deducted a total of 17 points. Therefore over the past seven years they have made amazing leaps and well done to them. Who would have envisaged such a rise five seasons ago? Not many I doubt. It would be fantastic if they are able to make their mark in the top flight next season. They have proved it can be done. Well done to them.

It never rains but it pours for poor old JLS, to top everything Shaun Whalley has been arrested in connection with the Ricky Miller case. He has now lost three players in the course of four days, with McGeehan's injury also. I am not sure if found guilty such players are wanted at Kenilworth Road. I know it is incorrect to be too judgemental, because we all have our flaws, however if true, such unacceptable behaviour.

Give the young ones a chance for the last game, may well shock us all, nothing to lose but much to gain.

Wednesday April 29th 2015

Firstly, a sad task, former "Hatter" Chris Turner passed away earlier.at the young age of 64. Chris had suffered from Frontal Lobe Dementia, being diagnosed with the disease in 2006. Something his wife placed the blame solely on his football career. The defender, signed by David Pleat was a pivotal member of the side whilst at the club. Making thirty four appearances and scoring five goals, Chris then departed to the United States, from where Pleat acquired him, the fact that he missed his time there was one reason he was allowed to leave so early.

In his youth he was on the books of Peterborough United, where he made over 300 appearances. He also played in the US for Connecticut Bicentennials and the New England Tea Men. On his return to the UK signing for Cambridge United before moving to Swindon Town and finally Southend United. Following retirement from his playing career he returned to the Abbey Stadium as manager in 1985, from there he moved to nearby Peterborough United where he not only managed them but took over the ownership of the club. Chris will be greatly missed and condolences to his wife and family. Another "Hatter" now reunited with those that passed before him. Rest in Peace Sir.

Only days after his marriage Ian Feuer gives me reason to smile again, the man is an enigma, the giant ex-goalkeeper is now in the movie business. He has been cast as The Predator in the new Predator movie being filmed at the moment. Super-star indeed.

Ian in the Predator costume during filming. Re-produced by kind permission Ian Feuer

Ian in the Predator costume during filming. Re-produced by kind permission Ian Feuer

Jonathan Smith has at last been offered a new contract it has been confirmed by the club. It is now up to the 28 year old midfielder to make his decision. I an all probability he will do so, especially following his recent declaration that he would like to stay at the club. I for one would be most pleased if he does decide to sign and extend his stay at Kenilworth Road. In my own humble opinion the perfect choice to replace Steve McNulty as skipper when the time arises. A very dependable and intelligent player although a little rash at time maybe. Other players that will definitely be at the "Kenny" next season are Alex Lawless, Luke Guttridge and Luke Wilkinson. I know there are some out there that will question the fact that Lawless will be staying, however, given the opportunity and staying fit, the chances are he will bring some much needed experience into the side. Some actually question his level of fitness. I argue the fact as with a number of other players this season Lawless was bought back from injury on more than one occasion too early, simply because they were required to make a team. That was another problem facing John Still and the squad, I also wonder if in fact the very strict and hard training regime the squad was put through pre-season was instrumental in a number of the injuries. However, that is just my own thoughts on the matters, I have seen similar with horses, where they are driven too hard in training and pay the price in the latter parts of the season. Athletes and footballers are no different to horses in many ways when it comes down to maintaining fitness, over training causing strains and the like that do not show immediately but can produce problems at a later date.
One player I would expect to see on his way in the close season may be Andy Drury, unless JLS decides to keep him in a coaching capacity maybe. For myself, he has not fulfilled his expectations of many. As said before I am not one that really welcomes bringing successful players of the past back for a second tenure, they seldom shine as much as they may be expected to. Drury for me definitely under achieved.

Thursday April 30th 2015
I am not really sure where to begin today.
Here we go, Nigel Pearson the Leiccster City manager has again shown his not so public friendly side again following his walk out during a press conference after his side had been mauled by Chelsea, despite taking an early lead, beaten 1-3.
During the press conference Pearson claimed that his players have received too much criticism over the season. Before continuing, as did the journalist Ian Baker, I am a little bewildered because I have always read and heard through the media that the Leicester players have been superb in their commitment to the club and the way that they have played the game, they have put their all into their play all season. Sometimes, very unlucky to come away without any points. So, when Pearson responded by asking where the journalist had been all season, after questioning the managers statement, Pearson dived into him quite disrespectful and unnecessarily asking Ian Baker if he was stupid, silly or daft. I would have found that most offensive, he also called him an Ostrich, having his head in the sand and then as he walked from the table muttered something to the words of "Fucking reporters" as he went through the door. This is not the first time, earlier in the season it is recalled that he named another journalist a prick. The man is not only an arrogant, ignorant man but also most obnoxious and offensive. He has a catalogue of discredits behind him, including grabbing Crystal Palace Midfielder James Macarthur by the throat after the player, it has to be said, accidentally crashed into the 51 year old manager during a game on the touchline. Something the FA never took further, which in itself was surprise to many people. It really is time

this vile individual was bought down by the footballing authorities as he is beginning to believe he is untouchable.

The big clubs are at it again, attempting to grab schoolboy players from the smaller clubs. This time it is a Luton Town based schoolboy, eleven year old Charlie Patino. All Luton would receive for finding this boy and nurturing him through his early years would be £10,000 plus a further £100,000 if the when the time is right he makes a Premiership appearance. This for me is all that is wrong with English football, the bigger clubs allowed to take the young stars of tomorrow and make the bigger bucks when the player is older, denying the smaller clubs much required revenue. Another case of keep them where they belong, below us. No wonder clubs are dubious to even bother looking for such young raw talent these days. This is not the first time that Luton have lost a player so young to a bigger club and gained nothing from it of true value. Jack Wilshere a prime example. Maybe the time has come that this poaching is put an end to and the young players stay where they are and keep their feet firmly planted on the ground and when the time is right, they not their parents make the decision where they would like to go. As correctly pointed out though, the fact that all the papers are suddenly aware of the boy's situation is most probably due to his parents contacting either the Press Association or all the large papers to make the story public. Seeking the publicity to maybe get even more of the bigger clubs interested where in time they can name their own price for the boy's talents. I am not saying that is the fact, just a thought. If that is so whose interests would the move really be in? Just a hypothetical question, I am not questioning Charlie's parents' actions for one moment.

One piece of good news this morning regarding Cameron McGeehan is that his arm injury is not as bad as initially feared, not broken. Although, it is most unlikely he will be available for the final game of the season against Stevenage unless the "Hatters" win by an unimaginable margin. So failing that it will be holidays imminent.

May

Friday May 1st 2015

The countdown begins, is this the eve of the Town's final game of the season or is something quite spectacular about to happen for the "Hatters" Wouldn't that be a shock to the system?

Back to yesterday's thoughts on the young lad Charlie Patino and Paul Gallagher, a fellow "Hatter" came up with a most interesting point. He said this:

The 2006 World Cup England and have gone out again on penalties to Portugal. England's best player in that tournament was Owen Hargreaves.

Eyes were raised initially when he was named in the final squad of 22. However, some didn't see the bigger picture. He was a Champions League winner with Bayern Munich. Hargreaves being their most outstanding player, when they played Real Madrid in the semi-final.

Hargreaves was by far the fittest player in the England squad at that time. He also possessed that extra touch of technical ability.

When clubs discovers their next young prodigy in this country, the easy option is to loan them out to a lower league club. The obvious thinking is that it will give them first team experience.

Yes that is generally the case, however, it can also prove them falling into the trap of developing bad habits.

Paul believes from the ages of between thirteen and eighteen, the ones who have potential and the right attitude should learn their trade in Germany.

They will learn to be more versatile and efficient, the will become more aware when it comes to conditioning their body, also how to conduct themselves when away from the pitch.

You only have to look at the difference in, for good example an English player and an Italian, the Euro 2012 match England v Italy.

The English have this theory that you have to play with passion, which is basically in English terms, put in some crunching tackles run around and get your kit dirty.

Pirlo of Italy, however, was pinging passes, orchestrating the middle of the park, he wasn't running around like a headless chicken.

If you want a fine example of an efficient team effort, one should go back to Germany v Portugal at the last World cup. The Portuguese were just trying to get the ball to Christiano Ronaldo, the Germans just looked for the nearest player in a white shirt.

The Germans kept their shape, no fancy flick-on and step-over just pure efficient football. The results were there for all to see an efficient engine working together as one, not singular parts attempting to do too much unnecessary motions, having to work harder to compliment another part. No cohesion between each player, unlike the Germans, perfectly tuned as one.

It does make me chuckle, people trying to convince themselves that Luton will get into the play offs, it is all well and good to positive, nothing wrong with that, however, despite our position we have not in all realms of reality been good enough with the sides we have been able to put out. It does not matter that we have had injuries and whatever, the fact is the replacements have not been up to the mark and it really does get a little tedious when one reads the same old thing day in day out. Sorry guys, but we have not been good enough, however saying that we have done extremely well for our first season back and that should be enough in itself. That is not "happy clapping" that is being simply realistic of the facts.

Tomorrow it will all be done and dusted, if by the miracle of footballing Gods Luton do go marching on I will be the first to jump in the air with joy, however I will also sit back and say good job done, if the Stevenage game is the last competitive game until August.

During a Belgian reserve league game last Monday, against Genk, Lokeren player Gregory Mertens collapsed with a heart complaint. Yesterday however, the sad news of his death was released. At twenty four years of age, he had a full life to look forward to. It brings all the pointless discord we as fans throw at one another into full perspective. At the end of it all, after all the complaining, the abuse and sadly sometimes the violence, it is only a game. I wonder how his family are feeling at this terrible time. How will his team mates pick themselves up for this weekend's league programme? Will they even be able to place themselves on the field so early after losing their friend, comrade and colleague?

It is moments such as this that makes us realise that there is more to life, although I fear some will not agree with me. "Such a sad day for football" I am sure some will be saying. For me this is never adequate, it is a tragic and upsetting day for all, the loss of a fellow human being.

Whether a side wins promotion or escapes relegation is not important at this moment. I often see tears at the end of the season for a side being relegated or beaten in a cup final. I do understand that, more than most, I have cried on numerous occasions during my years in the horse racing industry, but nothing can compare to losing a friend and colleague. How traumatic is this for all concerned, one cannot begin to imagine. May he rest in eternal peace.

Saturday May 2nd 2015

My goodness not twelve hours since I was writing such words regarding twenty four year old Gregory Mertens untimely passing, we now awaken to read of the death of Rio Ferdinand's wife Rebecca following a short battle with cancer. Yet another young and beautiful life taken from us. To think she leaves three young children without a mothers grace is so upsetting in itself, But again a young life taken away much too soon. Thoughts and prayers are with Rio and his children and Rebecca's family also at this terrible and sad time. Our hearts are with you all.

It was fifty six years ago today, however I am saving that for the penultimate chapter. So after forty five games it all fizzles down to this, win 8-0 and Plymouth lose its all good for another three weeks or so at least, otherwise it will be feet up time until August, for some anyway.

I am not going to go into all the obvious name calling stints that have seen bandied about all week, with all that has gone down over the past couple of days not appropriate. However, I could not stop the laughter a minute or so ago, does the name Atdhe Nuhiu deserve some relevance in the Luton Town supporter's hall of fame for future generations to say "Who the f**k is that?" with one of us older ones able to reply, "that is the man who ruined the dreams for a nest of hornets from down the road".

Congratulations to Eddie Howe and his AFC Bournemouth players in clinching the Championship trophy and their promotion to the Premiership. It can be done Gary Sweet.

What is in reality expected to be the final line-up for Luton Town of this rocky but still rolling on down the football league river season of 2014-2015 is:

Elliot Justham, Michael Harriman, Steve McNulty, Luke Wilkinson, Scott Griffiths, Cameron McGeehan, Jonathan Smith, Nathan Doyle, Jake Howells, Elliot Lee and Mark Cullen. With those in the starting stalls waiting for the tape to raise: Alex Lacey, Alex Wall, Nathan Oduwa (I thought he had gone home, has been so quiet of late), Luke Guttridge, Craig King, Lewis Kinsella and Ryan Hall.

Luton Town 2 Stevenage Town 0

Suddenly I am feeling slightly younger again with the sight of Dave Beasant sitting in goalkeeper kit on the Stevenage bench, are times really that hard? I wonder how they will manage if they somehow manage to win promotion in the play offs. Maybe they will look at signing Jimmy Greaves, Pat Jennings and Frank Mclintock to give them some depth in the squad.

In all honesty Luton's opponents were not at the races today. The "Hatters" Started the quicker of the two sides. Despite Stevenage slowing the game down at every given opportunity. Maybe they were worried Beasant would have to make an appearance.

It was not long before the Town made the point that they were not going to sit back and allow Plymouth into the play-offs without a fight. On the break from a Stevenage corner, Elliot Lee picked up the ball on the left, powering down the line before taking the ball infield, he played the ball nicely off to Harriman, who over hit an attempted Cross to Jonathan Smith who was able to collect the ball anyway passing the ball to Lee who was running in, his hot was parried by the Stevenage keeper Gray, but only as far as Mark Cullen who calmly slotted the ball inside of the far post. The "Hatters" were on the chase. With Plymouth away to Shrewsbury surely they were going to get beaten and Luton's opportunity would be there for the taking.

It must be questioned why we could not have played like this all season, but then we also have to remember that in all honesty Stevenage did field a much weaker side than normal, although nothing must be taken away from Luton's work rate, whoever a team plays, results do not come from waiting for the other side to falter, it comes from the work put in against those sides.

Lee and Cullen played well as a partnership, but with the fact that it was the last time they would be playing together maybe a little too late.

Luton's second came in injury time added before half time, McGeehan passing the ball for Harriman to latch on to with his left foot.

At Half time the news from Shrewsbury was a kick in the teeth for the "Hatters", Plymouth leading 1-0. Did I hear someone say a conspiracy against Luton getting promoted? Surely not! No doubt there will be a few somewhere around though.

The second half continued much as the first with Luton doing most of the pressing. No further goals were added, but in fairness it was not for lack of trying.

The dream for some was over, no promotion, no play-offs. I any case the score from Shrewsbury was a sobering realisation that it would not have mattered anyway, Plymouth 2-0 victors.

So congratulations to Burton Albion and their supporters. Clinching the League Two trophy, in all fairness deservedly so, with a 3-2 win at the Abbey Stadium. Let's hope for a change Richard Money was just a little more gracious in defeat than normal.

Shrewsbury finished in second place despite their home defeat to Plymouth Argyle.

The final promotion place was settled in the final minutes of the season. One has to be feel a little sympathy for Wycombe who thought they had made it, however Bury spoilt their hopes in the closing minutes with a last gasp win at Prenton Park, beating already doomed to the Conference, Tranmere Rovers 1-0.

The play offs then will be contested between Wycombe Wanderers, Southend United, Stevenage Town and Plymouth Argyle. Good luck to all teams concerned.

1959 and All the Razzmatazz.

1959 was to most without doubt one Luton Town's most savoured seasons in its long history. Playing in the top flight of the Football League, then known as Division One. Although not a memorable league campaign, the Town had finished eighth the previous season, finishing above Arsenal and Manchester United in doing so. Their biggest wins of the season included beating Arsenal 4-0 at Kenilworth Road, including a hat-trick from Allan Brown and also John Groves getting on the score sheet.

There were high expectations for the 1958-59 season following that. But things did not go to plan, despite going the first ten matches unbeaten including 4-1 wins against West Ham and Preston North End, also a 5-1 demolition job against Manchester City. The run ending on October 4th 1958 at Filbert Street home of Leicester City. That began the slide, the following game at Nottingham Forests City ground they succumbed to the same score.

Boxing Day the Town recorded a magnificent victory at home against Arsenal, who eventually finished third in the table, six goals to three, in what can only be described as most enthralling. A brace apiece from Billy Bingham and Allan Brown with Scotsman Jimmy Adam and Local lad tony Gregory scoring also. The following day the two sides met again at Highbury Stadium where Arsenal managed to turn the tables winning the game 1-0. This meant that Luton would enter 1959 in thirteenth place of twenty two teams, having twenty two points. (It has to remembered that in 1958-59 it was 2 points for a win and point for a draw, unlike the 3 points now allocated for a win.).

Luton, exempt until the third round, as it is still practiced today for the top two divisions, spectators they won easily 5-1 with goals from Billy Bingham and Tony Gregory two each and the other from Bob Morton.

The fourth round bought Luton together with Leicester City, on meeting Luton had now slid down the table to eighteenth place with Leicester just below in twenty second position, it was going to be a tight game. The Town managed a draw at Filbert Street and so the replay four days later at Kenilworth Road was expected to be another tight fisted affair, however from the kick off Luton had other ideas and Allan Brown scored his first hat-trick of the season, he was to score a second a couple of weeks later and a four goal match tally in April, along with Tony Gregory to win 4-1 and put the "Hatters" into the fifth round draw. Against Ipswich Town, themselves, experiencing a mediocre season in the second division. But prior to that game Luton had to negotiate two league encounters, the first away to Bolton Wanderers that they lost 2-4, Luton's goals coming from Bingham and Brown. The second at home to Burnley, and another hat-trick for Brown, with other goals from Dave Pacey and a brace for Bob Morton, the Town winning 6-2.

The Ipswich game was played on Valentine's Day, however there was no love given to the opponents that afternoon and in front of a sell-out 26,700 crowd Luton paved their way to the sixth round with a resounding 5-2 win with the two goals from Morton and one each for Pacey, Bingham and Gregory. The Town were in the quarter final draw and all over Luton the radio' were tuned in on the Monday lunchtime for the draw. Blackpool were listed as the next possible victims, but it was going to be a hard game against the top half of the first division side, especially on their home turf at Bloomfield Road. Their top scorer Ray Charnley was having a season not different to Luton's Allan Brown scoring freely. There was a fortnight to wait and one league game at home to Leicester City. The Town, managed to beat off the Foxes with a 4-3 win.

234

The trip to Blackpool the longest trek for the fans for a cup match to date in the season and 30,634 fans watched a hard fought game that ended in a 1-1 draw, Billy Bingham Luton Town's scorer. Since October the Town teams had been chosen each week from a team of selectors, strange, however it seems even in those days Luton town did not do things in an orthodox fashion. Dally Duncan, ten years at the club, had packed his bags and waved goodbye to the "Hatters" and shook hands to say hello to Huddersfield Town, leaving Luton without a front-line manager. The selection team included Captain Sid Owen, trainer Frank King, and three board directors including former team skipper come public house landlord Tom Hodgson. Yes, Luton Town innovative in moving forward, however one wonders if in this instant it was actually moving in a backward motion.

The replay was another tightly fought game with just the solitary goal from Brown enough to take the "Hatters" into the semi-final draw. Norwich City at Tottenham's North London home of White Hart Lane the chosen venue. The other semi-final to be played at Sheffield Wednesday's Hillsborough, Nottingham Forest versus Aston Villa. The Nottingham side winning a scrappy event 1-0.

Luton made heavy work of the game in front of a packed 65,000 crowd and came away with a 1-1 draw, courtesy of Allan Brown. The replay four days later took the two sides to Birmingham and St. Andrews Park. Luton winning 1-0 from Billy Bingham, a smaller crowd of 49,500 witnessed the "hatters" victory.

The town was being drawn into football frenzy, straw boaters the order of the day, manufacturers never knew what had hit them. The day, Saturday May 2nd could not come quick enough for many. However, there was a league programme to fulfil first and foremost and a battle for division one survival. Through the month of April the "Hatters" played no less than ten league matches. I cannot imagine in our day and age that being found acceptable by most clubs up and down the Football League, but as my dear departed Dad would often say, that was the time when footballers were made of iron not frilly skirts and women's hair do's. In actual fact, if he had still been around now, he passes away in 2000 I dread to think what he would make of it all. Dad was quite a footballer himself, representing the RAF on a number of occasions, in the times when that meant something. He also trained and helped manage Kempston Rovers in the late fifties when they themselves were quite a formidable team in the United Counties, winning the league no less than twice and maybe more, the memory lapses somewhat these days. Six of those ten games away from home was not helping matters. There was an FA cup final rehearsal, Nottingham Forest at Kenilworth Road and the whole of Luton must have been rubbing the palms of their hands in anticipation of Wembley as the "Hatters" ran out 5-1 victors, Allan Brown notching four of those goals, taking his seasonal total to 19 league goals to be added with his FA Cup tally of five. The other goal being taken by Billy Bingham. But the amassing of games took its toll winning only two, drawing four and losing four. Champions elect Wolverhampton Wanderers clubbing the Town 5-0 at Molineux. The "Hatters2 only other win and their last win of the season was at home to Portsmouth on April 22nd with goals from Pacey, Gordon Turner and George Cummins.

The league fixtures concluded a week before the final at home to Blackpool with a 1-1 stalemate. Gordon Turner Luton's sole scorer.

Luton finished the season in eighteenth place.

Pl. 42 W12 D13 L 17 GF68 GA71 Pts 37

The 78th FA CUP FINAL, May 2nd 1959

One, or should I say two of the reasons I chose to finish the book with this chapter was in recognition of two guys who were instrumental in getting the book published.

Mike Thomas, who you will already know and read has been the driving force when things may have become a little distant for me. Mike's Father Howel Thomas is the fine gentleman that suited out the entire Luton town team and relevant staff for the FA Cup final during his employ at Blundells on Cheapside. Howell Thomas was born in Swansea before moving to Bedfordshire. Mike recalls that his father started at the bottom as junior and eventually worked himself up to Director. It is so upsetting now how things do not happen like that these days very often, I have noticed men and women work for years giving loyal service and getting to know the company and the daily routine and schedules as well as anybody, but forever getting overlooked by University graduates, who work from text book scenarios, have no common sense and have no idea or respect of loyalty. That is the problem in this day and age, their bank balance and CV credentials more important than the people that work so hard to keep those above them at the top. However, when things go pear-shaped the buck passed down the line and the main culprits sit pretty with their overindulging salary whilst those that do all the graft get nothing but the blame for others. Sorry a case of digress.

Mike can recall when a young boy in his short trousers, now that I would love to have seen, helping himself with delight to ice cream bombs smothered in oodles of chocolate and the most brilliant feeling, acting the big fellah by saying what we would all love to say, "charge to Mr Thomas' account please" with a satisfied grin on his face.

When Debenhams bought out the local department store they made Mike's Father redundant, not at all counting on what would transpire next. Mr Thomas hiring a top London QC and taking Debenhams for a princely amount for unfair dismissal. Top man I say, top man indeed.

Paul Stillwell who has kindly donated his talents to design the book's cover also has fond memories of the Cup Final, or at least his family does. His late Mother's brother being a Town favourite at the time, locally born Tony Gregory who made a total of 78 appearances for the "Hatters" scoring 23 goals, following the cup final season Tony moved to rival neighbours Watford, before moving to Bexley United, Bedford Town, Hastings United and Dover. He later managed both Stevenage Town and Wolverton as player-manager.

The media of the day were not overly impressed with the two sides competing at Wembley for the end of season showcase. The main reason being that there were no big names going to be on show, therefore it would obviously be not a game to write home about. What that has to do with games not being entertaining has always troubled myself somewhat, one can make of a game what it is, without big names to carry it through.

In the history of Luton Town, this was their biggest game by far, to date. Never before having reached the final of the FA Cup.

The teams lined up as follows:

Nottingham Forest (Red shirts, white shorts): Thomson, Whare, McDonald, Whitefoot, McKinlay, Burkitt (Captain), Dwight, Quigley, Wilson, Gray and Imlach.

Luton Town (White Shirts, black shorts): Baynham, McNally, Hawkes, Groves, Owen (Captain), Pacey, Bingham, Brown, Morton, Cummins and Gregory.

Forest began the better of the two sides, and they took the lead after only nine minutes. A superbly taken goal by Dwight, a first time left footed shot, sent flying past Baynham in the Luton goal, flying into the top left corner. The goalkeeper well beaten.

With the crowd still buzzing from that opener, it was only five minutes before the team in red struck for a second time, Forest tearing Luton apart all over the pitch. Wilson putting the ball out of Baynham's reach to make the score 2-0 and Nottingham Forest cruising.

Luton at last began to make more of a challenge, giving the Forest keeper something to think about at last.

In the thirty third minute Forest were down to ten men when goal scorer Dwight was carried from the pitch through injury. Which meant for nearly an hour of football with one man down on the demanding Wembley turf not something to be desired.

Luton's heads began to lift and a chance to pull a goal back was thwarted by Billy McKinlay's dogged defending when not allowing Bob Morton any room to manoeuvre.

At half time the sides returned to their relevant dressing room as the band marched onto the pitch playing a medley of tunes to keep the crowd entertained at the break.

The second half saw Luton beginning to make the one man advantage show. Just after the hour mark Ken Hawkes, from a short corner placed drove the ball into the centre which Dave Pacey gathered and slotted the ball home. Luton were back in the hunt, 2-1.

Allan Brown was given a fantastic opportunity to draw the game level with a dramatic diving header from a Billy Bingham cross, however the ball agonisingly wide of Thomson's goal.

With only minutes remaining Luton are also forced to withdraw McNally who looked to be suffering from a bad case of cramp.

Injury time beckoned and three minutes in, another sublime cross into the middle from Bingham that found Tony Gregory at the far post, alas his header wide of the target. Luton's efforts to equalise in vain as the full time whistle sounds.

Nottingham Forest had held on superbly to claim the FA Cup, preventing Luton from collecting their first major trophy in their seventy four year history.

Following the presentation of cup and medals from Her Majesty the Queen, both the players and crowd stood respectfully for the national anthem. Can one imagine such a thing in this day of modern football? No, not really!

Forest then with a jovial step in their foot commenced what is now tradition, for the very first time at the cup final, a well-deserved lap of honour to show off their newly acquired trophy.

Luton Town F.C.   **F.A. Cup Finalists 1958-59**

Back Row (*left to right*) Ken. Hawkes, John Groves, Ron. Baynham, Dave Pacey, Brendan McNally.
Front Row (*left to right*) Billy Bingham, Allan Brown, Bob Morton, Sid. Owen (now Club Manager), George Cummins, Tony Gregory.

The Final Chapter

So there we have it the 2014-2015 football season concludes for Luton Town Football Club. It certainly was a typical Luton season, no easy ride for anyone including the coaching staff, playing squads and definitely not us the supporters. But had it been any different it would not have been Luton Town. A club that throughout recent history has always done its utmost to have all concerned sitting on the edge of our seats, sometimes crying into our beer, or whatever tipple we enjoyed most when suffering. The roller coaster certainly oiled its wheels in preparation and done itself proud.

We did not win automatic promotion, neither did we reach the play offs, but right until the final day our hearts were there, in our throats. The hopes kept alive.

We all have our own personal views on the season and how John Still managed what in all truth was not the easiest of seasons. I wonder in fact, if he has experienced anything like this before his joining Luton Town Football Club. We are not easy that is a fact.

But one thing I will say despite all the moans, the groans, the season of discord between one fan and another, we are all "Hatters" at heart.

If I have upset anyone during this publication, I promise each and every one of you it was not my intent. Every word has been written with passion and honesty. In moments of anger I may have said more than I should have, in moments of joy, over the top. If I have contradicted myself throughout the season, it is solely because it is a journal and at the start I promised myself whatever said would remain that way nothing changed. That is why I asked my good buddy Mike Thomas to see each entry as written, as well as help, he is able to confirm nothing was changed in accordance with later results and incidents.

Throughout this season I learned a great deal about Luton Town supporters. Yes, I was already aware that we are a most resilient breed. However, I also saw another side to a minority. Some people are never satisfied. I quote from a fellow "Hatters" remark that was made only a couple of weeks prior the end of the season and she was absolutely correct. "Some would even moan about Lionel Messi, if he was a Luton Town player, such are some who support this club, some are never happy whatever happens" How true that is.

Before we had the internet, Twitter, Facebook and other World Wide Web delights, to support ones club was simple, enjoyable and less complicated. We would go to our match on a Saturday afternoon, enjoy the game, sometimes win, sometimes lose and of course draw games also. Then a few hours after down the pub, putting the world to right's, analyse between mates the game we had earlier witnessed, all done in good banter on the whole. Then we would slip off home watch Match of The Day. It would be a case of getting on with our lives and wait for the next game to come along.

How things have changed now so drastically. One is able to discuss for hours on end day and night, the finer parts of games. Analyse each tackle, goal and foul in such minute detail. We all have our individual opinions and thoughts and on the whole it is a good feeling to be able to discuss with the world on ones reasoning, one way or another.

I have learnt though this season that, not all discussions are healthy, if someone has a differing opinion most will accept your own and discuss in a friendly tone why they believe their opinion to be more feasible than your own. But then there are those that have the notion that their opinion is the only one that counts and all else is wrong, when challenged they become offensive, such is their arrogance. But their offensiveness is not justified and this begins quite heated argument, the offensive behaviour builds into sheer insults that are for myself unacceptable. For goodness sake, it is a game of football not a matter of life or death. There are so many more important things to concern ourselves about in the world these days surely. We have realised that only over the past weeks with Nepal and Indonesia. In addition to the sad losses we have read about this very weekend as the season concludes

Already I am awaiting the back lash from this publication, not because I have insulted or been offensive in anyway, but simply because I have given my honest opinion and thoughts throughout, I have never and will never allow anyone to sway those thoughts. So if I have upset anyone, I cannot apologise, because it is my true thoughts. To be honest this season has put me off frequenting the supports forums for next season, as I am tired of reading insults made towards fellow supporters and also the hypocrisy that I have discovered within. It is though the minority that have messed much up for the majority.

On the other hand, I have met some most amazing people and become friends with some. So not all bad.

I hope on the whole that my writings have at least been enjoyed and you will find next seasons rant and raves on my website www.chrislukesportinglives.co.uk where we will be building a page during the close season dedicated solely to Luton Town amongst other sports disciplines.

As the new season comes ever nearer we shall say goodbye to quite a few players. We must say goodbye today even to Nathan Oduwa, Lewis Kinsella and thank them for their support as players. There are also two others whom we would hope will be amongst us next season, Cameron "Cameroon" McGeehan, we all know is all but a Luton player, but the fact at the moment is he is on loan, however to see you back young fellah would be a great plus. Secondly Michael Harriman, who as we have Cam, we have taken to our hearts, you have been a star from start to end, I for one would be overjoyed to see you here at the "Kenny" next season as a permanent player. Thank you guys for your excellent support throughout.

Some favourites I fear will be leaving us, as much as I like Fraser Franks, I have the feeling he has not done enough to stay. Not all his doing, as many others injuries have marred his progress.

Will we see young Lee Angol amongst the squad next season, personally I hope so. However, that is down to John and the team, not us the fans.

One last word from myself then there is room for a few words from you the supporters, in a special last page addition.

Thank you Gary Sweet, Nick Owen and the rest of the board. We do give you all some stick. That is true, however, despite everything, it is common knowledge we would not have a club, leave alone players, management staff, board members and fellow supporters to complain about. We should never forget that fact. Who would have thought eight years ago we would be in such a position financially to even mention a new stadium. Who would have believed we would be packing the ground week in week out in the football league again, for that matter in any league. If it was not for you guys who knows we could have been by now in the same predicament as Hereford (I will not say United because they are no longer). We are fortunate and we thank you.

John Still and staff, you have taken criticism that no human being deserves. You have made mistakes, but then no manager who is honest to themselves can ever deny that. What is different about you guys in contrast to recent managers of the past is simply that you have not hidden behind excuses. Not once have you given up, not once have you given us reason to believe you were going to give up. Too many supporters have short memories. Continuity in football is everything, in my humble opinion, for myself, I still believe despite all I may have said at times, you are the right team for the job. Thank you kindly.

Enjoy the break and look forward to another fantastic season back in the football league, because, yes

Supporters Games of the Season.

I requested, via Twitter and Facebook, for Luton Town supporters submit their favourite, or most memorable game of the season to be submitted to the book via the website.
These are the replies we received.
Thank you kindly gentlemen.

Peter Bulkely:
Carlisle away on the opening day - not just because we won. The feeling of watching Luton Town walk out before a game as a Football League team was amazing, made me proud to be a Hatter.

Richard Armstrong:
The first home game back in the league vs Wimbledon was special. There was a real buzz in the whole town that day. To see the shopping centre filled with fans wearing Luton tops made me realise we were indeed back.

Harry Ivey:
For the first time in years Luton visited Plymouth and not only came away with three points, but played with a composure and assurance, with Doyle running the show, which gave me, and I am sure many other fans an opportunity to enjoy the game without many fears of Argyle coming back as they usually do with late winners!

Dale Williams:
Luton 1 v Northampton 0
This win was our seventh straight, that took us to top of league two. Game was a proper localish derby. Both teams cancelled each other out. But one moment of magic, by Luke Guttridge against his old club in last min of the game, made it 1-0 to the hatters. The noise around the ground, seeing Luton go top of league. We was back. COYH.

Paul Hugh Gallagher:
My favourite Luton Town game from this season, has to be away to Carlisle United.
The reality that we were back in the football league after a five year absence made it a special occasion. Cheered on by 1,200 mad hatters who made the long trip via train car and coach we got off to the perfect start when Mark Cullen's goal secured a 1-0 win.

Alan Adair:
Luton 2 Southend 0
The Shrimpers were on a good run leading up to the game, but we were excellent that day.
Cracking goal from Lawless too.

Acknowledgements:

There are so many people who have taken time out to give some assistance, therefore, if be any chance you have been omitted, my most sincere apologies, it will not be intentional.

As at the commencement of the book, without Jimmy Duggan, Alan Hudson and Paul McCormack I do not think I would have had the confidence to have even dreamt of starting this journal, not to be submitted for print anyway. So a massive thank you to the three of you.

Then the two guys who have been in one way or another here with me right from the start, Mike Thomas, who was hassled most mornings with emails long before any sensible human being was awake. It has to be understood that both Mike and myself are far from normal, three and four am. Never seeming to be a problem. Together also with Paul Wright, who's relentless travels up and down the country with pen paper, Dictaphone, tablet or i-pad in hand never failed to give the best accounts of this season's matches. With Paul's assistance I was able to at least attempt to give a more reliable view of the game than I could ever hope to do. No, I did not use his words, however, his reports were most helpful and I thank him most appreciatively for his most valued assistance.

Paul Stillwell, who so kindly donated the artwork for the cover. Could not have asked for better. Thank you kindly Paul. Magnificent work my friend.

Also I must mention Tom Wright, Kenny Cook, Thomas Palmgren, Paul Hugh Gallagher, Danny Clubb and Paul Stanyon for putting up with my rantings and the occasional preview of a chapter being sent via email to give them moments of sheer boredom.
Finally my family, especially the younger daughters Jacyntha and Zaffiyyah who have been chased away on numerous occasions, with the words, I am busy you will have to wait. Sorry girls. I will try to do better. (Famous last words).
Thank you also to Luton Town, without you these past months would have been so much less nerve racking.
Enjoy the summer break everyone.

The final word goes to the surviving twin brother Paul, of whom this book was dedicated at the very beginning. I will say it again, a miserable old so and so, but he is my mate, and that counts more to me than anything and he deserves the last say as he missed not one game this season home or away.

The first game of the season was an away game against Carlisle United on Saturday August the 9th 2014.
The final game of the season was a home game against Stevenage Saturday the 2nd 2015.
LTFC finished 8th on 68 points. I did not miss one game during the season. Cup or League. Let's just say it has been an interesting journey around this great country of ours during the course of the season.
Mistakes have been made by myself and LTFC.
The way I see this season is like an old School report. "Can do better"

Have a good summer. See You Next Season.

Cannot say better than that…

JE SUIS CHARLIE.

Printed in Great Britain
by Amazon.co.uk, Ltd.,
Marston Gate.